The Rise of Organised Brut

Challenging the prevailing belief that organised violence is experiencing historically continuous decline, this book provides an in-depth sociological analysis that shows organised violence is, in fact, on the rise. Malešević demonstrates that violence is determined by organisational capacity, ideological penetration and microsolidarity, rather than biological tendencies, meaning that despite premodern societies being exposed to spectacles of cruelty and torture, such societies had no organisational means to systematically slaughter millions of individuals. Malešević suggests that violence should not be analysed as just an event or process, but also via changing perceptions of those events and processes, and by linking this to broader social transformations on the interpolity and intergroup levels, he makes his key argument that organised violence has proliferated. Focussing on wars, revolutions, genocides and terrorism, this book shows how modern social organisations utilise ideology and microsolidarity to mobilise public support for mass-scale violence.

Siniša Malešević is a professor of sociology at the University College Dublin. His recent books include *Nation-States and Nationalisms* (2013), *The Sociology of War and Violence* (Cambridge, 2010), *Identity as Ideology* (2006), *The Sociology of Ethnicity* (2004) and the edited volumes *Ernest Gellner and Historical Sociology* (2015), *Nationalism and War* (Cambridge, 2013) and *Ernest Gellner and Contemporary Social Thought* (Cambridge, 2007). His work has been translated into Croatian, Persian, Turkish, Portuguese, Chinese, Serbian and Spanish.

The Rise of Organised Brutality

A Historical Sociology of Violence

Siniša Malešević

University College Dublin

CAMBRIDGE
UNIVERSITY PRESS

University Printing House, Cambridge CB2 8BS, United Kingdom

One Liberty Plaza, 20th Floor, New York, NY 10006, USA

477 Williamstown Road, Port Melbourne, VIC 3207, Australia

4843/24, 2nd Floor, Ansari Road, Daryaganj, Delhi – 110002, India

79 Anson Road, #06–04/06, Singapore 079906

Cambridge University Press is part of the University of Cambridge.

It furthers the University's mission by disseminating knowledge in the pursuit of education, learning, and research at the highest international levels of excellence.

www.cambridge.org
Information on this title: www.cambridge.org/9781107095625
DOI: 10.1017/9781316155332

First published 2017

Printed in the United States of America by Sheridan Books, Inc.

A catalogue record for this publication is available from the British Library.

ISBN 978-1-107-09562-5 Hardback
ISBN 978-1-107-47949-4 Paperback

For Luna and Bilja and the better world they represent

Contents

Acknowledgements	*page* viii	
Introduction: The Faces of Violence	1	
1	What Is Organised Violence?	9
2	Violence in the Long Run	41
3	How Old Is Human Brutality?	67
4	The Rise and Rise of Organised Violence	99
5	Warfare	142
6	Revolutions	174
7	Genocides	211
8	Terrorisms	249
9	Why Do Humans Fight?	281
	Conclusion: The Future of Organised Violence	308
	References	313
	Index	337

Acknowledgements

While working on this book, I have received a lot of help, support, suggestions and comments from many friends and colleagues. In particular, I would like to thank Miguel Centeno, Chris Coker, Randall Collins, Manuel Eisner, Robert Gerwarth, Antonio Giustozzi, Peter Halden, John A. Hall, John Hutchinson, Jan Honing, Richard Jenkins, Stathis Kalyvas, Krishan Kumar, Sean L'Estrange, Jonathan Leader Maynard, Steve Loyal, Michael Mann, Aogan Mulcahy, Niall O'Dochartaigh, Christian Ollson, Larry Ray, Kevin Ryan, Stacey Scriver, Martin Shaw, Jennifer Todd, Sylvia Walby and Andreas Wimmer. I have also benefitted from the discussions and comments of colleagues and students at various venues where I presented some of the ideas and arguments developed in the book: the Academy of Sciences and Arts of Bosnia and Herzegovina, Sarajevo; the European University Institute, Florence; Free University of Brussels–ULB; Institut Barcelona d'Estudis Internacionals–IBEI Barcelona; the Institute for Philosophy and Social Theory, Belgrade; the Inter-University Center, Dubrovnik; McGill University, Montreal; National University of Ireland, Galway; Swedish Defence University, Stockholm; University of Edinburgh; University College Dublin; the University of Copenhagen; the University of Kent; the University of Lancaster; the University of Oxford; Queen's University Belfast; and Olympia Summer Academy, Olympia, Greece.

Most of all, I am indebted to the continuous love and support of my family: my wife Vesna, and our now big boys, Luka and Alex.

Chapter 3 is a substantially revised and extended version of the paper originally published as 'How Old is Human Brutality: On the Structural Origins of Violence?' *Common Knowledge*, 2016, 22, Number 1: **81–104**. I am grateful to the Duke University Press for permitting me to use this paper.

Introduction: The Faces of Violence

When we look into the past, we tend to be horrified by the apparent prevalence of cruelty. This comes across in the novels, art, religious scriptures, school textbooks and many popular outlets that record mass slaughters, violent riots, excessive torture, incessant wars, bloodthirsty conflicts and gruesome punishments against ordinary individuals. From ancient China and India to Africa, Roman Europe and the pre-Columbian Americas, the focus is on the prevalence of brutal practices and inhumane behaviour of our predecessors. The typical examples that one can encounter in these recordings of the past include detailed descriptions of torture, such as the Chinese Lingchi protracted method, involving small knife cuts of human limbs and torso (known as 'death by a thousand cuts'); Ashoka's Hell, an elaborate torture chamber in ancient India; or the Aztec human sacrifices accompanied by live heart extractions. However, at the nadir of this macabre theatre is medieval Europe, habitually depicted as an age of perpetual torture, grisly murders and celebration of the most extreme forms of violence. In the popular imagination, this period of human history is firmly associated with the complex instruments of torture, such as the breaking wheel; the head crusher; or the infamous Iron Maiden, an iron cabinet with a hinged front and spike-covered interior, developed to enclose a human being. For this reason, 'medieval brutality' has become a phrase identified with gruesome forms of violence and as such is commonly used to denounce one's opponents.

However, as contemporary medievalists demonstrate, historical reality does not square well with these popular perceptions of medieval Europe. As Klemettilä (2009), Kleinschmidt (2008), Carrel (2009), Baraz (2003) and others show, despite violence-prone rhetoric and some ghastly artis-tic depictions, medieval Europe was not a particularly violent period in human history. Kleinschmidt (2008: 170) emphasises that 'the early medieval sources provide little explicit evidence for war-proneness or outright delight in atrocities on the side of those engaged in war'. Baraz (2003) identifies complex realities where cruelty is used sporadically and

1

almost never without a specific instrumental reason. In a similar way, Carrel (2009) argues that the medieval justice system was not centred on public torture and inhumane forms of execution. Instead, most criminal acts were sanctioned with mild sentences focussed on the public shaming of an individual, who would often receive charity from the townspeople. The executions were usually reserved for murderers and for some types of blasphemous behaviour. Klemettilä (2009) emphasises that common misconceptions about the medieval period stem in part from the literal reading of the chronicles, visual representations of the crusades and the administration of justice and in part from latter-day reinterpretation of this period in the light of the Renaissance and Enlightenment movements. While medieval chronicles and visual materials of torture and martyrdom cannot be taken at face value, as they were written with specific propagandistic and didactical aims, the latter-day framing of 'the barbarous medieval period' owes a great deal to the Renaissance and Enlightenment movements involved in the deliberate 'Othering' of the past. In order to disseminate their massages of progress, reason and liberty successfully, it was necessary to define their projects in opposition to what they constructed to be 'the backward past'. This applies equally to Europe and other continents. We now know that Ashoka's Hell chamber was a literary invention, that the Iron Maiden was never used for torture in medieval Europe and that even Aztec human sacrifices were not as prevalent and as deadly as previously assumed (Schild 2000; Obeyesekere, 2002; Graulich 2000).

None of this is to say that there was no violence or cruelty in premodern times. On the contrary, violence was an important mechanism of social control, and the periodic, but mostly sporadic, instances of excessive cruelty were integral to the various justice systems and to some practices of warfare. The point is that the cruelty was not part of everyday life, and its intermittent gruesome practice should not be confused with its pervasiveness. As I emphasise later in the book, the use of torture is often a sign of coercive weakness rather than strength, and those who rely on macabre killings regularly lack other organisational means to inflict large-scale casualties.

These widely shared images of the past as being excessively violent are not only confined to the mass media or popular stereotypes but have been reinforced by highly influential academic voices. An early scholarly version of this view was already articulated by John Stuart Mill in his essay 'Civilization' (Mill 1836), where civilised action was counterpoised to barbarism. In particular, for Mill violence is a defining feature of barbarism, while civilisation stands for peace, cooperation and empathy:

In savage life there is little or no law, or administration of justice; no systematic employment of the collective strength of society, to protect individuals against injury from one another; every one trusts to his own strength or cunning, and where that fails, he is generally without resource. *We accordingly call a people civilized, where the arrangements of society,* for protecting the persons and property of its members, *are sufficiently perfect to maintain peace among them*; i.e. to induce the bulk of the community to rely for their security mainly upon social arrangements, and renounce for the most part, and in ordinary circumstances, the vindication of their interests (whether in the way of aggression or of defence) by their individual strength or courage (Mill 1836, section 1, my italics).

In Mill's account, once established, civilisation continues its development, reaching the pinnacle 'in modern Europe, and especially in Great Britain, in a more eminent degree, and in a state of more rapid progression, than at any other place or time'.

A similar yet sociologically more grounded view was also developed by Herbert Spencer (1882), who distinguished between militant and industrial societies, where the former were defined by the use of unremitting violence and 'compulsory cooperation', while the latter were characterised by liberty and 'voluntary cooperation'. In Spencer's evolutionary schema, social development was associated with the gradual move from the less advanced, militant societies towards more sophisticated, industrial social orders.[1] Hence here too violence was understood as the 'Other' of civilisation.

Although contemporary social science and theory are less sympathetic to such simplified evolutionary schemas, there is still a strong perception that violence and civilisation are mutually exclusive phenomena and that the modern world is less violent than its historical predecessors. For example, this view underpins Norbert Elias's theory of the civilising process, which is explicit in the view that that 'medieval societies were – compared with our own – very violent' (Elias 1998: 198). In a similar way, social historian Marc Bloch argued that in medieval Europe, 'violence was ... deep-rooted in the social structure and in the mentality of the age' (Bloch, 1961: 411). More recently, Steven Pinker (2011: 1) has written a book that depicts the premodern world as 'a foreign country' where 'brutality' was 'deeply woven into the fabric of daily existence'. In this interpretation, violence declines with the arrival of civilisation and particularly with the onset of modernity. Pinker (2011: xxi) goes further and argues that 'today we may be living in the most peaceable era in our species' existence'.

---

[1] To be fair to Spencer, he was more cautious about the direction of social change than Mill, as he envisaged the possibility of historical reversals from the industrial to the militant models of social organisation.

In this book, I challenge such highly popular social diagnoses of violence. In particular, my focus is on the historical dynamics of organised violence as exemplified by such social phenomena as wars, revolutions, genocides and terrorisms. I argue that careful exploration of these phenomena indicates that they have not experienced decline with the development of civilisation and the advent of modernity. On the contrary, the social trajectory of organised violence points in the other direction – as civilisations and bureaucratic models of rule develop and expand, so does the organisational and ideological capacity for violence. This is not to argue that the organisational development inevitably leads to violence, nor that organised violence is bound to continue its upward trend. There are enormous historical and geographical variations in the way violent action operates. Moreover, since violence does not have a fixed and predetermined essence but multiple forms of existence, it is extremely difficult to fully capture its historical transformations. This also includes changing attitudes towards the use of particular forms of violence. For example, while through much of premodern and early-modern Europe blasphemy was considered to be a more serious form of crime than wife battering, today it is the other way around. Hence, while our predecessors severely punished blasphemous acts, seeing them as the extreme form of violence against God, our normative parameters place the highest value on the preservation of one's bodily integrity.

Much of the contemporary debate on the decline of violence is premised on the idea that violence is a stable, transhistoric and transcultural phenomenon. These arguments are grounded in the view that brutality and civility are two mutually exclusive phenomena characterised by fixed boundaries built around the physicality and intentionality of violence. However, such a rigid dichotomy is conceptually too narrow and historically too limited. To explain the character of violence, it is necessary to place it in a much wider historical, geographical and social context. Today our legal and moral systems deem that deliberately touching the body (i.e. breast or penis) of a person one does not know is a violent/ criminal act. At the same time, severe psychological pressures generated in the workplace or education systems rarely qualify as a form of violence, although they usually have more profound consequences to one's health and well-being (i.e. from the persistent existential insecurity often underpinned by ever-increasing workload targets, unrealistic work-life demands, the ever-growing social isolation of individuals, the impact of new forms of public shaming, the institutionalised lack of empathy outside of one's organisation, etc.). In contrast, in the premodern world, social isolation and public shaming were considered to be much more serious forms of coercion than most forms of physical punishment. For example, as Carrel (2009) shows, in fourteenth-century England, most individuals preferred to have their feet fastened into stocks than to spend even a short time isolated in jail. An expulsion from one's village was generally considered to be much crueler than most forms of physical injuries inflicted as a form of punishment. All of this indicates that violence is a dynamic social phenomenon that changes through time and space. To better understand these long-term historical processes, it is necessary to move away from our present-day obsession with the corporal and actor-centred concepts of violence. The contemporary reinterpretation of violent action as being solely a material act, a physical event that involves the deliberate use of force on one's body, develops quite late in human history and as such requires historical contextualisation. There is little doubt that in the last several decades, modern social order has become overly centred on corporal forms of violent acts at the expense of all other types of violence. One could even argue that late modernity is defined by fetishism of the body, which ranges from the personal control reinforced through body decorations (i.e. tattooing and piercing) to body-centred consumerism to our perceptions of what constitutes an attack on one's body. In all of these cases and many others, the focus is firmly on the physical aspects of bodily integrity. While the physical dimensions of violence remain crucial in understanding the trajectory of organised violence, they have to be supplemented with the nonmaterial and nonintentional forms of violent action. In addition, to better comprehend how violent acts emerge and expand, it is crucial to refocus our attention from intentional acts of individual or collective agents towards unintended actions of social organisations that foster violent practices (see Chapter 1).

In this book, I attempt to explore how organised violence transforms over the course of human history. In this context, I argue that rather than experiencing a dramatic decline, most forms of organised violence have undergone a major social transition resulting in a greater organisational and ideological capacity for violence. This means that violence has gradually been transfigured into coercive and ideological power of social organisations, which have become able to utilise diverse forms of micro-level solidarities to extend their reach and legitimacy. To fully understand how coercive and ideological powers develop, expand and transform, one needs to engage with the long-term historical processes that have fostered this change. The ever-increasing state's monopolisation of the legitimate use of violence, increasing literacy rates, mass education, the proliferation of mass media and public sphere, bureaucratisation of authority and mass ideologisation have all contributed towards the reframing of violence. Nevertheless, rather than extinguishing violent acts, the last three centuries have in fact witnessed a substantial increase in the scale of organised violence. Much of this period was characterised by the gradual expansion of mass destruction, the nadir of which was the twentieth century, with over 250 million human casualties (White 2012). Most of these fatalities were confined to the first part of this century. However, the organisational and ideological scaffolds that have generated these casualties have not been dismantled. On the contrary, the last seventy years have witnessed the continuous increase of the coercive and ideological powers of social organisations: from nation-states, business corporations, religious institutions and social movements to civil society groupings. The rise of this organisational and ideological capacity has created a social environment where, on the one hand, social relations are coercively pacified, and, on the other hand, such coercive pacification provides conditions for periodic explosions of mass-scale violence.

This book aims to develop a sociologically and historically grounded approach to analyse the social transformation of organised violence in different historical and geographical contexts. This approach builds on my previous studies (Malešević 2013a, 2013b, 2013c, 2011, 2010) that attempted to articulate a longue durée analysis of organised violence by emphasising the workings of three interconnected historical processes: the cumulative bureaucratisation of coercion, centrifugal ideologisation and the envelopment of microsolidarity. My aim is to provide a systematic historical sociological analysis that traces the social dynamics of organised violence through time and space.

The Layout of the Book

In order to understand the relationship between organised violence and society over long stretches of time, it is necessary to define and situate this slippery concept. Hence in the first chapter I critically engage with the leading approaches in the study of violence with a view towards developing a theoretically and empirically sustainable concept of organised violence. The attempt is made to move away from the dominant understandings of violence, which are either too wide or too narrow. I argue that the wide definitions relativise violence, while the narrow concepts cannot account for noncorporal and nonintentional forms of violent action. This conceptual debate is then expanded to engage critically with the three leading approaches in the study of organised violence (Weber, Foucault and Elias). I briefly assess each of the three perspectives in order to pinpoint their strengths and weaknesses and to identify an analytical space for an alternative interpretation of organised violence.

In Chapter 2, I provide a theoretical framework for the study of organised violence. Drawing in part on the tradition of comparative historical sociology of the state, I articulate a version of the longue durée model that centres on the historical dynamics of organised violence. More specifically, I identify three long-term historical processes that, I believe, played a key role in the development and transformation of organised violence over the past twelve thousand years: the cumulative bureaucratisation of coercion, centrifugal ideologisation and envelopment of microsolidarity. The chapter explains how each of these three process works and also how they relate to each other in the context of organised violence.

Chapters 3 and 4 critically review the available evidence on the prevalence of organised violence over the course of human history. In particular, Chapter 3 explores the archaeological, anthropological and documentary historical evidence to assess how violent the early humans were. I argue that organised violence developed quite late in human history and that its proliferation is closely tied with the expansion of organisational power. While Chapter 3 largely focusses on prehistory and very early history, Chapter 4 looks briefly at the transformation of organised violence from early history until the present day. In line with my general argument, I emphasise that there is no evidence that violence declines with social development, civilizational advancement or modernity. On the contrary, the case is made that since organised violence is firmly linked with the coercive-organisational and ideological structures, it expands as these structures continue to grow. While Chapters 3 and 4 provide a general overview, the next four chapters focus more specifically on the main forms of organised violence: warfare, revolutions, genocides and terrorisms.

In Chapter 5, I explore the historical dynamics of war. I look at the relationship between warfare and social change and argue that the ever-increasing organisational and ideological capacity of war was decisive for both its destructive and socially productive outcomes. In this context, the recent decrease in the number of interstate wars and the frontline casualties cannot be interpreted as the inevitable demise of warfare but instead as a form of structural advancement whereby wars become organisationally and ideologically embedded in everyday life.

Chapter 6 explores the historical dynamics of revolutions. I critically review the dominant theories of revolution and then articulate an alternative interpretation centred on the role of organisation capacity, ideological penetration and the embedment of microsolidarity. In this context, I also shed some light on the uneven trajectories of revolutionary experience.

Since genocides are generally regarded as the most extreme forms of organised violence, I analyse their social origins and their historical trajectories in Chapter 7. Although most of the research on genocides focusses on the legal and ethical dimensions, there is a need to shift these debates towards sociology. Hence, in this chapter, I engage with the sociological approaches of genocide with a view towards developing a longue durée interpretation of this social phenomenon.

Although terrorism generates a much smaller number of human casualties than other forms of organised violence, it often attracts more attention than it merits. In Chapter 8, I analyse what is terrorism and why it entices so much public attention. More specifically, I provide a critical analysis of the influential sociological and nonsociological approaches to terrorism. I argue that while nonsociological analyses overemphasise psychological, economic and political factors, the leading sociological approaches offer culturally determinist explanations. In this context, I offer an alternative approach that explores terrorist acts through the prism of organisational and ideological powers and microsolidarity.

Since I see microsolidarity as one of the key mechanisms that mobilises social action, it is critical to examine how this process works in practice. Thus in Chapter 9 I take a closer look at how group cohesion operates. I argue that human beings are not naturally gregarious creatures, and that the group dynamics often entail organisational and ideological support. The chapter explores the historical dynamics between organised violence and microsolidarity.

In her essay 'On Violence', Hannah Arendt (1970) distinguishes sharply between power and violence. She argues that rather than being an extreme instance of power, violence is antithetical to power: unlike power, which is generated in the collective will and popular consent, violence is the absence of power. In this book, I take the opposite view: collective violence is the product of organisational and ideological powers, and as these powers grow and expand, so does the capacity for organised violence. Unlike Arendt, who shares the Enlightenment dream of social reality completely devoid of violence, this book is premised on the argument that violence is an integral and irreducible part of the human historical experience.

1   What Is Organised Violence?

What Is Violence?

In everyday life, the term *violence* is used for variety of very diverse situations. In most instances, it refers to a particular type of action with deleterious results, but it can also denote a lack of any action. Deliberately killing or physically injuring another human being is something that almost everybody would characterise as a violent act. However, the same label is also used by some to describe severe punishments of humans and animals; destruction of property and one's habitat (i.e. environmental devastation); the use of particularly offensive and insulting words; stern forms of emotional blackmail; and threats to one's life, health or mental well-being. Nevertheless, acts of omission, including indifference towards activities that generate violent outcomes, the neglect of human or animal suffering or withdrawal of support for highly vulnerable individuals have also been characterised as forms of violence. Furthermore, this term has often been applied to such activities as breaking a promise or an agreement (i.e. to violate a treaty), affecting adversely one's senses including smell or taste (i.e. 'that food was repulsive, it violated my taste buds') and harming one's dignity or self-image (i.e. 'this behaviour destroys my self-respect'), among others. Although most forms of action/inaction labelled as violent refer to the concrete events in the past or present, in some instances this label is also used in relation to the future events (i.e. 'by increasing CO_2 emissions, we are destroying the future of our children and grandchildren'). The concept of violence is also used in more metaphoric ways, such as 'winning the battle with cancer', 'fighting against poverty' or 'waging war on corruption'. Since this term has strong normative connotations, it has also often been applied as a political tool to justify or delegitimise a particular course of action. For example, in a team sport encounter, a robust tackle might be seen by one coach as sign of the player's hard work and commitment, while the coach of the other team might interpret the same act as a deliberate violent provocation. Similarly, an incident on the border between the two inimical neighbouring states might provoke fury of denouncements from each government about the premeditated aggression of the other side.

All these different uses and interpretations of what constitutes violence indicate that there are no unambiguous, universally accepted criteria to differentiate a violent from a nonviolent act. This is not to say that one should accept a relativist position and treat all action as being equality violent or nonviolent. Instead, this great interpretative variation implies that every violent act is situated in the specific social and historical context and as such is dependent on particular social perceptions and experiences. In other words, violence is a historically framed and socially dynamic phenomenon, the meaning of which changes through time and space. Nevertheless, unlike 'culture' or 'rights', which are extremely plastic concepts that can acquire profoundly different, almost mutually exclusive, meanings and have done so through time, violence is dynamic but much more constant phenomenon. For example, the concept of 'rights' has substantially shifted its meaning throughout history: from the inherited entitlements of a single family ('the divine rights of kings'), to group privilege of a particular status category (aristocracy, large land-owners, property owning white men, etc.), to becoming a legal prerogative of all citizens inhabiting a specific nation-state. In contrast, the concept of violence has not undergone such a dramatic transformation: the act of killing another human being was considered a violent deed ten thousand years ago just as it is now. Nevertheless, the specific social and historical framing of what a particular killing means has been substantially altered. While in some periods of history an aristocrat was entitled to take a life of a disobedient peasant, the legal and ethical principles of contemporary world make no room for such acts today. Hence although the historical interpretations of what constitutes violence change, this is a much slower and more limited process than is the case with many other social phenomena. Furthermore, violence is also different in a sense that it is a scalar concept: it includes diverse practices which vary in scale, magnitude and intensity of physical, moral or emotional damage. Obviously, there is a substantial difference between shouting obscene insults at somebody and taking one's life, yet both of these have been character-ised as forms of violent behaviour. However, this is not to say that this scalar nature of violence is historically and geographically universal and fixed. On the contrary, if one is to compare various social orders through time and space, it becomes apparent that in some contexts verbal insults might be deemed much more offensive and violent than the killing of another human being. For example, a blasphemous insult against divine authority might generate an instant death penalty, whereas the lynching of a blasphemer or an apostate might be regarded as a virtuous deed.

This pronounced contextual, dynamic and slippery nature of violence has generated vibrant conceptual debates around the question: What types of action/inaction constitute violence? The principal bones of contention have been the two issues: the corporality and intentionality of violent acts. While some scholars define violence in narrow terms as the intentional use of physical force that generates bodily harm or death (Tilly 2003, Eisner 2009, Ray 2011, Pinker 2011), others employ wider definitions that centre on the long-term impacts of the specific social action that ultimately produce harmful effects (Scheper-Hughes 2004; Žižek 2008, Schinkel 2010, Bourdieu 1990, Galtung 1969). For example, both Eisner (2009) and Tilly (2003) emphasise the physicality of violent experience. For Eisner (2009: 42), violence is simply 'the intentional but unwanted infliction of physical harm on other humans', while for Tilly (2003: 3) violent acts are to be distinguished from non-violent activity in terms of immediate infliction of 'physical damage on persons and/or objects'.

In contrast, other scholars argue that violence cannot be reduced to its corporal dimension, as both physical and emotional pain can be produced by nonphysical means. A regular exposure to episodes of relentless humiliation can foster suicidal behaviour; prolonged experiences of fear and tension can ultimately cause heart attacks; a stress-generating working environment might impact the escalation of domestic violence; being regularly exposed to the hazardous working environment or contaminated food can cause severe illness, pain or death; and so on. As Scheper-Hughes and Bourgois (2004 1) insist: 'Violence also includes assaults on the personhood, dignity, sense of worth or value of the victim. The social and cultural dimensions of violence are what give violence its power and meaning.'

In addition to challenging physicality, scholars have also contested the idea of intentionality. Although many acts of violence are planned, premeditated and calculated, most violent outcomes are produced unintentionally. For one thing, when analysing a violent episode it is necessary to distinguish between one's motive and the outcome of specific action. As Felson (2009) rightly points out, to explain adequately the processes that led to violence it is important to take into account all those involved, not only the victims and observers but also the perpetuators, as their motives often vary too. In many instances, the motivation of the violence perpetrator may not necessarily be linked to the violent outcomes produced. This point can be extended further to differentiate between the legal and sociological concepts of violence. Although legal systems all over the world are, for obvious reasons, centred on the victims of violence and as such have to operate with the fixed meanings of what constitutes a violent act, the sociological understandings of individual and collective experiences of violence are inevitably more nuanced. While in legal systems the emphasis is on the individual, or occasionally collective, responsibility and intentionality for violent acts in line with how the law defines criminal activity, in sociology the focus is on explaining the complex dynamics of violent episodes. Since every violent episode or situation is different and many are caused by the confluence of different factors, some of which might not have a single source or are not necessarily intended, sociological analysis will rarely yield answers that would satisfy legal experts. For example, a physical assault on a police officer is something that is clearly defined and severely punished in most legal systems all over the world. Since the assault on the police force is interpreted legally and almost uniformly as an attack on the state, the severity of legal punishment is not determined by an individual experience of a violent act but by the threat this type of attack represents to the authority of the state. So beating up ruthlessly and relentlessly a homeless drug addict will regularly count for less than spitting at or slapping a police officer. Although the degree of violence deployed is substantially greater in the former case, the legal systems would judge the latter as being much more violent. Furthermore, even though all human beings experience pain, the degree of physical and emotional injury that individuals experience can differ substantially, but this is usually not captured by criminal law. In legal eyes, all categories of violent behaviour/crime entail an equal degree of punishment, so the key issue is how a particular form of violence is legally categorised. As criminal legislation sharply distinguishes between an assault on the police and on civilians, it pays little attention to similarity or difference between the individual experiences of violent acts.

This complexity of violent experience in relation to the intentionality and corporality has led many sociologists to embrace much wider definitions of violence. For example, Johan Galtung's (1969) concept of structural violence was one of the first attempts to include nonintentional and nonphysical behaviour into the definition of violent action. In this understanding, structural violence encompasses all structural constraints that prevent human beings from realising their full potential, including the unequal access to resources, health, education, legal protection and political power. More specifically, structural violence is seen to be rooted in the unequal social relations that have disproportional effect on the individuals and groups who are at the bottom of stratification systems. Galtung identifies structural violence as a force that causes premature deaths, long-term disabilities, malnutrition or hunger. In his later work, Galtung (1990) also introduces the concept of cultural violence, which is interpreted as a social mechanism for the legitimisation of structural violence. This term refers to variety of cultural discourses that are deployed to justify the existence of structural violence, including ideological doctrines, religious teachings and artistic idioms as well as the use of scientific reasoning.

Pierre Bourdieu (1990) has expanded this view further by linking the processes of cultural legitimisation with the habitual reproduction of dominant social relationships. In this context, Bourdieu developed the idea of symbolic violence, which he sees as something that is often a more significant and effective form of dominance than individual acts of physical aggression. In his view, symbolic violence stems from the symbolic power that permeates social orders: it is a tacit form of social practice ingrained in the everyday social habits which is used to maintain existing hierarchical relationships. As Bourdieu and Wacquant (1992 167) argue, this type of violent activity is not characterised by visible physical injuries or by the intentional acts of specific agents, but it is a form of 'violence which is exercised upon a social agent with his or her complicity'. Typical examples of symbolic violence are the class, status and gender divisions in contemporary societies: the class and status distinctions are maintained through the popular acceptance, shared by the majority of all strata, that middle classes deserve their better social and economic situation on the grounds that they are more capable or more gifted. Furthermore, their artistic tastes, lifestyles and speech practices are deemed superior and as such are popularly accepted to be a universal measure of cultural competence in a given society.

This much wider understanding of violence is also present in Žižek (2008), who distinguishes between the subjective and objective violence. In his view, the conventional understandings of violence such as those associated with the 'clearly identifiable agent' and represented by acts of crime, terrorism or civil unrest are forms of subjective violence, which are highly visible but not the dominant forms of violent action. Instead, Žižek's (2008: 2) focus is on what he terms 'objective violence': unlike subjective violence, which is usually perceived as the disruption of everyday normality, objective violence is its opposite, the social reality that upholds the existing status quo. In his own words: 'Objective violence is invisible since it sustains the very zero-level standard against which we perceive something as subjectively violent'. The two types of violence are deeply interlinked, as subjective violence often emerges as an attempt to confront the dominance of objective violence. In Žižek's account, objective violence is further differentiated into symbolic and systemic violence. While symbolic violence is more or less identical to Bourdieu's own concept, with its emphasis on habitual reproduction of speech and

[handwritten margin annotations: "Subjective" bracketing the subjective violence paragraph, "Objective" bracketing the objective violence paragraph]

language forms, systemic violence is related to 'the often catastrophic consequences of the smooth functioning of our economic and political systems' (Žižek 2008: 2). For Žižek (2008 9), this type of violence is 'inherent in a system'; it involves direct physical force, 'but also the more subtle forms of coercion that sustain relations of domination and exploitation, including the threat of violence'. In this interpretation, the principal agents of systemic violence are the liberal elites who maintain the asymmetric economic and political relationships in the world through their attempts to control the subjective violence: 'the same philanthropists who give millions for AIDS or education in tolerance have ruined the lives of thousands through financial speculation and thus created the conditions for the rise of the very intolerance that is being fought' (Žižek 2008: 37).

Galtung, Bourdiou and Žižek are right that the violent acts and violent outcomes do not have to be a result of someone's intent and can be produced by nonphysical means. Violence cannot be simply reduced to one's corporal experience and to deliberate acts. Intimidation, neglect, omission, coercive pressure, threats and other forms of the noncorporal action or inaction can have mentally and physically just as harmful effects as those produced by the intentional physical injuries. Nevertheless, it is also important not to conflate the concept of violence with other social phenomena. For example, Galtung's definition is so wide that incorporates any form of inequality and lack of possibility to achieve one's full potential under the label of 'structural violence'. In this context, it is almost impossible to distinguish between the violent and nonviolent forms of structural action, as any individual can make a claim at any time that she is prevented from fulfilling her full potential by the presence of various structural obstacles. Similarly, both Žižek's and Bourdiou's concepts of symbolic and objective/systemic violence are equally so broad that they render the concept sociologically meaningless. If violence is used as a mere synonym for inequality, capitalism, socialisation or gender and class relations, then this concept becomes superfluous. Moreover, introducing such extremely wide definitions relativises the meaning of a violent act. Although violence often involves asymmetrical relationships of power and individual and collective inequalities, nothing can be gained analytically by reducing violence to inequality or asymmetric power relations. Violence is much more than inequality or power disparity. Obviously, there is a substantial difference between governments' introduction of a regressive tax system that privileges wealthy and the same government's direct involvement in a genocidal project. This is not only a question of scale; these are two very different social phenomena. Both Žižek's and Bourdiou's concepts of violence are economically determinist in a sense that they link all expressions of organised violence to the economic foundations of capitalism. Does this mean that there was no violence before capitalism, or that once capitalism is out of the picture we will live in a violence free world? For example, for Žižek systemic violence is integral to the everyday life of capitalism, and subjective violence is its direct counterpart: the acts of terrorism, civil unrest or crime reflect the inherently violent character of the capitalist order. This type of argument cannot account for the presence of organised violence for much of the precapitalist world, nor it can explain violent behaviour outside of the capitalist contexts. Furthermore, these overly structuralist definitions cannot adequately capture the microdynamics of violence. Much more can be gained analytically by shifting the focus of our analysis from individuals, groups and imprecise theoretical abstractions (i.e. capitalism) towards social and historical contexts that create conditions for the emergence of violent action. As Collins (2008a) rightly argues, violence is a situational process. On the micro level, violence is 'a set of pathways around confrontational tension and fear'. More specifically, his point is that violence is a form of social situation rather than an attribute of an individual or a group: 'we seek the contours of situations, which shape the emotions and acts of individuals who step inside them. It is a false lead to look for types of violent individuals, constant across situations' (Collins 2008a: 1). So both capitalists and capitalism can produce violence, but this is far from being a uniform, constant and permanent phenomenon.

Thus to avoid the Scylla and Charybdis of too narrow, too wide and structurally fixed definitions, it is crucial to reconceptualise violence in a way that incorporates nonphysicality, nonintentionality and the rich microdynamics of social situations without losing the analytical capacity of this concept. Hence I define violence as a scalar social process in which individuals, groups or social organisations find themselves steeped in situations whereby their intentional or unintentional actions generate some substantial coercively imposed behavioural changes or produce physical, mental or emotional damage, injury or death.

This working definition of violence aims to emphasise the situational and contextual nature of all violent action. However, as violence is a scalar phenomenon which operates at different levels, changes through time and space and is dependent on the specific social and cultural codings, it is difficult to capture all this complexity at once. Hence in order to provide an in-depth analysis, it is necessary to differentiate between the three principal layers of violence analysis: (1) interpersonal; (2) intergroup; and (3) interpolity (Malešević 2013b). Although, as this book shows, these three layers are often deeply interlinked, there are important differences in how violence emerges, develops and operates at each of these three layers.

The interpersonal layer relates to all forms of violence that emerge in direct face-to-face contact. It involves great variety of situations, from street fights, pub brawls, domestic abuse, nonorganised football hooliganism and duelling, to gang rape, suicide bombings and domestic cases of animal cruelty or child kidnappings, among many others. This type of violence generally involves a small number of individuals who find themselves in a direct physical interaction with other individuals. As such, these micro-level violent encounters exhibit a particular situational logic that characterises much of face-to-face confrontational interaction: as a rule, violence is messy, chaotic, emotionally intense and of relatively short duration. As Collins (2008a) emphasises, most forms of micro-level violent episodes are defined by the actor's incompetence at performing violence, are dependent on the synchronisation of bodily rhythms and are shaped by the dynamics of physical interaction, including postures, facial expressions and verbal and nonverbal communication.

In direct contrast to interpersonal violent encounters, where corporal contact dominates, the other two layers, the intergroup and interpolity, are for the most part characterised by the lack of direct physical interaction. Instead, the social action is here mediated by the presence of formal or informal organisations where individuals and groups are involved in violence on account of their membership/affiliation in the specific social organisations. This is not to say that in intergroup or interpolity violence individuals never come in close proximity with other individuals. Rather, the point is that when such interaction occurs, it is generally governed by the principles of organisational membership/affiliation. For example, when two soldiers fight each other on the battlefield, they are engaged in a direct interpersonal violent encounter, but this violence is a product of the organisational mediation, the fact that two polities are at war with each other. In a similar vein, intrusive racial profiling or young women' exposure to constant humiliation through verbal insults on the street have regularly more to do with broader intergroup ethnic and gender relations than with the interpersonal conflicts between the individuals involved.

Although both intergroup and interpolity violent action are forms of organised violence, the two differ in terms of their organisational capacity, legitimacy and sense of solidarity. While intergroup violence can be more or less formalised, interpolity violence is completely dependent on the existence of organisational structure. For example, violent class-based conflicts can involve well-established trade unions, social movements, radical political parties, organised militias or paramilitaries. However, class-based violence can also happen outside any organisational channels, such as when a desperate manual labourer goes on a rampage and kills the entire board of directors of a large private corporation. In contrast, violence between two or more polities inevitably entails deployment of organisational apparatuses to initiate and wage violent conflict. Of course, the leaders of respective polities can pinpoint an individual violent act as a motive for their decision to deploy organised violence against other polities, as was the case with the alleged burning of the Reichstag or Princip's assassination of Franz Ferdinand, but interpolity violence cannot ensue without the organisational structure.

Furthermore, intergroup and interpolity violence also differ in the ability of the two to secure internal and external legitimacy. While the established polities, from empires, city-states, city-leagues to nation-states, regularly acquire external legitimacy through regional and international treaties, diplomatic relations, military might or economic strength, this is not the case with nonstate collective actors. Instead, the external legitimacy of many groups might be regularly contested, regardless of whether they are formally organised or not. As most collectivities, be they defined in terms of religion, ethnicity, class, gender, age or any other social attribute, tend to be represented by more than one social organisation, there is always a question of who has the right to speak in the name of a particular collectivity. For example, when a particular violent conflict is defined as a religious strife between Shiia and Sunni, it is rarely clear which social movement, party, military group or clerical association has legitimate right to represent their co-religionists. In contrast, in wars between states, such as the Falklands–Malvinas war of 1982, it is usually more apparent who the legitimate adversaries are. Although particular governments' right to rule can be contested (i.e. Argentine Junta), the legitimacy of the polities involved (i.e. the United Kingdom and Argentina) is rarely questioned.

Although internal legitimacy and a sense of solidarity are necessary for all social organisations and informal groupings, these qualities are often achieved differently by polities and groups. Throughout history, the rulers of various polities had to rely on different sources to justify their right to rule, from mythology, religion, divine rights and civilising missions to nationalism, among others. In the modern era, the states have also been able to establish a monopoly on the legitimate use of violence over their territories and to justify this monopoly they had to deploy the language and ideologies of statewide collective solidarity. Nonpolity collective actors have also utilised the rhetoric of group solidarity to achieve internal legitimacy. However, as such groups generally make appeals to the particular constituencies (i.e. religion, ethnicity, class, gender, age, etc.), their internal sources of legitimacy and solidarity remain confined to the selected social strata. In contrast, as modern polities largely monopolise not only the legitimate use of violence but also taxation, education and legislation over their territory, their very existence is premised on developing and utilising politywide ideological discourses capable of internally justifying such social and political arrangements (Malešević 2013a).

Organising Violence

Most scholars recognise that interpersonal and organised violence exhibit different social properties. Despite substantial disparity between inter-group and interpolity violence, both of these types involve an important commonality: they are mediated phenomena, built around abstract organisational categories and enacted through organisational structures. Unlike interpersonal violence, which entails direct physical interaction, organised violence necessitates the presence of structured and abstract entities, such as social movements, established institutions or functioning social organisations which initiate, regulate and undertake violent acts. Although both organised and interpersonal violence often remain deeply interdependent, the gap between the two has widened over the past twelve thousand years of human history, and this process has intensified in the past three hundred years (Malešević 2010). One of the reasons for this is the ever-increasing organisational power of social orders at the expense of face-to-face interaction. Whereas for much of prehistory and early history violent acts tended to take place in the direct interaction between individuals or small, poorly organised groups facing each other directly, the development of complex social organisations has resulted in the ever-increasing social mediation of violence. In other words, the advancements in science, technology and administration on the one hand and the staggering increase in the population size on the other have fostered the emergence and proliferation of specialised social organisa-tions responsible for violent action as well as for coercive coordination of the large numbers of human beings (i.e. military, police, private security companies, armed militias, etc.). Whereas a handful of individuals living in a flexible foraging band could freely roam African savannahs and engage occasionally in violent interpersonal disputes, millions of individ-uals inhabiting Ptolemaic Egypt could not survive without the presence of the well-established polity able to generate enough food and establish internal order and external security, including periodic warfare with its neighbours.

Furthermore, as organised violence is dependent on the presence of effective and durable structural mechanisms, once these structures are put in place they tend to maintain their presence and expand in time. For example, while a pub brawl might result in a vicious fight between several individuals, such individual-level violence is unlikely to last for days or to spread further outside that particular pub. In contrast, once the police force or a private security company is established to preserve order and provide safety of a particular social organisation, it is unlikely to disband even when deemed by many to be unnecessary.

Although most scholars differentiate between interpersonal and organised violence, very few actually use these terms. Instead, the tendency is to distinguish between political (i.e. terrorism, war, genocide, etc.) and nonpolitical forms of violence (i.e. domestic abuse, violent crimes, etc.) or, in contrast, collective/social and individual violence. For example, Donatella Della Porta (2013: 6) employs the concept of political violence, which is defined as a particular form of violent activity that 'consists of those repertoires of collective action that involve great physical force and cause damage to an adversary to achieve political aims'. Tilly (2003: 3) prefers the term 'collective violence' and defines it as 'an episodic social interaction that immediately inflicts physical damage on persons and/or objects ..., involves at least two perpetrators of damage, and results at least in part from coordination among persons who perform damaging acts'. Leaving to one side their rather narrow understandings of violence in terms of its physicality and intentionality, both of these definitions overemphasise agency at the expense of the structural dynamics of violence. While Della Porta, who works within the social movements tradition, understands violence through the prism of collective action, for Tilly, a doyen of contentious politics paradigm, violent activity emerges through social interaction. Of course, collective action and episodic group interaction are significant ways through which violence transpires, but they are not the only nor the dominant types of violent experience. Instead, most violence is produced and inflicted not at the intergroup but at the inter- and intrapolity level. In other words, organisational structures, including states, political parties, private corporations or paramilitary organisations, among others, are responsible for more violence than any group or individual. Moreover, even in the typical cases of violence emerging from collective action/interaction, used by Tilly and Della Porta to illustrate their arguments, the presence of organisational structures, and particularly the state, is quite apparent. For example, Tilly (2003: 1–5) introduces his concept of collective violence by invoking the cases of Rwandan genocide, cowboy shootings in the Wild West and the combine harvesters' destruction in rural

Malaysia, all of which are seen to be instances of episodic social inter-action. Similarly, Della Porta (2013: 1–2) exemplifies her key arguments with cases of 9/11 terrorism, ETA's violent struggle for Basque inde-pendence and Breivik's massacre at Utøya Island to make a point that political violence constitutes a diverse range of collective action. Never-theless, in all of these cases organisational structures loom large: the Rwandan genocide could not have happened without reliance on the state apparatus, combine harvesters' sabotages were violent peasant reac-tions to the agricultural production changes introduced by the modern state and private corporations, both Al Qaida and ETA terrorism were a structural product of the geopolitical blind spots initiated by the long-term behaviour of particular states (i.e. the United States and Spain, respectively) and themselves are potent social organisations, and even the Wild West cowboy shootings and Breivik's mass murder have happened in the context of specific organisational structures: the U.S. state-sponsored frontier expansion and the Norwegian Labour Party youth camp gathering.

This almost omnipresent dominance of the state and other powerful social organisations in many instances of violent action suggests that there is something distinctive about the organisational power and its link with the different forms of violence. Terms such as political, collective or social violence cannot adequately capture this significance as the concept of organised violence can. The term 'political violence' is perhaps more precise as it focusses on the specific political aims of agents involved in violent activities. However, as it is difficult to distinguish between polit-ical and nonpolitical action, this precision can also be too reductionist and misleading. Furthermore, this term presupposes the presence of a political intent while much of violence, as already discussed, may not be intentional or agency-driven at all. Taking all these points into account, my working definition of this key concept is similar to the definition of violence I provided above notwithstanding its distinct historical and organisational features. Thus I define organised violence as a scalar and historical social process through which social organisations, including organised collectivities, find themselves steeped in situations or influ-enced by structural conditions that, intentionally or unintentionally, foster some substantial, coercively imposed behavioural changes or pro-duce physical, mental or emotional damage, injury or death.

Organised Violence and Historical Change

Defining organised violence as a historical process indicates that its character changes in time. One of the central debates in social science has unfolded around the question of whether violence has been constant throughout history or has experienced significant rise or decline. This particular question has equally vexed leading social theorists and empirically minded social analysts, many of whom have provided very different answers to this question. I will focus here briefly on the three most influential accounts of this relationship between organised violence and historical change, which provide contrasting answers to this question. While the Eliasian perspectives identify a downward trend in all forms of violent action throughout history, the Weberian and Foucauldian approaches emphasise the upward trajectory of violence over the last three hundred years of human development. Nevertheless, the Foucauldian and Weberian accounts differ substantially: while the former insist on the substantial discursive shifts in the framing and practice of violence in modernity, the latter emphasises the gradual expansion of institutional mechanisms for violence. My aim is to critically engage with these approaches in order to better understand the historical trajectories of organised violence but also to situate theoretically and conceptually the conceptual and empirical analysis that is developed in the rest of this book.

Discipline and Violence

Max Weber is traditionally associated with the idealist epistemology as exemplified by his well-known studies on Protestant ethics and the spirit of capitalism or his theory of social stratification, which gives more explanatory weight to the cultural factors such as social status and prestige than material ones, including class divisions or economic structures. However, this rather Parsonian, one-dimensional characterisation of Weber's work neglects the fact that the great German sociologist was first and foremost a theorist of conflict (Hall 2013; Collins 1986). Although Weber does not offer us a systematic theory of organised violence, his opus is saturated with the sophisticated sociological analyses of coercion and violent action. The starting point of Weber's approach is his perception of political life as being ultimately grounded in violence. In this view, politics is primarily about power, while power rests on one's coercive capacity. In his own terms: 'the essence of all politics is conflict', and power is the 'probability that one actor within a social relationship will be in a position to carry out his own will despite resistance, regardless of the basis on which this probability rests' (Weber 1968: 53).

Weber understands social life in part through the prism of Nietzschean ontology, where conflict is seen as something inherent to human beings. Moreover, Weber extends Nietzsche by placing this idea in a specific historical and sociological context. Thus on the micro level Weber conceptualises social relations as being shaped by the political, cultural and economic conflicts (i.e. his tripartite theory of stratification), all of which fundamentally remain dependent on the use or the threat of use of force. Political associations and individual politicians fight for the control of state apparatuses; economic groupings and individuals compete, often viciously, on the marketplace; and different social strata as well as their individual members are engaged in the perpetual status struggle. On the macro level, Weber interprets the great religious worldviews as well as state power as being defined by intense violent contests. Whereas religions espouse competing eschatological visions that are grounded in irreconcilable ultimate values, the very existence of state structure is premised on its ability to establish a monopoly on the legitimate use of violence over the territory under its control. In this context, both micro- and macro-level environments are shaped by violent conflictual situations: while individuals and groups compete over material resources, prestige and the control over the political institutions, and world polities are engaged in the incessant status and power struggle in the broader geopolitical arena (Weber 1968, Collins 1986).

This conflict-centred view of social relations is discernible in Weber's analyses of the state, war and social change. For Weber, the state is primarily a coercive institution defined by its monopoly of force. He agrees with Trotsky that 'every state is founded on force'. However, unlike Marxists, for whom the state has a specific purpose (to serve as an instrument of class rule), Weber argues that the state has no particular reason for its existence but instead can only be defined in terms of its violent means. In Weber's (1994: 310) own words: 'the modern state can only be defined sociologically in terms of a specific means which is peculiar to the state, as it is to all other political associations, namely physical violence'. Nevertheless, the monopoly on the legitimate use of violence is a historical product that mostly characterises modern polities, as premodern rulers usually did not have the organisational and infrastructural capacity to control their territories. One of the key historical developments that fostered state monopolisation was the ascent of discipline. In Weber's view, the expansion of disciplined action was a precondition for the spread of rationalism, which in itself was the cornerstone of modern-day bureaucratic organisation, technological development and economic growth. Although rationalisation was a generator of social development, it is also important to recognise that its origins are distinctly nonrational: it transpired through the proliferation of violence. Weber (1968: 1152–1155) makes this point explicit when he argues that the discipline was born in war: 'The sober and rational Puritan discipline made Cromwell's victories possible ... gunpowder and all the war techniques ... become significant only with the existence of discipline ... the varying impact of discipline on the conduct of war has had even greater effects upon the political and social order .... military discipline gives birth to all discipline'. The war experience has proved significant in making the actions of soldiers more coordinated, efficient, precise, timely and disciplined, thus moulding soldiers into effective rational killers while also helping advancement of rationalisation of the institutions they populate.

However, for Weber organised violence does not only stimulate rationalisation; it also generates unique emotional, collective happenings. It is only in war and similar life-threatening exceptional circumstances that human beings develop intense communal attachments and formulate strong meaningful moral visions. The catastrophic environment of war creates unique conditions where individuals develop strong communal pathos, which are often reflected in one's unconditional willingness to sacrifice for others. As Weber (2004: 225) puts it, war experience fashions 'community until death', where a soldier willingly dies for his comrades and where these intense emotional bonds create a new collective sense of meaning: 'Death in arms, only in this massiveness of death, can the individual believe he knows that he dies "for" something'.

Both of these processes that emerge as a result of organised violence, the organisational rationalisation and the emotional bonding, have historically been crucial for the direction of social change. In Weber's account, the expansion of organised violence in the premodern Europe has proved highly instrumental in generating a multipolar political environment that ultimately fostered the development of rationalised social orders, capitalism and the nation-state as we know them today. For Weber, the latter-day dramatic 'rise of the West' versus the rest originated in the continent's unusual geopolitical situation. The structural weakness left over after the collapse of the Roman Empire fostered an unstable and war-prone environment where numerous warlords waged violent conflicts but were unable to establish a powerful and unified continentwide empire as in the other parts of the world. However, this inherent structural weakness together with the emergence of an independent religious authority able to impose ideological monopoly, the universalist Catholic Church, in the long term proved beneficial for the development of a multipower feudal structure (Hall 1985). In contrast to the rest of the world, where the military remained the private possession of the emperor, European feudalism, with its contractual arrangements between aristocratic warriors, stimulated the gradual rationalisation of social order, thus giving impetus to advancement of state formation, capitalism and civil society.

Nevertheless, although rationalisation brings about greater efficiency and development, it cannot be divorced from its coercive structure. Moreover, as Weber emphasised, ever-increasing rationalisation, rooted in rational calculation, control and teleological effectiveness, is likely to further increase organisational power. Hence, as in the modern-era, bureaucracy becomes prevalent in most spheres of human life, social relations acquire an increasingly formalised and detached character. While the traditional patrimonial orders were inefficient, stagnant and nepotist, but have also thrived on the warmth of communal bonds, the contemporary bureaucratic world is effective, energetic and meritocratic but also steeped in 'the polar night of icy darkness'. Simply put, the increased organisational capacity comes at the high price: bureaucracy dispenses with the traditional ineptitude and institutional wastefulness in favour of functionality and instrumental achievements, but this also helps damage the emotional and ethical dimensions of human relations. In this context, high modernity is an iron cage, or more precisely 'a shell as hard as steel', where individual lives become ever more regulated by technical orders and rigid rules and where spontaneity and unpredictability give a way to organisational and technological superiority. Thus for Weber, coerciveness increases with social development. This is pronounced on both the interpersonal and interorganisational levels. One of the key features of interpersonal relationships in modernity is that kinship and friendship ties became replaced with the legally enforced rules of conduct. On the interorganisational level, one can witness increased competition between different social organisations, some of which end up in violent conflicts (from corporate takeovers to interstate warfare).

Weber's approach to the study of organised violence has stood the test of time much better than that of many of his contemporaries. Despite never articulating a comprehensive theory of violent action, his insights still remain highly illuminating and thought provoking. Unlike much of twentieth-century sociology, which was deeply wrought by the Enlightenment principles that conceptualised social development in terms of progress, reason and peace, Weber was well aware that most organisational advancements entail a substantial degree of coercive action and that force remains the bedrock of stable institutional order. It is no coincidence that the most significant periods of historical transformations were also the periods of excessive organised violence. More precisely, Weber links a variety of social institutions and group relations to force: from military and ascetic discipline to the iron cage of organisational rationality, to group solidarity and social meanings born on the battlefields to the state's monopoly on the use of violence over its territory. Although Weber's contribution to the understanding of organised violence is substantial, there are also some evident weaknesses in his position.

Firstly, even though Weber is a subtle analyst who acknowledges that the origins of organised violence can be multiple and historically varied, his micro-level understanding of violent action is much less flexible. In other words, for Weber interpersonal violence has a strong primordial quality as it is implicitly embedded in all political relationships. For example, in *Politics as a Vocation*, he argues that 'the specific instrument of politics is power, backed up by violence', or that 'for politics, the essential means is violence'. Moreover, violence is seen as having an inescapable inner logic: 'violence and the threat of violence inevitably engender by the inescapable logic of all action ever new violence. In this Reason of state pursues, both internally and externally, its own inner logic' (Weber 1994: 357–387). While one can agree that political and other forms of social action can rely on the use of or the threat of its use, not all of collective political interaction is inherently violent. Instead of clinging to the Hobbesian ontology that reduces interpersonal relations to violence, it is important to differentiate between the micro and macro contexts. As I argue throughout this book, unlike the macro-organisational level, where social and political relations are built around coercive dominance and rely extensively on the use or the threat of use of violence, most interpersonal relationships, including those in the political sphere, are often violence-free. The main point here is that rather than violence being an intrinsic quality of human essence, it is much more plausible to see violent action as a product of organisational dynamics. Simply put, an overwhelming majority of violent episodes are not generated by solitary individuals or small groups but by large-scale organisations.

Secondly, despite the emphasis placed in Weber's writings on the importance of coercion and force, his concept of violence remains wedded to concrete corporal and intentional acts. As violence is closely tied to politics, there is no room in Weber's opus for violent acts that result from unintended social actions nor for coercively imposed behavioural change that produces nonphysical forms of harm, including emotional, mental or existential damage. Although Weber is careful to differentiate between violence and the threat of violence, in both of these instances reference is made to the physicality and the intentionality of the violent experience.

Finally, Weber offers a highly persuasive analysis of the transformation of coercive power through time with its focus on rationalisation and bureaucratisation of social order. Nevertheless, while the trajectory of this gradual transition is well charted and explained, it is less clear why human beings accept the life under the iron cage. There is no doubt that the contemporary world is dominated by organisational/bureaucratic power, but to understand how and why individuals tolerate such a social condition it is necessary to explore the role ideology and solidarity play in the legitimisation of social organisations. Although Weber has devoted more attention to political legitimacy than any other sociological classic, his theory of legitimate authority does not spell out the specific social mechanisms that generate popular legitimisation. More specifically, Weber identifies three principal ideal types of legitimate authority which are associated with the different forms of social orders: legal-rational domination is linked with modern bureaucratic social organisations, and traditional authority is seen as dominating patrimonial and many other premodern social orders, while charismatic authority is understood as a temporary phenomenon emerging in times of profound crisis and structural transformations. For Weber, these different types of legitimate domination correspond to the different belief systems present in each of the three social orders. This type of argumentation has been described as tautological since it assumes that the mere existence of a particular regime confirms legitimacy on this regime. For example, Grafstein (1981: 456) insists that as Weber's concept identifies legitimacy with obedience it empties this concept from its true meaning: 'In Weber's hands ... legitimacy no longer represents an evaluation of a regime; indeed, it no longer refers directly to the regime itself. Rather, it is defined as the belief of citizens that the regime is, to speak in circles, legitimate'. Although, as I have argued elsewhere (Malešević 2002: 103), this type of criticism does not take into account that for Weber legitimacy is not only about the popular perceptions of a particular social order but also about the ability of those in power to secure societywide support. Grafstein also does not take into account that even in this form, the theory still allows for the analysis of different models of popular compliance. Nevertheless, a more important problem is that Weber does not provide a convincing account of the social dynamics involved in the legitimisation process. It is far from clear why, how, when and for how long individuals are inclined to consider particular social orders as being legitimate. This is particularly important in the context of violence analysis, as violent action requires a substantially more popular legitimation than other types of social action. For example, to understand how, when and why citizens of the modern nation-states provide tacit or explicit consent for the use of violence on a mass scale in times of war, one needs to dissect the long-term relationships between the organisational and ideological power of nation-states. As I argue in Chapter 2, although social organisations rely extensively on their coercive capacities, this coerciveness is in fact enhanced by the popular legitimisation generated through the various ideological mechanisms. However, ideology is not something that leaders of social organisations impose on the unwilling populations. Instead, ideological power is often the byproduct of organisational development, and as such it originates in the same complex historical transformations that give birth to specific social organisations. Furthermore, the success of both organisational and ideological power is nearly always dependent on the ability of social organisations to ideologically penetrate everyday life and to become embedded in the micro-universe of close networks of kinships and friendships. Hence, to benefit from the Weberian theory, it is crucial to broaden this analysis by attempting to explain the long-term dynamics of organisational and ideological power as they contribute to the transformation of organised violence.

Violence and Civilisation

The relationship between organised violence and civilisation is something that has puzzled analysts since antiquity. From Confucius and Mosi to Plato, Aristotle and Ibn Khaldun scholars have attempted to identify whether civilisations tame or ignite violence. Nevertheless, most such studies, including the highly influential works of Spengler (1918), Toynbee (1950) and more recently Huntington (1996) tend to focus more on the differences between specific civilisations and less on the intrinsic qualities of the relationship between violent action and civilisation. In contrast, Norbert Elias (2000[1939]) develops an original theory that centres on the interdependence of civilising process and violence. For Elias, violence and civilisation have a complex relationship. In some respects, Elias follows Weber arguing that the monopoly on the use of violence is a precondition of civilisational advancement, as it pacifies the social order. However, in other, more pronounced, respects, for Elias violence is the exact opposite of civilisation. More specifically, his most celebrated book, *The Civilising Process* (2000), traces the steady decrease in individual and collective forms of violence to lasting processes of expanding external social control, coupled with a gradual internalisation of self-restraint. Exploring the long-term changes in the everyday manners of different social strata throughout Europe, Elias contends that the overcoming of violent action, in both its interpersonal and structural forms, is the central feature of the civilising process. In his interpretation, aggressiveness is an inherent human predisposition linked to our animal nature. Hence, in Elias' view, the further one delves into the past the more one is likely to encounter wild and uninhibited human beings who are not very different from their animal counterparts.[1] For example *The Civilizing Process* is littered with references to humans as essentially animalistic creatures motivated by biological impulses, which are presented in the form of 'elementary urges', 'drives', 'instinctual tendencies', 'animalistic activities' and 'animalistic impulses' (Elias 2000: 107–116; 119–120; 158–159; 216, 218, 230, 252, 365). In more recent publications, Elias makes frequent references to 'the animal nature of humans', to 'the elementary constraints of human nature', and to 'instinct control' whereby human beings are seen as coming to this world as 'wild, helpless creatures' (Elias 1996: 32–33; 1991: 22). In Elias's analysis, socialisation is given exceptional transformative power in the way that it moulds children, turning the 'semi-wild human animal' into a fully fledged and self-constrained person.

This distinctively Hobbesian/Freudian conception of the human subject is equally pronounced in Elias' understanding of interpersonal and organised violence. Rather than conceptualising violent action as a product of (changing) social relations, for Elias violence has a naturalistic quality. Not only does he fail to distinguish between the psychological phenomenon of aggression and the sociological process that is violence, but he also views violent behaviour as innately pleasurable. When writing about 'medieval society', he alludes to the 'original savagery of feeling' and contends that for most people 'the pleasure of killing and torturing others was great'. And because 'belligerence, hatred and joy in tormenting others were more uninhibited', so these were 'socially permitted pleasure[s]' (Elias 2000: 163). In this view, violence is seen as an 'elementary urge' and 'a means of satisfying lust'. Thus violence is an integral component of human nature which if not controlled is bound to lead towards never ending bloodshed and the abuse of others (Elias 1998: 23). Those who inhabited the medieval world are depicted as governed by insatiated 'drives' which were 'wild, cruel, prone to violent outbreaks and abandoned to the joy of the moment'. They apparently found 'delight in plundering and rape', and this gave expression to their 'desire to acknowledge no master' (Elias 2000: 241–242).

In a similar vein Elias approaches organised violence. Drawing indirectly on Weber, Elias (2005, 2000: 344) explores the consequences of political and military 'elimination contests' through which states have gradually established monopolies of violence and taxation. In his view,

---

[1] This section of the chapter draws in part from Malešević and Ryan (2013).

the internalisation of self-restraint and consequent behavioural change goes hand in hand with structural transformations in Europe whereby military and fiscal might, coupled with demographic change, urbanisation, a greater division of labour, the expansion of trade and the emergence of a money economy, fostered internal pacification and state centralisation. The rise of free towns and the steady growth of a money economy allowed former feudal rulers to bypass warlord landed nobility and monopolise the means of violence and taxation, thus enabling them to wage further wars of elimination and expand their realms of rule. European feudalism thus reached its absolutist stage with the formerly independent warrior aristocracy becoming replaced with highly dependent courtiers. For Elias, absolutism/court society expanded the internal pacification of states while simultaneously facilitating behavioural changes as the declining aristocratic courtier class relied on the symbols of greater self-restraint to distinguish itself from the rising middle classes. Ultimately, the values and practices of self-restraint and refined mannerism became status markers gradually imitated and embraced by other groups in society, leading towards more civilised social conduct. Therefore, structural changes such as state formation generated external mechanisms of restraint that eventually became internalised in the form of self-restraining behaviour which gradually spread throughout Europe (Elias 2005, 2000). Ultimately, the Eliasian perspective purports that as the civilising process intensifies, both interpersonal and organised violence are destined to decline.

This theoretical position has received much attention, and a number of scholars have attempted to provide an empirical verification of its core arguments. Although a great deal of this empirical research has focussed on the long-term decrease in interpersonal violence (Eisner 2003, Speiernenburg 2008), more recently scholars have also attempted to show the existence of the identical trends for many types of organised violence (Pinker 2011; Goldstein 2011; Morris 2014). While the next two chapters will engage with these empirical studies, it is also important to probe and question some of Elias' key ideas.

One of the central paradoxes of the Eliasian position is that despite its firm commitment to developing a figurational, process-oriented, dynamic theory of social relations, the epistemological building blocks of this approach are constructed on the Freudian and Hobbesian ontology of an essential, primordial, human nature governed by (unchanging) drives and instincts. One can leave to one side his uncritical reading of the old documents, where the rhetorical bravados of medieval warriors are simply understood as statements of fact reflecting one's biology rather than a specific social context. Instead, let's focus only on

Elias' theory of organised violence, which, I would argue, does not hold up to analytical scrutiny.[2]

In Elias' writings, the civilising process is understood as a dual phenomenon through which individuals learn how to constrain their own 'natural' violent impulses and through which entire social orders become more pacified. However, not only is it the case that civilisation and violent action are fully congruent, as all coordinated collective violence requires a substantial degree of self-restraint, but more importantly, civilisation is the cradle of organised violence. Despite the popular view that human beings have engaged in warfare since time immemorial, numerous archaeological and anthropological studies have shown that organised violence emerged only in the last twelve thousand years, and large-scale warfare only in the last three thousand years of human existence (see the next chapter). Organised violence appears on the historical stage, together with sedentary cultures – with the domestication of plants and animals, organised farming, land ownership, fortified towns, institutionalised religions, political orders and elaborate forms of social stratification. In a word: civilisation. What distinguished the first known civilisations – Sumer, ancient Egypt, Shang China, Harrapan India and later Mesoamerican worlds – from the earlier social formations was their ability to use organised violence and fight wars of conquest. The pristine states of early civilisations were created through warfare, and distinct civilisations have expanded through organised violence. Hence violence is not the 'Other' of civilisation but one of its most important components.

Secondly, by focussing almost exclusively on medieval and early modern Europe, the theory of a civilising process misinterprets the direction of historical transformation of violence. According to Elias, as external and internal constraints of civilisation gradually advance, violent action becomes simultaneously repressed and outlawed through the state's monopolisation of coercion. In other words, violence decreases with the arrival and expansion of modern, civilised, social orders. Thus Elias shares a popular stereotypical view which contrasts 'medieval barbarism' with the alleged increasingly peaceful modernity. Nevertheless, while the medieval world was characterised by episodes of gruesome cruelty, witch hunts and intermittent torture, these macabre practices often conceal their low efficiency as a means of destruction. In the medieval ages, wars were no more than ritualistic skirmishes between

---

[2] My spotlight here is only on organised violence. For an extensive critique of Elias' understanding of both interpersonal and organised violence, see Malešević and Ryan (2013).

aristocrats, and while organised violence might have been more ghastly, it certainly could not compare to what transpired with the advent of civilisation. As recent macrosociological research demonstrates convincingly, ethnic cleansing and genocide are modern phenomena inspired by modern ideological blueprints, modern means of organisation, modern and mutually exclusive state-building projects, and conflicting visions of modernity (Mann 2005; Levene 2005; Bauman 1989; see also Chapter 7). While the modern subject might avoid spitting or blowing her nose in the table cloth, the populations of modern states are complicit in many episodes of mass violence, whether detonating atomic bombs, perpetrating 'targeted assassinations' or launching 'preemptive' and 'surgical strikes', and the reality of these actions is often sanitised through the language of 'collateral damage'.

Thirdly, the theory of a civilising process cannot adequately explain the persistence and proliferation of warfare. As violence and civilisation are conceptualised as inversely proportional, the logical corollary of this explanatory model would be the gradual decrease of violent action in all its forms. And this is exactly how Elias (2000: 318) interprets the historical trajectory of European societies, contrasting the situation of 'pure enmity to the death', which he associates with the premodern world, and an essentially peaceful social environment of 'highly developed societies' where individuals are pacified through the 'ambivalence of interests'. However, instead of steadily disappearing, wars, revolutions, terrorism and other forms of violent action have expanded and have also become more deadly. As Tilly (2003: 55) has documented, the twentieth century alone was witness to over 250 new wars with more than a million deaths annually. This was a century that gave birth to total war, the Holocaust, gas chambers, gulags, organised suicide bombings and the atomic annihilation of entire cities. In contrast to Elias' diagnosis, 'pure enmity' is not characteristic of the premodern world, where violence was theatrical, macabre and inefficient, but something that emerges with total wars. The two World Wars were the embodiment of industrialised total wars where all the resources of the state and society, including all healthy men and women, transport, trade, industrial production and communications were placed at the disposal of the state at war. War became not just a conflict between two armies but between entire populations. Mass production, mass politics and mass communications were mobilised for mass destruction, as total war eliminated the distinction between state and society, military and civilian and the public and private spheres. The military ideologies and strategies behind these two wars were conceived and implemented by highly refined and self-disciplined gentlemen bent on implementing Clausewitz's (1997: 6) dictum of absolute war as a realm of 'utmost violence' where one side is determined to annihilate the other. The theory of the civilising process has no answer for this development. For Elias, war is just an epiphenomenon that is bound to gradually disappear. In his own words, the excessive atrocities of World War I are 'merely a very slight recession, one of the fluctuations that constantly arise from the complexity of the historical movement within each phase of the total process' (Elias 2000: 157). Rather than seeing warfare as an integral component of the civilising process – one of the crucial constituents of modernity as we know it – Elias sees it as a temporary 'regression to barbarism' (Elias, 1996: 308).

Finally, when facts fly in the face of his theory, Elias utilises concepts such as 'decivilising spurt' to rescue his explanatory model. An example is how Elias accounts for Nazism and the Holocaust, where he argues that the civilising process can occasionally go into reverse. So concentration camps, gas chambers, extensive systems of torture and genocide are understood as no more than a 'deepest regression into barbarism' whereby war removes all internal and external constraints and individuals revert to their 'animalistic selves'. In particular, Elias (1996: 311) emphasises the role of specific social agents wedded to irrationally held belief systems with 'high fantasy content' that provided them with 'a high degree of immediate emotional satisfaction'. In other words, a decivilising spurt strips away the civilising benefits of detached thinking and marks the return of emotionally charged communal fantasies: '[the] national Socialist movement was mainly led by half-educated men'; 'the Nazi belief system with its pseudo-scientific varnish spread thinly over a primitive, barbaric national mythology ... that it could not withstand the judgement of more educated people' (Elias 1996: 315). As most recent studies of the Nazi movement show (Mann 2004, 2005; Burleigh 2000; Jarausch 1990), much of its leadership as well as its support base were very well educated. Many German intellectuals, university professors and broader cultural elite were sympathetic to National Socialist ideas, and its core constituency was much more educated than the rest of German society. For example, '41 per cent of SD [Nazi intelligence service] had higher education at the time when national average was 2 or 3 per cent' (Burleigh 2000: 186); the SS recruits and officers were highly educated; majority of doctors, judges and solicitors were members of NSDAP. As Müller-Hill (1998) shows the majority of the commanders of Einsatzkommandos (mobile killing squads), who were the main protagonists of genocide, were highly educated individuals: economists, solicitors, academics. More than two-thirds of these commanders had higher education and one-third had doctorates. In a similar vein, 'half of the German students were Nazi sympathisers by

1930'; 'university-trained professionals (i.e. "academic professionals")
were overrepresented in the NSDAP and in the SA and SS officer corps'
(Mann 2004: 165–166; Jarausch 1990: 78). While National Socialist
ideology did attract many social strata, some of which had little or no
education, its core ideological support base were young and educated
males: 'Fascism was capturing the young and educated males because it
was the latest wisdom of half a continent. Its ideological resonance in its
era ... was the main reason it was a generational movement' (Mann
2004: 167).

To sum up Elias provides an original theory of organised violence
which has clear merits. He builds on Weber to emphasise the significance
of violence in social life and to trace the historical contexts that generated
the state's monopoly on the legitimate use of violence. However, unlike
Weber, who is much more ambivalent about the relationship between
violence and civility and is sceptical about the idea of decline of violence,
Elias is adamant that violence and civilisation are diametrically opposed
and that as civilisation advances violence is bound to decrease. This view,
deeply rooted in the Hobbesian ontology, cannot explain the staggering
rise of organised violence in modernity.

Violence and Carceral Power

In contrast to the Eliasian perspective, which understands violence as the
Other of civilisation and something that contains strong biological, if not
primordial, quality, Foucaldian approaches conceptualise violent acts as
profoundly contingent and linked to specific historical formations.
Unlike Weber or Schmitt, for whom violence is an integral and indispensable aspect of political life, for the Foucauldians politics and violence
represent two fully autonomous spheres of social action. More to the
point, Foucauldians conceptualise politics in agonistic terms, but they
also argue that the political conflicts differ substantially from violent
action. Their view is that precisely because political power can dispense
with violence it is able to dominate modern social orders. As Foucault
(1982: 219–220) argues in *The Subject and Power,* rather than being
inherently violent, political power actually stops where violence prevails.
Unlike power, which is understood as a dynamic relationship, something
that 'exists only when it is put into action', violence is seen to be more
static, as its direct opposite 'can only be passivity'. Foucault recognises
that violence can be part of some power relations, but he is adamant that
'in itself the exercise of power is not violence'.

In this perspective, the distinction is made between modern and premodern forms of governance. For Foucault, premodern orders tended to

focus on achieving and expanding their sovereign powers and in this process have extensively relied on violence. In the era of absolutism, the king's power was unquestioned and violence was used to imprint king's sovereignty on those who resisted. Some of this violence was theatrical, such as displayed in the public hanging and elaborate torturing techniques that functioned as forms of public spectacle: 'the penal ceremony had the effectiveness of a long public confession', while 'a successful public execution justified justice, in that it published the truth of the crime in the very body of the man to be executed' (Foucault 1975: 44). Once the royal power was dethroned, violence was still utilised by the revolutionaries to establish the boundaries of what was now the popular sovereign power of the state. Nevertheless, Foucault argues, over the past three hundred years sovereign power has gradually given way to disciplinary power. In other words, instead explicitly relying on violence, modern social orders control their subjects indirectly through expert knowledge, administrative regulations and technology. Simply put, the highly visible, corporal and personal power of sovereign transforms into an invisible and anonymous power of disciplinary practices.

This new type of domination, which Foucault calls 'disciplinary power' and in later works 'bio-power', dispenses with the use of violence and instead maintains its control by relying on surveillance, bureaucratic rules, statistical codification and the apparatus of science. In this new context, the use of violence is largely delegitimised as the governments are capable of disciplining and pacifying social orders through their affirmation rather than the denial of life. The focus is on establishing specific 'technologies of normalisation' which encourage self-censorship and publically delegitimise those who do not conform. Hence instead of labelling those who question state power as traitors or regicides, new categories of social deviance are simultaneously produced and policed: perverts, delinquents, terrorists and so on. The epitome of disciplinary power for Foucault is Bentham's design of Panopticon as an ideal model of prison. As Panopticon envisages prison cells with windows at the back arranged in a circular mode around a central viewing tower, each prisoner is constantly visible to prison guards. This architectural arrangement is extremely efficient in a sense that a small number of guards can observe large number of prisoners. More significantly, as prisoners cannot know when and if they are observed, they have to behave as if they are under perpetual surveillance. For Foucault, Panopticon is a metaphor for modern-day disciplinary power, where individuals internalise disciplinary normalising techniques and as such tend to police themselves and individuals around them. Although Bentham's blueprint was designed for prisons, Foucault sees the same principles (panopticism) present in most other modern institutions, from "lunatic" asylums, schools, factories, militaries to state bureaucracies. In this way, panopticism is 'an important mechanism, for it automatises and disindividualises power. Power has its principle not so much in a person as in a certain concerted distribution of bodies, surfaces, lights, gazes; in an arrangement whose internal mechanisms produce the relation in which individuals are caught up' (Foucault 1975: 202). Hence unlike the premodern world, where punishment was profoundly corporal, as violence was stamped on the actual human bodies in public displays of cruelty including torture, dismemberment and excessive killings, in modernity the place of violence is taken over by the practices of normalisation, self-disciplining, surveillance and the internalisation of dominant rules of behaviour. In short, this is a historical shift from 'a culture of spectacle' to 'a carceral culture', where 'carceral' stands for a set of punitive disciplinary mechanisms that generate what Foucault calls 'docile bodies'.

Foucault's key point is that the disappearance of violence in modernity does not mean that contemporary individuals live in less oppressive social environments. On the contrary, the idea is, as Foucault (1975: 82) puts it, 'not to punish less, but to punish better', as unlike a sovereign power which could not go beyond punishment of one's body, the carceral power is capable of penetrating individuals' minds and souls, thus controlling both the physical bodies and inner thoughts of modern-day individuals.

Although discipline constitutes an important mechanism of power relations in the modern era, Foucault's notion of disciplinary power differs substantially from Elias or Weber. Whereas both Weber and Elias analyse discipline through the prism of large-scale historical transformations where structural forces generate institutional conditions that foster disciplinary action, for Foucault discipline is not to be associated with specific institutions but with the particular technology of power. In his own words: '"Discipline" may be identified neither with an institution nor with an apparatus; it is a type of power, a modality for its exercise, comprising a whole set of instruments, techniques, procedures, levels of application, targets; it is a "physics" or an "anatomy" of power, a technology' (Foucault 1975: 215). In other words, rather than associating discipline with concrete rationalist-driven institutions such as ascetic monasteries, small Protestant churches (Weber) or civilising institutions such as the modern state or aristocratic courts (Elias), Foucault's understanding of disciplinary power is largely nonorganisational. Interestingly, enough unlike Elias, for whom violence is the exact opposite of civilisation-induced rationality, for Foucault rationality is closely linked with violence:

All human behaviour is scheduled and programmed through rationality. There is a logic of institutions and in behaviour and in political relations. In even the most violent ones there is a rationality. What is most dangerous in violence is its rationality. Of course violence itself is terrible. But the deepest root of violence and its permanence come out of the form of the rationality we use. The idea had been that if we live in the world of reason, we can get rid of violence. This is quite wrong. Between violence and rationality there is no incompatibility (Foucault 1980: 299).

There is no doubt that Foucault provides an original and persuasive theory of coercive power. As such, this account is able to identify and get the grips of coercive forms of domination, which may not necessarily have violent outcomes. In some respects, Foucault succeeds where Elias fails. What for Elias is a sign of civilisational advancement, the internalised self-control which pacifies violence, for Foucault is the epitome of coercive repression: modern-day surveillance techniques, self-censorship and the invisible yet pervasive control of individual bodies and souls. In this sense, Foucault's account is a major improvement on Elias' diagnosis. Nevertheless, the Foucauldian perspective still does not offer a satisfactory explanation of organised violence. There are four pronounced weakness in this position.

Firstly, the Foucauldian sharp distinction between violence and power is not analytically sustainable. Although both social conflict and politics are obviously possible without violence and an overwhelming majority of human interactions are violence-free, this in itself does not mean that political power can be completely divorced from violence. For example, it seems quite difficult, if not impossible, to envisage the operation of Panopticon without the institutional recourse to violence: prisons, just as mental hospitals, militaries or even factories, all rely on the threat of violent punishments. If prisoners, soldiers, patients or employees do not behave as stipulated by the rules of their respective organisations, they will all be penalised, sometimes with elaborate violent punishments: soldiers that escape from the battlefield will be court-martialled with the strong possibility of the long-term imprisonment, accompanied by harsh shaming rituals or even the firing squad; mental patients who break the rules and are deemed a threat will regularly experience physical brutality; prisoners who misbehave will end up in the solitary confinement or be beaten by guards; and even protesting factory employees might experience not only instant dismissal and the loss of earnings and social protection but also physical threats and beatings by the company's security personnel. The key issue here is that, as Weber (1968) was well aware, there is no lasting political power which ultimately does not rely on the threat of violence. As Poggi (2001: 30) specifies: 'What qualifies the power ... as political is the fact that it rests ultimately upon, and intrinsically ... refers to, the superior's ability to sanction coercively the subordinate's failure to comply with commands'. Simply put, the control that an individual or an organisation has over other individuals or organisations remains dependent on the capacity to inflict mental, physical or emotional pain, anguish or even death. As Foucauldians identify violence narrowly with physical force resulting in injuries to one's body (i.e. Foucault 1975; Oksala 2012), they have difficulty in accounting for noncorporal forms of violence. In this perspective, as Foucault himself states (1982), violence is passive, uniform, almost empty phenomenon, the exact opposite of power, which is seen as being active, historically dynamic, creative, destructive and so on. Nevertheless, if one takes a more nuanced view, it is possible to see that, just like political power, violence too is far from being an empty, passive vessel but is a highly vibrant phenomenon that appears in a variety of guises and fosters profound social change (Malešević 2013b, 2010; see Chapter 2).

Secondly, another of Foucault's principal dichotomies seems also to stand on a shaky ground. Opposing sovereign and disciplinary power might be a useful conceptual exercise, but it does not hold up well against empirical[3] scrutiny. While there is no question that with the onset of modernity technical, scientific and administrative capacities of social and political agents have dramatically increased, this is not reliable indicator that the character of power has changed completely. It is true that the modern social orders are now organisationally much better equipped to police and control their citizens than their historical predecessors were. As Mann (2013, 1993) and Lachmann (2010) show, it is only in the last 150 years that the states have acquired such infrastructural capacity to be able to fully control their territories, police their borders, tax income at the source, collect and recall an enormous amount of personal data on all their citizens, implement successful mass requirement programmes in times of war, nationalise private ownership when deemed crucial for state's purposes, make obligatory the use of personal identification papers and so on. However, these enhanced disciplinary mechanisms did not emerge in opposition to the sovereign powers. On the contrary, they are the key organisational ingredients of political sovereignty, as state power is largely defined by the ability of states to monopolise the

---

[3] The term 'empirical' is used here in a general sense. I will not focus on the conventional historical criticisms of Foucault, which point out his highly arbitrary dating of events and processes. For example, Foucault dates the shift to disciplinary power to a period between 1760–1840, but Spierenburg's (2004) data indicate that the changes in the punishment practices predate and also continue after this period.

legitimate use of violence, taxation, education and jurisprudence over the territories under their control. Rather than being displaced by the carceral/disciplinary and nonviolent forms of power, contemporary states have in fact effectively utilised these organisational controls to substantially enhance their sovereign powers (Malešević 2013a; Mann 2013, 2012). This is particularly pronounced in this so-called age of globalisation when, unlike their early modern predecessors, most world states have only recently acquired full sovereignty that includes control of such areas as mass media, public education, health, welfare, immigration, labour and employment, fiscal policy, urban surveillance, environmental planning, etc. (Malešević 2013a: 183; Meyer et al. 1997). That sovereign power, embodied by the nation-state, remains the dominant form of politics today is damaging to Foucault's argument, but even more damaging is that this dominance continues to be rooted in the polity's capacity to inflict violence on the subjects under its control. Instead of acting as opposing forces, the disciplinary and sovereign power reinforce each other.

Thirdly, unlike Elias, for whom the civilising process brings about a less violent world, Foucault understands the historical shift towards disciplinary power in terms of ever-increasing oppression. Nevertheless, his diagnosis of the past has much in common with Elias as they both emphasise discontinuity between the modern and premodern role that violence plays in society. Simply put, they both agree that unlike the contemporary world, the premodern world was excessively violent. They also share idea that increased self-control has fostered a decrease of violent action, although Elias sees this largely as a sign of civilisational advancement, while Foucault interprets it more pessimistically through his idea of 'technologies of the self'. However, both of these types of arguments are empirically unfounded. As explained above, Elias provides a misdiagnosis of violence in modernity. Although Foucault's point about less visible forms of coercion in late modernity is significant, as modern social orders have developed complex and often well-concealed mechanisms of social control, this does not suggest that in modernity violence experiences an inexorable decline. On the contrary, there is more violence in contemporary times than ever before. The problem with Foucault's account is that his focus is almost exclusively on interpersonal and intergroup violence as embedded in specific structural contexts while ignoring the level where the majority of explicitly violent acts have taken place in modernity – the interpolity level. Thus instead of looking at the violent action that takes place in wars, genocides, ethnic cleansing, terrorism or even revolutions, Foucault's eye is fixed on the prisons, schools or mental hospitals. However, if one takes into account the fact that the last 250 years have witnessed an unprecedented increase in the number of human casualties – the culmination of which were the two total twentieth-century wars and large-scale genocidal projects exemplified by the Holocaust as well as by the Namibian, Armenian, Circassian, Cambodian, Rwandan and many other episodes of mass murder – then any idea about the decline of physical violence seems implausible. Although one can agree that carceral power is on the increase, that in itself does not suggest that its relationship with sovereign/violent power is mutually exclusive. On the contrary, it is the rise of disciplinary might that has been highly instrumental in providing new and improved organisational means for the proliferation of mass killings. The ultimate result of this organisational synergy between the carceral and sovereign powers is at least 300 million deaths caused by wars, genocides, revolutions and insurgencies over the last 250 years, which easily dwarfs human losses from organised violence in the premodern era (White 2012; Malešević 2010; Eckhard 1992; see the next two chapters).

The final point concerns Foucault's rather unusual overemphasis on the role of discourse in the transformation of coercive power. Trying hard to distance himself from the Marxist theories of domination that highlight the significance of political economy but also ideology in the expansion of violence in capitalist modernity, Foucault explicitly downplays relevance of either. Hence instead of emphasising the 'economic of untruth', he shifts his gaze towards the 'politics of truth', and in this process finds the concept of discourse as a much better analytical replacement for both ideology and political economy. In this view, discourse is understood as something that constitutes subjects, or more precisely, 'subjects are not the producers of discourse but rather "positions" in discourse which can be occupied by any individual' (Foucault 1975: 115). Although this concept attempts to incorporate both ideas and materiality of social agents as well as the historical structures that foster social change, it is far from clear how exactly discursive transformations take place. More specifically, it is not clear how and why carceral power replaces sovereign power and why and how this historical transition is popularly legitimised. As I have argued before, Foucault's concept of discourse is too vague and too general to help explain subtleties and complexities of historical change. Moreover, despite its nominal critique of the structuralist and Marxist ideas, his concept still retains much of the same analytical trappings that shackle these theories of power (Malešević 2006: 58–80). The concept of discourse is particularly inadequate in trying to understand the dynamics of violent action, as it blurs the macro-organisational, ideological and microsolidary levels of social action. Rather than being a product of almost mystical, invisible normal-ising techniques, violence is primarily generated in concrete organisa-tions, is legitimised by specific ideological doctrines and appeals to particular networks of solidarity (see the next chapter).

There is no doubt that Foucault offers a more persuasive theory of organised violence than Elias. In some important respects, Foucault extends the Weberian analysis (via Nietzsche) to account for the complex dynamics of power and violence in the modern world. However, Foucault's approach also departs from Weber in its sharp differentiation between power and violence and between the disciplinary and sovereign powers as well as in its relativist epistemology. Ultimately, the Foucaul-dian diagnosis of organised violence is unsatisfactory, as it leaves a little room for the study of organisational and ideological continuities through time and space.

Conclusion

Violence is a precarious concept, prone to multiple interpretations. While there is an agreement over extreme instances of it, such as killing, there is no consensus on the other pole of this continuum. While for some violence is primarily physical and intentional, for others most forms of inequality between human beings would qualify as violent acts. In this chapter, I attempted to find a middle road by moving away from the too intentionalist and the too corporal definitions while also maintaining a firm distinction between violence and inequality. Hence violence is defined as a scalar social process involving intentional and unintentional action that generates coercively imposed behavioural changes resulting in physical, mental or emotional injuries or death. More specifically, the chapter focussed on organised violence, which is understood as a histor-ical process through which the social organisations engender coercively imposed outcomes. To situate this discussion within the broader debate, I briefly engaged with the three leading sociological theories of organised violence: the Weberian, the Eliasian and the Foucauldian approaches. By identifying the main strengths and weaknesses of each approach, I lay a theoretical ground for an alternative sociological approach to the study of organised violence which is elaborated in the next chapter.

2   Violence in the Long Run

Introduction

Unlike many other social processes, the act of violence often demands an immediate response. The injured party might quickly strike back or ask for the retribution, revenge, legal sanction or at least a justification for such an attack. Since violence does not come naturally to human beings, violent acts often invoke surprise, tension or shock and as such entail an attempt towards instant redressing of this unusual situation. This emphasis on the immediacy is also reflected in the social science explanations that largely focus on the direct and instantaneous causes: frustration, anger, disrespect, lack of empathy, lack of self-control, sense of injustice, religious fanaticism, pathological disturbances and so on. While such factors might motivate some instances of interpersonal violence, they are unlikely to explain the transformation of organised violence over long periods of time. Whereas frustrations, anger or sense of injustice can all play a part in the individual motives to participate in the revolutionary action, war or genocide, such psychological states cannot explain how and why revolutions, wars and genocides happen in the first place or why such emotions materialise in some instances and never materialise in most other cases. Hence to gauge the direction of violent action over the centuries, it is necessary to explore the broader structural contexts and how they influence the dynamics of violence over time. In this chapter, I articulate a version of the longue durée approach that aims to understand the historical dynamics of organised violence by looking at the role organisational and ideological powers play in this process. I also analyse how the growth of the organisational capacity and the ideological penetration links with the transformation of group solidarity.

The Sociology of the Long Run

This book explores the origins and transformations of violence through a longue durée theoretical perspective that emphasises the significance of

41

slowly evolving structural changes. The concept of a longue durée is largely associated with the second generation of the French historical *Annales* school, including Fernand Braudel, Georges Duby, Pierre Goubert, Robert Mandrou, Pierre Chaunu, Jacques Le Goff and Ernest Labrousse. These scholars rejected the so-called event history which was linked with the short-term time frames and the attempts to generate causal explanations on the basis of the specific and immediate factors. In contrast, the Annales school articulated an approach that focusses on the well-established and slowly changing structures. Hence, while the conventional, event-centred, historiography was preoccupied with chronicling the specific historical episodes and the dominant personalities, a longue durée approach was centred on the large-scale processes. Whereas the event history studies elite biographies, the longue durée history gives primacy to the historical reconstruction of the structural patterns and the long-term collective action. Instead of biography, the emphasis is on prosopography – a study of the common features of distinct historical groups and structure (Stone 1971). As Collins (1999: 1) rightly argues, this type of the longitudinal historical analysis requires not the social microscope of historiography but the social macroscope capable of tracing the identifiable patterns that emerge from the long-term processes. Among the Annales school, Fernand Braudel's work had the most cross-disciplinary impact. His monumental books, such as *The Mediterranean in the Time of Philip II* (Braudel 1973[1949]) and the *Civilization and Capitalism* (Braudel 1979), shifted away from the conventional nation-centric and time-specific understandings of historical change and emphasised the long-term structural transformations. Although Braudel's focus was on the role of the macroeconomic and social factors, his studies also identified the long-term complexities and contingencies that have shaped the centuries of European history.

Over the years, the longue durée has become not only a methodological strategy but also a distinct theoretical frame of analysis. Historical sociologists in particular have embraced the idea of the long run in order to trace the large-scale social change. This form of sociological analysis has evolved in different directions, with some scholars expanding Braudel's original socioeconomic approach to account for worldwide historical changes – the world system theory (Wallerstein 1989, Arrighi 1994, Chase-Dunn 1989). Others have deployed the idea of longue durée to develop culture-centred analyses of nation formation (Smith 2009a, 1986; Hutchinson 2005; Armstrong 1982). Nevertheless, within the comparative historical sociology the long-run perspective had most impact in the study of the origins and development of the state (Mann 2013, 2012, 1993, 1986; Tilly 2003, 1992, 1985; Hall 1985; Collins

1999). Unlike the traditional accounts that took the states as given and unproblematic entities, these comparative historical sociologists attempted to identify the contradictory long-term historical processes involved in the formation of statehood. In particular, these studies focussed on the role that geopolitics and military conflicts played in the rise and fall of the state power in Europe and other continents. Thus Tilly (1992) explores how seventeenth- and eighteenth-century military revolutions had different impacts on state formation across Europe, as some rulers extracted money from the urban merchants while others opted to conquer the agrarian lands. These initial differences had a long-term impact in terms of the fiscal capacity of individual states, which ultimately determined their military prowess. In a similar vein, Mann (1993) analyses how the protracted European warfare and the continuous increase in military expenditure led to the gradual penetration of the state into civil society. In order to secure the funding, recruits and resources that were necessary to win the wars, the European rulers were forced to cooperate with their civil societies and to accommodate the popular demands to extend citizenship rights. Although warfare and other forms of organised violence play an important part in these studies, they are still secondary to the main object of their research – state formation. My intention in this book is to build on this tradition of research with an aim of pushing the longue durée analysis more explicitly towards the study of organised violence. To do so, it is necessary to develop an adequate theoretical framework which centres on the origins and the transformation of organised violence over very long stints of time.

More to the point, I argue that the social dynamics of organised violence are captured best when one focusses on the three long-term historical processes that have shaped its development: the cumulative bureaucratisation of coercion, the centrifugal ideologisation and the envelopment of microsolidarity (Malešević 2013a, 2010). To emphasise these three processes does not mean to imply that they cover all aspects of social change or all forms of violent action throughout history. In this sense, the theoretical framework used is not envisaged as a causal model capable of explaining all or most significant instances of organised violence through time and space. Instead, my aims are much more modest. The ambition is to articulate and utilise a particular conceptual and analytical apparatus to assess the direction of social change in relation to violence over long stretches of time. In other words, rather than attempting to identify lawlike generalisations or statistical probabilities on the origins and trajectories of violence, the idea is to look at the patterns of violent action through the prism of these three historical processes. As I have argued in my previous work (Malešević 2004: 178–181), positivist ambition to treat the social and natural world as if they are the same is not only impossible to achieve in social sciences but more importantly such attempts regularly lead towards explanatory dead ends. However, rejection of positivism does not suggest acceptance of relativist subjectivism. Instead, the aim is to work within a softer, reflexive, historically rooted version of objectivism which maintains the view that the interpretative generalisations are possible and desirable as long as they take into account that the human world is highly contingent, filled with the social meanings and unintended consequences of individual and collective action. Hence this is an interpretative historical approach that focusses on the origins, rise and transformation of social organisations, ideologies and patterns of solidarity and the impact they have on violence. Although these three processes are deeply interdependent and mutually constitutive, it is also important to carefully distinguish the key features of each.

Social Organisation and Violence

There is a tendency, dominant in the public discourse and still just as entrenched in academia, to treat groups as generators of social action. For example, newspapers, TV reports, influential websites and many academic publications regularly refer to the violent ethnic and religious conflicts between Sunnis and Shia in Iraq, Russians and Ukrainians in Ukraine or Palestinians and Israelis in the Middle East. Similarly, references are often made to the clashes between civilizations (West versus China), classes (Bolivian indigenous peasants versus white landowners), races (killing of the African American teenagers by white police officers) or between groups with contrasting ideological affiliations (the liberals versus the conservatives in Poland). However, since the early works of Weber (1968, 1946), social scientists operate with a more subtle understanding of group action which aims to differentiate between the category affiliations (i.e. Sunnis, Russians, indigenous peasants) and the mobilised social action (i.e. specific organisations that claim to speak in the name of Sunnis, Russians and indigenous peasants). This argument has been recently extended further to challenge the notion that groups as such are capable of prolonged collective action. Instead, the argument is made that social organisations, not groups or individuals, are the principal agents of conflict (Malešević 2006, 2010; Sinno 2008).[1] For one

---

[1] Brubaker (2004:186) goes even further, arguing that one needs to deconstruct the idea of groupness altogether and replace the analytical category of 'a group' with much more

thing, it is very rare to see entire groups of individuals engaging in conflict with each other. For example, even in total wars such as World War II, when a huge proportion of the population was successfully mobilised for the conflict, only a minority of French, British or German citizens were deployed to the battlefields. For example, the United Kingdom had the highest percentage of mobilisation among all the states involved, reaching 22 per cent of its total population at one point (Axelrod and Kingston 2007). However, even in this case not all soldiers ended up on the battlefields, and close to 80 per cent of the population were never mobilised.

More importantly, as individuals espouse different interests, values, cognitions and emotions and might perceive the same situations differently, it is extremely difficult if not impossible to generate a large-scale collective action without some form of organisation. As the scholars of revolutions show (see Chapter 6), there is no such a thing as a spontaneous popular uprising capable of overthrowing a particular government. The revolutions, rebellions and uprisings can succeed only when led by well-functioning social organisations. Simply put, to fully understand the dynamics of social action, one has to focus not on amorphous groups or self-interested individuals but on concrete social organisations.

So what are social organisations? Jenkins (2014: 170) defines organisations as a particular kind of institution where: 'there are always members ... [who] combine in pursuit of explicit objectives, which serve to identify the organisation; there are criteria for identifying, and processes for recruiting, members; there is a division of labour in the specification of the specialised tasks and functions performed by individual members; and there is a recognised pattern of decision-making and task allocation'. What is also worth emphasising is that members of specific social organisations do not have to be either voluntary or active participants. For example, a prison or a concentration camp is a social organisation composed of individuals who, apart from the guards and technical personnel, are all coerced to be its members (Sofsky 1997). The strong coercive element is also present in our membership of nation-states: as we are all now born in nation-states, we are obliged to pay taxes; observe their legal systems; send our children to their educational institutions; provide variety of personal information to the state authorities when asked; participate in the elections (which is compulsory in some states); respond to the draft calls; and acquire state-approved documents in order to travel, build a house, start a business, etc. Hence social

---

dynamic concepts such as cognitive schemas, practical categories, cultural idioms, organisational routines, discursive frames, political projects, etc.

organisations establish particular and prolonged patterns of relationships between the individuals, where every individual is part of the larger organisational network. In the contemporary world, human beings are members of numerous social organisations, and much of their everyday life is dependent on these organisational networks (see Chapter 3). Nevertheless, humans have not always lived in durable social organisations. Instead, for much of our existence on this planet, social life was largely disorganised and precarious, as early Homo sapiens sapiens struggled to survive among carnivorous predators inhabiting the African savannah. Survival in this life-threatening environment required constant mobility and flexibility, which stimulated development of weak social ties centred on supple and small packs of humans built around mother and child dyads and triads[2] (Turner 2007: 23). Once humans developed survival techniques and left primordial savannahs, they tended to congregate in larger, but still highly malleable and mobile, social units, such as foraging bands. The social life of the simple hunter-gatherers did not require much organisation. As such, these nomadic groupings were characterised by quite egalitarian, kinship-centred social relations; lack of clearly developed division of labour; weak discipline; and absence of distinct hierarchical structure. It is important to emphasise that Homo sapiens sapiens lived in such small, nonsedentary, mobile and fluid entities for almost 1.8 million years of their existence on this planet. Although one could argue that such bands, and the latter-day larger tribal units, did possess rudimentary forms of social organisation (often linked to relatively mild status distinctions in terms of age and gender), this was still far cry from the institutionalised, disciplined, hierarchically established social orders that have been in existence since the early Neolithic (see Chapter 3).

Hence when I use term 'social organisation', I refer to the complex hierarchical entities defined by the regulated division of labour, coordinated and disciplined social action that involves mobilisation and control of large numbers of individuals and resources. Social organisations tend also to establish durable means of communication, transport, knowledge

---

[2] Surveying evidence from archaeology, palaeontology and biology Turner (2007:23) shows that contrary to the common-sense evolutionary understanding where apes have trumped monkeys that in fact 'humans are descendents of species that lost out in competition with monkeys' and were forced to leave the trees and start settling on the ground, where they were exposed to predatory carnivores. In this context, their very survival was dependent on their capacity to maintain weak social ties: 'To limit the size of ape groupings in the forest canopy, natural selection hit upon a solution to this potential problem by wiring apes for the female transfer pattern that, in essence, breaks the group apart at puberty and by weakening ties among all adults so that they could move alone or in temporary and small foraging parties in the forest canopy'.

generation and a degree of shared cultural practices. Such entities developed very late in human history, around twelve thousand years ago, but once they came into existence they managed to establish themselves as the dominant form of social life. Obviously, as archaeological records show, this was not a smooth, evolutionary process, and many attempts to establish complex organisations ended in failure; some long-lasting organisations have collapsed or were destroyed/absorbed by more powerful competitors while some complex regulated entities have reverted back to the preorganised foraging bands. Although there were many individual instances of organisational disintegration throughout history, there was no turning back (as of yet) from the complex organisational form as such.

Moreover, once the first social organisations, such as chiefdoms, pristine empires, city-states and city-leagues, were firmly instituted, the tendency was to expand the organisational capacity and power of such entities. In other words, once established, organisational power as such has experienced continuous and cumulative growth over the past twelve thousand years. While organisational power appears in variety of forms, including, among others, patrimonial, gerontocratic, sultanic and bureaucratic modes of administration, all these forms have proved to be much more effective in coordinating the large numbers of human beings than its preorganisational predecessors. Nevertheless, as Weber (1968) argued convincingly, it was the birth and expansion of the bureaucratic model that was central for the emergence of most successful social organisations. The historical record demonstrates that bureaucratic organisation is the most efficient and practical social mechanism to maintain order and govern complex social formations. In contrast to its alternatives, bureaucratic rule favours the use of knowledge, meritocratic division of labour, professional recruitment, a transparent and consistent system of rules and regulations and the existence of impersonal hierarchies. Even though bureaucracy is often identified as a modern type of administrative rule, its presence can clearly be traced back to the ancient civilizations, including Sumer, Egypt, Rome and China. There is no doubt that the first bureaucratic orders were quite rudimentary by our standards, as they did not possess technological and infrastructural capacities to penetrate deeply into the societies under their control (Burbank and Cooper 2010; Mann 1986). Nevertheless, the organisational competence of early empires was so overwhelming when compared to their hunting-gathering neighbours that they were able to quickly expand their influence over the large swaths of territory and regularly swallow the neighbouring foraging bands and tribes. It is no coincidence that the rise of first bureaucratic social organisations, and hence civilisations, emerged at the same time as the institution of warfare and other forms of organised violence.

As I have argued before, to understand this historical development it is crucial to study bureaucracies through the prism of coercive power (Malešević 2010). What sets apart effective social organisations from their less organised predecessors is discipline. Weber (1968: 1152) insists that the discipline is the key ingredient of bureaucratic rationality. However, discipline is not something that develops spontaneously and willingly. On the contrary, both discipline and self-control are products of intense social pressure. In the world of hunter-gatherers, this is occasionally and temporarily achieved through the specific cultural practices (such as taboo, manna, magic, etc.) that foster a degree of restraint allowing prolonged collective action. With the development and expansion of bureaucratic organisations, disciplinary action becomes more permanent and more pervasive as the very existence of social organisations depends on their ability to enforce and maintain disciplined order. As human beings are not naturally predisposed towards restraint and discipline, the tendency is to rely on coercive (and ideological) mechanisms to implement such action. Hence the other side of discipline is obedience and acceptance of external control, which entails a coercive threat. In order for social organisations to be effective, they have to have a clear chain of command, well-established hierarchies, elaborate and regulated division of labour, strict compliance with rules and regulations and so on. While most social organisations deploy effective legitimacy strategies for the existing organisational order (see below), the ultimate deterrent for the noncompliance with rules remains coercion – from financial penalties and demotions to the loss of a role in the organisation to prison to death, depending on the character of a particular bureaucratic enterprise. The key point here is that very success of bureaucratic model of rule is premised on its effective coercive capacity.[3] Although patrimonial or sultanic forms of organisation are nominally much more belligerent as the central rulers retain the ultimate right of life and death over their subjects (i.e. Genghis Khan or Attila the Hun), the internal composition of their respective organisations mitigates against the ability to enhance organisational (and ideological) power which would allow effective use of coercion. In other words, precisely because patrimonialism, sultanism and other nonbureaucratic forms of domination are

---

[3] As Chapman (1970:82) noticed a long time ago, the coercive logic of policing inevitably leads to the perception of all individuals as the law breakers: 'the complexity of administration in modern societies is such that if all laws and police ordinances were to be universally enforced, all citizens would be criminals'.

centred on the individual rulers, they remain organisationally weak and unable to fully penetrate the social order under their nominal control. It is highly indicative that once the patrimonial/sultanic ruler is dead, the tendency is for the entire order to collapse. This rarely, if ever, happens with the bureaucratic systems, as they can withstand change of leadership without much turmoil.

In addition to having this intrinsic coercive quality, bureaucratic social organisations generally aspire to and often succeed in accumulating ever more organisational power. In this process, some social organisations fall prey to their stronger or more efficient counterparts, others overreach their possibilities and collapse and some deliberately pursue full integration with other organisations. Nevertheless, the coercive organisational capacity as such has continued to increase since its inception twelve thousand years ago. Although Roman or Chinese empires are often considered to be the epitome of omnipotent organisational machines that controlled millions of individuals and huge territories, their infrastructural capacities were feeble when compared to any present-day small European state. For example, at the peak of its powers the entire civil administration of Roman Empire, which controlled over 3 million square kilometres and over 70 million people, consisted of only three hundred to four hundred civil servants (Mann 1986: 266, 274). Similarly the administration of the enormous Chinese Empire under the first Ming emperor (1371) was carried out by less than 5,500 mandarins (Hall 1988: 21). Today even the smallest states, just as well as the medium-sized private corporations, have enormous bureaucratic apparatuses. Hence in 2009, tiny Montenegro, with a population of about six hundred thousand, had over fifty thousand state employees (Cohen 2010: 47). Moreover as the organisational capacity remains dependent on technology, science, literacy levels, communication and information networks among others, no premodern polity could master such organisational might that characterises contemporary bureaucracies. Simply put, there are objective, structural reasons why organisational power increases throughout history and in particular why this increase expanded dramatically in modern era. This same structural rationale has made this process (so far) cumulative. Hence I call this longue durée phenomenon the cumulative bureaucratisation of coercion. This is an open-ended historical process that so far has been defined by continuous increase of organisational capacity and coercive (as well as ideological) power, which has been used to pacify the social environment under one's control. This growth of bureaucratic power has been most visible in the state formation, as the modernising empires replaced capstone empires, city-states, composite kingdoms or tribal confederacies and were themselves in turn largely replaced by the nation-states. However, increased organisational and coercive power is also a feature of the nonstate entities from private business corporations, well-established social movements, clandestine political and terrorist associations and institutionalised religious organisations to international establishments such as the World Bank, the European Union or the United Nations. Some of this power is reflected in the ability of nation-states to monopolise the use of force over their territories while the nonstate organisations utilise this power to control their membership and to exact symbolic or real damage to the coercive and ideological monopolies of nation-states. In most instances, the accumulation of coercive/organisational power for both polities and nonpolities has been cumulative as they have continued to increase over the past twelve thousand years, and this has only intensified in the last three hundred years. Furthermore the organisational capacity continues to develop in terms of its infrastructural reach, deeper social penetration and wider territorial scope (Malešević 2013a, 2013b, 2011).

Since the backbone of social organisations is the coercive power, they are the main vehicles of violence. The popular views, reinforced by the dominance of the Hobbesian paradigm in social science, see human beings as intrinsically violent creatures (Fukuyama 2011; Pinker 2011, Elias 2000). In this understanding, our primordial inclination to violence has been gradually constrained and overcome by the establishment of powerful and long-lasting institutions such as the state, civil society, capitalism or civilisation. The argument is that as such institutions gain in strength, they thwart conflicts, thus removing violence from the human everyday interactions and securing lasting peace and order. In contrast to this view, I argue that human beings are not naturally predisposed either for violence or for peace: we lack recognisable biological prerequisites for fighting, and we are not naturally prone towards living in very large congruous associations (see Chapters 3 and 9). Instead, it is in fact the development of complex social organisations that has given impetus to proliferation of violent acts. Hence, rather than stifling alleged genetically programmed aggressive impulses, social organisations create conditions for conflict and also foster expansion of violence among human beings. Organisational power has proved crucial for successfully mobilising the large groups of individuals as well as for maintaining those individuals in their specific roles. There would be no wars, revolutions, genocides, insurgencies or terrorism without durable social organisations. The bureaucratic entities are there to make sure that individuals pay taxes, levies or tributes that will finance violent conflicts; that they are available for recruitment when the organisations require fighters; that they are producing weapons, equipment and resources for future clashes;

that they provide popular support for the use of violence in organisational causes; and that human beings comply with so many other organisational demands. It is the coercive might of organisations that has historically proven decisive for the popular compliance.

This is not to say that organisations are superhuman entities with a will of their own. My intention is not to reify organisational power. As Sinno (2008: 25) rightly argues, this term is a form of a metaphor used as a 'simplified parsimonious model' for the specific 'set of relations that generally function far less coherently and convincingly than the metaphor would imply'. In other words, just as with any other major sociological concept, this term is an attempt to impose analytical order on always messy historical reality. In line with the constructivist thinking, the categories of language we use to describe and explain social relations are inevitably provisional as they can never fully reflect complex, contradictory and dynamic social realities. Nevertheless, in order not to end up in self-defeating relativist traps, it is necessary to devise and use concepts to understand and identify similar historical trends. In this context, I see social organisations as the primary locus of violent social relations throughout history. Moreover, as I argue in this book one can observe an inversely proportional relationship between the rise of organisational capacity and peace: as bureaucratic organisations develop, expand and penetrate social orders under their control, they tend to gain greater coercive capabilities and are more likely to generate violence. As argued in Chapter 4, the historical records indicate the dramatic and continuous increase in both the bureaucratic organisational structure and the coercive power of such organisations. Moreover, up until the second half of the twentieth century, this enlarged organisational capacity has regularly translated into the intense violent action resulting in ever-increasing human casualties and the destruction of the environment. Although the staggering scale of violent excesses reached in the early twentieth century has not been repeated in the last few decades, the continuous expansion of coercive and organisational power suggests that such a possibility is still very much present.

Ideology and Violence

The ever-increasing organisational expansion is often associated with the image of a coldly rational bureaucratic machine where humans are no more than mere cogs in this giant and highly detached mechanical system. Both Weber's (1930) metaphor of an 'iron cage' and Mann's (1986) concept of a 'social cage' express something of this alienating character of bureaucratic organisations. There is little doubt that the fully functioning and efficient organisations built around the principles of instrumental rationality, regulated division of labour and goal achievement tend to foster uniformity. The ultimate ambition of any bureaucratic order is to fulfil all requirements associated with what Weber (1968) called an ideal type of legal-rational authority: the order which follows a consistent system of abstract and written rules and regulations; meritocratic professionalization of staff who are required to undergo long, institutionalised training; existence of fixed and transparent systems of promotion based on skill, competence and experience; and a power structure that is impersonal and regulated by the written rules while authority is derived from one's place in the transparent hierarchical system. Although no social organisation in the world has ever managed to fully resemble this ideal type, the universal aspiration is to work towards fulfilling these requirements as much as possible. However, as modern social organisations aim to emulate these bureaucratic principles, they inevitably tend to resemble each other. The ideals of instrumental rationality foster the development of an organisational environment which is very similar if not identical. As Weber (1968) emphasised, once social action is centred only on the rational calculation, control and teleological efficiency, it generates a substantial degree of sameness. Bureaucracy rationalises social relations and in this way fosters dissolution of strong personal attachments, kinship bonds, clan loyalties or even family allegiances which are regularly built on arbitrary principles associated with emotional and other personalised bonds. While modern-day corporations pride themselves on employment of strict meritocratic rules that do not discriminate against their employees in terms of their gender, ethnicity, religious or sexual orientation, no loving parent would be willing to apply these same criteria when dealing with one's own as opposed to somebody else's children. We still love more and privilege our kids over anybody else, and this is never premised on their efficiency, productivity or success. In this sense, Tolstoy's maxim about all happy families being the same while unhappy ones being all unhappy in their own ways applies to some extent to social organisations just as well: whereas ideal-type bureaucracies resemble each other, the nonbureaucratic orders are all ill fated or happy in their own way.

Nevertheless, as human beings are not robots but complex creatures who thrive on the strong emotional commitments, they generally resent this nearly universal pull towards sameness. Nobody is delighted to work or live in an environment where everything looks the same and where social relations are reduced to codified rules of conduct. Even in organisations that insist on rigid uniformity, from prisons and military barracks to the cubicles of large corporate organisations, individuals find ways to resist this uniformity by making their environments and social relations personalised (i.e. from displaying posters, stickers and family photos in the workplace/prison/military establishment to socialising with coworkers inside and outside of the bureaucratic gaze).

While coercion and economic remuneration are important for establishing and making sturdy social organisations work, they are not sufficient in the long term. In addition, nearly all durable bureaucracies require also a more specific social glue that motivates its members and holds these entities together. Throughout history, social organisations tended to rely on different cultural mechanisms to secure organisational legitimacy as well as to mobilise a degree of popular support. For example, composite kingdoms and pristine empires utilised religious principles, including the idea of the divine rights of rulers, to justify the existing social structure. In a similar vein, chartered companies such as British East India or Dutch Verenigde Oostindische Compagnie regularly deployed the idiom of civilising mission both to legitimate their colonial expansion and to justify their existence to their own employees. Today, nation-states rely on nationalism to maintain popular support as well as to mobilise public opinion for a particular course of action.

Nevertheless, this is not to say that the premodern world required as much popular justification as it is needed today. While when waging wars or domestic persecutions rulers of pristine empires and early kingdoms were interested in acquiring as much support as they could muster, their target audience was usually very small – fellow aristocrats and the top clergy. As the majority of the largely peasant population were excluded from the body politic and military affairs and were traditionally perceived as inferior, almost subhuman, rabble, there was little organisational demand to justify political decisions. Hence the divine rights principle and other religious doctrines were really more proto-ideologies than fully fledged ideological doctrines (Malešević 2013a, 2010). In contrast, the birth and expansion of modernity are associated with a much deeper ideological penetration. Once the ideals of humanity, equality, liberty and fraternity take centre stage and replace supernatural authorities as the dominant source of organisational legitimacy, ideological power becomes much more significant. Ideological penetration entails substantially increased literacy rates; mass printing of cheap and affordable books, pamphlets, popular magazines and newspapers; the development of public sphere; the existence of a military draft; enlarged urbanisation; and the existence of mass educational systems, among others; all of which help politicise ordinary citizens (Breuilly 1993, Gellner 1983, Nairn 1977).

Since the French and American revolutions, popular ideological doctrines have proliferated as answering the question of what constitutes a just and desirable social order was not a sole prerogative of the elites anymore. In this historically changed context, cumulative bureaucratisation of coercion is regularly accompanied by what I call centrifugal ideologisation (Malešević 2013, 2010). This too is a historical phenomenon, an organisationally generated mass-scale process, characterised by the ever-increasing impact of specific ideological tenets in the everyday life of populations. As both the Enlightenment and Romanticism have generated a variety of diverse, mostly secular, doctrinal visions of the world, these ideological principles have been gradually embraced by both new social organisations as well as by the newly politicised populations. Although the emerging ideological discourses tended to appeal differently to diverse social strata, most successful social organisations were able to articulate narratives that have proved attractive to wider sectors of the population. Hence versions of conservatism often appeal to small farmers and soldiers just as much as to clergy, former aristocrats or big landowners; liberal discourses attract businesspeople just as much as middle-class university students or intellectuals; socialist narratives draw unionised labour and landless peasants equally as much as the radical intellectuals whereas the different forms of nationalism generally appeal to the majority of populations inhabiting nation-states. Even though ideological doctrines are usually formulated and propagated by elites, in the modern era they gradually develop into a mass phenomenon. Modernity stimulates ideological bifurcation as diverse social organisations have to compete for the 'souls' of their future adherents. This includes political parties, social movements, civil society networks and associations, clandestine organisations, nation-states, churches and business corporations, which are all required to offer distinct normative vistas and blueprints for the better future. This competitive feature of ideologisation indicates why this process is centrifugal in nature: although it regularly projects the images of ideological unity and social harmony, as ideologisation operates in the world of highly competitive social organisations, it inevitably fosters both organisational and ideological polarisation. Consequently, there is never one form of liberalism, socialism, conservatism, nationalism, anarchism, republicanism, environmentalism or religious or market fundamentalism on offer. Instead, chief ideologues of different social organisations formulate and disseminate diverse articulations of these and other ideological doctrines, aiming to convince the public that their interpretations are better, more truthful, more practical to implement or more ethical or that they are the only organisation capable of achieving these ideological goals. Hence ideologisation is a centrifugal process in two senses. For one thing, it develops and operates from the centre of the particular organisation outward. The specific ideological discourse radiates from the top of distinct social organisations (i.e. nation-state, church, social movement, etc.) towards broader sectors of population. In the same way as a centrifuge in the washing machine spins wet laundry at high speeds to remove the excess water and in this process sheds thousands of water drops, so does the organisational vortex, which spins and scatters its ideological message around to the receptive audience. For another thing, this is a highly competitive process that engages two or more rival social organisations that struggle to disperse their doctrine to a wider population while also attempting to delegitimise their rivals.

Although ideological projects are cornerstones of modernity, as exemplified by the staggering rise and fall of fascism, Nazism, Stalinism, Maoism, anarchism, classical liberalism and many other modern -*isms*, ideologisation is particularly important in the context of violence. As violent acts are by definition generally regarded as illicit and immoral, they necessitate much more justification than other forms of social action. Throughout history, even the most powerful and most revered rulers had to provide some form of justification to torture or kill other human beings. For example, when in the book of Exodus Pharaoh orders Israelite midwifes to kill all firstborn male children, it is explained that this is done because the birthrate of Israelites has increased so much that they started outnumbering Egyptians (1:9). Although this is a biblical story rather than a real historical event, it still demonstrates that even omnipotent rulers such as the Pharaohs were expected to justify the use of violence. This in part stems from the nearly universal propensity of human beings to proscribe the use of excessive violence in everyday life. It obviously is not a coincidence that all major religious traditions condemn violence and many regard killing of another human being as a mortal sin. Hence all social organizations have to provide believable justificatory mechanisms for the deployment of coercive action. This is even more the case with organisations that specialise in the use of violence, such as militaries, police, private security companies, militias, paramilitaries, clandestine armed units and so on.

Nevertheless, as the premodern social orders did not require as much justification as is expected today, the killing or torturing of those who were regarded as threatening to the specific social organisations such as empires, free towns, clerical establishments or entrepreneurial guilds was more acceptable. In the world where human beings were not regarded as being of equal moral worth, the use of violence was often condoned and approved if it fitted the established social structure. In Medieval Europe, aristocracy was entitled to torture or kill disobeying peasants. For example, in the fourteenth century, peasant rebellions were crushed with utmost severity since aristocrats perceived peasantry as no better than animals. The Froissart Chronicles document the dominant attitude: 'the knights did not have to treat their enemies according to the law of arms. The peasants were not human; their behaviour, as well as their appearance, betrayed them as animals' (Brown 2011: 271). In a similar vein, religious doctrines often justified the use of violence against those who were considered to be pagans or followers of other religions. All three major monotheistic religions, Judaism, Christianity and Islam, have provided theological arguments for legitimisation of violence in this context – from religiously mandated wars in the Hebrew Bible (stories of Amalekites, Midianites, the battle of Jericho), to the just war theory of Saint Augustine, the Crusades and the Inquisition in Christianity, to jihad in Islam.

In the post-Enlightenment environment, such forms of proto-ideological justification have lost much of their impact. One of the principal legacies of the French and American revolutions was the idea of moral equality of human beings. While it took long time for this principle to crystallise once it acquired popular recognition and became entrenched in the legal systems of modern nation-states, it had profound implications on the legitimisation of violence. When all human beings are recognised as being of equal moral worth and when violence is conceptualised as a barbaric leftover from the past, as is the case with the Enlightenment doctrine, then one cannot deploy violent action using premodern normative criteria. Instead, in modernity violence is generally utilised and justified in reference to implementation of the better or more just world. Since there is no universally accepted set of parameters of what constitutes an ideal social reality nor how to achieve this ideal world, modernity stimulates proliferation of diverse ideological doctrines. Although they offer very different and often even mutually exclusive vistas of a better future, such ideological programmes tend to exhibit a great deal of similarity in terms of their doctrinal and organisational zeal. Simply put, many modern ideological discourses embrace totalising images of social change. In contrast to traditional belief systems, some of which were nominally purist but in the everyday reality tended to operate in a messier, and thus flexible, fashion, many Enlightenment- and Romanticism-inspired modern ideological movements take their purism much more seriously. Moreover, modern ideologies, including the modernising religious fundamentalisms, are often built around projects intent on large-scale social engineering. If a particular ideological doctrine is understood by its proponents as possessing universal knowledge and the blueprint for a perfect social order, then any opposition to realisation of such a utopia is likely to be interpreted by its adherents as being a product of evil. And there is no compromise with evil; it can only be crushed. Hence, rather than using violence to suppress demands of inherently inferior peasantry or devilish unbelievers, as was the case with premodern worldviews, modern ideologies shift their focus towards punishment of those who deny equal rights for all. In other words, whereas in the premodern universe violence is used to reaffirm the existing, deeply hierarchical social order, in modernity violence is often deployed to advance social change. Nevertheless, the totalist ambitions of modern ideologies, underpinned by superior organisational might, scientific knowhow and a particular kind of moral universalism, have proved extremely potent in justifying and generating large-scale popular support for an unprecedented magnitude of violence. As argued in Chapters 4 and 7, this peculiar combination of sophisticated organisational and ideological power has proved decisive in escalating organised violence and coercive social relations in modernity.

Although the modern era has witnessed a high degree of compatibility between the organisational and ideological power, there are also pronounced structural tensions in this relationship. As modern social organisations embrace the bureaucratic model of development, they are pulled towards principles that privilege science over alternative types of knowledge acquisition. As Weber (1968) emphasised, a legal-rational form of authority is essentially domination through knowledge. In this context, for bureaucratic organisations to succeed they have to generate and utilise the most reliable and up-to-date information and data. For example, if ExxonMobil Corporation or Toyota intends to expand its production, the corporation requires the most trustworthy information available about its organisational capacity to expand further; the long-term viability of potential markets; costs of production, transport and energy; unionisation of the workforce; etc. The corporation also needs specific data on the quality and availability of oil or materials for car production in different parts of the world, respectively. One can secure this type of information in variety of ways: by pure guesses made by the leadership of the corporation; by consulting the oracle or a witchdoctor; by asking the advice of eldest employees in each company; by waiting for the sign from the gods; and by employing scientists to conduct detail empirical studies on each of these issues. Obviously, all bureaucratic corporations will pursue the latter option, as science is considered to be the most reliable mechanism for the generation of trustworthy information. Moreover, the entire bureaucratic enterprise is built around an idea that privileges (scientific) truth over the communal values. Whereas premodern organisations tended to rely on the variety of epistemological principles, modern bureaucracies recognise only one principle, as the use of scientific knowledge has proved decisive in running an effective and successful social organisation.

However, as scientific knowledge is cold and rational it cannot bind members of particular social organisations together. As Gellner (1988: 272) argues powerfully: 'social cohesion cannot be based on truth. Truth butters no parsnips and legitimises no social arrangements'. As pure knowledge is factual, dry and coldly rational, it cannot in itself bind human beings nor provide comfort. The truth does not set you free; explanations are inevitably cold, blunt and heartless. Telling a simple truth to a small child that there is no Tooth Fairy or Santa Claus will make her more knowledgeable, but it is bound to hurt her feelings. While Marx and Durkheim saw alienation and anomie, respectively, as modern processes that lead away from one's true self, it is really truth that alienates, not illusions. Unlike religion, culture or ideology, which provide human beings with meanings and communal warmth, scientific truth is chillingly unsentimental. The sincere believers who attend a religious ceremony, tribesmen who take part in the rain dance or co-nationals who experience the shiver in their spines when the national anthem is played forge an intensive sense of belonging not by way of truth but through the shared untruth. Once one realises that dancing does not bring rain, that there is no god or that nationalist rituals are recent inventions, one attains knowledge at the expense of communal solidarity. The cold, rational truth brings enlightenment, but the price is very high: solitude, emotional deprivation and the lack of meaning.

Hence, as human beings are first and foremost emotional creatures, all social organisations require potent and cohesive social glue to keep them together. Much of this glue is generated through the centrifugal ideologisation which supplies ideational ingredients for doctrinal organisational cohesion. Nevertheless, this is never a smooth and uncontested process but is regularly riddled with tensions, as bureaucratic and ideological principles clash and collide. To resolve or bypass these inherent tensions, the most efficient social organisations have managed to link organisational and ideological processes with microsolidarity.

Solidarity and Violence

So far, my focus has largely been on macro-level processes. Both cumulative bureaucratisation of coercion and centrifugal ideologisation entail presence of the large-scale structures: nation-states, empires, private corporations, civil society networks, social movements, clandestine political organisations and so on. The ideological potency of such organisations is generally wide, and the content of their doctrinal messages regularly reaches huge public. In this sense, ideologisation operates as a broad adhesive holding together vast institutions and numerous individuals. All of this might suggest that agency does not matter and that human beings are no more than pawns of giant structural forces beyond their control. Moreover, the focus on organisations and ideologies could also imply that the reception of ideological discourses is simple and automatic and that humans are naturally predisposed to live under outsized organisational structures. This certainly is not the case. Individual wills matter a great deal, and social organisations and ideologies can only operate successfully when the individual cognitive, emotional and conative needs and wishes are addressed. It is precisely because the behaviour of individual and collective agents matters on so many levels that the history of organised violence is full of unpredictable episodes, utterly contingent outcomes and the unintended consequences of social action. If this were not the case, it would be difficult to explain why very similar complex social organisations, infused with almost identical ideological principles, experience completely different trajectories. For example, it is not completely clear why during the Great Recession in 2008 some investment banks were allowed to collapse while others were bailed out by governments. If one compares the rise and fall of Lehman Brothers with that of Goldman Sachs, it becomes apparent that the relatively arbitrary political decision was made to save the latter and not the former. Similarly, the individual will of rulers has often been a determining factor in the history of warfare. In this context, the collapse of a particular polity was often premised on the contingent individual decisions made regarding which neighbouring polity should be attacked and which would be spared. For example, during the Spring and Autumn and the Warring States period in ancient China (656–221 BCE), over thirty small kingdoms were engaged in the periodic and intense warfare where allegiances were in complete turmoil and alliances were shifting on a constant basis depending chiefly on relatively arbitrary decisions made by the rulers (Tin-bor Hui 2005).

Furthermore, as the records from the prehistory and early history demonstrate, large-scale structures do not come naturally to human beings (see Chapter 3). On the contrary, it seems that our predecessors were reluctant to embrace life under complex and durable social organisations even when this has proved beneficial in terms of security and the regular supply of food and shelter. This might be in part linked to the loss of individual and communal freedoms, sharp rise in inequalities and general worsening of quality of life.[4] In contrast to popular perceptions, reinforced by evolutionary thinking, our late Palaeolithic predecessors had better health, were taller, had greater pelvic inlet depth index and had a slightly longer lifespan than average individuals living from the fifteenth to the nineteenth century (Mann 2014; Cohen and Armelagos 1984). This nearly universal resistance towards organisational structures is much better documented with the contemporary foragers from Amazonia to Papua New Guinea, who generally tend to reject all attempts by the state authorities to bring them into the fold of the established organisational structures. Such reactions are understandable if one takes into account the biological, cognitive and emotional predispositions of hominids.

As argued above, human beings are not intrinsically social, as our predecessors were probably the least social of all apes. This minimalistic sociability has expanded to some extent over time as humans started inhabiting foraging bands. Nevertheless, as early humans lived in very small and highly flexible groups whose membership would constantly change, it was paramount to recognise whom to trust and how to develop secure networks of individuals. As much of recent research indicates it seems that this highly threatening natural environment has proved to be decisive for the advancement of the cognitive and emotional capacities of human beings (Damasio 2003; Collins 2004; Turner 2007). By becoming emotionally and cognitively attuned with other members of their small, and initially ever-changing, group, early humans were able not only to survive but also in the long term to utilise these new skills to ultimately dominate this planet. Cognitive, emotional and conative skills allowed early humans to interpret and remember the meanings of emotions expressed in the face-to-face interaction, all of which eventually stimulated the development of better systems of group interaction and coordination (including language). Furthermore, as emotions and cognition are vital ingredients of group solidarity, continuous emotional and cognitive development has fostered the emergence of emotionally much tighter groups than those present among other animals and early hominids. In other words, precisely because humans are not naturally predisposed to a sociable life, they have developed unique cognitive and emotional skills which have proved to be highly functional for the

---

[4] As Mann (2014: 12) documents the shift from hunting-gathering to agriculture had number of negative outcomes, such as deterioration of health: 'Early agriculturalists had more nutritional deficiencies and dental diseases than hunter-gatherers because they were dependent on a narrower range of food crops, while greater population density produced more infectious diseases, worsened by the proximity to the diseases of domesticated animals'.

preservation and ultimately dramatic expansion of our species. Moreover, this evolutionary functionality has in the long term fostered emotional interdependence so that human beings now thrive in very small
groups. In this context, microsolidarity is the foundation of all human
sociability. Although human beings might change individual preferences
regarding whom they like or dislike over time, an overwhelming majority
derive their emotional stability and ontological security from very small
networks of close individuals: family members, lovers, intimate friends,
trusted neighbours, peer groups, etc.

The decades of research on small group behaviour have confirmed that
all such small-scale groupings exposed to adverse conditions tend to
develop intense *espirit de corps*: from platoons of soldiers on the battlefields, to clandestine organisations of conspirators, revolutionary activists, terrorist cells and perpetuators of genocidal projects to members of
close-knit social movements (Della Porta 2013, Collins 2008a, 2004,
Malešević 2013a, 2013b, Mann 2005, du Picq 2006 [1880]). In all of
these cases, it is the emotional commitment, moral obligation and similarity of lifestyles that transform a functional/operational unit into something much more: an almost sacred community where individual
members are willing to sacrifice for each other (see Chapter 9).

However, while these processes are most visible among the combatants
exposed to everyday life-and-death situations, they are just as present
among most other human groups involved in prolonged and coordinated
social action. The emotional attachment that one has towards one's
children or parents, siblings, lovers and friends might often be very
intense so as to parallel the mutual affection expressed by soldiers on
the battlefield. In fact, when such soldiers attempt to describe their
feelings towards comrades, they tend to rely on kinship and friendship
metaphors (i.e. 'they were like my brothers or my children'; 'they were
the best friends one could have'; etc.). As I have argued before (Malešević 2013a), and in contrast to Durkheim, the inhabitants of modern
social orders require ties of solidarity that are not profoundly different
from those that bound our predecessors. Simply put, there are some
cognitive and emotional limits to how far human interactions can
expand. Since the early 1990s, scientists have identified cognitive restrictions of the human brain in terms of its ability to maintain stable social
relationships. Thus Dunbar (1998, 1992) and McCarty et al. (2000)
among others have demonstrated how an average human brain cannot
maintain a large number of social interactions. For Dunbar, who has
done experimental studies on the social organisation of gelada baboons,
the maximum number of stable relationships for an average human brain
is 150. Further psychological and microsociological studies indicate that

there are even greater limits in establishing prolonged relations of mutual affection. For example, two recent studies show how despite the huge number of Facebook 'friends' and Twitter followers, most Facebook and Twitter users maintain regular contact and interaction with a very small number of individuals: the average female Facebook user with five hundred 'friends' leaves comments on only twenty-six friends' photos, status updates or wall and chats with sixteen friends, while for the average male the numbers are even lower – seventeen and ten, respectively (Smith 2009b).[5] In other words, and to stand Durkheim on his head, there is still much more mechanical than organic solidarity in the modern world, as genuine ties of solidarity require protracted emotional commitment and face-to-face interaction, which very large collectivities simply cannot provide. Just as our predecessors did, we too have a need of emotional and cognitive attunement to a very small, intimate circle of those who are quite similar to us – our family members and friends.

This well-entrenched human affinity towards small, intimate group attachments stands in direct opposition to memberships in large-scale social organisations. Whereas cumulative bureaucratisation of coercion tends to foster uniformity, instrumental rationality and cold organisational detachment microsolidary networks are built and exist as hubs of close emotional affection, informal bonding, intense friendships, love and personalised care for others. Hence these two forms of group structure are likely to pull individuals in the opposite direction: one cannot easily reconcile kinship favouritism with the meritocratic distribution of rewards and organisational roles nor formal hierarchies with strong emotional commitments. While the organisational logic is underpinned by the ideas that emphasise individual effectiveness and organisational utility, the logic of microgroup solidarity is built around the principles that abhor such values. Simply put, whereas the cumulative bureaucratisation of coercion stimulates relationships of formal and instrumental reciprocity, the tight networks of microsolidarity reject instrumental exchange and privilege deep emotional bonds. Hence the central question here is, how can social organisations accommodate such incongruous principles at work?

In the classical Weberian account, the effectiveness of bureaucracies is dependent on their ability to formalise and rationalise social relations. The more a particular enterprise displaces personalised and other non-meritocratic arrangements, the more it is likely to efficiently achieve its organisational goals. In other words, the closer one is to the image of the

---

[5] The Twitter networks seem to be a bit larger but are still well below one hundred to two hundred members (Goncalves et al. 2011).

'iron cage', the greater is its ultimate organisational payoff. This normative ideal still governs much of the managerial ethics which underpins the
majority of complex bureaucratic systems, from militaries, state administration and hospitals to universities and private business, all over the
world. Nevertheless, as the decades of research in industrial relations
show, the rigid implementation of such instrumentalist models of authority generally do not result in greater productivity. Since the well-known
Hawthorne studies[6] of Elton Mayo (1949) and others, it has become
evident that successful organisational output entails a substantial degree
of emotional interaction. Although human beings respond well to coercive threats and economic rewards, they are usually much more motivated by the emotional attachments. People work, study, compete and feel
better when such collective activities are accompanied by the affective
ties with significant others. Since Durkheim's early studies (Durkheim
1952 [1897]), it has become apparent that the altruistic suicide has
played an important role in traditional orders exposed to extreme external dangers. Intense emotional commitments inspire willingness to sacrifice oneself for others. Whereas no sensible individual would accept a
material reward to commit suicide, there are many instances throughout
history of ordinary people dying voluntarily for others. Hence the ultimate success of any social organisation is dependent on its ability to either
provide or simulate social environment infused with recognisable emotional bonds. To achieve this, bureaucratic systems tend to deploy variety
of short-term means, such as depicting their organisations as being more
effective or more just than their competitors, creating a distinct organisational culture, providing incentives for loyalty to one's organisation and
so on. For example, a particular private corporation might emphasise to
its employees that their work practices are family-friendly and that they
provide a collegial and affable work environment. Others might highlight
equitable and welcoming social relations filled with regular team-
building trips and so on. In a similar vein, most world militaries encourage development of unique identity of its military units. By calling
attention to the superior status of the particular platoon or battalion,
military organisations can encourage a stronger sense of emotional
attachment with that particular unit of soldiers.

---

[6] The Hawthorn studies were commissioned to analyse the levels of productivity on the
assembly line in relation to higher or lower levels of light. The study found that workers'
productivity increased regardless of which type of change was made (more light or less
light) and that productivity slumped once the researchers completed their study. The
conclusion was made that the increase in productivity was not linked to environmental
factors such as light, but it was generated through increased motivation as the workers
were being observed.

Nevertheless, to attain a durable and more concentrated sense of belonging to a social organisation, it is essential to articulate a potent ideological narrative and the corresponding practice that would appeal to most of the organisation's members. In other words, it is difficult to image how networks of microsolidarity can be linked with bureaucratic units without centrifugal ideologisation. In this sense, all complex, long-lasting social organisations tend to utilise specific ideological discourses to integrate large numbers of people. When successful, centrifugal ideologisation helps to bridge this huge gap between the hyperrationality of bureaucracy and intimacy of family and friendship. However, to accomplish this difficult task, ideologisation has to penetrate the hubs of microsolidarity and glue them to the organisational scaffold. This is usually achieved over long periods of time after many years of attempting to project the image of organisations as those resembling one's family and friends. In some instances, the effort is made to develop ideological narratives that directly subsume networks of microsolidarity. For example, both ethnonationalism and some religious fundamentalisms embrace the kinship metaphors and refer to the actual or potential members of their organisations as 'brothers', 'sisters', 'sons' or 'daughters'. Thus both ISIS and Al Qaeda address their constituencies in such familial terminology, insisting that all Muslims are brothers and sisters, part of the great *umma*. Similarly, the newspapers and websites of Basque nationalist organisations refer to the Basque population as 'sons and daughters of the Basque land'. The ambition here is to represent a particular bureaucratic social organisation (i.e. ETA, ISIS) as resembling an extended family. When social organisations are successful in projecting this kinship image, they are in position to attract a degree of strong emotional attachment that individuals usually reserve only for their closest friends and family. In this context, loyalty to organisational goals is understood in terms of the moral responsibility towards one's family members: if I do not work towards fulfilling these goals, I will disappoint my brothers and sisters or bring shame on my family.

In situations where social organisations cannot make such a direct shift to kinship ties, this ideological translation is achieved indirectly. For example, a business corporation such as Google or BP cannot easily deploy such familial images as its employees are unlikely to conceive of such organisations as resembling their kinship networks.[7] Hence, instead the focus here is on building a particular representation of organisational culture as being fully in tune with the emotional and other needs of its

---

[7] Although some large corporations, such as the Japanese companies, have attempted to project kinship imaginary and speak of their companies as large families (Gerlach 1992).

members. This is usually done by fostering the image of an organisation as being highly responsive to demands of its (unionised or un-unionised) labour, respectful of their family lives and the plurality of individual beliefs and supportive of their future ambitions. However, to succeed in binding their employees together, such organisations also require development of specific ideological glue. Simply put, neither Google, BP nor any other complex corporation can function smoothly by relying on the coercion or financial incentives alone. Rather, all such organisations utilise ideological messages which attempt to link the pockets of microsolidarity into a meaningful, all-encompassing, organisational whole. That is why powerful corporations put a lot of effort into branding and building a unique corporate 'identity'. Such practices are often seen as a form of advertising that is centred on the potential consumers of their products and services. Nevertheless, these activities are equally aimed at the employees of these corporations, who are encouraged, and ultimately expected, to identify with their core organisational goals. Moreover, by projecting an image of the highly successful, progressive or pioneering enterprise, these social organisations appeal to the individual social status of their workforce and in this way often manage to incorporate family and friendship networks under the organisational umbrella. Thus ordinary BP workers, as well as their families and friends, can and often will recognise themselves in the success of the company they work for. Similarly, individual programmers employed at Google are likely to develop intense friendships that are formed around the company's activities and can be well infused with the ideological messages that such an organisation disseminates.

This link among ideologisation, bureaucratisation and microsolidarity is most apparent in the context of organisations that are the principal purveyors of violence. As soldiers, police officers, paramilitaries, terrorists and revolutionaries are regularly involved in the violent encounters, they need to know that their actions are legitimate and morally acceptable. This means that their respective organisations have to devise and implement effective and believable ideological mechanisms capable of bringing together organisational aims and micro-level attachments. Since ordinary human beings, as individuals, are not particularly comfortable with the use of violence, it is paramount that when such violent episodes occur that they are interpreted through the prism of a specific ideological frame. For example, the battlefield experience of soldiers who fought in the trenches of World War I was dependent not only on the capacity of a military organisation to force individuals to shoot and kill other human beings but also on their ability to establish and successfully disseminate an ideological narrative which explains and justifies this experience. Only when soldiers recognised that they were fighting for a noble cause were they willing to kill and die for such a purpose. For military organisations to achieve this type of mass recognition, it was necessary to integrate the wider nationalist ideology with the sense of moral responsibility that soldiers expressed for their family, friends and close neighbours back home. Hence when this noble cause is articulated in the language of life preservation of those who are dearest to us, then ideology, organisation and microsolidarity become successfully fused.

Conclusion

There is no protracted collective violence without social organisation and some kind of plausible narrative to justify such action. In this chapter, I have attempted to theoretically formulate how organisation, ideology and microsolidarity work in the transformation of organised violence over long stints of time. I argue that as organisational and ideological powers expand and link with the existing pockets of microsolidarity, the possibility of organised violence grows too. This is not to say that this is a simple causal relationship and that the greater bureaucratic incorporation and ideological penetration inevitably lead to mass destruction. I also do not argue that this is a straightforward evolutionary process, as the cumulative bureaucratisation of coercion and centrifugal ideologisation develop quite late in human history (less than 5 per cent of our species' existence on this planet) and continue to spread very unevenly throughout the world.

Instead, it is necessary to emphasise that this is a contingent, flexible and fragile relationship wrought by persistent internal tensions and contested action. It is this flexibility and fragility that keep social organisations alive as they adapt and transform with time and place. This flexibility also allows for the violence to change over long periods of time. This change is rarely completely haphazard, but it often happens on the terms and along the tracks of powerful social organisations. In this context, the constant growth of organisational and ideological powers contributes to the continuous rise of capacity for violent action. Since the bureaucratic shell is not a natural environment for a human being, the bureaucratisation entails a degree of permanency: social organisations need to expand in order to survive. This equally applies to ideology: as bureaucratisation expands, so does a need to justify this process. Hence the dynamics of organised violence remain rooted in the workings of organisational and ideological powers as well as their capacity to penetrate the micro-interactional world. Let us see how this works in practice.

3   How Old Is Human Brutality?

Introduction

To properly understand the contemporary instances of human brutality, it is necessary to explore the long-term historical dynamics of human relationship with violence. In this chapter, I critically review and analyse available data and existing interpretations of this relationship. Given the paucity of evidence, much scholarship remains deeply divided over the question: How old is human violence? However, despite sharp disagreements where some scholars see humans as intrinsically violent and others emphasise their nonviolent character, there is a pronounced tendency among both of these perspectives to rely on simple naturalist epistemology. In contrast, I articulate an alternative interpretation which focusses on the structural foundations of violent action: instead of tracing violent or nonviolent behaviour to 'human nature', I link the origins of violence to the rise and proliferation of complex social organisations.

The chapter is divided into four parts. The first part briefly explores whether humans are more or less violent than other living beings. The second part provides a critical analysis of archaeological, anthropological and documentary evidence on the origins and prevalence of violence in prehistory and early history. The third section looks at the cultural determinants of violent action, whereas the last part develops an alternative interpretative position that stresses the organisational roots of violence.

Are Humans More Violent Than Other Animals?

It is difficult to dispute the fact that human beings have been responsible for more deaths and destruction than any other species. The continuous population increase together with climate change, devastation of habitats and pollution have generally been identified as decisive factors causing the extinction of various animal species. Hence the International Union for the Conservation of Nature (IUCN) estimates that animal extinction caused by human action is more than one thousand times higher than the natural extinction rate (www.iucn.org/). Although this process has dramatically intensified in recent years, it is important to remember that since the emergence of Homo sapiens, animal extinction has accelerated. For example, it is estimated that in the Americas 80 per cent of all large animals became extinct once humans started settling these continents. In Australia, animal extinction was also paralleled with the appearance and expansion of first humans about sixty thousand years ago. In some cases, the extinction of animals come about as the result of excessive hunting for food or entertainment (i.e. the dodo, Tasmanian wolf or red gazelle), but many more species were destroyed as a result of the increased number of human settlements, which negatively impacted the local habitat.

Nevertheless, as humans have historically been dependent on other species for food, clothing, labour, protection, companionship and entertainment, many animals have been destroyed or enslaved in this process. For example, the number of slaughtered animals used for consumption in the United States alone is regularly over 25 billion per year. In 2011, 29 billion animals have been killed for food, including 23.1 million ducks, 38 million cattle, 109 million pigs, 256 million turkeys, 7.8 million chickens, 2.4. million rabbits, 14 billion fish and 40 billion shellfish (Mohr 2012). The world consumption of animal food has experienced staggering increase since 1860s, and it now amounts to over 63 billion animals killed per year (Mohr 2012). As Cudworth (2015: 2) documents, 'at least 55 billion land-based non-human animals are killed in the farming industry per year'. Bourke (2011: 276) vividly describes the enormous scale of animal destruction[1]: 'In factories for killing pigs, "hog stickers" can slit over a thousand throats an hour. In the UK, twenty-eight animals are slaughtered for food every second – a total of over 883 million animals each year'. At the same time, the number of humans killed by animals is miniscule. Apart from the mosquitoes that carry malaria and other diseases, which kill up to 3 million humans per year, no other animal is likely to cause more than a handful of human

---

[1] Although the food industry is the main arena for animal destruction, animals are killed for clothing, display, hunting, pharmaceutical products and scientific experiments among others. For example, over a billion animals are killed for leather products worldwide every year: 'Buenos Aires recorded exports between 1977 and 1979 of 21,534,299 animal skins from pumas to lizards. ... Between 1980 and 1985 the US imported between 2 and 4 million reptile skins and 125 million live ornamental fish. ... The British Home Office statistics on animal experimentation for 2002 list a figure of 2,655,876 animals used' (Baker at al. 2006: 2–3).

casualties in one year[2]. For example, in the United States only one person dies from shark attack, three from bull attack, thirty-one from dog attack and fifty-three as a result of bee/wasp attack per year (HL 2008: 1). The statistics are similar in other developed nation-states. While the rest of the world experiences more animal attacks, their number too is extremely small compared to that of the number of animals killed by humans. Animals are also used as the material for domestic uses, from soaps, dyes, lubricants, plastic, rubber, strings and fertilizers to cosmetics, adhesives and cleaning products. Although human beings could for the most part exist without the use of animal food, products and labour, the foundations of all human civilisations have been built on the subjugation, exploitation and consumption of animals.

The fact that humans now completely dominate the animal world and have largely been responsible for the destruction and extinction of various species might suggest that human beings are inherently violent creatures. Moreover, the staggering asymmetry in the killing ratios between animals and humans would simply imply that even the most dangerous carnivorous animals such as tigers or crocodiles could never match the aggressive drive of the human being. This perception of humans as being intrinsically violent dominates contemporary popular attitudes worldwide and is also reinforced by many influential social scientists. The recent and highly influential books by such authors as Steven Pinker (2011) and Azar Gat (2006) among others articulate a vision of a human being as being genetically predisposed to violence. For example, Gat argues that the aggressive impulses are biological means used to acquire potential reproductive mates and food and as such violent action is an 'innate but optional tactic' utilised by human beings to maximise their genetic potential for self-reproduction. For Pinker too violence is a genetic proclivity. In his own words: 'most of us – including you, dear reader – are wired for violence' (Pinker 2011: 483). For evolutionary theorists such as Pinker or Gat, aggressiveness is something that we share with the rest of the animal world, but as humans evolved the repertoire of their violent acts and aggressive strategies has only increased.

To assess the genetic roots of human violent behaviour, neo-Darwinian scholars tend to focus on our closest animal relatives – the big apes. More specifically, much sociobiological research on violence draws on the comparisons between humans and chimpanzees. Hence as chimpanzees are

---

[2] Even in this case, it is the diseases (i.e. viruses and bacteria) that are the direct killers, not the mosquito as such.

found to be domineering, aggressive and disposed to regular attacks of other animals, including competing troops of chimpanzee (van Hooff 1990; Goodal 1986), evolutionary scholars argue that this in itself is a reliable indicator that early humans exhibited similar traits. Furthermore, they insist that in all big apes, including humans, violent behaviour was a necessary strategy for the long-term survival of the species. Thus the view is that in all carnivorous animals and many other species, violence is an inborn disposition that allows specific species to exist. In other words, mere survival in the animal kingdom is premised on one of the two most common evolutionary tactics – fight or flight – and the species which develop successful fighting capacities are likely to substantially increase their potential for procreation. The fact that humans largely control all other animals is viewed by sociobiologists as the ultimate empirical proof of their unprecedented aptitude for violence.

However, any attempt to assess whether humans are more or less violent than other animals has to deal with the two major obstacle: (a) the dominance of the anthropocentric understandings of violence; and (b) the problematic nature of the analyses based on simple analogies. Firstly, when humans observe how a tiger attacks, kills and devours an antelope, the tendency is to regard such behaviour as extremely violent. This view is premised on the idea generally shared by most human beings that taking one's life is the ultimate form of a violent act. Although we recognise that tigers have to kill in order to live and apply the same parameter to ourselves when opting to eat meat, we still employ the same concept of violence to both animals and humans and judge lions to be more violent than, for example, a cone snail. Nevertheless, this is a clear case of an anthropocentric logic which relies on the human moral yardstick to evaluate animal behaviour. In other words, when identifying a particular act as violent or aggressive, the tendency is to treat all processes aimed at the destruction or harm of one's body as being products of violent behaviour. In this view, one inevitably conflates different forms of action, such as tigers' killing for food, as very different from our own deployment of violence. This is not to say that tigers are not violent. Of course, they use their physical strength to impose their will within their streak or against other streaks and other species that encroach on their territory. The point is that one has to sharply distinguish between the biological requisite such as the tiger's killing of an antelope for food and more voluntary uses of force to establish one's dominance. In this context, if biological stimuli for food is removed from the picture and if violence is understood in terms of social relationships, then it would be possible to see that even the tigers may not be particularly violent creatures: they rarely injure or kill other tigers (within or outside of their streak) and they very rarely if ever kill or injure species that they do not eat. Although tigers and many other species rely on coercive behaviour and threats in most instances, their action could not be regarded as particularly violent, even in human terms. Since carnivorous animals have to kill in order to survive, their acts of killing and physical domination greatly differ from species such as ours which uses violence for strategic, symbolic, instrumental, ideological, economic and other reasons. We do not have to kill to live; we kill for a variety of other reasons.

Secondly, the common tendency among sociobiologists and several other groups of scholars is to infer about early humans through in-depth studies of big apes and especially chimpanzees. Although it is true that the great apes are our closest living biological relatives, as we share more than 98 per cent of DNA with the chimpanzees and gorillas, this in itself is far from being a reliable indicator of what early humans were like. For one thing, DNA similarity patterns should not be taken as an absolute measure of behavioural tendencies, for humans also share over 90 per cent of genes with cats, 82 per cent with dogs, 80 per cent with cows and 69 percent with rats. As geneticists show, 99 per cent of mouse genes have analogues in human beings and even a tomato and a human share more than 60 per cent of genes. More significantly, genomewide variation from one human to another can be as much as 0.5 (that is, 99.5 per cent similarity). Furthermore, why make inference about early humans on the basis of 'aggressive' species such as gorillas and chimpanzees and not about bonobos (pygmy chimps), with whom we also share over 98 per cent of genes and who are generally nonhierarchical, nonpromiscuous, peaceful and tend to use sex rather than violence to settle in-group disputes (Goldstein 2001::184–194)? While genetics certainly has significant impacted our behaviour, no individual member of any species is biologically regulated to blindly follow a predetermined and fixed course of action. Thus extrapolating conclusions about human behaviour on the basis of any animal species and particularly a single species such as chimps or gorillas is very likely to lead towards flawed analysis. Furthermore, as recent studies on animal behaviour indicate, widely shared assumptions about animal social life have been questioned and the researchers now recognise that we know much less about animal sociability than previously thought (De Waal 2013; Weiss and Buchanan, 2009). In some important respects, the similarity of animals and humans is almost the exact opposite of simple sociobiological analogies: rather than humans sharing 'animalistic drives', it seems that animal social life is highly complex and as such resembles complexities of human sociability. Simply put, instead of attempting to show that humans are ultimately animals, it is much more fruitful to explore how animal social life is in fact more akin to human social life.

Notwithstanding these popular views about ever-present violence among humans and animals, much contemporary social science research indicates that in fact most violent acts do not have strong biological foundations. Moreover, as Collins (2008a) convincingly argues and documents, human beings, as individuals and as members of distinct species, are not inherently violent. Engaging in violent acts is difficult and emotionally demanding, and such acts regularly generate tension, fear and a sense of insecurity. Moreover, most large mammals are biologically much better equipped for violence than humans. Unlike many other large animals, Homo sapiens sapiens is not biologically well endowed for aggressive action. In contrast to mammals, reptiles and birds, who either have sharp and strong teeth able to hold and kill a prey (lions, tigers, wolves, etc.), robust razor claws (bears, cassowaries, dogs, etc.), sturdy, sharp and pointed horns (rhinoceros, mouse, bison, etc.), strong and powerful jaws able to inflict lethal bites (shark, crocodile, hyena, etc.) or possess deadly venom (komodo dragon, slow loris, snakes, stonefish spiders, box jellyfish, etc.), human beings are very poorly provided by nature for violent action. In addition, as our species also lacks a strong sense of smell, exceptionally sharp eyesight, ability to fly or run at the speed of rapacious animals, it is safe to say that early humans were not only biologically unequipped for fight but they were just as much unfit for flight from the carnivorous predators. In contrast to other species, a five-year-old human child is still almost completely defenceless outside its group. The early humans inhabiting African savannahs were regularly at the mercy of various dangerous animals and were continuously at the brink of extinction.[3] As Turner (2007) convincingly shows, it is this constant existential insecurity that fostered the development of cognitive and emotional capacities of Homo sapiens sapiens. The latter-day unprecedented rise of humans owes a great deal to our biological weakness, not our strengths. It is very likely that if our species acquired any of the offensive or defensive biological attributes that other animals have, we would never evolve to the present-day level whereby humans rely not on their 'aggressive impulses' but on their complex social organisations and ideologies to dominate, and justify such domination, over the rest of the animal world. In other words, many species of animals are evolutionary built to possess and rely on what humans would describe as aggressive and violent traits, while human beings as such largely cannot depend on

---

[3] Unlike Homo sapiens sapiens, most other species of walking apes did become extinct long before humans became the masters of this planet.

this biological equipment. Nevertheless, the lack of such biological attributes did not prevent humans from generating much more destruction and death than any other species. Hence the key question is: If human beings are not biologically wired for violence and are as individuals not very good at violent behaviour, why and how has this species become responsible for mass murder and destruction of most other species (including its own) on this planet? To answer this question, it is necessary to look at the origin of human violence and especially the development of organised violent action among early humans.

How Old Is Human Violence?

Since the material evidence on the behaviour of early humans is extremely scarce, scholars have generally tended to rely on three sources of data to generalise about the origins of human violence. The first option, which has already been discussed, is to draw analogies between early humans and the great apes. Although this strategy has generated interesting and relevant findings about some similar biological qualities and shared genetic composition of apes and humans, it has largely proved to be a too crude and unreliable technique for identifying patterns of early human behaviour. Human beings do share a great deal with other large apes, but the fact that different species of apes have developed different social practices, including very diverse approaches to violence, means that such findings cannot tell us much about the origins of human violence.

The second, more popular, option is to look at the concrete material artefacts available from the past – documentary records and the archaeological and paleontological evidence. Although much of the historical reconstructions of the past depends on the data generated from the written material (such as certifiable testimonies, court records, medical records, etc.), such evidence is problematic for variety of reasons: the written records cannot be taken at face value, as they might reflect the prejudices or deliberate misinterpretations of those who compile them. More significantly, as Carman (1997: 2) emphasises, for most of the human past no such written records exist: 'there are no survivor's accounts, no official reports, no verbal record, no written transcripts'.

Archaeological digs provide more material artefacts, but human remains do not speak for themselves – they require scholars' interpretation, and no interpretation is immune from biases. Furthermore, archaeological and paleontological evidence is rarely if ever uncontested, as in many instances it is difficult to differentiate between human-made injuries and those generated by disease or taphonomic changes (i.e. decaying bones, tissues, etc.). For example, Leakey (1981) argues that popular views shared by some academics such as Ardrey (1976) and Courville (1967) that the disappearance of Neanderthals from Europe can be explained in terms of genocidal practices of early humans, as evidenced from skull fractures, are deeply problematic, as such changes on the skull could also result from animal scavenging, soil and water damage and other forms of environmental interaction with the prefossil bone.

It is extremely difficult to corroborate unquestionable proof of a violent act. Even contemporary cases of violent conduct have great difficulty in passing the relatively low thresholds set by the legal systems of modern nation-states: judges and jurors want to be convinced that there is indisputable evidence that violent action has taken place. As most injuries, concussions, fractures, bruises, swellings, strap marks, haematomas, thermal burns and bites heal, time is of the essence when attempting to capture such evidence. The further one moves in time, it becomes almost impossible to find reliable proof of violent behaviour. In addition, many acts of violence do not leave lasting physical damage, while at the same time physical injuries do not have to be caused by violence. Wakely's (1997) comprehensive analysis of prehistoric human skull injuries demonstrates that in many instances such physical damage was caused by a variety of nonfighting contexts, including accidental injuries, self-inflicted harm that accompanied mourning rituals, damage caused by animals and the deliberate opening of the skull to expose the brain in an attempt to heal an ill person (trephination). She emphasises that early humans who lived in caves and forests were often prone to accidental injuries of the head, and self-injuring head rituals such as trephination were common practices in the Neolithic, Bronze and Iron Age Europe, Andean America, Africa and Pacific Islands (Wakely 1997: 37–40). Obviously, nonphysical forms of violence, including psychological abuse, emotional harm or coercive behavioural change, cannot be verified through the archaeological evidence.

The third and probably the most popular method for data collection is ethnographic and anthropological case studies of contemporary hunter-gatherers. Although there is general awareness that the remaining hunter-gathering bands and tribes are 'contaminated' by the modern world, many scholars believe that in some crucial respects their social life resembles the life and everyday practices of our Neolithic predecessors. Hence nearly everything we know about the prehistorical social world of foragers we owe to the anthropological and ethnographic studies of the nineteenth-, twentieth- and twenty-first-century hunter-gatherers. Certainly there are some major advantages to this type of data collection: spending months or in some instances years immersed in the everyday life of such isolated communities can prove highly instrumental in generating indispensable knowledge about the social structure and social practices of the hunter-gatherers. There is no doubt that most foraging bands share some common structural features, such as nonhierarchical social relations; fluid, mobile and very flexible group attachments; a nonsedentary lifestyle; and a strong egalitarian structure (Malešević 2013: 21–27; Fry 2007; Service 1978). However, since many such contemporary bands and tribes have been to some extent influenced by their modern or modernising neighbours, they have developed very different social arrangements, including their attitudes towards, and practices of, violence. Thus one can encounter some hunting-gathering collectivities which shun any expression of violent conduct and never engage in inter- or intragroup violent conflicts (i.e. Semai, Mbuti, Siriono, Paliyan, etc.) and those that have been described as very violent and war prone (Yanomamo, Angu, etc.). The problem is to figure out how much of this social behaviour is a product of contact with the modern world[4] and how much it resembles the 'original' features of early human social life. Some scholars are adamant that this modern impact is so profound that using present day hunter-gatherers as proxies for generalisations about our ancient predecessors is pointless if not counterproductive, as contemporary hunter-gatherers are not archaeological remnants of previous communities but very different social groupings. There is no society which has not changed through time (Scott 2012).

Taking into account all these methodological caveats, let us see what we know about the presence of violence among the early humans. Given the paucity of the reliable data, it is no surprise that the scholarly views have tended to be quite polarised. While some analysts insist that available data indicate that Homo sapiens sapiens was from the beginning a violent creature, others vigorously dispute such findings and emphasise the relatively peaceful character of our prehistoric predecessors. For example, Keeley (1996: 37) argues that human prehistory is full of violence: 'Whenever modern humans appear on the scene, definite evidence of homicidal violence becomes more common. ... Several of the rare burials of early modern humans in central and western Europe, dating from 34,000 to 24,000 years ago, show evidence of violent death'. In contrast, Sponsel (2015: 1) is adamant that 'the accumulating scientific evidence proves beyond any doubt that

---

[4] The contact has to be understood in wider terms, as nearly all such groups, including those that live in remote jungles of Amazon or Papua New Guinea, have been influenced by changing environmental and other conditions caused by the modern lifestyles.

nonviolent and peaceful societies not only exist, but are actually the norm throughout human prehistory and history'.

Obviously, relying on the documentary evidence to ascertain the scale of violence in prehistory and early history does not make much sense. While illiterate foragers could not leave written records, much of the available documentary records from the early history depicting their own past is not trustworthy. Some scholars rely on the cave paintings to make a case that violence was prevalent in the Upper Palaeolithic if not before. For example, the Jebel Acacus cave painting shows scenes of intergroup violence.[5] Nevertheless, what is really interesting about Palaeolithic and Mesolithic cave paintings is that there is a conspicuous absence of violent images, and when these appear they generally tend to depict animals, not people (i.e. Altamira, Lascaux, Chauvet-Pont-d'Arc). Although there are preserved cave paintings as old as forty thousand years, it is only in the last twelve thousand that one can find depictions of interhuman violence in Stone Age art. As Guthrie (2005) points out, 'Palaeolithic art shows no drawing of group conflict, and there is virtually no indication from late Palaeolithic skeletons of murderous violence'.

The invention of writing, in Sumer Mesopotamia around 3200 BCE and Mesoamerica around 600 BCE, has provided historians with documentary records which chronicle prehistoric events. Thus some scholars of violence such as Pinker (2011) and White (2012) draw heavily on early available documents to argue that both prehistory and early history were characterised by excessive violence. For example, Pinker invokes various passages from Homer's *Odyssey* and *Iliad*, the Hebrew Bible and the New Testament to show that torture, massacres and war were prevalent in the ancient world. The typical example of Pinker's (2011: 6) reasoning, which is solely based on simple quantification, is the Biblical story of Cain and Abel: '... Cain talked with Abel his brother: and it came to pass, when they were in the field, that Cain rose up against Abel his brother, and slew him. With a world population of exactly four [i.e. Adam and Eve and their two sons], that works out to a homicidal rate of 25 percent, which is about a thousand times higher than the equivalent rates in Western countries today'. Similarly, quotes from *Iliad,* such as Agamemnon's proclamation that all Trojans 'must be wiped out of existence', or Achilles' description of his life as being filled with 'sleepless nights and bloody days in battle', are interpreted as evidence of the genocidal mindset of the ancient Greeks, Israelites and other peoples. Although Pinker recognises that most of the events depicted in such

---

[5] However, this cave painting is only twelve thousand years old, so it cannot act as a proof of violence before this period.

books are largely fictitious, he contends that 'they offer a window into the lives and values of Near Eastern civilisations in the mid-1st millennium BCE. Whether or not the Israelites actually engaged in genocide, they certainly thought it was a good idea' (Pinker 2011: 11).

However, there is a near-consensus among historians that such literary and religious documents, as well as early court and church records, tend to exaggerate the numbers of injured and killed in various periods of time. For example, Flavius Josephus' *War of the Jews* (75 CE) has throughout history been used as reliable documentary evidence for the scale of warfare in ancient Middle East. In this book, Josephus claims that the siege of Jerusalem caused more than 1.1. million deaths. How-ever, the up-to-date archaeological evidence indicates that this number is wildly exaggerated since 'a cautious estimate suggests that Jerusalem at that time could have had a population of [no more than] sixty thousand to seventy thousand inhabitants' (Sand 2008 131). Similarly, the cele-brated Battle of Megiddo (1457 BCE) between 'Egyptians' and 'Canaan-ites' was described by several ancient sources as involving millions of warriors and hundreds of thousands of human casualties. Nevertheless, as archaeological digs demonstrate, only eighty-three soldiers died in this battle (Eckhardt 1992: 30). Furthermore, many ancient documents tend to employ metaphoric language to highlight the significance of particular event or to impart a particular didactic massage to scare their audience, to provoke a sense of awe, to dramatize the past in order to motivate support for particular policies, etc. Obviously such documents should never be taken at face value in the same way we do not judge the behaviour of modern-day humans by looking at highly popular and extremely violent video games, films, books, Internet sites, etc. What could the Grand Theft Auto III game say about everyday life in the early twenty-first century United States to a twenty-eighth-century anthro-pologist? Probably just as much as *Iliad* could tell us about everyday life in the pre-Homeric Greece.

Even though archaeological records are more trustworthy, their pau-city and the scale of bone decay involved prevent researchers from reaching unambiguous conclusions. The general benchmark for the evidence of a violent act involves the combination of an artefact lodged in human bone and corresponding skeletal damage or clear presence of lethal bone lesions. This is usually taken as a reliable indicator of interhu-man violence. In this context, the earliest possible evidence of hominid violence with skeletal damage is traced to Sima de los Huesos Atapuerca in Spain, dating to between six hundred thousand and three hundred thousand years ago. This site includes twenty-eight skeletons of Homo Heidelbergensis, with several fractured skulls and possible signs of cannibalism. Nevertheless, it is far from clear that skeletal injuries were caused by violent interaction between hominids, whereas cannibalism was probably caused by starvation and most likely was practised on already dead corpses (Wakely 1997; Ferguson 2013). Most other very early findings such as Kasies River (South Africa) circa ninety thousand years ago, Predmosti (Czech Republic) circa fifty thousand years ago and the late Palaeolithic digs in Italy (San Teodoro Cave, Sicily, and Grotta dei Fanciulli, Balzi-Rossi) include solitary human victims – a women injured by what could be an arrow and a child with a flint in its vertebra.

Much better evidence comes from Jebel Sahaba, Cemetery 117 (present-day Egypt), where archaeologists have discovered a late Palaeolithic graveyard (c. 13,140 to 14,340 years old) containing fifty-nine burials with twenty-four skeletons that had flint projectile points embedded in the bones or were present in the grave. The general view was that around 40 per cent of individuals found in these burial sites experienced violent deaths. Nevertheless, some archaeologists and paleosteologists question such interpretation. Jurmain (2001) and Wendorf (1968) emphasise that some lithic fragments which are described as 'arrowheads' are in fact thin flakes, chips, debitage, debris and scrapers, some of which were found inside skulls but with no entry wounds. For Jurmain (2001: 20), all of this indicates that the number of violent deaths in Jebel Sahaba is less than 10 per cent (that is, four out of forty-one complete skeletons). Most scholars see the scale of violent deaths at this archaeological site as rather unusual for its time, as there are no other similar sites which contain evidence of interhuman violence involving more than two or three individuals in the Palaeolithic era. Some archaeologists argue that these deaths were linked to vanishing resources and large-scale environmental pressure and as such might be more of an exception than the rule for the presence of organised violence in the late Palaeolithic (Ferguson 2013: 117; Wendorf 1968). As Ferguson (2013: 117) notes: 'If the early date [i.e. 12,000–10,000 BCE] is correct, it puts the Jebel Sahaba cemetery within a major ecological crisis, as Nile cut a gorge that eliminated the previous broad spectrum subsistence base, including marsh resources. After this, the area was entirely abandoned by humans'.

The oldest European evidence of a substantial violent conflict comes from the Dneiper rapids region in Ukraine (Voloshkoe and Vasilyevka) dated between 10,000 and 9000 BCE. The several sites and cemeteries in this region contain human remains, some of which show clear signs of trauma: 'At Voloshkoe, of 19 individuals, 5 have some combination of embedded or associated points and missing appendages (26.3 per cent)', whereas at Vasilyevka I this amounts to one (or two) of nineteen, and at

Vasilyevka III five of forty-four skeletons have embedded points (two sites combined account for an 11.1 per cent violent death rate) (Ferguson 2013: 118; Lillie 2004: 87–91). Although these Mesolithic sites show quite a high rate of violence, they are not representative of their times but, as Ferguson (2013: 118) emphasises, are 'an outstanding exception to the general record'.

Another significant site is the Ofnet cave in Bavaria (8,500 years ago), which contained damaged skulls and vertebrae of thirty-eight people. The majority of individuals in the two pits found were children and women, suggesting that this might have been an attack on the community while the adult males were absent. The later analysis showed that half of the individuals were wounded before death by blunt weapons and the skulls were buried in a ceremonial fashion. While it seems plausible to conclude that these sites indicate the presence of violence, none of them prove conclusively that this was systematic and organised violence on display. What is truly remarkable about archaeological evidence is not only the fact that there is very little unambiguous proof that humans have engaged in intergroup violence before twelve thousand years ago, but also that there is not much empirical evidence that interpersonal violence was widespread either.

The anthropological studies provide much more information on the structure and organisation of foragers. However, there is very little consensus among anthropologists on the question of origins of violence. For one group of scholars, most hunter-gatherers inhabit a world where violence is ubiquitous. For example, Bowles (2009), Le Blanc (2007) and Keeley (1996) among others argue that on average hunter-gathering bands engage in more violence than more complex societies and as result have very high death rates. Some estimate that up to 30 per cent of adult male deaths in foraging societies have been caused by homicide (Winegard and Deaner 2010: 434; Van Vugt and Park 2008: 5). Keeley (1996: I) insists that conflicts among the hunter-gatherers are 'more deadly, more frequent and more ruthless than modern warfare'. The representatives of this approach share the view that 'from the !Kung in the Kalahari to the Inuit in the Arctic and the aborigines in Australia, two-thirds of modern hunter-gatherers are in a state of almost constant tribal warfare, and nearly 90% go to war at least once a year' (Economist 2007). These and similar conclusions are drawn on the basis of ethnographic studies conducted among several hunting-gathering communities. Typical and often quoted examples are the Yanomamö of Amazon rainforest, the Dani of Western New Guinea or the indigenous populations of the Great Plains in the United States and Canada. These tribal groupings have been characterised as having an extremely violent social life. Chagnon

(1992, 1967) described Yanomamö as living 'in the state of chronic warfare' and emphasised that aggressive behaviour is integral to the structure of a social order which privileges those men who take part in armed conflicts against other tribes. Moreover, Chagnon claims that Yanomomi men who were more violent and took part in killings out-reproduced their less violent tribesmen. He estimated that up to half of Yanomami male deaths were caused by violent confrontations over scarce resources with the neighbouring tribes. Chagnon also documented the prevalence of domestic violence, with women regularly experiencing physical abuse. In a similar vein, Berndt (1962) and Diamond (2012) identify the proclivity for violence among several hunting-gathering tribes in Western New Guinea. For example, Dani culture is seen as being shaped around cycles of war: the preparations of weapons, treating injuries, observing the movements of the potential enemies, etc. Diamond (2012: 120) depicts Dani wars as frequent, involving ambushes, open battles and occasional massacres 'that exterminate a whole population or kill a significant fraction of it'. According to Diamond, Dani and the neighbouring tribes engage in the regular demonisation of their enemies and train their boys for armed conflicts from early childhood. The Great Plains tribes have also been regularly characterised as extremely violent (Keeley 1996; Pinker 2011). For example, Keeley's (1996: 194–198) calculations indicate that in proportional terms the violent conflicts between Great Plains tribes have generated more human casualties than both world wars combined. Thus in all these accounts, hunter-gatherers are understood to be prone to an excessive use of violence.

In sharp contrast, other anthropologists maintain that foraging bands rarely engage in violence and generally do not wage wars or other large-scale armed conflicts. Hence Fry (2013b, 2007), Ferguson (2013) and Sponsel (2015), among others, emphasise that simple hunter-gatherers generally avoid violent encounters. Since they inhabit small, isolated, nonsedentary bands which live off scavenging, they have neither rudimentary organisational means nor interest to take part in violent action. The foraging populations are usually on the perpetual move in search for food while trying to avoid and escape large carnivores. The band structures are very loose and flexible, and individuals usually shift among different bands. As such, they are not territorial, do not have strong group attachments and are not well equipped for violence: they generally do not possess weapons. Significantly, bands are as a rule egalitarian in the sense that they lack hierarchical structure and tend to be organised around kinship segments. Taking into account that for 98 per cent of their existence on this planet human beings have lived in such bands, the anthropologists such as Fry (2007) and Ferguson (2013) argue that protracted violent action is a phenomenon that developed quite late in human development. As Fry (2007) argues, this is not to deny that some contemporary hunter-gatherers are prone to very violent behaviour. However, to understand present-day dynamics, it is necessary to bear in mind that all existing societies have been influenced by a variety of worldwide social changes. In other words, despite a similar social structure and congruent belief systems or nearly identical means of substance used, present-day hunter gatherers are not representative of our prehistoric predecessors. There are no historically static societies, and some contemporary hunter-gatherers have been found to be 'remnants' of historically more complex social organisations that have reverted to hunting-gathering for environmental, demographic or other structural reasons. Furthermore, many twenty-first-century hunting-gathering communities are also different from the prehistoric foragers in the sense that they are complex sedentary hunter-gatherers as opposed to the simple nomadic hunter-gatherers who dominated our prehistoric past.

Hence as Fry (2007: 71) explains, complex sedentary hunter-gatherers are socially ranked and hierarchical societies governed by powerful chiefs – chiefdoms. Such chiefdoms have higher population densities than simple foraging bands and usually emerge in geographical areas abundant with rich natural resources (such as the Nootka of British Columbia, who exploit the salmon runs of the Canadian northwest coast). Unlike simple hunter-gatherers, the complex sedentary hunter-gatherers are characterised by the excessive use of violence. For example, the Nootka chiefdom was well known for their ambushes, violent raids, massacres of the neighbouring tribes and taking of enemy heads as trophies (Service 1978:238). Nevertheless, chiefdoms tend to be historically a very rare phenomenon and as such cannot tell us much about the prevalence of violent action among early humans. Ferguson (2013), Sponsel (2015) and Fry (2007) argue that nearly all examples of violent hunter-gatherers provided by Bowles, Keeley and Le Blanc and other representatives of the 'violent past' approach are in fact contemporary complex sedentary hunter-gatherers who have been in contact with the outside world for long periods of time. For example, as Ferguson (1995: 6) argues:

Although some Yanomami really have been engaged in intensive warfare and other kinds of bloody conflict, this violence is not an expression of Yanomami culture itself. It is, rather, a product of specific historical situations: The Yanomami make war not because Western culture is absent, but because it is present, and present in certain specific forms. All Yanomami warfare that we know about occurs within what Neil Whitehead and I call a 'tribal zone', an extensive area beyond state administrative control, inhabited by nonstate people who must react to the far-flung effects of the state presence.

To illustrate this argument about the general lack of propensity to violence among simple foragers, many anthropologists have identified and analysed social life of variety of simple hunter-gatherers who as a rule avoid violent conflicts. There are at least seventy known cases of such groups, some of which are also sedentary hunter-gatherers, who very rarely if ever practice intra-or intergroup violence. For example, the Mbuti of South Africa, the Semai of Malaysia, the Siriono of Bolivia or the Paliyan of India are often identified as typical representatives of collectivities that shun violence and have developed social mechanisms for resolving disputes through peaceful means (Holmberg, 1968 Service, 1978; Gardner, 2000; Fry, 2007). The semisedentary Semai, who have no formal leaders, rely on public shame to regulate in-group disagreements. Most disputes are settled at a periodic public assembly (*becharaa*), which can last for days until agreement is reached. Such assemblies involve extensive discussion of the motives, causes and possible solutions to conflicts and disagreements where all members of the community, including the disputants, can and usually do contribute. The final decision is generally the result of public deliberation, which is articulated by the (temporary) headman, who tends to reprimand one or both disputants and ask that similar acts are not repeated in the future. In the Semai world, disputes are perceived as threats to the whole community, and this is clearly stated in the popular saying that 'there are more reasons to fear a dispute than a tiger' (De Waal 2005: 166). Furthermore, the early socialisation of children is one of the key social devices that promote nonviolent attitudes and behaviour: there is no corporal punishment or forcing children to do something against their will, and they are taught from early age on not to be stubborn but to 'give way' to others (*mengalah*) in order to maintain peaceful relations with the group. Although parents tend to invoke the fear of strangers, spirits or nature (lightning, thunderstorms, etc.) to discipline their children, no child is compelled to follow the wishes of his or her parents. Furthermore, children's games are completely noncompetitive, with the focus on exercise, playfulness and group integration. When contemporary sports such as badminton or football are adopted, they are played in a noncompetitive fashion (scores are not kept, nets are not used, etc.)(Bonta 1996). In addition to homicide rates being negligible, suicide among Semai is also extremely rare (Dentan 1968; Robarchek and Robarchek 1998).

While anthropologists recognise that Semai, Siriono and other peaceful hunter-gatherers, just as Yanomami or Dani, have been profoundly influenced by contact with the modern world, the fact that they have not automatically embraced violence might be a good indicator that aggressive behaviour is not an evolutionary absolute necessary for the reproduction of our species, as claimed by sociobiologists. A number of recent studies confirm that simple foragers are wary of most forms of violence, and when they engage in violent acts they are usually sporadic, disorganised and personalised disputes between individuals, not groups (Fry 2013b, Fry and Soderberg 2013; Ferguson 2013; Kelly 2000). For example, Kelly (2000: 51) demonstrates that 'there is a very strong association between the unsegmented organisational type and a low frequency of warfare among foragers'. In simple foraging groups, killing is not understood in group-centric terms, so violence usually does not escalate: '... murder is an isolated event that does not engender a sequel. The violent death of an individual is experienced as a relational loss – the loss of a father, mother, sister, brother, cousin, or others of like kind – rather than as the diminution of the kindred as a conceptualised group or abstract group concept' (Kelly 2000: 56–57). Similarly Fry and Soderberg 's (2013) analysis of the patterns of lethal aggression on the standard cross-cultural sample of twenty-one mobile foragers reveals that the overwhelming majority of lethal events in such communities stem from personal disputes rather than intergroup or intragroup conflicts: 'More than half of the lethal aggression events were perpetuated by lone individuals, and almost two-thirds resulted from accidents, interfamilial disputes, within-group executions, or interpersonal motives such as competition over a particular woman' (Fry and Soderberg 2013: 270). Therefore, if one differentiates simple nomadic foragers from the complex sedentary hunter-gatherers, it becomes clear that the available, although still scarce, anthropological and archaeological evidence supports the argument that early humans were generally most likely to be wary of violence.

Are Some Human Groups More Violent Than Others?

The anthropological and archaeological research clearly indicates that there are pronounced regional variations in the scale, timing and forms of violent action. Although one can observe more geographical and continental uniformity in the patterns of violent behaviour before the Mesolithic – with only intermittent instances of collective violent action throughout the world – from the Neolithic onwards, this evidence increases and becomes substantially varied. Hence it becomes apparent that violence proliferates in the regions where foraging is gradually replaced with sedentary lifestyles. This is evident from many archaeological sites all over the world and is best exemplified by the relative abundance of violent artefacts (i.e. weapons, fortifications, skeletal injuries, etc.) in the ruins of the first known civilisations such as the Middle East (Sumer), ancient Egypt, Indus Valley (Harappan) and ancient China, among others. The similar type and scale of protracted violent action emerge much later in the Americas (Zapotec, Olmec, Maya, Aztec, Purepecha, etc.) and other parts of the world. The fact that different regions of the world have experienced different patterns of violence proliferation might suggest that some cultures, civilisations or groups of individuals are more prone to violence than others. Moreover, anthropological studies of the surviving hunter-gatherers also demonstrate great variation in their attitudes towards and practices of violence. This too could imply that some collectivities are inherently predisposed for aggressive behaviour whereas others lack such intrinsic attributes. For example, John Keegan (1993) is one of the leading exponents of the idea that violent conflicts are products of diverse cultural traditions. In his view, war and other forms of armed struggle have less to do with politics (pace Clausewitz) and a great deal to do with culture: 'war embraces much more than politics ... it is always an expression of culture, often a determinant of cultural forms, in some societies the culture itself' (Keegan 1993: 12). In this context, he analyses several 'violent cultures' of different levels of organisational complexity, from the Easter Islands, the Zulus, the Mamelukes, to the Samurai, aiming to show how collective violence has deep and particularist, cultural roots. In a similar way, as already mentioned, Keeley, Chagnon and Diamond identify the Great Plains Native Americans, Yanomamo and Dani as being the typical representatives of the tribal groupings whose cultural practices and entire lifestyle are shaped around regular cycles of excessive violence. In most of these accounts, violence is perceived to be an ingrained characteristic of some cultures.

While it is certainly true that there are pronounced differences between various social orders and organised collectivities in terms of their reliance on violence in everyday life, the origins of this difference are mostly structural, not cultural or biological. As I have argued elsewhere (Malešević 2013, 2010) not much is gained if violence is understood through the prism of cultural difference or biological stimuli. Both biological and cultural explanations tend to utilise functionalist and circular logic which confuses causes and needs. There are many culturally (and biologically) similar collectivities in the Amazon and Western New Guinea that do not engage in violent acts on the scale associated with Yanomami or Dani, or at all. If culture or biology is to be the principal explanatory variable, why is it possible to witness such diverse collective responses? While some social orders glorify violence and socialise their youth in the spirit of the warrior ethos, these cultural practices cannot explain by themselves how and why they have been embraced and maintained by members of a particular tribe. Moreover, why do children who have been socialised in a similar, if not identical, way develop into different adults, as not all Danis or Yanomami are vicious killers? How come individuals who grew up in very violent communities can easily adapt to life without violence, as was the case of many settled hunter-gatherers over the past fifty years?

All cultural specificities have distinct structural origins. In other words, invoking culture as something given, primordial and fixed is not only problematic but more importantly cannot help us explain the historical trajectories of violent action among diverse groups. If the overwhelming majority of simple hunter-gatherers shun violence and rarely if ever engage in protracted violent confrontations, then the key question is, why have some complex hunter-gatherers developed 'cultures of violence' in response to their changing social environments? To answer this question properly, it is necessary to explore the structural complexities of this social change.

Perhaps it is best to start from these three examples, as they are regularly seen to represent the epitome of violent culture. The tribal groupings of the Great Plains, such as the Blackfoot, Arapaho, Cheyenne, Comanche, Crow and Kiowa Apache, among others, have often been described as being war prone and having strong warrior cultures. The popular images of scalped enemy heads, raped women, pillaged villages and tortured war prisoners are typically associated with many of these tribes. Nevertheless, as Farb (1991[1968]) demonstrates, rather than having an intrinsic proclivity for violence from time immemorial, these tribes were, for the most part, a historical product of the European colonialism, as an overwhelming majority of these groups did not exist as such before the European conquest. Simply put, the Great Plains Indians developed from the descendants of refugees of various precontact tribes. As European colonisation advanced, most native populations were decimated by disease and colonial expansion, while the remnants of these populations created new social orders and cultures built around horses, guns and alcohol, all of which were introduced by the European invasion. Hence there is nothing inherently violent about the Great Plains hunter-gatherers: their violent cultural practices are not ubiquitous but were a product of the specific structural transformation.

Similarly, Chagnon's (2013, 1992) highly influential accounts of Yanomami as 'the fierce people' and 'dangerous tribe' who engage in regular violent raids, feuds and wars with the neighbouring tribes has been vigorously challenged by much recent research. Ferguson (1995), Sponsel (1998), Harris (1984) and Lizot (1985), among others, have shown that Yanomami violent practices are a relatively recent development influenced by changing social, environmental and demographic conditions. For some, such as Harris, violence developed as a response to the lack of nutritional resources in their territory. For most others, the shift to violence was a gradual development caused by the colonial expansion in South America. Thus Ferguson (1995) argues that the Yanomami lifestyle was directly influenced by the changing regional, national and global political economy, including differential access to metal trade goods. Lizot (1985) and Sponsel (1998) further question Chagnon's findings about the prevalence of violence in everyday life.[6] Sponsel insists that the Yanomami's periodic raids cannot be characterised as warfare but rather as blood feuds that are common among sedentary hunter-gatherers. Lizot (1985: 16) argues that the Yanomami's violence is actually not as frequent as Chagnon would have us believe: 'Violence is only sporadic; it never dominates social life for any length of time, and long peaceful moments can separate two explosions. When one is acquainted with the societies of the North American plains or the societies of the Chaco in South America, one cannot say that Yanomami culture is organized around warfare as Chagnon does'.

The third example of supposedly highly violent culture, the Dani, seems also to be an exaggeration. Much of anthropological research emphasises that most armed conflicts between Dani and their neighbours result in a small number of casualties (Centeno and Enriquez 2016). What some, such as Diamond, term primitive wars are in fact small-scale ritualistic skirmishes which are less focussed on killing or injuring an enemy and much more on insulting and ritually humiliating the adversary. Instead of aiming to capture territory or material goods, such armed encounters are centred on establishing a sense of ritualistic domination. Consequently, such conflicts typically involve a handful of injuries and very few deaths. It is true that over the twentieth century, these conflicts have intensified and became more destructive, but here again this was a result of the external transformations caused by European colonial expansion.

Thus in all of these cases biological and cultural explanations seem to falter. The sedentary hunter-gatherers embrace violence in the context of a profound structural change. These changes are sometimes direct, as

---

[6] It seems Chagnon was in part responsible for making some Yanomami violent as he facilitated a violent raid 'by taking a 10-man raiding party upstream in his motorised canoe' (Chagnon 1992: 201–202; Fry 2013a: 531).

when the colonial power invades a particular world region and establishes new rules of the (coercive) game (i.e. the Great Plains populations), but in many other instances this impact is less direct, as the global transformations trickle down circuitously (as in the cases of the Yanomami and Dani). This indicates that to properly and fully understand the origin and the long-term dynamics of violence, it is crucial to shift our gaze from biology and culture towards the organisational foundations of violent action.

The Organisational Foundations of Violence

Despite the obvious paucity of evidence on the behaviour of early humans, what comes across from the various anthropological, archaeological, paleontological and other studies is that there is no proof that early humans were particularly violent creatures. This is not to say that violence was completely absent from daily life nor that our predecessors were peace loving and harmless beings. There is no evidence for such claims either. The romantic portrayals of the early Homo sapiens sapiens as inherently peaceful – which dominate some strands of anthropological scholarship – are as problematic as the sociobiological, violence-centred accounts. As I have argued in my previous work (Malešević 2010; 2008), neither the Hobbesian nor the Rousseauian paradigm can adequately explain the dynamics of violent action. Just as Hobbes and Rousseau were in some important respects representatives of the similar philosophical tradition (i.e. the social contract theory), so are contemporary Rousseauian and Hobbesian anthropologists of violence: despite their diametrically opposed views on human relations to violence, they both embrace an essentialist understanding of social relations. Simply put, instead of analysing violent interaction through the prism of changing social and structural relations, these scholars tend to focus on the spurious and sociologically meaningless question, that is, are human beings inherently violent or peaceful? Hence for Sponsel (2015: 2), 'nonviolence and peace are natural, ubiquitous, and normal in the human species throughout its evolution and adaptation. In fact, for well over a million years evolution has selected for a human nature that is naturally inclined toward nonviolence, peace, cooperation, reciprocity, empathy, and compassion'. In stark contrast, for Pinker (2011) and Shaw and Wong (1989), human beings are genetically wired for violence.

Nevertheless, if one understands social relations as complex, changing and flexible, then the starting point of any historical analysis of violent action should not be the inherent predispositions but its social dynamics. Human beings are processual creatures prone to very diverse forms of social conduct. Nobody is born a murderer or a saint, and everybody can find herself in a social situation that will stimulate violent or nonviolent courses of action. Violence is first and foremost a social relation between two or more living organisms; it is not a biological quality. It is a particular form of social action that human beings alone categorise as violent. It is not a fixed trait but something that is historically generated, structurally shaped and ideologically framed. Not every form of bodily injury is characterised as violence. For example, when two boxers hit each other in the face causing bloodletting injuries, we called this a sporting encounter, and when a random passerby touches a breast of a woman he does not know, this is legally and morally defined as a violent act (i.e. the violation of bodily integrity) likely to result in a prison sentence if charges are pressed. Although the boxers experience much more physical pain than the caressed woman, the contemporary definitions categorise the former as substantially less violent than the latter. Obviously, these two examples are historically and culturally specific as in other periods of history, and in other cultural contexts such social acts would be deemed very differently. The key point here is that all assumptions about the inherent propensity of human beings to either peace or violence are built on the highly problematic, naturalistic foundations. However, there is no such a thing called human nature. Human beings are not invariable and static creatures. Obviously, our biological and genetic makeup plays an important part in our actions, but human beings are also sufficiently plastic and adoptable creatures that engage in the variety of social action. There are no natural-born killers, and the same individuals can at some point in time behave as vicious executioners and at other times as compassionate life preservers. To understand the dynamics of violence, it is crucial to look at the social contexts that generate violent outcomes. In other words, to explain the origins and expansion of violence entails shifting one's attention from biology and simple evolutionary logic towards historical sociology.

Once the focus of our analysis is on the social and historical context instead of biological traits, it becomes apparent that violence proliferates in specific structural conditions. More specifically, large-scale violent action necessitates the development of durable social organisations, as disorganised violence does not last and is unlikely to have any long-term impact. Therefore, unlike some scholars who attribute violent acts to individual or collective motivation and see violence as the property of specific groups,[7] it is much more fruitful to look not at groups or

---

[7] For convincing critique of such groupist epistemologies, see Brubaker (2004).

individuals but at social organisations as the dominant purveyors of violent, and other, action. This is not to say that individuals and groups do not matter. Of course they do, as their motivation and willingness to take part in social organisations make such organisations possible and meaningful. Organisations can exist only as long as there are concrete individuals and groups willing to support or operate in such organisations. Nevertheless, as large-scale social organisations depend on hundreds of thousands of individuals and can last for hundreds of years, no single group or individual is as significant as the organisation itself, and all individuals are ultimately replaceable. For example, the Catholic Church is a powerful social organisation which has been in existence for two thousand years. Although its membership constantly changes and is replaced with new popes, cardinals, priests and ordinary believers, its organisational structure, in many crucial respects, largely remains intact.

Once established, social organisations can be very efficient and if effectively run can expand substantially. Much of human social development is reflected in the growing complexity of social organisations and, as Weber noticed long ago, one of the key defining features of modernity is the dependence of human beings on (bureaucratic) social organisations. We now live in a world which is completely permeated by organisational power. We are born in organisations (hospitals); we are raised and educated in organisations (nurseries, schools, colleges); we work in organisations (private companies or public sector entities); we depend on protection of organisations (police, military, private security agencies); our transport and communications are managed by organisations (public and private corporations); our roads, utilities and houses are built by organisations; and our citizenship rights are confirmed and enacted by social organisations (nation-states).

Although social organisations are usually perceived as the most effective devices for undertaking a variety of tasks in complex societies, they also have a pronounced coercive edge. There is no doubt that organisations are necessary in order to manage the large numbers of individuals: while small families, neighbours and groups of friends can accomplish everyday tasks without much hierarchy, division of labour or specialisation, large entities such as private businesses, religious denominations or social movements would not be able to exist without well-established organisational shells. One of the key taxonomic contributions made by Max Weber (1968) is his distinction between bureaucracy and patrimonialism: while patrimonial forms of authority rely on tradition, kin-based loyalties, arbitrary decision making and clientelism, bureaucratic authority is rooted in professionalism, impersonal hierarchies, strict division of labour, consistent and transparent rules and knowledge-based decision making. Weber is of course right that the legal-rational bureaucratic mode of administration is likely to regularly trump its patrimonial alternatives as in the long run it has proved to be much more efficient. However, what is generally missing from this account are two things: (a) the historical analysis of organisational power which would help us understand the logic of transformations from one to another type of rule and authority; and (b) the exploration of the coercive foundations of all social organisations. To understand the historical dynamics of violence, it is necessary to tackle both of these issues.

The Historical Trajectory of Organisational Power

Weber's distinction between bureaucracy and patrimonialism is valid and illuminating, but it does not really tell us much about the prepatrimonial social world. Is there a year zero in the development of social organisations, or have patrimonial and other forms of traditional authority always existed? In one sense, organisational power predates Homo sapiens sapiens, as our hominid predecessors were involved in a variety of coordinated action, some of which did acquire clear organisational shape. Moreover, hominids are not unique in developing organisational structures, as ants, wasps, monkeys, apes and many other animals and insects have hierarchies, division of labour, specialisation and other key features of organisational power. Nevertheless, in another, more central, sense, durable, effective, transformative, large-scale complex social organisations developed very late in human history. While simple hunter-gatherers do create and rely extensively on organisational mechanisms such as the gendered division of labour, age and, in some cases, status hierarchies, none of these life practices led to the development of lasting, transformative and efficient large-scale social organisations. This is not to say that hunter-gatherers are fixed and unchangeable social forms, as clearly they are prone to change, but only that such nonsedentary lifestyles are highly unlikely to generate powerful organisational structures.

The predecessors of modern-day social organisations emerge only in the last twelve thousand years of human existence on this planet. The Neolithic revolution/demographic transition was a key moment in world history, as it gave birth to the first sedentary congregations which gradually replaced gathering and hunting with agriculture as the principal means of daily subsistence. This was also a period when humans have managed to domesticate many species of animals and plants, and with the greater availability of food the planet experienced a demographic explosion. Thus with the Neolithic revolution, the world of nomadic foragers became gradually replaced with the sedentary social orders where individuals inhabit settled urban and rural congregations and specialise in agricultural production (i.e. the techniques of irrigation, deforestation, crop cultivation, food storage, etc.). The last twelve thousand years of human development witnessed the co-evolution of sedentary lifestyles with relatively densely populated centres, elaborate division of labour, professional specialisation, the development of relatively centralised political structures, regulated private ownership and established and legitimate social hierarchies. In a nutshell, the main distinguishing feature of the pre-Neolithic and post-Neolithic world is the emergence of durable and well-entrenched social organisations. While there is a general consensus that the Neolithic brings about a completely different form of human social life, it is far from clear how and why this unprecedented large-scale social transition unfolded.

Marxist-inspired scholars insist that such a transition was rooted in the changing modes of production, as agriculture allowed the creation of surplus food which was quickly monopolised by the nonproducing ruling strata (Mandel 1968). For Sahlins (1972), the capacity to store surplus food was crucial as it, on the one hand, stimulated development of organisational competence (i.e. coordination of large groups of people necessary for building big food storages, etc.) and on the other hand it provided control of the continuous economic resource (i.e. food), which could be used for both economic and political ends. Nevertheless, as I have argued elsewhere (Malešević 2010: 253–259), such explanations overemphasise economic factors such as production of food surpluses and downplay the role of coercion in this historical process. It is far from self-evident that those who create surpluses are also the ones who experience the exploitation of their labour. While not denying that such exploitative relationships have developed over time, this may not necessarily be the case at the dawn of the Neolithic. It seems much more logical to assume that those individuals and small groups who initially demonstrated skill, organisational competence and coercive dominance to produce more food than others may have been just as skilled in relying on these qualities to safeguard their food surpluses. As a number of anthropological studies indicate (Waiko 1993; Strathern 1971; Sahlins 1972), the nascent hierarchies in the prepatrimonial world were usually built around the distribution, not appropriation, of goods. The so-called Big Men tended to distribute food surpluses and protection in order to attain group support and maintain their Big Men position. This is still evident among the existing hunter-gatherers and was particularly pronounced in the complex hunting-gathering communities (chiefdoms). What seems to be of more importance than the accumulation or distribution of economic goods is the social mechanisms through which such processes take place – the creation of social organisation itself. Binding individuals together around a shared long-term project gives impetus to the development of organisational power. So regardless of what a particular undertaking is (the hunting and storage of animal flash, cultivation of land, coordinated distribution or appropriation of resources, etc.), what really matters is the ever-increasing organisational capacity that such joint undertakings generate. As Michels (1939[1911]) noted long ago, organisations are the epicentres of all power, as the organised minorities generally tend to overpower the disorganised majorities.

In this context, it seems plausible to argue that once humans realised the benefits of social organisation it gradually became a cornerstone of social action. Of course, this was far from being a straightforward evolutionary development. Instead, it seems more likely that this was a highly contingent and in many respects an unlikely process. One could compare the invention of social organisation to the invention of fire: both were present in the world before they were adopted by hominids; both were accidental human inventions involving simultaneous discoveries and rediscoveries in different parts of the world and at different moments in time, and both had profound and lasting impacts on the development of human history. Nevertheless, unlike fire, which once adopted was generally acknowledged as being beneficial to the hunter-gathering lifestyles, organisational power was usually resisted. As both archaeological and anthropological records show, foragers as a rule do not like organised structures (Mann 2014). The historical records demonstrate many instances of foraging bands being integrated into wider imperial or other state structures and their prolonged struggles to break free from such organisational shells (i.e. from the neighbouring tribes of Akkadian Sumer to the indigenous populations of Australia, South and North America, etc.). Even today, most existing hunting-gathering communities reject all attempts to bring them into the fold of the modern nation-state. Hence the shift towards social organisations was extremely slow and turbulent, involving numerous reversals and countless new beginnings. It is far from being clear what ultimately caused the transition from nomadic and seminomadic fluid lifestyles towards sedentary relatively stable and durable social organisations such as chiefdoms, city-states and pristine empires. Some scholars argue that the combination of environmental pressures and demographic increases generated conflict over scarce resources, thus forcing foraging groups to settle and embrace social organisations in order to survive. For example, Carneiro (2012, 1970) argues that in parts of the world where arable agricultural land is limited, population pressure leads to violent conflicts over the land and food, which ultimately stimulates the evolution of the state. This circumscription theory of the state origin has been criticised for not being able to explain many instances where early state formation was not linked to the 'ecological trap' or demographic pressure such as in Sri Lanka, East Africa and Polynesia, among other examples (Claessen 2000). Other scholars have identified the confluence of various factors, including demographic change, macroeconomic issues, cultural transformations and environmental causes. However, most such theories overemphasise instrumental motivations of individuals without devoting enough attention to the structural contexts that make such unprecedented large-scale historical change possible. In other words, instead of focussing on the long list of possible causes for the transition from foraging towards sedentary social life, it might be more fruitful to look at the development of organisational power as such, for it is this power that is at the heart of this staggering transformation.

The Coercive Foundations of Social Organisations

There is no doubt that planned and coordinated social action involving clearly defined goals, division of labour, transparent hierarchy and internal legitimacy is likely to trump noncoordinated, chaotic collective action that lacks clear goals, legitimacy, division of labour or well-established hierarchies. This is especially the case when one encounters very large groups of people. While it is still possible when building one's wigwam or a hut to rely on ad hoc and spontaneous arrangements with several relatives or neighbours, to build a massive bridge, multistorey building or an aqueduct involving thousands of labourers and constructors, one needs an elaborate organisational structure. Simply put, it is almost impossible to manage large-scale tasks involving huge numbers of individuals without well-established organisational devices. In this context, social organisation is the backbone of all historical development.

When comparing simple foragers and complex hunter-gatherers (chiefdoms), it is noticeable that the key defining difference between the two is their organisational capacity. While forging bands consist of very small, fluid, nonhierarchic, mobile and generally disorganised groups, the chiefdoms are much more populous and better organised entities built around a centralised leadership and possessing distinct social hierarchies in terms of age, gender, marriage and military role. Furthermore, unlike disorganised foragers who tend to scavenge for food and run away from external attacks (by carnivorous animals or organised human groups) and are generally unable to establish collective resistance, the chiefdoms are characterised by their political and military prowess and are capable of utilising organised collective action for both attack and defence. However, unlike chiefdoms, which are able to mobilise relatively large numbers of individuals and as such can force those individuals to act against their will, the foraging bands enjoy almost unlimited individual freedom. As Mann (1986: 12–14) convincingly argues, in the context of state formation the increased organisational power is a trade-off whereby an individual gains more security and food in exchange for the lack of liberty. In this sense, Mann describes the pristine states as 'social cages' which provide military protection, economic resources and some political rights at the expense of curtailing individual freedoms that the prestate social life offered. Mann's point is very convincing, but it has to be extended further to all social organisations, not just the state. Obviously, the chiefdoms did not have a state structure but have established a very similar inversely proportional relationship between security and resources on the one hand and liberty on the other. This has also been the case for many other nonstate organisations throughout history (from city-states, city-leagues, guilds, free towns and trading companies to private corporations, etc.). A Microsoft employee is provided with a regular salary, pension, health insurance and social security protection as long as she abides by the strict rules of that organisation and devotes eight or more hours per day to Microsoft. This historical trade-off between individual liberty and organisational security is at the heart of both social development and organisational power. When comparing the simple foragers and chiefdoms, one can instantly recognise that chiefdoms are much more effective, resource productive and cohesive than the foraging bands. As a direct result of the better organising capacities, an individual living in a chiefdom is less likely to die from hunger or an animal attack than his foraging counterpart. However, at the same time inhabitants of chiefdoms have less individual freedom than those living in loose foraging bands. More significantly, unlike the simple foragers who lack security and often experience constant hunger but are also rarely if ever involved in protracted violence, the complex hunter-gatherers are generally prone to bursts of intense organised violence, from blood feuds to warfare. To understand this substantial shift to violence, it is necessary to focus on the key defining feature of these two types of social orders: the complex social organisation.

Once human action is institutionalised in specific organisations, it develops a particular *sui generis* quality. In other words, once human beings legitimately devolve a degree of their individual power to relatively abstract organisational structures, such as chiefdoms, city-states, empires, nation-states or private corporations, such entities acquire unique potency with a life of their own. Since social organisations are the backbone of coordinated human action once in place, they attain and, if successful, are able to maintain and increase organisational power which individual humans could never have on their own. Such organisational capacity is a prerequisite for any social development: if it was not for the emergence of complex social organisations, human beings would never create civilisations, agriculture, technology, science, industry, art, philosophy, etc. Nevertheless, all organisational power is a double-edged sword: it is a potent mechanism for production as much as for destruction. The early complex hunter-gatherers relied on the developed organisational power to generate more food, better accommodation and clothing, but this very same organisational power was also used to dominate, enslave and kill one's neighbours in the new thrust for territory, resources, status and other acquisitions. There is a tendency to keep these two sets of processes separate as the organised production is regularly opposed to the organised destruction, but in fact these two are outcomes of the same phenomenon – organisational power. Once organisational power is generated, it can be deployed in variety of ways, some of which are likely to be perceived differently by those who utilise such power and those who become objects of this power. While well-established commercial fishing fleets such as American Seafoods or Trident Seafoods use their superior organisational power to catch hundreds of tonnes of fish per year which feed millions of humans, such undertakings are also premised on the destruction of particular ecosystems and the lives of millions of seabed animals and also negatively impact the livelihoods of local fishing communities. There is no social development without coercive costs. Even the nominally most benevolent social organisations retain their coercive underbelly as organisational complexity is rooted in force. For example, Google might pride itself at having the most advanced employee friendly-work practices, at being at the forefront of empowering its workers and of supporting distinctly humanitarian goals,[8] but like all complex corporations it too has to rely on very elaborate coercive practices. As Fuchs (2012: 46) emphasises, for Google to provide its services, it 'necessarily has to exploit users and to engage in the surveillance and commodification of user-oriented data'. Unparalleled surveillance and data-gathering capacities enable Google to generate and use an astonishing amount of personal information which can be used for a variety of purposes, many of which are far from being benign. One does not have to be Foucauldian to highlight the links between knowledge and power in this instance, and the U.S.

---

[8] Google's official philosophy is that 'you can make money without doing evil', and its self-perception is of 'a company that does good things for the world' (Jarvis 2009: 99).

government's recent use of Google's data for security purposes is highly indicative of this tight link. Moreover, Google employees have also to observe strict company regulations, meet performance targets, obey supervisors and respect the hierarchical structure of the organisation and engage in many other activities where nonperformance is penalised in a variety of ways: from the loss of earnings and deductions of annual leave days to the instant loss of employment.[9]

Therefore, violence is not an unnecessary addition or an avoidable byproduct of organisational power. Instead, violence is the core of all organisational social action, and this link between organisation and violence has its structural logic. The origins and development of violence are rooted in the dynamics of organisational power. As I have argued in my previous work (Malešević 2013a, 2010), since organisational power is born in and through coercive processes, its coerciveness can be soothed and made less visible – as in the case of Google or the modern-day nation-states that monopolise the use of violence on their territory – but it cannot be eradicated. In some significant respects, coercive organisational power that generates violence is similar to accumulated nuclear energy: both enable human beings to achieve much more than their muscles would allow them; and both can be controlled, contained, transformed, enhanced or moved from one destination to another, but once created it is extremely difficult if not impossible to dispense with such force. The nuclear power can be stored and moved from one place to another, but it is extremely difficult to extinguish such power. Similarly, once created, the coercive organisational power can be contained by the modern constitutional state through its monopoly on the use of violence, but if the state stops functioning this monopoly is likely to crumble, making large-scale violence visible in the everyday life. This is well illustrated with the cases of contemporary Somalia and Syria, both of which were extremely stable and highly coercive states before they collapsed during protracted civil wars.

In other words, the historical trajectory of organisational power has for the most part been cumulative: although individual social organisations experience rise and fall and many disappear quickly, organisational

---

[9] This coercive character of Google's policy is well illustrated by the e-mail exchange between the head of recruitment in Google and one of the owners (Eric Schmidt). When an employee tried to recruit somebody from Apple, the Google recruitment boss' response was the following: 'sourcer who contacted this Apple employee should not have and [her employment contract] will be terminated within the hour'. Schmidt's response was as follows: 'Please make a public example of this termination within the group. Please also make it a very strong part of new hire training for the group. I want it clear that we have a zero-tolerance policy for violating our policies' (Malkin & Miano 2016: 327).

power as such has undergone a cumulative expansion over the past twelve thousand years. While human communities did not experience significant organisational change for 98 per cent of their existence on this planet, once the first complex social organisations emerged the rise of organisational power became astounding. The chiefdoms tend to trump simple foragers in terms of their organisational capacity; empires trump chiefdoms and city-states and modern nation-states have more infrastructural and other organisational prowess than any of their historical predecessors. It is no accident that this increase in the organisational capacity is followed by the increase in destructive potential as the modern nation-states have been involved in more killings than any of their predecessors. If one looks only at the death casualties of wars over the past seven centuries, it is possible to see the exponential rise: for the fourteenth and fifteenth centuries, the total war death toll is less than 1 and 4 million, respectively; this jumps to 7 and 8 million for the sixteenth and seventeenth centuries and rockets to 19 million for the nineteenth century alone. However, the twentieth century surpasses all of the recorded history combined with its 135 million war deaths (Leitenberg 2006: 9; Eckhardt 1992: 272–273). This rise in death tolls is clearly linked with the increase in the organisational capacity of polities: even though some rulers of the premodern empires might have been more inclined to kill than their modern counterparts, the emperors lacked the organisational means (i.e. technology, infrastructure, communications, transport, etc.) to achieve such bloody ends.

Therefore, to understand the origins and proliferation of violence, one has to shift the analytical focus from individual and collective agents towards organisational contexts. Rather than looking at the origins of violence through the prism of biological or economic competition or through the lenses of cultural difference, it is much more plausible to explore the dynamics of organisational power as it expands through time. There is no systematic protracted violence without substantial coercive capacity at one's disposal, and this capacity is always firmly rooted in organisational power. Hence, simply and bluntly put, the existence of organisation is a precondition for violent action. Of course, this does not mean that every form of organised power will lead to a bloodbath nor that simply having the requisite social organisation is enough to generate sustained violent activity. As I have argued elsewhere (Malešević 2013a, 2013b, 2010), organisational capacity is one of several key structural elements that facilitate the historical transformation of violence. This organisational process is coercive, cumulative and bureaucratic, so I called it the cumulative bureaucratisation of coercion. By this I mean the ability of social organisations to coercively pacify and discipline the

domain under their control through a variety of means, including corporal punishments, direct surveillance, strict legislation or normative
control, among others. Although individual organisations experience
periodic cycles of rise and decline, this open-ended historical process
has resulted in the continuous and cumulative increase in organisational
power throughout the world. Furthermore, as the bureaucratic mode of
organisation has proved more successful than its alternatives, the most
durable large-scale social organisations have gradually embraced bureaucratic principles of administration. Hence to fully understand the historical dynamics of violence, one has to grapple with the long-term
transformations underpinned by the cumulative bureaucratisation of
coercion.

Conclusion

Human beings do not have a natural proclivity either for violent or
nonviolent behaviour. As the historical record demonstrates, human
groups are capable of both compassion and cruelty, although they have
no special physical predispositions for either. Given their biological
feebleness, including the absence of the substantial prerequisites for fight
or flight, our prehistoric predecessors gave priority to defence over
attack: for much of their existence on this planet, Homo sapiens sapiens
had to find ways to escape dangerous carnivorous predators and had little
time or reason to contemplate violent struggles against other members of
its species. The archaeological and paleontological research does not
indicate that intrahuman violence was prevalent in prehistory. Similarly,
many anthropological studies show that simple hunter-gatherers are wary
of protracted violent interactions. Nevertheless, once sedentary, organised and stratified populations managed to replace the egalitarian
nomadic foragers, violence dramatically expanded. In other words, there
is an unambiguous historical link between the rise of civilisations and the
proliferation of brutality: social development and mass destruction
emerge together on the historical scene. Hence the origins of human
violence are to be found in the increasing organisational capacity of
sedentary lifestyles. It is the social organisation which is the backbone
of both productivity and destruction: violence stems from the coercive
capacity which is in itself generated through organisational advancement.
There is no sustained violence without effective social organisation.

4   The Rise and Rise of Organised Violence

Introduction

From de Saint-Pierre and Kant to Leibniz, Mill and Spencer, many scholars have articulated an argument that modernity and violence are inversely proportional. For classical Enlightenment thinkers such as de Saint-Pierre, Kant and Leibniz, the idea of perpetual peace was linked to the development of reason and progress, two key elements of the modern world. For liberals such as Mill and Spencer, violence was nothing more than a remnant of the intransigent past, destined to disappear in the near future. Although these were highly popular ideas then (and now), they largely did not have the empirical corroboration. Thus, it is only in the last few decades that attempts have been made to provide a sound empirical backing for such arguments. In this context, a number of influential researchers have made a case that all forms of violence are on the wane and that in particular organised violence has experienced a continuous downward trend over the past centuries (Morris 2014; Pinker 2011; Horgan 2012; Goldstein 2011). Since this book as a whole challenges the declinicist thesis, the main aim of this chapter is to lay the groundwork for an alternative interpretation. More specifically, this chapter briefly reviews the historical data on organised violence in order to identify its general trajectories. While the dominant forms of organised violence are dissected in a great deal in the later chapters on wars, revolutions, genocides and terrorism, this chapter aims to show that there is no evidence for the claim that organised violence has experienced a long-term decline. On the contrary, the argument is made that as organised violence is deeply linked to organisational and ideological structures, as these structures continue to grow so will the potential for the large-scale violence.

How to Measure Organised Violence through History?

Violence is a slippery concept. Since scholars disagree over what types of activity constitute a violent act, there is no consensus on how to measure

99

its extent either. As discussed in Chapter 1, those analysts who utilise a narrow definition, which identifies violence with the intentionality and materiality, tend to gauge violence through such parameters as battle deaths, homicide rates, rape figures, hate crime murders, execution rates, lynching episodes or documented instances of child physical abuse, among others. In contrast, scholars who understand violence in wide terms, as something that involves structural conditions that generate violent outcomes, use different measures, from the documented cases of psychological abuse[1], the economic disparities among diverse social groups, the tacit pedagogical practices that inflict symbolic violence, to differences in life expectancies between various societies. For example, while White (2012), Eisner (2003) and Gleditsch at al. (2002) focus almost exclusively on human death rates, Kohler and Alcock (1976) and Galtung and Hoivik (1971) measure structural violence through the difference between optimal life expectancy and actual life expectancy. While both of these sets of measures are beneficial in assessing the changing patterns of violence through time and space, as they focus on very different phenomena, they tend to generate contradictory results. Hence for those who analyse only human fatalities, the world as a whole is seen as having experienced substantial and continuous decline in violence over the last several centuries (Pinker 2011; Gat 2013). More specifically, looking at the homicide rates, Eisner (2003) documents how violence has decreased in much of Western Europe from the sixteenth to early-twentieth centuries. Similarly, Pinker's (2011) data indicate that all regions of the world have followed similar pattern of decline in violence with dramatic decrease in the number of war casualties, homicides, acts of revolutionary violence and terrorism and so on. In contrast, studies that empirically analyse patterns of structural violence find continuous increase in the scale of structural and symbolic violence in different parts of the world. For example, using the Human Development Index as a comparative measure of structural violence, Iadicola and Shupe (2012) show that many underdeveloped regions of the world have experienced a rise in different forms of violence: from the decrease in life expectancy (in DC Congo and Somalia, only forty-four years), to the increased number of stunted development of children due to malnutrition (58 per cent in Yemen and 54 per cent in Guatemala), to the substantial rise of serious

---

[1] As Hajjar (2013: 26) emphasises, psychological torture often 'fuses tactics of sensory deprivation and self-inflicted pain', and, 'unlike beatings and other tacticts that violently attack the body, this combination targets the mind', thus causing 'victims to feel responsible for their suffering' and making them more likely to capitulate to their torturers.

diseases and deaths caused by pollution (where the underdeveloped countries experience thirty-three times more deaths than those in the developed world).

The main problem with these perspectives is not so much the data they gather and interpret[2] but whether such statistics can fully capture the long-term dynamics of violence. As argued in Chapter 1, to get a better sense of how violence transforms through time and space, it is of paramount importance to move away from both too narrow and too wide definitions of violence. This means that violence cannot be reduced to intentional and corporal forms of individual injuries and death tolls, but also that violence is not just a mere synonym for inequality. It is highly probable that inequalities generate violence, but not all forms of inequality stem from violent acts, and there are many forms of violence that involve socially equal participants. Hence, to circumvent both of these conceptual and methodological models, it is necessary to focus analytical attention on different incarnations of violence. More to the point, as this study explores the character of organised violence, I will attempt to gauge the configurations of violence by identifying not only the physical forms of violent action but also, where possible, coercively induced behavioural changes and other forms of noncorporal and unintentional violence[3].

However, before such analysis takes place, it is also necessary to determine its range and scope. Much of the available comparative data on organised violence are collected and framed around organisationally set categories such as the nation-state, empire, city-state, private corporation or religious institution. Leaving to one side the question of the trustworthiness of such data, which is inevitably tainted by the organisational demands of such large-scale entities[4], what is even more important is that such a strategy of data collection cannot adequately capture information on organised violence. For one thing, most organisations gather only data that are relevant and useful to their own activities. Hence, most imperial powers had no interest in gathering information on casualties of their colonial policies or on violence that was not threatening their rule. Thus many domestic conflicts, uprisings, state-induced famines and other types of violence were not recorded. As Mann (2012: 37–38)

---

[2] Steven Pinker is an exception, as his use of data has been criticised extensively (Herman and Petterson 2014; Epstein 2011; Corry 2013; Malešević 2013a; Cirillo and Taleb 2016).

[3] Unfortunately, as noncorporal forms of violence are difficult to document, such data are very scant. Hence much of my analysis will inevitably rely on the 'corporal' evidence.

[4] There is an extensive literature on the state's manipulation of censuses and other data collection practices (Thompson 2010; Kertzer & Arel 2002).

shows, most colonial conflicts did not fit the conventional one thousand casualties per year threshold, so they were often not recorded as wars or at all. For another thing, until quite recently most organisations had no interest in assembling information on the indirect casualties of wars, revolutions, rebellions or uprisings and had no means to regularly collect such information on direct casualties. In this sense, much of the information we possess on premodern and early modern times is highly problematic, as it is framed through the methodologically nationalist practices that reinterpret the past through the prism of present-day (national) categories. For example, the longitudinal data on wars between France and Germany are built around the wrong idea that these two contemporary nation-states have been in existence for the past millennium or so. However, the political and cultural entities that occupied the territories of present-day Germany and France had virtually no resemblance to the contemporary states (Geary 2002, 1988). More importantly, such entities had no ability to permanently control large-scale territories, with local rulers making mutually exclusive and crisscrossing claims over the same patches of territory (involving at times up to ten local rulers). Such polities also had no administration to collect reliable data on violence, had no transport or communication networks to organise such data collection and had no literate population to assemble such information (Mann 1986, Malešević 2013a). These organisationally framed statistics also feed into the worldwide data sets on violence. Hence the most commonly used such databases, including the Correlates of War (Michigan) or Uppsala Conflict Data Programme, utilise existing information collected mostly at the level of nation-states. Thus when one conducts a global level analysis, this too often stands only for the sum of individual (organisationally shaped) parts.

With these caveats in mind, let us establish what a unit of a violence analysis should be. Some scholars such as Pinker (2011) and White (2012) take the whole world as an analytical unit to assess the historical direction of organised violence. Furthermore, Pinker downplays absolute numbers and favours the use of relative death rates to measure the scale of violence through time. This means that the casualties of violence are calculated as a proportion of the world population. Using this measure, Pinker ranks the eighth-century An Lushan revolt as the most violent event in human history, which is then followed by the thirteenth-century Mongol conquest and the seventh- to nineteenth-century Mideast slave trade. In this table, World War II's 55 million casualties are ranked somewhere in the middle of the world's worst atrocities (number 9) while World War I's 15 million dead rank somewhere at the bottom of the scale (16). Leaving to one side Pinker's wildly inflated numbers for many prehistoric cases such as An Lushan revolt or Mongol Conquest[5], this type of analysis is problematic on several accounts. First, such crude use of statistics does not differentiate the timescale involved in each case. There is a huge difference between the casualties occurring during the Mideast slave trade lasting twelve centuries and those resulting from several months of killing, such as the battles of Verdun, Stalingrad or Kursk, to name a few. Hence the annual or even in some instances monthly rates of killing for these two cases are profoundly disproportional in a sense that twentieth-century death tolls are higher than anything seen before.

Second, the calculation of the simple proportion between the total casualties and the total world population does not differentiate between the specific places, towns, regions, polities, populations or continents where such violence has taken place. To make a point about decreasing or increasing levels of violence, one has to focus on the specific places rather than including populations where violent events did not take place. For example, when assessing the scale of violence in World War I or World War II, it does not make much sense to include populations which did not actively take part in these wars, as the increasing/decreasing scale of violence is not in any way related to their death rates. That the overall violence has decreased because the relative death rates are lower has nothing to do with the populations of world which did not actively participate in the two world wars. The fact that such populations might have experienced a demographic boom during the two world wars has very little to do with the bloody realities of the war taking place elsewhere. What does a substantial population increase in 1939–1945 Brazil or India have to do with the mass slaughters on the battlefields of Stalingrad, Verdun and Kursk? In Pinker's strange and deeply misleading system of calculation, these non-war-related population increases were used to offset the casualties taking place elsewhere[6]. Methodologically, it would be much better to focus on the specific

---

[5] For criticisms of these inflated figures, see Mann (2016), Weatherford (2004), Fairbank (1992) and Fitzgerald (1985). The claim that the An Lushan revolt resulted in 36 million fatalities is based on the comparison of the highly unreliable census results before and after the events followed by floods, diseases and starvation and not on the actual death rates. Mann (2016: 8) and Weatherford (2004: 118) regard Pinker's claims about the casualties of the An Lushan revolt and the Mongolian invasions as 'preposterous'.

[6] A similar point is made by Herman and Peterson (2014): 'what relevance did the large population of Asia in the first-half of the 20th century (accounting for more than one-in-two people worldwide) have to the fact that the machinery of death available at the time of the Second World War set new records in mass violence, with the most civilized countries leading the killing process? Should the Nazi holocaust be downgraded in importance because the populations of China and India were so large?'

randomly selected world regions and then assess the scale of violence over the course of history.

Third, it is difficult, if not impossible, to clearly separate specific violent historical episodes, as they are usually connected to many other processes. For example, the Atlantic or Mideast slave trades were not isolated specific events, but were long-term historical processes that took place over centuries involving a variety of wars, revolutions, uprisings and many other forms of violence that cannot be neatly separated from each other. Similarly, as Mann (2016:27) points out, the early-twentieth century instances of mass killings such as the two world wars, revolutions, civil wars and famines in Russia and China are all deeply connected events taking place in a relatively short period of time (twenty to thirty years) and as such resulting in by far the highest death toll in history.

Fourth, as the organised violence involves also noncorporal and non-intentional injuries and coercively induced behavioural changes, it is necessary to pay attention to data that can capture these types of violence: the organisational inaction to prevent violent outcomes, changing incarceration rates, suicide rates, the size of security apparatuses (i.e. police, military, private security agencies, etc.), the military and police spending, the number of court cases[7] related to the violent events and so on[8]. Thus taking these methodological issues on board, one can assess the direction organised violence has taken over the past twelve thousand years.

The Early History

In the world of foragers, violence is sporadic and largely comes from the outside: ever-threatening carnivorous animals, unpredictable weather changes, natural disasters, contagious and life-threatening diseases or ever-present starvation (Chapter 3). In contrast, the permanent sedentary social life is characterised by the presence of violence that is produced internally. This is violence caused by the human action, including wars, uprisings, feuds, assassinations, mass slaughter, torture, etc.

---

[7] As Ginsberg (2013: 140) documents in the U.S. context, the number of criminal court cases keeps expanding enormously: 'the expansion of federal criminal law has contributed to a 300 percent increase in federal criminal prosecutions from slightly more than 20,000 in 1980 to 80,000 in 2009 and an eightfold increase in the federal prison population during the same period'.

[8] Tracing down all this gamut of difficult-to-access information is a project in itself. Hence to illustrate my key points, I will only identify and make use of a very small section of these data. Obviously, the further one moves through time the information on the noncorporal forms of violence becomes less accessible.

Whereas simple hunter-gatherers largely did not engage in protracted violence, complex hunter-gatherers, and particularly those who establish chiefdoms, often participate in excessive violent acts (Fry 2013b; Ferguson 2013). As argued in the previous chapter, this gradual shift from the nomadic foraging to the sedentary lifestyle has proved decisive in the proliferation of violence worldwide. Although chiefdoms are largely unstable forms of polity, they still represent an organisational watershed in human history (Fry 2013b; Malešević 2010: 255; Kradin 2004, Service 1978: 6). Unlike simple foragers, who have no lasting organisational structure, chiefdoms possess established hierarchies built around centralised leadership. Most chiefdoms are profoundly unequal and comprise of two or more social strata. Nevertheless, such systems of stratification tend to be fluid in a sense that an exceptional warrior can climb up the social ladder and become a member of the elite rank. Most chiefdoms were underpinned by kinship order, with the chiefs maintaining their power through family links. Some chiefdoms developed a very complex organisational structure, with the tributary relationships and lesser chiefs. For example, some so-called tribal confederacies, including the various groupings of Germanic and other populations that later conquered Roman Empire (i.e. Visigoths, Ostrogoths, Vandals, Huns, Suevi, etc.) or the Indian confederacies of the third century CE, were in fact conglomerates of chiefdoms (Geary 2002, 1988; Chatterjee 1993). It is interesting that the largest contiguous territorial conquest in world history was a product not of a fully fledged state organisation but of a relatively unstable chiefdom – Genghis Khan's Mongol empire that at its peak stretched over 33 million km^2 (Taagepera 1997). Since chiefdoms entail relatively complex organisational structure, they develop quite late in human history – only in the last thirteen thousand years or so (Kelly 2000: 302; Fry 2007: 71). What is striking here is that the historical expansion of violence follows the expansion of organisational structure. Simple foragers lack organisation and are generally egalitarian and less violent. Chiefdoms possess contours of complex organisations and are also deeply hierarchical and violence prone. For example, Genghis Khan's conquests (1206–1227) are often considered to be among the most violent episodes in human history, amounting to as many as 40 million casualties[9] (White 2012; MacFarlane 2003). Obviously, this is no

---

[9] However, one should be wary of such huge projections as they are based on indirect calculations focussing on the general population decline within a particular timeframe. Since such declines are usually consequence of famine and contagious diseases, it is not clear what the direct casualties of war were and what the long-term consequence of social change were.

coincidence. It is one of the main principles that can be encountered throughout history: the better, more complex and durable social organisations possess greater coercive capacities which often generate more violence. Although chiefdoms are a crucial organisational development in history, their inherent instability suggests that their very existence was dependent on their ability to transform into more permanent organisational form – the pristine state. While most chiefdoms collapsed, some did evolve into durable imperial and other structures[10].

Unlike chiefdoms, which are often effective in waging wars and conquering neighbouring territories but are weak in maintaining such territories, empires possess greater infrastructural capacities to coordinate the everyday life of large populations. Since nomadic and seminomadic military structures have no effective mechanisms to supply their soldiers with food, clothing, weapons and other resources on a regular basis, such armies are forced either to engage in regular pillages or cease military undertaking when they run out of resources. In contrast, pristine empires develop permanent systems of military supply which integrate individual military missions with the entire state structure. Hence the rise of the first river valley civilisations, such as Akkadian Sumer, ancient Egypt, ancient China or the Harappan in India, was decisive in making coercive organisational power the bedrock of social development (Mann 1986, Malešević 2010). The long-term consequence of these organisational advancements was the increase in the scale of violence. As emphasised in Chapter 3, documentary evidence for much of the early history is scant and when available usually is not reliable. There is consensus among academics that most official documentation describing wars, uprisings and other instances of organised violence tends to exaggerate the number of casualties. For example, the depictions of war victories of Alexander the Great constantly inflate the number of enemy soldiers and their casualties. Similarly, the death tolls of the ancient Chinese wars are regularly reported in the millions while in fact they were much smaller (Cioffi-Revilla and Lai 1995). In India, the Ashoka's conquest of Kalinga (261 BCE) is depicted in an edict as involving enormous casualties: '100,000 were slain and many times that number died' (Sewell 1987: 10). However, contemporary historians insist that these numbers are wildly inflated. The habitual exaggeration of war fatalities had several

---

[10] The transition from chiefdom to empires is just one of many historical possibilities of state creation. It is important to recognise that the institution of the state has also developed via unification of different city-states, religious centres, 'tribal' organisations, city-leagues, etc., or through the conquest of various forms of social organisation (Mann 1986; Malešević 2010).

purposes: to emphasise the scale of victory against impossible odds so as to enhance one's social status, to frighten the enemy, to generate a pedagogical narrative for the future generations, etc. In addition to deliberately inflating death tolls, the ancients also had less interest in recording the exact numbers. Without standardised systems of weights and measures, most records utilised provisional estimations relying on imprecise calculations. For example, both Chinese and Greek administrators used 10,000 (a myriad) as an equivalent to an indefinite large figure, meaning essentially 'huge number' (i.e. along the same lines, we would say, 'there were a million problems with these policies'). So both military units and death tolls were often defined in such a loose way. Nevertheless, even when all the available numbers are taken with a grain of salt, it is still possible to conclude that the shift from the nonsedentary to sedentary lifestyle, defined by the formation of the first imperial states, resulted in the substantial increase in organised violence. Obviously, it is impossible to estimate the total number of casualties for the entire world, but looking at the recorded violent events in Ancient Egypt, China or the Hellenic world it becomes evident that there is a strong link between the rise of civilisation and the increase in the scale of violence. Thus the famous battles involving the ancient Egyptian armies such as Kadesh (c. 1457 BCE against the Hittite Empire) or Megiddo (1479 BCE against Canaanites) included a relatively large number of soldiers (up to fifty thousand including both sides) and in the case of Kadesh also substantial number of casualties. The better-documented large-scale ancient Greek warfare typically involved tens of thousands of soldiers and thousands of casualties. For example, Sorokin calculated that the Corinthian War (394–387 BCE) and the Spartan–Theban War (379–362 BCE) each accounted for up to 34,000 casualties. The devastating Peloponnesian War (431–404 BCE) resulted in around 18,800 deaths. According to one general estimate, between 500 and 146 BCE the Hellenic world has experienced around 300,000 casualties (Sorokin 1957).

The ancient Chinese wars and uprisings are more difficult to assess, as the estimates tend to fluctuate enormously depending on the sources and they are usually reported in millions. Hence the Three Kingdoms Wars (189–280 CE) are recorded as involving 34 million fatalities (de Crespigny 1991) while the figures for the An Lushan revolt (756–763 CE) range from several million to 13 million to 36 million (White 2012; Pinker 2011). Most of these projections are based on highly unreliable sources and cannot be taken at face value. Mark Lewis (1999: 625–626) dismisses these numbers as wild exaggerations. He emphasises that the ancient Chinese documents tend regularly to refer to their armies as having millions of soldiers, while in fact such use of numbers was 'purely notional and serve[s] only as rhetorical terms to suggest a great size'. Thus one should be highly sceptical about such enormous estimates of casualties. However, it also seems plausible to conclude that the scale of organised violence has escalated when compared to the populations inhabiting the same region before the emergence of the Chinese Empire. For example, Cioffi-Revilla and Lai (1995: 469) demonstrate empirically that in China, 'warfare increased across epochs, particularly during the Zhou epoch, reaching an onset frequency of approximately 10% of the modern-world frequency (1816–1980 A.D.) for international and civil wars combined'.

Since the Roman Empire had a regular system of data recording of its population, its war and other casualties are a better measure of the long-term change in this part of the world. Thus the evidence indicates that the combat-related mortality rate in Rome for the period 200–168 BCE was at around 5.6 per cent of soldiers per year (Rosenstein 2004: 124). Rough estimates suggest that from 400 BCE to 500 CE the Roman armies suffered somewhere between 500,000 and 885,000 direct casualties (Sorokin 1957; Hanson 2001; White 2012). However, even in this instance the casualties of major wars and battles seem to be highly overestimated. Hence the Punic wars are often referred as causing hundreds of thousands of casualties: the First Punic War (264–241 BCE), 400,000; the Second Punic War (218–202 BCE), 770,000; and the Third Punic War (149–146 BCE), 250,000 (Gabriel 1990; White 2012). In a similar vein, the destruction of Carthage (146 BCE) is reported as involving up to 400,000 deaths. However, scholars who specialise in the history of these conflicts offer much lower figures. For example, Goldsworthy (2007) calculates that in the First Punic War, the Roman Empire lost not 200,000 as suggested but fewer than 50,000 soldiers. In a similar way, the casualties of the Second Punic War and the destruction of Carthage seem to be inflated. Although this certainly was one of the most destructive wars of early history with a staggering number of casualties, it seems that the number was still lower than that presented by early historians. The death toll of the destruction of Carthage, which came about at the end of the Third Punic War, is now estimated at 150,000 deaths (Kiernan 2009), if not even much lower.

The rise of statehood in the Islamic world demonstrates a similar pattern. There are many more war fatalities and other forms of organised violence recorded, although these sources tend also to inflate the death toll figures. Hence the so-called early Islamic conquests (al-Futūḥāt al-Islāmiyya) from the seventh until the eleventh century are often depicted as involving large numbers of casualties. These conflicts stretch from the Byzantine–Arab wars (634–750), to the Rashidun conquests of Syria, Armenia, Egypt,

North Africa and Cyprus to Umayyads conquests of Hispania, Georgia and North Africa and the siege of Constantinople. As this period involves numerous undocumented violent conflicts, it is impossible to provide an accurate figure of casualties. Using Gibbon's (2003 [1776]) calculations from the *History of Decline and Fall of the Roman Empire*, White (2012) comes up with around seven hundred thousand war fatalities. However, this is a completely speculative figure based on the anecdotal estimates of an eighteenth-century historian, which can hardly been taken as reliable information. Nevertheless, by zooming in on the better-documented battles and sieges such as those of Yermuk (636), Alexandria (642), Constantinople (717–718) or Amorium (838), one can reach a clearer sense of the scale of violence involved. Although the Battle of Yermuk is often seen as the decisive victory of Rashidun Arab forces under caliph Khalid ibn al-Walid over much larger Byzantine armies, resulting in 60,000 casualties, in fact better estimates indicate around 5,000 and 15,000, respectively. Similarly, the siege and the conquest of Amorium by the Abassid Caliph al-Mu'tasim (over the Byzantines) is documented as involving over 70,000 military fatalities. Nevertheless, recent research leans towards fewer than 30,000 casualties (Tucker 2010).

The main point of listing these war, siege and uprising death tolls is not to identify the precise number of worldwide casualties in the early history, which would be an impossible task. Instead, these figures are presented as a rough illustration of the trends that emerge with the rise and expansion of the state worldwide. While not all new state institutions were involved in mass-scale violence, those that have exhibit a very similar pattern, with substantially increased rate of casualties when compared to their nonstate predecessors. This is not to say that some complex hunter-gatherers such as those who formed chiefdoms were involved in less violent conflicts than some pristine states. Obviously, that is not the case, as the Mongol or early European nomadic invasions illustrate too well. Nevertheless, unlike chiefdoms, which were unstable and flexible entities that had no organisational means to maintain long-term control of captured territories and populations, the pristine states were capable of translating their violent conquest into a prolonged coercive power. Hence, despite the relative strength of some chiefdoms vis-à-vis some early states, it is the organisational (and ideological) form of the imperial state that has ultimately proved much more effective in terms of generating and utilising organised violence. While one can rightly question the habitual exaggeration of death tolls recorded in early history, it is difficult to question the fact that this period has witnessed substantial increase in the scale of all forms of violence when compared to the world of nomadic foragers.

The Premodern World

Most scholars of early history agree that the emergence of civilizations was paralleled with the substantial increase in the scale and scope of violence (for synthesis, see Bowden 2013, Malešević 2010; Mann 1986). There is wealth of evidence that early empires, city-states and other forms of statehood were much more belligerent than those of their nomadic foraging predecessors. The establishment of complex hierarchical polities with permanent, usually densely populated urban settlements, elaborate division of labour, established patterns of social stratification and power centralization, was crucial for the increase in the coercive capacity of early civilizations (Osborne 2006; Mann 1986; Malešević 2010, 2014). These organisational advancements often developed together with elaborate proto-ideological belief systems, ceremonial centres of worship and the practice of the elite-level writing that helped justify the use of violence on a large scale. However, this does not mean that the transition from a nomadic to a sedentary lifestyle was smooth and evolutionary. On the contrary, such structural breakthroughs were rare and uneven, with only small number of polities managing to achieve and preserve this organisational form. The early history is littered with the cases of failed state making, and many prospective polities have reverted back to nonstate forms or have simply been gobbled up by the more powerful neighbours. Nevertheless, once complex and durable social organisations were established, their coercive and ideological powers continued to increase, with the more powerful empires, religious organisations and trading networks replacing their weaker opponents and predecessors. This is not to say that the cumulative bureaucratisation of coercion and centrifugal ideologisation are unidirectional evolutionary processes. On the contrary, the social change is multidirectional and reversible. The typical examples of this are the collapse of the Western Roman Empire (476 CE) and the gradual decline of Han dynasty China (189–220 CE), both of which experienced organisational reversal and pronounced ideological bifurcations. The decline of these two empires resulted in the proliferation of many new and initially weaker polities and gave rise to ideological cacophony that often was not able to sustain organisational advancements. However, the long-term consequence of these organisational breakdowns and transformations did not automatically lead to decline in the scale of violence. On the contrary, the historical record indicates that the collapse of regional and world hegemons has regularly been followed by an increase in the levels of violence. In both the Roman and the Chinese cases, imperial dominance was eventually responsible for the prolonged periods of peace on the imperial terms (Pax Romana and Pax Sinica) that actually prevented emergence of mass-scale violence well into 200 CE (Pollard 2015). With their organisational collapse, new polities emerged that attempted to reclaim the hegemonic mantle, thus initiating long periods of violent turbulence. In Europe, this proliferation of violence took a variety of forms: wars, uprisings, religious crusades, expansion of torture, feuds, religion- and status-based massacres and so on. While most premodern warfare was not characterised by huge direct human casualties, this did not mean that violence declined. Instead, the relative organisational weakness of early polities changed the nature and dynamics of warfare. Hence, unlike the Roman type of fighting that relied on large-scale and well-trained heavy infantry units (i.e. legions) which were sustained by the powerful organisational and infrastructural systems of the Roman Empire, the new small and weak polities prioritised a cavalry- and defensive-style of fighting.

Despite popular images of the Dark Ages as being an exceptionally brutal period in European history, post–Roman Western Europe experienced quantitatively less violence than its imperial predecessor. The collapse of the Roman Empire in the West paralleled an increase in the number of violent conflicts, but the overwhelming majority of these conflicts were small-scale ones, usually involving a miniscule number of human casualties. For example, some of the most important wars of this era, such as the Norman conquest of England (1066–1088), the War of the Sicilian Vespers (1282–1302) or the Hundred Years' War (1337–1453), took place over very long periods of time but resulted in a comparatively quite small number of direct casualties. Hence the Battle of Hastings, which is often referred to as one of the most destructive events in early medieval European history, involved fewer than five thousand casualties. Similarly, the two decades of the Sicilian Vespers conflict generated fewer than four thousand casualties, while the major battles of the Hundred Years' War, such as Agincourt or Crecy, involved only a couple of thousands of casualties (about seven thousand and two thousand, respectively) (France 2010; Green 2010). The principal feature of the post–Roman Empire Western Europe was the lack of large-scale organisational infrastructure. With the collapse of the Roman imperial organisation, the violence that ensued was sporadic, often disorganised and mostly ineffective. In this context, indirect human casualties were much greater than those caused by actual fighting. As France (2010: 348) emphasises, even in the pitched battles, which were extremely rare in this period, most casualties were a product of disease and not of a military action: 'In 1166 Emperor Frederick I Barbarossa launched a great army into Italy crushing the Roman army at Tusculum and going on to besiege Rome. Plague then destroyed his army totally . . .

in 1415 Henry V of England landed with an army of about twelve thousand at Harfleuer. The town held until 22 September inflicting some casualties, but it was largely disease that caused the English army to dwindle to about seven thousand when it marched on into France'.

Most medieval warfare was highly ritualised, with clearly defined patterns of siege and duelling involving well-established mechanisms of attack and defence. In this context, the majority of fighting involved skirmishes between aristocrats, with the focus on defensive over offensive warfare. This period of European history is also well remembered through many peasant rebellions and uprisings, some of which were crushed with the utmost violence. Although for much of the early medieval period such uprisings were largely local and confined to a protests against tyrannical lords at specific manor houses, from the fourteenth century onwards such revolts developed into better organised and widespread movements. For example, between 1336 and 1525 the territories of the German states were the epicentre of militant peasant rebellions involving more than sixty such unrests (Blickle 1981). A similar phenomenon was also witnessed throughout Europe, from England and Flanders to France, the Baltics and the Balkans (i.e. the 1323–1328 Flanders revolt, the 1381 English Great Rising, the 1356–1358 French Jaquerie, the 1343–1345 St George's Night uprising in Estonia, etc.). The popular image of the period as being profoundly violent is to some extent associated with the aristocratic reaction to such rebellions. The development of elaborate techniques of torture (i.e. castration, amputation of limbs, eye gouging or thumbscrews, among many others) and the public display of tortured and killed victims (including hanged persons and severed heads decorating town squares and entrances to aristocratic estates) are often identified as the hallmarks of medieval Europe. While it is true that the use of these macabre forms of violence increased significantly in this period[11], this in itself is no reliable indicator of an overall increase in violence. On the contrary, the proliferation of torture can be interpreted as a sign of organisational weakness. Social organisations that fully control their constituents do not have to deploy extreme cruelty. It is mostly organisations that find themselves unable to control social change that have to embrace such techniques of fear.

As Collins (1974) rightly points out, the scale of mutilation and torture is often proportional with the levels of social inequality. Thus, highly stratified social orders engage more in such practices than more egalitarian societies. Nevertheless, not all deeply hierarchical systems

---

[11] Although most of these torture techniques were known and used in pre-Roman times as well.

practice mass-scale torture. This is much more evident in social orders undergoing substantial change or, more precisely, experiencing substantial pressure from below. In late medieval Europe, the peasant uprisings were rightly perceived by the aristocrats as an existential threat to the existing social order. In this context, torture was not driven by 'the institutionalised sadism', 'thirst for cruelty' or 'animalistic impulses' as suggested by Pinker (2011: 130–133) and Elias (2000: 107–116). Instead, these acts had a clear sociological rationale: torture was utilised as a means of communication in order to reinforce existing social relations. The burning of witches, the breaking rebellious peasants on wheel and the impalement of heretics were all deployed to send a similar message – do not dare to challenge the existing religious, social and political order. Hence the use of torture in late medieval Europe was not random or irrational. It was a logistical response to the organisational weaknesses of the social order. Lacking the organisational capacity to control hundreds of thousands of rebellious peasants meant that both the church and the aristocrats had to install fear through individual cases of grisly brutality. In this context, cruelty acted as a substitute for the lack of infrastructural power. This gruesomeness is often misread as pervasiveness. For example, Pinker (2011: 130–131) argues that 'Medieval Christendom was a culture of cruelty' where 'torture was woven into the fabric of public life', while Elias (2000) sees this period of European history as full of relentless violence. Nevertheless, this spectacle of cruelty should not be taken at face value as it was in the interest of the medieval elites to demonstrate their power through the imagery of horror. However, this visible omnipresence of brutality was intended to hide the inherent organisational weakness of the elite, who simply had no means to control large sectors of population. Hence many of the cruellest torture devices were rarely used, and when used they involved a handful of individuals. The notorious Iron Maiden, a casket with spikes on the inside which could be closed slowly, impaling the living person inside, was never used in medieval Europe. Other elaborate torture devices were also very rarely deployed. Their purpose was more to frighten the potential lawbreakers and heretics and less to inflict actual pain. The Spanish Inquisition, under the widely feared Tomás de Torquemada, has become a symbol of murder and cruelty, but its killing ratio was largely negligible, nothing comparable to daily killings and torture in contemporary conflicts from Syria to Mexico. Despite the vicious rhetoric and its horrifying image, the Spanish Inquisition was responsible for a very small number of deaths. For example, during its most violent period, between 1450 and 1500, under the rule of de Torquemada, only two thousand people were murdered

(Perez, 2006: 34). Much of this violence was ritualistic in character, focussed on legitimising the existing status quo, and as such the emphasis was on the spectacle of morbidity, not on efficiency of kill ratios. Some scholars have also questioned the prevalent view that the ordinary life of the late medieval world was full of violence. As Maddern's (1992) study of the fifteenth century shows, England was not particularly violent and its most urban areas such as East Anglia had miniscule levels of crime.

Nevertheless, the fact that the medieval Europe has largely experienced a substantial decrease in organised violence when compared to its predecessors should not be taken as an indicator that worldwide organised violence was in decline. On the contrary, the other parts of the world have witnessed a substantial rise in the scale of organised violence. This was particularly evident in central Asia, the Middle East and North Africa, which were the beacons of organisational and ideological expansion for much of this period. The so-called Islamic golden age (the eighth to the thirteenth centuries, with some scholars extending this to the fifteenth and sixteenth centuries) is generally regarded as a period when various Islamic empires were far ahead of Europe in terms of scientific, cultural and economic development. However, this is also a period when various Islamic caliphates fought for geopolitical primacy and in this process established powerful military organisations. This involved world-leading empires, such as the Rashidun (632–661), Umayyad (661–750), Abbasid (786–1258), Fatimid (909–1171), Ayyubid (1171–1260) and Mamluk (1250–1517) caliphates as well as the latter-day rise of the Ottoman Empire (1517–1923). In addition, this period also gave birth to several regional powers, such as the Caliphate of Cordoba in Islamic Spain (929–1031), the Volga in present-day Bulgaria (922–1236), the Golden Horde (1251–1502), the Crimean Khanate (1441–1783), the Mali Empire (1230s–1600s), the Songhai Empire (1340–1591) and numerous khanates, sultanates and emirates. All of these polities were involved in protracted wars and have experienced large-scale uprisings, rebellions and other forms of organised violence. For example, the staggering expansion of the Abbasid caliphate, which at its peak in 850s stretched from much of North Africa to India, was driven by its military might. The Abbasids fought numerous wars, some of which involved tens of thousands of casualties (i.e. the Zanj rebellion of 871; the Battle of the Zab in 750 against Umayyads; the Battle of Talas against the Chinese Tang dynasty; the Battle of Lalakaon in 863 against Byzantines; the Abbasid invasion of Asia Minor in 782; and so on). Similarly, the Umayyads and Mamluks were involved in frequent wars, crushing of rebellions and uprisings, resulting in large-scale destruction often triggering famine and starvation of hundreds of thousands of people. While there is scant documentary evidence on the scale of such devastating events, there is no doubt that that these wars and rebellions were as a rule much larger than the violent conflicts experienced in Europe at that time.

Nevertheless, the scale of organised violence in Central and East Asia in the thirteenth century seems to overpower even these quite substantial casualties. The Mongol invasions under Genghis Khan are regularly identified as being exceptionally violent. Pinker (2011) uses the staggering figure of 40 million fatalities. Most experts on Mongol conquest dispute this hugely inflated number and suggest something between 10 and 14 million casualties (Mann 2016; Clarke 2012). However, what is crucial here is to understand that most of these fatalities were not result of direct violence, battlefield deaths or massacres of civilians, as suggested by Pinker, but came about indirectly. As Phillips and Axelrod (2005) indicate, millions of individuals died as a result of massive flooding of the Yellow River that later triggered unprecedented famine and starvation. Bearing all these caveats in mind, it is still clear that the Mongol Empire possessed a highly effective organisational system capable of conquering and ruling the largest continuous territorial space in the history of the world. It is also evident that this organisation generated unparalleled destruction and a scale of violence never witnessed before. While Genghis Khan was instrumental in establishing this powerful empire, its organisational strength remained visible even after his death as the empire lasted for one hundred years (1250–1350). Although Genghis Khan's conquests are to some extent exceptional in terms of the level of destruction, a similar organisational machine, dependent on disciplined and loyal horse-riding warriors, was also deployed by latter-day Mongol emperors such as Kublai Khan or Timur, who both led powerful armies that destroyed many cities and killed hundreds of thousands of people.

Hence the principal feature of organised violence in the premodern world is its geographical oscillation. Despite the clear paucity of evidence, what is clear is that some parts of the world such as medieval Europe and post–Han dynasty China experienced substantial decline in the scale of violence while in the other regions such as Central Asia, the Middle East, North Africa and Mesoamerica organised violence continued to increase. Nevertheless, despite this diversity and pronounced regional variations, the organisational and ideological capacity upon which violence rests continued the upward trend overall. In other words, while some parts of the world underwent significant organisational decline, the cumulative bureaucratisation of coercion largely maintained its ascendant direction.

Organised Violence and Modernity

Early Modern Period

The early modern period of human history follows a similar pattern in terms of geographical oscillations and the overall continuous increase in the scale of organized violence. Whereas before Asia, North Africa and to some extent Mesoamerica had the upper hand in terms of coercive organizational and proto-ideological expansion, this period witnesses the gradual rise of Europe as the epicentre of organized violence. From the seventeenth century onwards, European empires, and then later nation-states, were involved in unparalleled and continuous growth in terms of both organisational and ideological capacity. The rise of science, technology and industry combined with the increasing centralisation and restructuring of state organisation created conditions for intensified organisational development. While until this period bureaucratisation of coercion was for the most part cumulative but rather slow and uneven, from this point forwards this process accelerates at an unprecedented scale and speed. As Tilly (1992), Hall (1988, 1985) and Mann (1986, 1993) document, this staggering social change was rooted in the ever-increasing interdependency among the state, society and war making. The Europe's relatively unique multipolar order of small and perennially weak polities proved in the long term advantageous for the organisational breakthrough. In contrast to the monopolistic large-scale empires in other parts of the world, which were powerful enough to contain hostile neighboring polities and were also independent from their ruling subjects, most early modern European rulers were weak and dependent on their societies. Hence to increase their military might and to fend off their agonistic neighbours, the rulers had to develop more effective fiscal systems capable of financing expensive wars, and to accomplish this they had to work with and accommodate their civil societies. As the efficient extraction of regular taxation depends on disciplined and relatively knowledgeable civil servants, it was of paramount importance to set up adequate administrative apparatuses. Once new bureaucratic systems were put in place, the regular fiscal income could fund protracted wars and consequently increase further the state's capacity. In this context, war making stimulated state making as preparations for war included building of better transport and communication networks and greater industrial capacities, implementation of novel scientific discoveries, more systematic development of military and other technologies and so on. Thus while the rulers of the Ottoman Empire and China experienced what Elvin (1972) and Darwin (2008: 201) call a 'high-level-equilibrium trap' which provided economic and political stability that ultimately fostered conservatism and rejection of new technologies and new modes of organisation, European rulers had no other option but to embrace social change. In this context, the proliferation of organised violence was directly linked with the expansion of organisational prowess. In addition to material transformations, this organisational advancement was also premised on (and gave impetus to) ideological growth. It is no accident that in this period states start to develop plans to educate some of their citizens (i.e. future civil servants, soldiers, bankers, etc.); increase literacy rates; allow the existence of independent book production; tolerate establishment of private mass media; and ultimately concede some civil, political and economic rights to their populations.

This interdependence of state and war making was crucial for the social development of Europe and ultimately fostered the long-term organisational and ideological dominance of European powers in the world. However, since this dominance was built on the ever-increasing coercive capacity of states and other social organisations, the ultimate result of this development was an extraordinary rise in the scale of destruction. This pattern is particularly pronounced from the early seventeenth century until the 1950s. There is no doubt that these 350 years are by far the bloodiest and most destructive period of human history. From the Thirty Years' War (1618–1648) until the end of Korean War (1950–1953), the dynamics of violent conflicts change in a sense that more and more people are sucked into the vortex of organised violence. The Thirty Years' War is often judged as one of the most devastating conflicts of seventeenth century, with the scale of human casualties and destruction unprecedented for its time: 8 million people (Davis 1996: 568). Even though most of these casualties came about as a result of famine, hunger, disease and pillage, direct military confrontations also generated more bloodshed than witnessed in previous wars on the European soil. For example, Lee (1991: 53) documents that at the Battle of Nordlingen (1634) Swedish forces lost almost half of their soldiers, while at the Battle of Wittstock (1636) the Holy Roman Empire lost more than 60 per cent of its troops. However, despite these large-scale casualties, the Thirty Years' War was still far from being an example of fully fledged modern warfare. This was still conflict fought by the aristocrats in the name of dynastic, religious and other traditional principles. Like the Hundred Years' War, this was more of a series of individual conflicts linked together by the changing geopolitical conditions and the shifting alliances of monarchs. Although the conflict was highly instrumental in stimulating long-term organisational development and ideological changes, it still was locked in the traditional framework of ritualistic warfare. What was distinct about these series of conflicts is that the main protagonists largely maintained the traditional understanding of warfare and attempted strenuously to follow that conventional logic of war while the state's organisational advancements pulled the conflict towards all-out war. In other words, regardless of the individual wills of generals and rulers, the increased coercive-organisational capacities of states had already set tracks for a more destructive conflict.

The similar cumulative rise in human casualties was also present outside of Europe, in regions where organisational and ideological capacity was also on the rise, such as India and China before they hit the 'high-level-equilibrium trap'. The Qing conquest of the Ming (1618–1683) in China is often identified as one of the most devastating events in human history, resulting in an enormous number of human fatalities. The conflict was initiated by Manchu rebellion in the far northwest, but over the years it spread throughout the China, including Beijing. Following the Manchu Qing's takeover of Beijing in 1644, the civil war ensued, involving the North-dominated Qing against the Ming loyalists in the South (and Taiwan). Some sources put the total number of casualties at 34 million (White 2012). However, this seems to be another case of a highly inflated figure, grounded in the latter-day nationalist interpretations of Chinese history. Experts on China are highly sceptical of this number (Purdue 2005; Cioffi-Revilla and Lai 1995; Lewis 1999) and emphasise that as in other premodern and early modern conflicts, most casualties were a product of dramatically changed weather conditions, floods, famine, starvation, infectious disease, etc. Nevertheless, even when all these factors are taken into account, it is clear that the Qing's war and state making did result in a substantial increase in the level of organised violence. What is equally important and this to some extent resembles the experience of the Thirty Years' War, is that the conflict increased organisational capacity of the two sides but also led ultimately towards protracted violence and organisational destruction of the two sides involved. Although the Manchu Qing were eventually victorious, the price of their victory was exceptionally high in human casualties on both sides.

The Islamic conquest of India is another instance where intensified state and war making generated an enormous number of human casualties. Although there is no reliable evidence on the total number of deaths generated over several centuries of warfare, uprisings and colonisation, some scholars insist that they number in the millions (White 2012). While the early periods of conquests are generally not documented at all or very poorly documented by highly biased locals, there is some external evidence on the Mughal rule. For example, a Venetian writer and traveller,

Nicolao Manucci, who worked on the Mughal court in the service of Dara Shikoh, wrote about war casualties in the Mughal India. According to his estimates, the protracted Deccan Wars (1680–1707) involved a very large number of casualties. He stipulates that during Aurangzeb's rule one hundred thousand soldiers died every year while another two million civilians died from starvation and disease (Wolpert 2004, Clodfelter 1992: 56). This too seems to be an inflated number, as other scholars believe that the twenty-seven-year conflict between the Maratha and Mughal empires did not involve more than 650,000 soldiers all together (500,000 Mughals and 150,000 Marathas). However, what is important to emphasise here is the organisational complexity of Mughal Empire, which was capable of assembling an enormous military and civilian machine that could be deployed relatively quickly to different parts of India. As Wolpert (1977: :56) puts it colourfully: 'Aurangzeb's encampment was like a moving capital – a city of tents 30 miles in circumference, with some 250 bazaars, with a $^1/_2$ million camp followers, 50,000 camels and 30,000 elephants, all of whom had to be fed, stripped the Deccan of any and all of its surplus grain and wealth'. Even though Aurangzeb's empire was powerful, he encountered even better organised and more disciplined Maratha soldiers, who despite much smaller numbers resisted for decades, thus corroding the Mughal military might. The outcome of this protracted and organisationally draining conflict was the Mughals' pyrrhic victory, achieved at enormous human costs. Nevertheless, in this case too most soldiers and civilians died from the famine and bubonic plague rather than from direct encounters on the battlefields.

These three early modern conflicts, fought in the three different parts of the world, are quite distinct in many ways, but they all exhibit an important similarity: the continuous increase in the scale of violence is embedded in the rising organisational and to some extent ideological capacity of the polities involved in conflicts. The Thirty Years' War, the Qing conquest of the Ming and the Deccan Wars all involved large-scale violence generated by the conflicts between two or more rising imperial organisations. Although in each of the three instances the warfare was still rooted in traditional trajectories, organisational expansion and complexity produced unintended consequences – long, drawn-out and quite deadly conflicts that utterly exhausted all the sides involved in the wars. This pattern was set to continue throughout modernity.

The Modern Period

The early modern conflicts were still governed by traditional rules of combat and by aristocratic proto-ideological principles which left no room for ordinary individuals. In contrast, the modern period was defined by new ideological vistas and by novel organisational developments. Although the French and American revolutions symbolically spearheaded these dramatic social changes, modernity is a complex structural and historical phenomenon that cannot be confined to the two spectacular events only. While the European and North American historical experience has initially shaped the new dynamics of organised violence, once unleashed these dynamics quickly infused other parts of the world. Pinker (2011) argues that the European and North American 'humanitarian revolution' was a key catalyst for the decline of violence as the principles of the Enlightenment, including individual rights and a widening sense of empathy, spread gradually throughout the world, thus helping pacify social relations. This epistemologically idealist view confuses causes and consequences. Profound ideational changes rarely if ever develop through the humanitarian proclamations of intellectuals and committed activists. Instead, they regularly emerge as a result of structural contexts: the shifting geopolitics, economic crises, political upheavals or environmental disasters, among others. Hence the key issue here was the relatively unique multipolar experience of Europe, where initially military and political weakness was ultimately translated into organisational strength. As both Tilly (1985, 1992) and Mann (1986, 1993) made clear, it was the interdependence of war and state making that eventually gave birth to the robust civil societies in Europe. Rather than 'humanitarian revolution' changing the political and military order, it was the other way around: the acceptance and implementation of Enlightenment principles were a byproduct of geopolitical and economic change. Although the ideas of individual autonomy, popular sovereignty and equal moral worth of all human beings were articulated a long time before the Enlightenment, it was only after the concrete structural transformations, including the two famous revolutions, that such ideas started to become acceptable to most.

Furthermore, and in contrast to Pinker, these ideas did not automatically pacify social order. Instead, these very ideas were inaugurated through some of the most violent episodes in human history. Not only were the American and French revolutions accomplished through a great deal of postrevolutionary violence[12], but once in motion these revolutionary ideas and practices quickly transformed into all-out warfare. Following the success of the revolution, the new French Republic was involved in numerous wars and crushing of domestic and foreign

---

[12] As explained in Chapter 8, the direct casualties of the two events were relatively miniscule, but the postrevolutionary period was exceptionally brutal in both cases.

rebellions. Initially the focus was on obliterating the clerical and monarchist opposition in Vendée and Brittany (1793–1796), where much of the local civilian population were exterminated as the 'enemies of the free republic'. While the conflict is usually depicted solely as an ideological conflict, the initial uprising was motivated by the peasant rejection of the mass conscription introduced by the new republic. Of course, ideology played an important role on the republican side as the revolt was interpreted to be a counterrevolution aimed at destroying the new republic. Consequently, the Committee of Public Safety made a conscious decision on 1 August 1793 to 'pacify' the entire region by killing all of its inhabitants. When the general in charge questioned the 'fate of the women and children', the Committee's order to him was 'eliminate the brigands to the last man, there is your duty' (Sutherland 2003: 222). The outcome of this deliberate policy of political cleansing was more than 160,000 locals killed out of the population of 800,000 (Townshend 2005: 179).

The external conflicts of the new republic were much deadlier. The postrevolutionary period was defined by twenty years of continuous warfare. Initially, these violent conflicts were stirred by external invasions of hostile antirepublican neighbours but also by the republican zeal for universal revolution. In the words of a parliamentary deputy of the new French Republic, Brissot: 'We cannot be calm until Europe, all Europe, is in flames' (Doyle 2001: 52). In this quintessentially modernist discourse, there was no room for moderation. Since the revolutionaries saw themselves as being in the possession of the ultimate truth and absolute justice, they were motivated by this 'scientific' understanding of righteous zeal. For example, the new National Convention, a republican parliament in Paris, issued the Edict of Fraternity in November 1792 declaring that their aim was to 'export the French Revolution' with the promise of 'fraternity and help to all peoples who wish to recover their liberty' (Rapport 2013: 25).

The consequence of this policy was a gradual transformation of what was essentially a defensive war into an expansionist conquest – the Napoleonic Wars (1803–1815). These wars were historically distinctive in a sense that they brought together advanced military organisation and societywide ideological mobilisation. Although Napoleonic armies did not possess more advanced technology than their adversaries, they were different in their capacity to combine mass participation with the organisational flexibility. The introduction of mass conscription (*Levée en masse*) and the more meritocratic modes of promotion revolutionised the character of war. The traditional scholarship tends to mythologise the military genius of Napoleon as being the decisive factor in the unprecedented victories of the revolutionary armies. However, recent analyses emphasise the organisational and ideological dimensions: the state's capability to recruit, train, arm, feed, clothe and coordinate huge numbers of ordinary recruits, some of whom were enthusiastic to fight but the majority of whom were mobilised through the combination of coercion and ideology. The ideological element was important as the soldiers tended to see themselves more and more as equal members of the abstract French nation. This is not to say that they joined the military because of a strong sense of French identity; rather, nationalism was in most cases a byproduct of military socialisation (Posen 1993). However, what really matters is the ideological (and organisational) capacity and willingness of the French state to turn 'peasants into Frenchmen' through its military machine. The Napoleonic Wars inaugurated the new form of a mass-scale fighting resulting in a staggering number of casualties. Unlike previous European conflicts, where direct battlefield fatalities were generally small and more soldiers died from the disease or hunger, now the battlefields became the arena of mass death and destruction. For example, at the Battle of Leipzig (1813), 500,000 soldiers were involved, out of which 150,000 were direct fatalities (Rapport 2013). As Doyle (2001: 96) documents, all these 'wars against old regime Europe between 1792 and 1815 cost the lives of well over 5 million Europeans'.

The early-nineteenth century was an exceptionally destructive period in Europe and North America. While the twelve years of Napoleonic Wars generated enormous military and civilian casualties, ranging somewhere between 4 to 6 million deaths (Gates, 2011; Esdaile, 2008; Bell 2007), the new American republic embarked on a series of violent conflicts of its own. In addition to the American Revolutionary War (1775–1783), these also include the early and later Indian wars, the First and Second Barbary War against Morocco, Libya/Tripolitania and Algiers, the 1812 war against the British Empire, the Mexican–American War (1846–1848), the Filibuster War in Nicaragua (1855–1857), the First and Second Cortina War (1859–61) against Mexico and the various brief invasions ranging from Fiji, Sumatra, Central America and China (Second Opium War, 1856–1859). Just as in the French case, here too organised violence was directed internally and externally. The main casualties of the internal violence were the Native Americans, who were largely decimated by the new state and the settlers, who often acted on their own. The colonial expansion and the struggle for territory in the Americas almost completely obliterated its native populations. It is estimated that in the period from 1490s when Columbus 'discovered' this continent until the end of the nineteenth century, 96 per cent of its original population was annihilated: from c. 50 million to 1.8 million

(Taylor 2002: 40). Although most deaths were caused by European diseases such as smallpox or even the common flu, there were numerous instances of deliberate policies to kill off the natives or not to interfere with the spread of diseases while having knowledge of their deadly effects (Anderson and Cayton 2005; Stannard 1993). White (2012) estimates that between 1775 and 1890 at least 350,000 Native Americans were killed through warfare and settler atrocities alone. With the native populations demolished by conquest and disease, the new labour force was provided through the import of African slaves on a massive scale. The chattel slavery peaked during the 1801–1825, when 109,545 Africans were brought to the U.S. soil. In total, over 300,000 slaves were transported alive to the United States, while hundreds of thousands have died on the slave ships (www.slavevoyages.org/assessment/esti mates). The total number of Atlantic slave trade fatalities is around 2.5 million, with 1.6 million slaves transported to different parts of the world (White 2012).

While the new U.S. republic was involved in numerous wars of conquest in North America, and further afield most of the human casualties transpired in the context of the American Civil War (1861–1865). This war is often described as the first industrial war, as it successfully mobilised large sectors of society together with industry, modern military technology, complex systems of transport and communication on the both sides of the frontline. Since the conflict was fought by the two organisationally and ideologically advanced polities capable of recruiting and arming millions of soldiers, the direct outcome of the war was enormous human costs. The traditional estimates indicate that the conflict involved over 3 million soldiers, resulting in more than 600,000 fatalities (Clodfelter 1992: 528). However, more recent calculations show that the actual casualties seem to be even higher – 750,000 (Hacker 2011). The scale of mobilisation and destruction in this war demonstrates yet again how the military and political leadership are often out of tune with the organisational and ideological changes produced by unforeseen structural forces. This conflict had all the hallmarks of a war where premodern tactics confronted modern technology, with most casualties coming from traditional mass infantry assaults being mowed down by industrial weaponry such as machine guns and long-range fast-firing weapons.

The nineteenth and early-twentieth centuries were also a period of intensified European colonisation of the world, which was often implemented through violence. Since by the beginning of nineteenth century European powers had at their disposal the most advanced organisational and ideological machinery, they could militarily dominate much of the globe with a relative ease. Yet colonial expansion generated numerous wars, rebellions, uprisings, genocides and many other forms of organised violence. Moreover, the native population was also exposed to other forms of violent action, including famine; starvation; diseases; and the destruction of the arable land, water and other natural resources. For example, Davis (2001) argues that the Malthusian laissez faire political economy implemented by the imperial administrators, businessmen and landlords was directly responsible for the waves of famine throughout the colonised world. In particular, he identifies three large-scale famine periods – 1876–1878, 1896–1897 and 1899–1902 – that affected numerous regions of the world, including China, India, Korea, Vietnam, Philippines, New Caledonia and Brazil, among others. According to Davis, these famines were caused by specific Malthusian economic policies that ultimately generated starvation, rural poverty and death. He concludes that between 32 and 61 million individuals lost their lives as a result of these policies, with China, India and Brazil taking the most of the casualties. Nineteenth-century Africa was at the brunt of European colonial violence. For one thing, the African population was for centuries the most significant victim of the slave trade. Although scholars disagree on the exact death toll from different forms of slavery, all estimates point in direction of millions. For example, Rummel (2005) argues that from 1451 to 1870 more than 17 million people died as a result of slavery, with a large majority dying either on the ships headed for the Americas or once they had settled on New World plantations (i.e. 13.7 million). Others believe that this figure is higher: White (2012) estimates range from 6 million to 58 million with a medium range of 17.8 million; Wertham (1966) believes that the total death toll is closer to 150 million. In addition to these enormous fatalities generated through the centuries of the slave trade, African populations were also decimated by colonial wars, massacres and economic exploitation. The two most infamous examples are the Belgian colonisation of Congo under King Leopold that resulted in 8 million to 10 million deaths and the Herero and Nama genocide in German South West Africa that destroyed more than 80 per cent of their population (i.e. 100,000 casualties).

The Congo Free State (1886–1908) is a particularly good example where different forms of organised violence were combined to generate an enormous number of human casualties. While a large number of people were killed directly by the colonial administration, many more died also as a result of a forced labour system, starvation and disease. In 1919, a Belgian government commission established that the total casualties amounted to no less than half of Congo's entire pre–Free State population. This was later verified by other scholars (Hochschild 1999;

Vansina 1966). When one takes into account that at the turn of the century the entire African continent had around 90 to 100 million people (Meredith 2005), the Congo genocide resulted in close to 10 per cent of all inhabitants of Africa. And this was just one of many colonial massacres. While the colonial administrative apparatuses were at the helm of mass murder, the native rulers were also involved in very destructive wars and massacres. For example, the rise of the highly militaristic Zulu Kingdom under Shaka kaSenzangakhona (1816–1828) was crucial in the escalation of mass-scale violence in Southeast Africa. Although there is no agreement among historians on what caused intensified and forced migrations, wars and chaotic struggle for arable land and resources in early-nineteenth century Southeast Africa, often referred to as Mfecane (1818–1840) 'crushing', there is no doubt that the rise of the Zulu Kingdom played a significant part[13]. Although there is no universal agreement on the scale of casualties, it is estimated that these violent events resulted in 1 to 2 million deaths (Walter 1969; Hanson 2001).

As I emphasise in Chapter 9, Shaka's staggering rise and military success was rooted in the Zulu Kingdom's organisational might. Similar processes, with the increased organisational capacity combining with the greater ideological penetration bringing about a huge number of human fatalities, were also at display in other parts of the world. Perhaps the most spectacular militant organisation of this kind was the Chinese Christian millenarian movement Heavenly Kingdom of Peace, which between 1850 and 1864 was involved in probably the most violent uprising in human history – the Taiping rebellion. This conflict, waged between the ruling (Manchu-dominated) Qing dynasty and the Christian millenarian rebels, had complex historical roots, including the Qing's previous military defeats against the Western powers (i.e. the First Opium War), the economic problems caused by the series of natural disasters and the lack of legitimacy of the Manchu government in the eyes of the Han elite and middle classes. In this context, as the central state power was weakened, Chinese regions developed alternative military organisations that challenged the central court. Hence the government was beset with periodic uprisings, including the Nian Rebellion (1853–1868), the Panthay Rebellion (1855–1873), the Dungan Revolt (1862–1877) and so on. Nevertheless, the very well-organised, highly disciplined and ideologically well-articulated movement Heavenly Kingdom of Peace proved to be

---

[13] Some scholars also identify the role of Portuguese slave traders who operated in what is today Mozambique and who fostered both the labour shortage and resource depletion as well as the role of British colonists who too contributed to environmental pressures that generated famine and migrations (Cobbing 1988).

the most serious military challenge. The movement was defined by its theological rigidity, egalitarian ethics and highly militarised organisation. It developed an effective administrative system (with the territory being divided among five provincial rulers), based on the merit which for the first time in Chinese history allowed women to take the civil service exams and join the military. It also rigorously pursued its ideological principles through the existing state, military and educational institutions, including biblical teaching, rigid gender separation and the abolition of private property. The movement was particularly ruthless in terms of its military discipline, and as a result it was successful in capturing several large cities, including Hangzhou and Suzhou in 1860. Since the majority of the movement's supporters came from poverty-stricken groups and the 'lower' classes, its military might was the product of large-scale mobilisation among these groups. At its peak, the army had more than five hundred thousand soldiers. The rebellion was defeated only with European military help (i.e. British and French forces). The rising organisational and ideological powers on both sides on the conflict contributed heavily to the enormity of the death toll that characterised this rebellion: 20 million to 30 million fatalities (MacFarlane 2003). While most of the casualties were a result of the famine, plague and other diseases, this conflict was different from previous Chinese conflicts in that it also involved large-scale battles resulting in a huge number of deaths. For example, the Third Battle of Nanking (1864) generated one hundred thousand casualties in only three days of fighting.

The Twentieth Century and Beyond

Despite some historical oscillations and geographical variations, it is clear that organised violence escalates with the proliferation of modernity around the globe. While the seventeenth, eighteenth and nineteenth centuries demonstrate a substantial increase in terms of the human death tolls through warfare, revolutions, state oppression, starvation, diseases, coercively imposed behavioural changes and other forms of organised violence, it is the twentieth century that is the pinnacle of mass destruction. As Rummel (2005: 3) rightly emphasizes, this century 'was by far the bloodiest in history both in total murdered and as a proportion of the world population'. He estimates that warfare, revolutions, uprisings, and many other forms of violence have generated over 100 million casualties (including 34 million direct war casualties, 54 million famine-related deaths and at least 12 million deaths by other violent causes). However, he is also adamant that majority of victims were killed outside of the battlefields by the state power. Rummel (2005) coined the term 'democide' to describe this practice of killing people through governmental violent action, including genocide, politicide and mass murder. Exploring over eight thousand government reports, he concluded that the twentieth century produced no fewer than 170 million deaths of democide, which combined with 100 million from above equals 270 million in total. Other scholars operate with somewhat different figures. Thus, Brzezinski (1993) calculates that in the twentieth century between 167 million and 175 million people were killed. Hobsbawm (2002) identifies 187 million, Leitenberg (2006) differentiates between 130 million to 142 million war casualties and another 214 to 226 politically caused deaths, while White (2012) estimates 203 million dead through the various forms of organized violence, including warfare, genocide, state oppression and human-made or intentional famine. However, before one analyses the patterns of organized violence in this period, it is important to differentiate its first and second half. The twentieth century is an extremely unusual period of human history in the sense that its first half is by far the deadliest era in human existence on this planet, while its second half (together with the beginning of twenty-first century) is atypical in yielding quite low levels of war casualties. In this sense, it is worth exploring these two periods separately, with the first period culminating with the end of Korean War (1950–1953) and the second period stretching all the way to the present.

The Earth's Darkest Period Yet

The first half of the twentieth century was inaugurated through a series of colonial wars and massacres, including the Congo Free State killings, the genocide of Herero and Nama, the 1898–1901 Boxer Rebellion in China, the Colombian Civil War (1899–1903), the U.S. occupation of the Philippines (1899–1902), the Boer War (1899–1902), the Russo–Japanese War (1904–1905) and the Mexican revolution (1910–1920), among many others. However, after the 'long peace' (1871–1912), Europe became an epicentre of violence. The violent European twentieth century was set off by the brutal Balkan Wars (1912–1913), which were initially misinterpreted as a throwback to the unenlightened past rather than what they actually were – an indication of the things to come in the rest of Europe. Although the Balkan states were quite underdeveloped in comparison to their West European neighbours, their late nineteenth century and early twentieth century modernizing rulers prioritized investing in the state and military building, thus creating conditions for a relatively quick buildup of large and potent militaries capable of mobilising up to 1 million soldiers (Malešević 2012). The intense organizational and ideological developments that underpinned the geopolitical rise of Serbia, Bulgaria and Greece have ultimately resulted in large-scale human carnage: the systematic massacres of civilians and enormous death tolls on the battlefields. The two Balkan wars resulted in close to 150,000 casualties (Hall 2000).

A similar disconnect between traditional strategy and modern organization, ideology and technology, witnessed in the American Civil War and the Balkans wars, was also present in one of the most destructive conflicts in human history – World War I. The Great War still had many hallmarks of the previous conflicts, with imperial rulers stumbling into a highly contingent series of unintended consequences that eventually sparked off warfare that nobody wanted (Clark 2012; Mann 1993, 2012). However, as the war developed it generated unprecedented social changes. For one thing, the huge scale of war stimulated intensive development of science, technology and the organisational capacity of most European and some non-European states. To quickly transport a large number of soldiers and to maintain communication in the theatres of war, it was necessary to develop one's infrastructure. Moreover, the warring sides invested substantially in new military technology, and World War I was responsible for many military inventions, some of which were later successfully deployed in the civilian sphere: from the sanitary napkins and air traffic control, to the hydrophones, aircraft carriers, rudimentary drones, tanks and flamethrowers. For another thing, the trench war paralysis and unparalleled death tolls fostered the mass mobilisation of different social strata who participated in the war on the promise that their postwar social conditions would substantially improve. Hence the shared war experience stimulated the societywide penetration of the nationalist ideologies while the wartime sacrifices imposed a moral obligation on the rulers to expand citizenship rights (Mann 1993, 2012; Tilly 1992). The increased organizational and ideological capacities of states contributed substantially to the scale of human slaughter. The total war casualties range from 15 to 20 million deaths and over 20 million wounded (Herwig at al. 2003: 511: White 2012). Although a huge number of victims were civilians (c. 6.6 million), most fatalities involved soldiers (c. 8.5 million) (White 2012: 345).

Here too one could see continuity in terms of the very short timescale of mass killings. While in premodern and even early modern conflicts it took decades to murder a large number of people in a modern conflict such as World War I, soldiers were killed on an industrial scale in a matter of days and hours. For example, the two famous battles of Somme and Verdun took several months each and resulted in over 306,000 and 305,000 deaths, respectively (White 2012: 350). On the first day of the

Somme, the British lost 58,000 soldiers (Rapport 2013: 83). The staggering speed of Somme was only surpassed twenty seven years later in the Nazi death camps: 'In Majdanek on "bloody Wednesday," November 3, 1943 ... some eighteen thousand Jews were shot within the space of a few hours' (Sofsky 1997: 232). By the summer of 1944, the gas chambers and crematoria of Auschwitz increased their speed of destruction so that '24,000 persons a day were killed and burned' (Sofsky 1997: 262).

The direct offshoot of this total war was also several devastating civil wars and genocides. In particular, the Russian Civil War (1917–1922) and the Armenian genocide (1915–1917) stand out for the unparalleled death toll of civilians. In both of these conflicts, ideology and organisation played a decisive role. The Russian Civil War, fought between several ideologically opposed movements with the dominance of the Bolsheviks on the one side and monarchist Whites on the other, generated close to 9 million human casualties, an overwhelming majority of which were civilians, 8 million (White 2012: 359). Although most deaths were caused by famine and disease, both warring sides also utilised the organisational and ideological means to implement extreme coercion against what they regarded to be their ideological enemies. Hence the Bolshevik Cheka carried out between 250,000 and 1 million summary executions of the 'enemies of the people' (Overy 2004: 180; 1997). Furthermore, some ethnic collectivities were coercively deported to other parts of the new state or were simply murdered on a massive scale. For example, up to five hundred thousand Cossacks were killed or deported while at least one hundred thousand Jews were murdered by the White forces in Ukraine (Allworth 1967: 232–233). No premodern polity had the means or elaborate ideology for this type of systematic murder.

Similarly the Armenian genocide undertaken by the Ottoman state authorities, the Young Turk movement, involved around 1.5 million civilian fatalities. This genocide was also conducted in a relatively systematic way by utilising the coercive and ideological apparatuses of the state. This was a two-phase process that initially involved the decision to kill all males of military age either through wholesale massacres or by forced labour in the military. The second phase involved death marches, where the women, children, elderly and sick were deported to the Syrian desert (Walker 1980; Mann 2005).

While World War I resulted in an enormous death toll and also triggered several large-scale conflicts and genocides, it is World War II that tops all the records in the levels of destruction. Although Pinker (2011: 195) lists this conflict as being only in the middle of his table of the twenty-one deadliest violent episodes in human history, almost every other scholar of violence regards this conflict to be the most devastating human-caused event that has ever taken place on this planet. Even Mathew White (2012: 560), on whose data Pinker largely relies, states that 'the Second World War was the most destructive man-made event in history'. The six years of conflict resulted in a staggering 66 million deaths with a substantially increased ratio of civilian casualties (around 46 million civilians and 20 million soldiers were killed). In some respects, World War II was a pinnacle of the organisational and ideological developments that were initiated in the early modernity. Such a devastating conflict could not take place without the highly advanced organisational capacity of states and militaries involved. The ability to mobilise, train, feed, clothe, arm, transport and communicate with millions of soldiers at staggering speed requires not only sophisticated infrastructural powers but it also entails organisational penetration of the wider societies to fully support and economically sustain years of large-scale warfare. In this context, all major warring sides 'mobilised between a half and two thirds of their industrial work-force, and devoted up to three-quarters of their national product to waging war' (Overy 2005: 154). The massive investment in the military industry galvanized new scientific and technological discoveries which were initially focussed on the military sphere but quickly found their mass application in the civilian life too: from the fast food, dynamo-powered torches, synthetic rubber and oil, penicillin and computers to pressurised air cabins, radar, jet engines and nuclear power. Without complex and hierarchical organizational systems, no polity would be able to wage this type of total war.

In addition to applying such organisational complexity, this war was also defined by societywide ideological penetration and mass mobilisation: Nazi and Fascist utopian ambitions directly challenged the ideological blueprints of Soviet communism and the liberal-conservative vistas of the several Western European and North American polities. Such ideological purity underpinned the main war goals and had profound impact on the levels of human carnage. The Holocaust and many other mass murders of civilians were firmly embedded in the specific and elaborate ideological narratives that justified annihilation of the entire groups of people and provided organisational means to accomplish such gigantic projects. In contrast to Pinker (2011:320), who argues that 'there is no indication that anyone but Hitler and a few fanatical henchmen thought it was a good idea for the Jews to be exterminated', the historical research indicates that there were '42,500 institutions set up to perpetrate the Holocaust' (Corry 2013). In addition, ideological discourses were also utilised to legitimise the carpet bombing of entire cities and the use of atomic bombs against 'enemy' civilians. While mass killings of civilians are not unique to modernity, it is only in this period that sophisticated organisations and elaborate ideological discourses blend together to achieve such devastating results in terms of mass murder. World War II also stands out in terms of the scope and speed of destruction. While the major World War I theatres of war already produced a staggering level of casualties, World War II battlefields topped anything seen before: the siege of Leningrad (up to 4.5 million people), the Battle of Stalingrad (1.8 million deaths), the Battle of Berlin (1.3 million); the Battle of Moscow (1 million); Operation Barbarossa (up to 5 million); the Dnieper campaign (up to 2.5 million); the Battle of Narva (550,000), Kursk (up to 400,000) and so on. The dramatically increased organisational capacities, reflected also in the use of sophisticated military technology, made mass killings instant while the mass-scale ideological mobilisation provided the means to justify such unprecedented acts of violence.

The first half of the twentieth century was also a time when people were killed and starved to death en masse outside of the war zones. The Soviet and later Chinese states were directly responsible for the systematic destruction of their own populations, either from direct atrocities or from the famine, disease and starvation. These policies caused around 20 million deaths in the Soviet Union during the Stalin's reign and up to 40 million deaths in the People's Republic of China under Mao (Hochschild 1999; Rosenburg 1995). Although famine, starvation and disease were the main killers throughout much of history, these two cases differ substantially from the premodern patterns. While in the premodern world the famines and diseases regularly were a consequence of the collapsing organisational structure after a devastating war, in the Soviet and Chinese cases such tragedies were a product of modern organisation and ideology. In other words, unlike the premodern world, where starvation was a result of organisational weakness and ideological incoherence, in these two cases famine and disease came about through the cognizant decision making rooted in fully articulated ideological vistas and implemented through the effective hierarchical systems of organisation. Stalin's extermination of kulaks was an ideologically driven project aimed at reducing the role of the agricultural sector while increasing industrial output, in line with the Marxist theory of history, where there was little room for peasantry. The resisting peasants were killed or sent to forced labour camps. This organisational upheaval generated a large-scale famine which was further exacerbated by the bureaucratic obsession of Soviet commissars to seize the remaining grain (indispensable for next year's planting) in order to fill centrally imposed quotas.

In addition, the Stalinist regime undertook the Great Purge of 'the counterrevolutionary saboteurs and spies', resulting in at least 1 million deaths (Conquest 1992; Elmann 2007). In this case, too, one could witness how the combined advanced organisational and ideological powers generated mass slaughter on a daily basis.[14] As Pipes (2001: 67) documents, during 1937–1938 the NKVD executed close to seven hundred thousand people, with an average of one thousand executions per day. This contrasts sharply with the Tsarist regime, which was also authoritarian but managed to kill fewer than four thousand people for political crimes for the entire period between 1825 and 1910. What monarchists did in eighty-five years the Soviets accomplished in fewer than four days. The similar pattern of action is visible in the Chinese case, where the human toll is even higher. Firmly relying on the tenets of the Marxist doctrine, Maoist rulers attempted to undertake a rapid industrialisation and urbanisation of China by moving 90 million peasants from their farms. The consequence of this policy was a famine at an enormous scale, killing close to 30 million people. Although the deaths and suffering caused by the Great Leap Forward were not intentional, this tragic outcome was still rooted in the ideological and organisational logic that underpinned this modernist project. Here too one can identify the violent consequences of the increased organisational and ideological power which can operate according to its own dynamics. As the early and mid-twentieth century is packed with a huge number of large-scale atrocities, wars and genocides, some scholars argue that these violent episodes should not be treated separately but as a deeply interconnected series of events and processes (Mann 2016; Levy and Thompson 2012). In this context, it becomes even clearer that this is by far the bloodiest period in human history whichever measure one uses. Moreover, although the scale of destruction experienced in this period surpasses anything seen before, its overall trajectory is not unusual as it represents a continuum: the cumulative rise of organised violence that starts twelve thousand years ago and reaches its pinnacle in the mid-twentieth century. What is much more unusual is the situation witnessed in the last fifty years.

The Last Fifty Years

Although Pinker's (2011) popular book has ignited a debate on the decline of violence thesis, his argument is far from being novel. On the

---

[14] To accomplish such grandiose tasks, the Soviet state had to build an enormous bureaucratic machinery of trusted spies. Hence by 1919, Cheka already had a staff of 37,000 and within two years it had expanded to a staggering 260,000 employees (Giustozzi 2011: 117).

one hand the Eliasian sociologists and criminologists have articulated a more sophisticated version of this argument since the publication of *The Civilising Process* (Elias [2000] 1939) and more recent empirical studies by Eisner (2003), Spierenburg (2008), Mennell (2007) and many others. All these studies make a case that violence has experienced substantial decline. They emphasise that there is a wealth of evidence that homicide rates have decreased substantially in Europe between the sixteenth and early-twentieth century (Eisner 2003) and that many other forms of serious interpersonal violence have also decreased in the same period. Similar findings have been corroborated in other parts of the world. On the other hand, political scientists and war studies scholars have provided abundant evidence that the worldwide fatalities of warfare have been in decline for several decades (Cederman et al. 2013; Lacina, Gleditsch and Russett 2006). As illustrated in Chapter 5, there is a significant level of agreement that the number of wars, the length of violent conflicts and the overall casualties of war have been on the substantial decrease over the last fifty years[15]. One could also accept the point that in most contemporary societies corporal forms of violence have experienced societywide delegitimisation and have also been rigorously criminalised. For example, while only a few decades ago disciplining one's children through corporal punishment was regarded as a normal or even desirable part of parenting, today no self-respecting parent would admit that she beats her children. Similarly, the habitual abuse or ridiculing of minorities is generally no longer tolerated. Variety of practices from wife battering to pub fights to animal abuse have all been delegitimised and legally proscribed as criminal behaviour. Even our attitude towards the use of animals in scientific experiments and entertainment has radically changed, with the pronounced slump in the popularity of circuses using trained animals and the frequent protests against the use of animals in laboratories. For some authors, such as Pinker (2011) and Gat (2013, 2006), these are all reliable indicators that all forms of violence are in decline and that we live, as Pinker regularly repeats, in 'the most peaceful era in our species' existence'.

However, this view is problematic on several grounds. Firstly, making a judgement about the long-term direction of violence on the basis of a very short period of time is a flawed strategy. Most historical sociologists are wary of any such grand pronouncements about the direction of social

---

[15] Although as recent studies (Neill & Wardenaer 2015; SIPRI 2016: 6) indicate the scale of organised violence and especially warfare has increased again since 2012. For example, from 2012 to 2014 there was 35% increase in war casualties while 'the number of active armed conflicts increased from 41 in 2014 to 50 in 2015'.

change over such a short period of time. As both Elias (1987: 223) and Mann (2006: 489–495) rightly point out, much of social science is ahistorical and tends to generalise on the basis of contemporary experience. Elias calls this the 'retreat of sociologists into the present', and Mann describes it as an obsession with the 'last five minutes of human history'. Although both Pinker and Gat claim to trace a long-term trend, much of their focus (and evidence) is really centred on the last forty to fifty years. Nevertheless, historically speaking this is too brief a period to identify a long-term trend. The historical experience is full of such apparent short-term peaceful periods that are then followed by devastating wars and other forms of organised violence. The typical examples include the Roman Pax Augusta, which lasted for over 200 years (27 BCE to 192 CE); the Japan's Edo/Tokugawa period, which was even longer, over 250 years (1603 and 1868); or the European Long Peace, which lasted 43 years (1871–1914). In all of these cases, the periods of prolonged peace were followed by highly destructive warfare. As argued in the previous chapter, the current era resembles several previous historical examples in the sense that peace is established on the victor's terms: the contemporary Pax Americana has a great deal in common with the Pax Romana and Pax Britannica of previous times (Mann 2003; Malešević 2015). Furthermore, as critics have pointed out, Pinker's notion of a 'long peace' is a statistical illusion. As Cirillo and Taleb (2016: 1–13) demonstrate, the less frequent wars do not automatically imply more moderation. On the contrary, they might suggest 'fewer but deeper departures from the mean. The fact that nuclear bombs explode less often than regular shells does not make them safer'.

Secondly, Pinker and Gat's view is premised on the idea that violence is a stable, universal, transhistoric and transcultural phenomenon. These arguments are grounded in the view that brutality and civility are mutually exclusive and characterised by fixed boundaries: being civil implies complete disengagement from, and disapproval, of brutal acts. Moreover, the key dividing line in this view is the use of physical force and in particular the kill ratios. Nevertheless, the extent of violence cannot be read at face value. While killing a human being is the ultimate form of extreme violent act, it is far from being the dominant form of violence. Historical criminologists use homicide rates as an indicator of the scale of violence in different periods of time and in different locations. Such data show that the homicide rates in the West have been in decline for centuries but have experienced a small increase from 1960s onwards (Eisner 2003). These data allow them to argue that interpersonal violence is declining. However, if one probes these datasets, it becomes clear that even though homicide rates have been higher in previous centuries they were never particularly high when compared to other forms of violent action. For example, there is a substantial difference between the homicide rates in fourteenth-century and early twentieth century Switzerland (37 and 1.4, respectively per 100,000 per year) (Eisner, 2003: 99), but even the extremely high figure of 37 only suggests that during an entire year in fourteenth-century Switzerland 0.037 of individuals lost their lives through interpersonal violence. Hence the question of whether the homicide rates increase or decrease should be situated in the broader context where this type of violence represents a rather miniscule number within the existing forms of violent action.

The focus on declining homicide rates could also be countered with the rise in suicide rates that usually account for a much larger number of violent deaths in late modernity. For example, according to all available statistics, global suicide rates have increased by 60 per cent over the past forty-five years, with more than 1 million individuals dying as a result of suicide each year. The suicide rates in most countries are substantially higher than rates of homicide, with the global suicide rate at 16 per 100,000 people (www.suicide.org/international-suicide-statistics.html). Furthermore, in most societies male suicide rates are often five or more times higher than male homicide rates: Lithuania 70.1 compared to 7 (in 2004); Guyana 70.8 compared to 17 (in 2012), South Korea 41.7 compared to 0.9 (in 2012) or the United States 20.7 compared to 4 (2013) (data.worldbank.org/indicator/VC.IHR.PSRC.P5; http://www.who.int/en/). Although suicide is conventionally excluded from statistics on violent deaths, there is no doubt that this extreme form of self-harm is a product of changing social conditions. Since Durkheim's (1952) early studies on altruistic, anomic and egoistic suicide, sociologists have become well aware that organisational and ideological pressure combined with the sense of emotional and moral responsibility towards one's family and friends has significant impact on suicide rates. Just as with homicides and war casualties, suicide too is first and foremost a social phenomenon. In this context, the continuous rise in suicide rates can be interpreted as a product of organisational and ideological development where this type of violence increases at the expense of homicides and other forms of violent action.

Therefore, the fact that the homicide rates have decreased cannot be taken as a straightforward indicator for the 'decline of violence' argument. Instead, one has to balance this figure with the rise of suicide rates and other forms of coercive action. Moreover, it is also important to understand that such decreases occur from an already very low base as both homicides and suicides are only a fraction of violent action that take place in the world. One could accept the point that the last fifty years have witnessed a decline in the number of intentional killings of human beings without accepting the argument that violence has declined as such. The overwhelming focus on deliberate murders alone prevents us from exploring the other, more prevalent forms of violence which have not decreased.

Furthermore, focussing exclusively on direct casualties one cannot capture the full extent of destruction in particular regions of the world. As Kissane (2016) shows more people now die and suffer in the aftermath of civil wars than during the actual fighting. This includes infectious diseases; inadequate access to food, shelter and health care; psychological disorders; suicides; and so on. For example, the 1990s U.S. strikes on Iraqi electric power grids 'were intended to have a bloodless psychological effect on the Iraqi citizenry', but without electricity, water purification facilities and sewage treatment plants could not work, thus contributing to mass poisoning from contaminated water and the plethora of other diseases. Consequently, over 111,000 people died (Downes 2008: 226). Moreover, such environments often generate extremely hostile and unhealthy social relations. For example, over 90 per cent of world's drug supply is produced in areas affected by civil war (Kissane 2016: 145–146).

Thirdly, the idea that violence as such can disappear through ever-increasing criminalisation, policing and securitisation is premised on a highly simplistic and essentially wrong view of social action. Since Pinker, Gat and many others understand violence through the narrow prism of intentionality and physicality, they cannot analytically capture its dynamic quality. As argued in Chapter 1, violence is not a fixed and stable event but a malleable and historically changing phenomenon. The exclusive focus on the deliberate injuring of one's body can decontextualise and dehistoricise violent action. Since violence is often generated in the process of establishing control, domination and specific power relations, one cannot simply decouple violence from power. Max Weber's work (1968) has made apparent that coercive action does not have to result in visible injuries or intentional deaths; instead, domination can be achieved through the coercive disciplining and self-disciplining. The key issue here is the credible threat and the ability to deploy violence at any moment of time. Both well-established gangs and modern nation-states maintain this ability and use it only sporadically to make sure that their threats are perceived to be credible. Hence gang leaders might send warnings to those who are unwilling to pay extortion money and can also beat up or kill some disobeying individuals. However, most of the gang's activity will not involve unnecessary killings. In a similar way, representatives of the nation-state can imprison and in some cases even kill their citizens for violent acts, treason or draft dodging. Nevertheless, in most instances the ordinary citizens will respect the established rules of the state and will not act unlawfully. In this context, the sole focus on the homicide rates and war fatalities can thwart more fruitful avenues of research, including the question of how violent action changes through time.

This is particularly relevant when studying collective forms of violence. As this type of violent action presupposes a degree of organisation, it can never dispense with coercion. In other words, as all large-scale complex social organisations have a coercive core, they maintain a potential for violence. The fact that modern wars involve fewer casualties is not a sign that violence is in decline, but only that the modern states and military organisations have greater organisational and ideological capacities to achieve specific political goals without resorting to mass mobilisation of conscripts and mass attacks. Whereas the early- and mid-twentieth-century generals relied on millions of soldiers to accomplish their military and political goals, today such goals can be achieved with much smaller number of better equipped and better trained professional soldiers. The fact that such wars and military interventions usually generate fewer fatalities is no indicator that violence declines but only that the violent action has become more effective. To rephrase Foucault (1975), late modernity is not so much about punishing better instead of punishing less but about killing better rather than killing more. In the same way as the hegemonic and well-established gang does not need to engage in indiscriminate killings to attain its goals and maintain its reputation, so modern twenty-first-century military machines do not have to pursue carpet bombings and burning of villages. Instead, they can opt for selective targeting and periodic displays of their military might. For example, during the conflict in Northern Ireland, British forces have caused only a small number of direct casualties (less than five hundred), but their coercive might was discernible in many other nonfatal ways: twenty thousand imprisoned individuals, three hundred thousand coercive house searches, two thousand people interned without charge and so on (O'Dochartaigh 2016: 152). Rather than dispensing with violence, modern social organisations continue to accumulate coercive power that can be unleashed at any moment in time. The best examples of this destructive capacity are nuclear warheads, which are largely invisible in everyday life but contain such devastating potential that only a handful of such bombs could annihilate the entire planet in a matter of minutes. It is estimated that there are at least fifteen thousand nuclear weapons in the world with the United States and Russia maintaining about 1,800 such weapons on high-alert status (www.icanw.org/the-facts/nuclear-arsenals/).

Hence violence is historically variable: there is no need to burn people at the stake when you can achieve much more through the threat of nuclear Armageddon or selective targeting by drones and ballistic missiles. Violence does not disappear but instead transforms in line with the character of social organisations that utilise coercive power. The decrease in homicide rates and war fatalities is not a sign of its decline but on the contrary it signifies a much greater embodiment of violent power in social organisations. Premodern rulers had no organisational means nor ideological capacity to enforce their will over large populations and vast territories and as such had to use macabre and inefficient violence to generate fear. In contrast, twenty-first-century modern states and many nonstate organisations have sophisticated coercive bureaucratic and ideological apparatuses at their disposal allowing them to accomplish much more through the use of more effective forms of violent action. To fully capture this change, it is necessary to analyse not only homicide rates and war fatalities but also the less visible means that induce coercive behavioural change: the rising number of imprisoned populations, the expansion of police powers, the increased number of coercive court orders, the greater penetration of state power into everyday life (i.e. policing spousal and parent–children relations, policing of sexuality, etc.), the expansion of state and private surveillance, zero-tolerance policing strategies, the greater control of excesses in everyday life (i.e. drinking, the use of recreational drugs, antisocial behaviour, etc.) and so on.

For example, the adult U.S. prison population has increased dramatically over the past hundred years: from about 150,000 in 1920s to 2.3 million in 2015. The United States has by far the highest incarceration rate in the world – in 2013, it stood at 716 per 100,000 of the population, which amounts to 22 per cent of all the world's prisoners (Walmsley 2013; www.prisonstudies.org). Russia too has a very high number of individuals behind the bars: 455 per 100,000. Several other states maintain large prison populations: Kazakhstan (275), Singapore (220), Saudi Arabia (161) and China (119) (www.prisonstudies.org). Furthermore, as Eisener (2014: 121–124) documents well, there is a strong link between the decline in the number of homicides and the continuous expansion of coercive policies of states. By zooming in on the NGRAM viewer data for the 'Western World 1950–2008', Eisener establishes 'a good correspondence between the beginning of the crime decline in the 1990s and the diffusion of the three indicators of a new culture of control, namely, CCTV surveillance, zero-tolerance policies in policing and schools, and a focus on anger management as a self-control-based therapeutic strategy'. This evidence seems to confirm earlier studies on increasing securatisation and the new culture of control (Farrell et al. 2011; Garland 2001).

There is no doubt that the coercive and ideological power of modern social organisations continues to grow and expand. It is quite telling that the two largest employers in the world are military organisations: the U.S. Department of Defence (3.1 million employees) and China's People's Liberation Army (2.3 million employees).[16] While modern states retain the power to quickly apprehend anybody who challenges its coercive monopoly (i.e. nobody can use violence except the state), other social organisations continue to increase their coercive capacity within their own domain (i.e. private organisations can quickly fire disobedient employees, and religious organisations can instantly delegitimize and excommunicate disobedient members). Thus, rather than disappearing, violence is largely undergoing transformation: from individuals and small groups towards large-scale social organisations.

Finally, the perception that violence is decreasing or disappearing is also premised on a specific set of beliefs and practices that differentiate sharply between the illegitimate and legitimate forms of violent action. While throughout history such distinctions were either nonexistent or less clear, modern social organisations have established and enforced particular parameters that delegitimise only certain forms of violence. Hence in modern nation-states, there is an unambiguous differentiation between internal and external violence: killing a compatriot is heinous crime punishable by death in some jurisdictions, whereas killing hundreds of young enemy soldiers in war is an act of bravery deserving of a medal. As both Mann (1986) and Giddens (1985) emphasise that this sharp distinction did not exist in previous historical epochs, as premodern rulers had no organisational power to enforce their will over huge territories and large populations. Furthermore, with the constantly changing alliances between the nobility on the one hand and the different types of popular uprisings on the other (i.e. peasant rebellions, marauders, banditry, pirates, fiefs, heretics, etc.), there were no fixed and elaborate ideological narratives in place to delegitimise all these different forms of violence. In contrast, modernity brings about greater organisational and ideological powers that allow rulers and other leaders to establish coercive monopolies vis-a-vis individuals under their control. Hence states legitimately monopolise their use of violence over specific territory while nonstate organisations acquire increased coercive capacity to control their members or employees. This allows for a significant structural transformation whereby violence becomes less visible as social organisations manage to pacify their surroundings. Hence state power shifts from 'the manifest use of violence to pervasive use of administrative power in sustaining its rule' (Giddens 1985: 188), and the same applies to private corporations, religious institutions and many other complex modern social organisations. This transition from the physicality of violence towards less discernible coercive power was mediated by ideological transformation too. As argued in Chapter 1, the distinction between internal/private and external/public violence presupposes popular acceptance of such dichotomy. The rise and expansion of centrifugal ideologisation has created conditions that made such dichotomous thinking fully legitimate. In this context, the continuous increase in the coercive capacity of states and other organisations went hand in hand with the greater ideological penetration that ultimately provided justification for this continuous increase. This process has largely proved to be inversely proportional: the expansion of organisational legitimacy came through the greater delegitimisation of others.

Hence no other social organisation can legitimately deploy coercive power or encroach on the space of its competitor, and this applies equally to states and nonstate organisations. In addition, no individual or a group, whether legitimate members of that organisation or externals, can use the coercive might within one's organisation. As organisational power grows, its coerciveness becomes hegemonic, and organisations became capable of projecting insecurity and fear so as to maintain its ideological grip on its members. Hence late modernity is paradoxical in the sense that even though physicality of violence decreases there is constant organisational demand for increase in coercive power. For example, over the last three decades the state's coercive capacity has extended deeply into the ordinary everyday life of most individuals: there is greater policing of sexuality, interpersonal and family relations, neighbourhoods and friendships (Mann 2013). States and other social organisations have developed extensive infrastructural powers and are capable of utilising sophisticated technology to monitor commercial transactions, personal phone and Internet exchanges, border crossings, antisocial behaviour and a variety of social actions defined as deviant or criminal. Nevertheless, this greater organisational coerciveness largely does not develop in opposition to popular attitudes. On the contrary, with pervasive centrifugal ideologisation there is a constant popular demand for even greater intrusion of bureaucratic apparatuses into everyday life. Much of this action is justified in relation to networks of microsolidarity. When states interfere in interpersonal and family relations, this regularly happens through the calls 'to protect our children', 'to help our deprived fellow citizens', 'to safeguard our family life', 'to preserve our way of life' and so on. Since ideologisation is anchored in the projection of microsolidarity, the legitimate expansion of coercive power is possible only through personalised ideological appeals. Hence, rather than disappearing, both violence and perceptions of violence undergo historical change. Any thesis suggesting a decline of violence fails to capture this transformation at all.

Conclusion

Despite popular perceptions, reinforced by recent scholarly contributions, that organised violence has been in steep decline for centuries, in fact the opposite is true. Although there are obvious geographical and historical variations in the scale and extent of violence, there is no doubt that over the last twelve thousand years organised violence has grown substantially. A brief review of the available historical data indicates that even though the epicentres of violence change and move through time and space, its direction remains largely constant: a continuous rise. Since violence originates in, and remains dependent on, organisational capacity and ideological penetration, it is difficult to envisage how violence can decline while organisational and ideological powers continue to expand. It is true that the last fifty years have experienced a drop in the number of human fatalities, but this in itself is no reliable sign that organised violence has substantially declined. Instead, this is a potent indicator that collective violence is in transformation as the coercive capacities of states and other social organisations have increased to such an extent that mass killings can be replaced with the alternative forms of violent action. To explore how this process works over longer periods of time, it is necessary to zoom in on the four main forms of organised violence: warfare, genocide, revolution and terrorism.

5   Warfare

Introduction

In his 2009 Nobel Peace Prize acceptance speech, Barak Obama stated that 'war, in one form or another, appeared with the first man. At the dawn of history, its morality was not questioned; it was simply a fact, like drought or disease – the manner in which tribes and then civilizations sought power and settled their differences'.[1] This statement summarises quite well a conventional and highly popular view that warfare is immemorial and that as human development progresses our world is bound to become less violent. Nevertheless, this view is built on the empirically mistaken assumptions. War is not a natural fact; it is a product of social development. Unlike droughts or diseases, which are environmental and biological phenomena, respectively, war is first and foremost a social phenomenon. As argued in Chapter 3, the institution of war develops quite late in human history, and its very existence remains dependent on the complex social relations of human beings and the organisations they create, not on human beings' nature. In this chapter, I analyse this deeply interdependent relationship between war and social change. More to the point, I explore the role that bureaucratisation, ideologisation and micro-solidarity play in the proliferation of warfare throughout the world. I argue that for much of our history, warfare was an important catalyst of social transformation. Wars brought about enormous destruction and bloodshed, but they also galvanised and changed social relations; generated new scientific and technological inventions; and fostered economic modernisation, political change and cultural development. Since its origins twelve thousand years ago, war has shaped most aspects of social life, and it is still the most significant social and political force in the world. Although the last fifty years have witnessed a decrease in the number of interstate wars and battlefield fatalities, this should not be interpreted as a sign that warfare is becoming obsolete. On the contrary,

---

[1] www.whitehouse.gov/the-press-office/remarks-president-acceptance-nobel-peace-prize

this change might signal that the institution of war has become more advanced, as it is now organisationally and ideologically better embedded in the everyday life.

War and Social Change

Even though the study of war is almost as old as war itself, there is no universally accepted definition of this phenomenon. However, since the 1970s onwards, most empirical, particularly quantitative-oriented, research on war has tended to congregate around Singer and Small's (1972) proposition that defines as war any armed conflict which results in at least one thousand battle deaths per year. This almost exclusive focus on the size of human casualties as the determining feature of warfare has proved useful for developing large-scale datasets for comparative analyses of wars. Nevertheless, excessive quantification was also highly detrimental for understanding the complexities and subtleties of social changes and the correspondingly diverse historical trajectories of war in time and space. While battle deaths might be a useful indicator to assess the scale and size of particular wars, they are not comprehensive enough to capture the full dynamics of social change instigated by specific wars. Many historically highly significant violent conflicts did not involve large number of casualties nor mass destruction. For example, the highly significant Indian Wars of 1865–1898 and the Mexican–American War of 1846–1848, events that have shaped the size and character of the future world superpower, each involved a quite small number of casualties, with only 919 and 1,733 dead American soldiers, respectively (Clodfelter 1992). Similarly, the NATO–Yugoslav war of 1999 involved only two fatalities on the NATO side (two killed pilots) and 956 Yugoslav casualties (Krieger 2001).

Furthermore, most warfare before the modern era was characterised by, comparatively speaking, small human casualties, with many wars resembling pushing matches (as in the ancient Greek world) or ritualistic skirmishes between nobility whereby the number of dead soldiers or civilians played a minor role in determining the outcome of war and even a lesser role in the social change that followed specific violent events (Mann 1993; Collins 2008a; Malešević 2010). In this context, war is better defined by shifting the focus from the number of casualties towards the character of the conflict and its relationship with the states and societies involved in such violent processes. Hence one could define war as a protracted and widespread armed conflict between social organisations resulting in significant social change. This involves the organised use of physical violence with the principal aim of coercing one social organisation to comply with the demands of other social organisations. Most wars are complex and historically contingent events that entail mobilisation of human beings, economic resources, coercive means, production and communication.

Traditional definitions of war, which overemphasise the quantity of human casualties, are also built around the misperception that war is a historically constant and uniform phenomenon shaped by similar, if not identical, transhistorical social processes. Nevertheless, this assumption is highly problematic. The key point here is that just as world societies have been in constant flux over the past twelve thousand years, so has the institution of warfare. When one talks about society and state today and the polities and social orders that occupied the world of two thousand or four hundred years ago, one is not discussing the same forms of social organisation.[2] The early forms of polity, such as chiefdoms, pristine empires or city-states, were entities that were profoundly different from contemporary nation-states. In contrast to nation-states, which derive their raison d'etre from the idea of popular sovereignty, moral equality and a substantial degree of cultural uniformity, premodern polities utilised very different sources of legitimacy – mythologies of nonhuman descent, divine origins of monarchs, imperial civilising missions and so on. Furthermore, unlike their premodern counterparts that adopted different versions of patrimonial rules of social organisation, nation-states are modelled on bureaucratic principles that emphasise efficiency, division of labour, knowledge, professionalism and the impersonality and transparency of hierarchical order (Malešević 2013a: 8–11, 20–54; Meyer et al. 1997; Weber 1968). The institution of warfare has also undergone a similar social transformation – from nonfighting simple foragers, the pushing matches of antiquity, the ritualistic tussles of the medieval world, the limited violent conflicts of mercenaries, the brutalising wars of revolutionaries and nationalists, the mass warfare of two total wars and eventually contemporary civil wars waged by warlords versus the high-tech interventionist wars of the Western professionals (Centeno and Enriques 2016, Malešević 2010, Howard 1976). The fact that one is forced to use the same term 'war' for a variety of highly distinct and historically specific forms of organised violence often leads to the misleading strategy that treats all these armed conflicts as if they are the same phenomenon. Nevertheless, to understand these fundamental changes it is necessary to briefly explore the organisational underpinnings of warfare.

---

[2] This section draws in part on Malešević 2015.

. In contrast to popular perceptions, shared by sociobiologists such as Pinker (2011) and van der Dennen (1995), war is, historically speaking, a relatively novel invention. As demonstrated in Chapter 3, much of the available archaeological and anthropological evidence indicates that the simple hunter-gatherers and other foraging nomadic groupings tended to avoid prolonged intergroup violence and had no organisational, technological, ideological or environmental means to wage wars (Fry and Soderberg 2013; Sponsel 2015; Fry 2007; Kelly 2000). As foraging bands are small, nonsedentary, egalitarian and fluid, there is no organisational prerequisite to wage wars. Thus war emerges on the historical scene together with social development – the rise of stratified group structures, sedentary lifestyles, agriculture, social hierarchies, and division of labour, among others. Most of all the proliferation of warfare is closely linked with the emergence of the first stable, territorially focussed, polities – chiefdoms, city-states and eventually pristine empires (Mann 1993; Malešević 2010: 92–101), all of which have taken root only in the last twelve thousand years. Furthermore, from its inception, war, state and society have developed and changed together. If one understands war as an instrument of social and political power, then as social orders change, so does the nature of warfare. It is no accident that both chiefdoms and early pristine empires relied extensively on violent conquests to maintain (and expand) the existing social order. The famous chiefdoms of yesteryear, such as those ruled by Arminius or Genghis Khan, were despotic and hierarchical but highly unstable polities whose very existence was premised on continuous territorial expansion and war conquests. Similarly, the early empires, from the Romans, Chinese, Rashiduns and Srivijayas to the Ottomans, were heavily dependent on resources, slaves, serfs and territories to maintain their internal social cohesion and prosperity (Burbank and Cooper 2010). In contrast, most city-states were more stable, less hierarchical and, with few notable exceptions such as Sparta or Venice, less conquest prone. In all of these cases, polity formation, internal social dynamics and warfare have had a profound and lasting impact on each other. The nature of war has often had significant impact on internal social stratification and vice versa. Protracted, symmetrical and all-encompassing wars stimulated development of citizenship rights and democratic institutions, whereas asymmetric and conquest-oriented warfare that utilised armies of highly skilled warriors and expensive weaponry was more likely to foster hierarchical and highly stratified social orders (Andreski 1968; Mann 1993; Malešević 2010). For example, both ancient Greece and medieval Switzerland were often hailed as the first examples of participatory citizenship and advanced democratic institutions, including their representative popular assemblies such as the Greek *ekklêsia* and the Swiss *landsgemeinde* (Sinclair 1988; Kobach 1993). However, it is often forgotten that this unusual degree of social freedom and popular decision making was built on large-scale participation in wars. These were societies composed of self-armed and self-equipped communities of farmers-soldiers who were able and willing to use their arms and military skills to maintain their rights.

War has also played a decisive role in the advent of modernity. As Tilly (1985), Mann (1993), Giddens (1985) and Hirst (2001) have convincingly demonstrated that the intensive preparations for war and the escalation of European warfare since late-sixteenth century onwards provided unprecedented stimulus for state development and social change. Ever-increasing geopolitical competition forced rulers towards greater fiscal reorganisation; the expansion of administrative structures; the growth of the banking sector; and investment in the development of science, technology and the military. The direct corollary of these transformations was the extension of parliamentarism, citizenship rights and greater welfare provisions as the rulers were forced to trade political and social rights for more popular support, increased public taxation and the willingness of citizens to fight in wars. The onset of industrialisation was heavily dependent on the technology pioneered in the military sphere, and from the mid-nineteenth century onwards social development in the civilian sector regularly went hand in hand with the industrialisation of warfare (McNeill 1982; Giddens 1985). The two total wars of the twentieth century were a culmination of this ever-expanding link among the state, war and society: mass production, mass politics and mass communications were all mobilised for mass destruction. What started off as a traditional military confrontation was gradually redefined as a vicious conflict to death between the entire populations. Nevertheless, the long-term consequence of these two extremely destructive conflicts was the further extension of citizenship rights, greater gender equality, delegitimisation of racism and the establishment of welfare states (Mann 2013). Hence, over the past several centuries one could notice the constant increase in the destructiveness of war, which was often preceded or followed by substantial social changes.

The War–State–Society Nexus and Social Organisations

What one can observe when looking historically at the nexus of war–state–society is that this social dynamic was largely shaped by similar processes that stretch over very long periods of time, and this has not substantially changed today. Since for 98 per cent of their existence on this planet humans were nomadic foragers characterised by malleable and weak social ties, it took millions of years for rudimentary social organisations to emerge. However, once the first elements of social order and statehood developed, they tended to arise in tandem with warfare. Hence what is truly distinct about the last twelve thousand years is how quickly and forcefully the nexus of war–state–society has transformed the face of this planet. One of the key processes spawned by the interplay at this nexus was the continuous expansion of organisational power. Since Weber's early works (1968, 1994), analysts have become aware that any effective social action entails the presence of organisations. Nevertheless, once in place social organisations are inclined to grow, expand, control its personnel and engage in confrontations with the competing social organisations. Hence nearly all influential social organisations have a coercive foundation (Malešević 2013a, 2010). The prevalence of warfare over the past centuries has helped expand and increase the coercive capacity of polities. This process was already visible at the birth of the first empires when the expanding state power depended on the proliferation of 'social caging', with individuals being forced to trade personal liberty for state-provided security (Mann 1993). Over the years, social caging was combined with 'political racketeering', that is, popula-tions being required to pay taxes and finance costly wars in exchange for some citizenship rights and protection from other states and domestic threats (Tilly 1985). Nevertheless, it is only in the past two hundred years that the cumulative bureaucratisation of coercion has significantly accel-erated. The transformation of empires, composite kingdoms and city-states into sovereign nation-states was accompanied by technological, scientific and production changes, all of which have had an enormous impact on the war–state–society nexus. As wars expanded and became more destructive and costly, the organisational power of states and their ability to control their populations grew exponentially. Not only have modern states increased their infrastructural reach and capacity but they have also managed, for the first time in history, to legitimately monopol-ise the use of violence, taxation, legislation and education (Weber, 1968; Elias 2000[1939]; Gellner 1983; Malešević 2013a). The pinnacle of this process were the two world wars. To wage such protracted and costly wars, states were forced to further increase their organisational powers, including their ability to mobilise millions of individuals to fight or labour for the war effort. The intensive popular mobilisation had long-term effects that galvanised intensive social changes. For example, the short-age of manpower on the battlefields fostered the introduction of universal conscription, which, among other things, expanded the citizenship and some welfare rights of urban poor and peasantry that could not be easily revoked after the war. In a similar vein, the mass deployment of men to fronts and the expansion of war industries caused a shortage of industrial labour. This ultimately compelled state authorities to open up the factories and other industries to women workers, thus introducing policies which have profoundly undermined traditional patriarchal relationships.[3] Once women gained economic independence, it was extremely difficult to reestablish the gendered status quo. Furthermore, mass war casualties and wartime ideals of national solidarity stimulated gradual delegitimisation of sharp class divides and forced state authorities to extend welfare policies and health protection in many European and, to a lesser extent, North American states. All of these substantial social transformations had a deep impact on postwar states and societies. Despite enormous human casualties and material destruction, postwar social organisations became stronger than ever. The further expansion of scientific knowledge, technology and industry together with the continuous growth of the administrative sector provided impetus to multiply organisational power in a variety of domains. Hence the second half of the twentieth century witnessed a dramatic acceleration in the state's ability to collect information on all of its population; to tax its citizens at source; to fully police its borders; to control public education, health care, employment and immigration policies; to interfere in family and sexual life; and to successfully introduce mass surveillance programs (i.e. biometric passports, ID cards, birth certificates, census data, CCTV cameras, etc.) (Lyon 2001, Dandeker 1990, Mann 2013). It is war that was a prime catalyst of these changes.

The fact that most of Europe, North America and the rest of developed world have not experienced much or any warfare on their soil over the past seven decades might suggest that the war–state–society nexus has been broken or displaced by the less coercive structural mechanisms of development. This, however, is not the case. The immediate aftermath of World War II was not permanent peace but instead a protracted and highly intensive cold war occasionally escalated by brutal and devastating proxy wars[4] (i.e. Korea, Vietnam, Afghanistan, Angola, Nicaragua, etc.) directly supported by the two superpowers. This period (1946–1991) was characterised by the continuous preparation for war together with the political mobilisation of citizenry, all of which have helped stimulate further increases in the organisational powers of states. Not only the United States and the Soviet Union but all members of the two military alliances utilised military advancements and the perpetual threat of war

---

[3] See more about relationship between gender and war in Malešević (2010: 275–307) and Goldstein (2001).

[4] As Mann (2013: 33) indicates, these proxy wars cost at least 20 million human lives.

to increase their organisational power. It was the political and military competition between the two power blocs that gave impetus to techno-logical, scientific, industrial and state development. As in the previous historical periods, most significant scientific and technological inventions were pioneered in the military sector and then gradually found their way into civilian use (Giddens 1985). Despite the lack of human casualties in Europe and North America, the proxy wars and the permanent threat of nuclear Armageddon proved to be key organisational devices for sub-stantial social change throughout the world. The cold war was certainly the golden age of economic prosperity, political stability, welfare provi-sions and social mobility for large sectors of the population on both sides of the political divide (Hobsbawm 1994, Mann 2012). Just as in the previous three centuries, social development, state enhancement and military expansion advanced together. The war–state–society nexus was not significantly dented; it just became accommodated to the different historical constellations.

Whereas the late-twentieth and early-twenty-first centuries have wit-nessed some significant changes in the relationship among war, state and society, these are far from being radical transformations. In fact, these changes indicate the continuous strengthening of the war–state–society nexus and further increase in the cumulative bureaucratisation of coer-cive power (Malešević 2013b, 2010). The popular view of globalisation as undermining the strength of nation-states and dramatically transform-ing social relationships between the states is an overstatement lacking empirical validation (Mann 2013, 2012; Hirst at al. 2009; Hall 2000). The argument that globalisation inevitably weakens state power is often premised on the idea that before the current wave of globalisation, nation-states were strong and sovereign. However, historically nuanced analyses show that for most of the nineteenth and early-twentieth cen-tury, full sovereignty and political independence were largely unachieved ideals, something that most rulers strived for but were unable to accom-plish. It is only the Great Powers that could attain and afford full state sovereignty and control of their territories, whereas most other states did not possess sufficient state capacity for, nor were they allowed to achieve, full sovereignty (Smith 2010). Hence the fact that some states have more political might and independence today than others is not particularly new. In fact, it is only in the last few decades that most states have gained more organisational power than even their strongest nineteenth-century predecessors could have imagined possible. Similarly, pre-2008 eco-nomic liberalisation was not profoundly different from its late-nineteenth and early-twentieth-century predecessor, and in both of these cases opening up world markets went hand in hand with increasing the organisational and coercive potency of the states (Mann 1993, 2013; Conrad 2006; Lachmann 2010). Instead of being mutually exclusive forces, neoliberal capitalism and bureaucratisation often underpin one other (Fligstein 2001; Vogel 1996). Even the appearance of new technologies has not substantially shifted this balance. On the contrary, new technological advancements and inventions – from satellites, the Internet, mobile phones, robotics and laser weapon systems to nanotechnologies and many others – have helped reinforce the organisational power of states, which are now much more able and willing to control and police their borders, populations, tax intake, transgressions of law, immigration, education, sexuality and so many other aspects of everyday life.

The continuous expansion of state power is also followed by the extension of its coercive reach and capacity both internally (policing one's own population) and externally (using military might to shape foreign policy). This growth of organisational strength allows most powerful states to engage in periodic but quite regular military interventions all over the world. Since the end of the cold war, the United States, the United Kingdom, France, Russia and Israel, among others, have been involved in a number of wars and military interventions, including Iraq, Syria, Afghanistan, Mali, Georgia, Lebanon, Palestine, Libya, Sierra Leon, Chad, Central African Republic, Ukraine, etc. It is true that these military undertakings have generated a smaller number of casualties than similar interventions before and during the cold war. However, the key point is that analysts' focus should shift from such a crude measure as military casualties in the direction of whether or not such wars make significant social and political impact. What sociologically matters in contemporary wars is what kind of social and political change they generate.

Outbreaks of civil war tend to emerge in regions where the existing state structures are already quite weak and are challenged by competing social organisations. These often include not only neighbouring states but also domestic competitors dissatisfied and capable of challenging the weakened state, as well as world powers pursuing their own geopolitical ambitions. This obviously is not a historically novel situation. As Tilly (1985: 15) shows, European state formation went through a very similar process – it started with one thousand polities in the fourteenth century which by the sixteenth century were reduced to five hundred, and by the early-twentieth century protracted warfare was instrumental in reducing this number to only twenty-five states. As the running of modern social organisations becomes ever more expensive, state structures that cannot keep up with the demands of cumulative bureaucratisation of coercion often lose their monopoly on the legitimate use of violence. In other words, the dominance of civil wars today is not a new phenomenon (Kalyvas 2001); they are just more visible as there are fewer wars between powerful states. What is distinct about these conflicts is that, unlike their fifteenth-, sixteenth- or eighteenth-century European predecessors, most contemporary civil wars cannot be 'played out' to their logical conclusion, the outcome of which would be fewer but more powerful states (Herbst 2000; Centeno 2002). The main reason why such conflicts are labelled 'civil wars' and contained within existing state borders is the coercive dominance of international regulations that explicitly prohibit any violent change of interstate borders. In previous historical periods, many wars that started off as intrastate conflicts were later, if and when insurgencies won, redesigned as interstate wars. However, the contemporary geopolitical context does not allow for such a transition from civil to interstate war to occur. In contrast to Mueller (2009) and Pinker (2011), who see the existing norms on the sanctity of interstate borders as a simple reflection of universally shared Enlightenment principles, it is much more plausible to view these rules as something initiated, imposed and policed by the winners of World War II. As such, these regulations are the ideological expression of contemporary geopolitical constellations, as they firmly reinforce the geopolitical status quo.[5]

Although the last twenty years have seen numerous high-tech wars and military interventions waged by the powerful states, most of these violent conflicts did not generate radical social transformations. The reliance on sophisticated technology, science and industry has reduced the need for the use of mass armies and has led to the abolition of conscription in Europe and North America. Although the introduction of mass conscription gave birth to the welfare state, there is no reliable evidence that the ever-increasing professionalization of the military directly causes the shrinking of welfare provisions (Lachmann 2013a, 2010). New technological advancements in military and medicine have also been instrumental in decreasing the number of human casualties among the military personnel of the powerful states. This is particularly visible in the ever-increasing ratio of wounds to death. For example, for U.S. soldiers World War I and World War II ratios of deaths to wounded were 1:1.75 and 1:1.65, respectively. This has increased to 2.6 wounded during the Vietnam War and 8.38 and 7.17 during the Afghanistan and Iraq wars, respectively (Centeno and Enriquez 2016: 34).

---

[5] The most memorable attempt to violate this norm was Saddam Hussein's invasion of Kuwait, which instantly triggered the U.S. and European armed punishment: the Gulf War of 1991.

However, these changes had very little to do with humanitarian ethics and civilising processes and much more to do with the organisational capacity of powerful states to use sophisticated technology to minimise political and military risks. As Shaw (2005) demonstrates, much of this warfare is premised on minimizing life-risks to Western military personnel by transferring these risks to the weaker enemy. From the Falkland War of 1982, to the 1991 Gulf War, the 1999 Kosovo War and most recent wars in Syria, Afghanistan, Iraq, Libya and Mali, the reliance on technologically sophisticated weapons has helped create the systematic transfer of risks from elected politicians to military personnel and from Western militaries to enemy combatants and their civilians. Nevertheless, the use of new technology and science did not alter the social and political context of warfare. In other words, what was pursued in the Korean and Vietnam wars and the Soviet war in Afghanistan relying on millions of recruits and the mass mobilisation of entire societies is now achieved through the use of high-altitude bombing, long-distance missile launches, remotely navigated combat drones, the use of demolition vehicles and other robotic devices. Simply put, when Pinker (2011), Goldstein (2011) and others use the statistics on the decline of human casualties in contemporary warfare to argue that we live in the least violent period of human history, they misread the present situation. The fact that recent wars have lower casualties is not a symptom of coercive decline but in fact is an indicator of its increased strength. As both Giustozzi (2011) and Kalyvas (2006) show, as social organisations develop and consolidate their monopolies of violence, they move away from indiscriminate killings towards what is much more effective, selected targeting. In Giustozzi's (2011: 14) words: '... these multiple processes of specialisation and taming of violence have at their core the attempt to make coercion (hence violence) more carefully targeted and selective, as opposed to the untamed, indiscriminate violence which tends to characterise the initial establishment of the monopoly of violence'. Since the cumulative bureaucratisation of coercion has increased substantially over the past three to four decades, state and military authorities have become aware that the armies of mass conscripts do not achieve much while bringing about huge numbers of human casualties. Hence, instead of deploying millions of inexperienced conscripts who regularly end up as a cannon fodder, thus generating long-term national traumas and enormous financial costs, present-day social organisations have switched to smaller numbers of well-trained and well-organised professional purveyors of violence (King 2013).

When war is conceptualised not as a simple political instrument of rulers but as an outcome of complex and contingent historical processes involving competition between social organisations, then its proliferation is heavily dependent on the strength and coercive reach of particular social organisations.[6] The historical record shows that the prevalence and expansion of warfare tends to be linked with the increased capacity of social organisations. Hence scholars have identified several periods of revolutionary acceleration of warfare ranging from southern Mesopotamia in the late-fourth and early-third millennia, the eastern Mediterranean and China at the end of first millennium BE and the European-induced warfare expansion between 1500s and 1945 (Levy and Thompson 2012; Gabriel 2002; Gray 2002). In all three of these cases, one can witness the significant interplay among war, state development and social transformation. The war–state–society nexus generated unprecedented social changes in military (army sizes, weaponry production, etc.), society (greater urbanisation, technological inventions, a shift to mass-scale production in agriculture and later in industry, etc.) and polity formation (greater political centralisation, expanding infrastructural power, etc.). The direct outcome of these changes was an escalation in wars as ever-expanding states attempted to establish regional hegemonies and/or prevent other such polities from becoming new political hegemons (Levy and Thompson 2012). In this context, the post–World War II period is not the end of (war) history. It is just the end of the long-term process that was initiated with the military revolution of early-fifteenth century.

However, the relative peace established in Europe and North America in the last several decades still remains grounded in similar historical processes that have shaped social and political life in the previous centuries – organisational power and the ability of large-scale social organisations such as modern-day nation-states to establish their political, economic, ideological and military dominance. During the cold war era, the bipolar stability, mutually recognised regional hegemony and threat of nuclear destruction prevented escalation of violence in the Northern part of the globe.

The further decline of interstate warfare after the cold war is tightly linked with the unprecedented military supremacy of the United States

---

[6] Although the nation-state remains the most powerful political actor in the contemporary world, there are other nonstate organisations which have also increased their coercive-bureaucratic power. These include private corporations (such as Shell, McDonald's, Toyota, etc.), religious institutions (the Catholic Church, Scientology, the Russian Orthodox Church, etc.), terrorist networks (Islamic State, al Qaeda, Hezbollah, Continuity IRA, etc.), established social movements (the Zapatistas, the Animal Liberation Front, the Earth Liberation Army, etc.). I explore this briefly in Malešević (2016).

and the combination of inability and unwillingness of other powerful social organisations (i.e. the European Union, Russia, China, Japan, etc.) to challenge U.S. military and political hegemony. For much of the past sixty years, American military power has been so overwhelming that no other state, not even the Soviet Union at the peak of its military might, would willingly provoke a war with the United States. The military omnipotence of this state is historically unprecedented: this is the only state that has a substantial military presence, including large-scale army bases, in more than 150 countries all over the world; the U.S. military budget is larger than the total combined military expenditure of its next ten competitors, China, Russia, the United Kingdom, France, Japan, India, Saudi Arabia, Brazil, Germany and Italy (SIPRI 2016); American airpower is so overwhelming that no other state is anywhere near its technological supremacy; and the U.S.'s military technology in laser-guided missiles, aircraft carrier ships, refuelling facilities, military robotics and many other areas is far ahead of any other military in the world (Collins 2013; Mann 2003). This unparalleled military hegemony remains the cornerstone of contemporary geopolitical stability in the world. U.S. military supremacy averts any attempts to engage in interstate warfare in the northern part of the globe and strongly discourages potential outbreaks of interstate war within the U.S.'s extremely wide interest zone. The fact that the American military shield (through NATO or other arrangements) incorporates much of Europe and Japan means that this Pax Americana acts as a brake on the escalation of any potential conflicts within its very wide domain. In this sense, as Burbank and Cooper (2010), Munkler (2007) and Mann (2003) remind us, U.S. military hegemony in many important respects resembles its imperial predecessors – the military supremacy of the Roman, Mongol and British empires were decisive in generating extensive periods of peace not so dissimilar to the period we are currently experiencing. Hence it is the geopolitical configuration, not the humanitarian revolution or civilizational advancement, so dear to Pinker and Mueller, which gave birth to Pax Romana, Pax Mongolica and Pax Britannica just as much as to Pax Americana.

Nevertheless, what distinguishes the contemporary world from its predecessors is the considerable increase in organisational capacity of most modern states and other social organisations. Whereas Roman, Mongol and other empires usually waged wars against polities with feeble organisational power, most contemporary states possess high infrastructural capacity, which makes any potential interstate war extremely costly and difficult to fight. Unlike their patrimonial counterparts, which in most important respects were puny leviathans, most present-day states are built around bureaucratic principles that foster the continuous expansion of their coercive capacity and reach (Malešević 2013a, 2010). For example, while the Roman Empire could subdue relatively quickly and cheaply the chiefdoms and composite kingdoms of the Sabines, Etruscans, Goths, Illyrians or Gauls, the late-twentieth and twenty-first-century interstate wars, typified by the Iran–Iraq war (1980–1988), have been extremely destructive, costly and difficult to win. Nevertheless, it is important to emphasise that ever-increasing organisational power is not just confined to states but also to other overtly and covertly coercive social organisations (including terrorist networks, private corporations, social movements, etc.). This is best illustrated by the fact that despite the enormous military presence of the United States, the United Kingdom and forty-seven other highly developed militaries in one of the poorest and infrastructurally least-developed countries in the world, the Taliban insurgency has been well able to wage successful guerrilla war for more than a decade. On the surface, this looks as if the most powerful state in the world cannot easily overpower one of the weakest polities in the world. However, the point is that the United States and its allies are not fighting the Afghan state, which is infrastructurally and organisationally extremely weak, but are engaged in a fierce struggle with a highly organised, effective, hierarchical and coercive insurgency network – the Taliban. In this sense, the Taliban is similar to other insurgency movements such as Islamic State, Hamas, Hezbollah or FARC: all of them have substantially increased their coercive organisational powers at the expense of the nation-state they inhabit (Malešević 2014, 2013a; Giustozzi 2011).

Hence, paradoxically even though the continuous expansion of organisational power was decisive for the escalation of the twentieth-century total wars, it is this very same process that plays a major role in containing interstate warfare today. Simply put, interstate wars have become rare and less deadly precisely because the organisational power of many contemporary states, and most of all that of the United States, has so substantially increased to the point that initiating an interstate war is extremely difficult, hugely expensive and, with the exception of a couple of powerful states, likely to generate enormous devastation if not complete self-destruction.

None of this is to suggest that the cumulative bureaucratisation of coercion will ultimately lead towards the obsolescence of war. On the contrary, as geopolitical and environmental configurations change it is likely that the long-term future will bring about more violent conflicts between social organisations with increasingly uneven power structures. Once Pax Americana weakens and other states and nonstate associations and networks gain even more organisational capacity, one is likely to see an enormous geopolitical worldwide transformation. Moreover, as climate change and other environmental variations intensify, including global warming, continuous population expansion and the excessive consumption of nonrenewable resources, the nature of the war–state–society nexus is likely to become even more prominent. As much of the available evidence-based forecasting demonstrates, climatic changes are bound to further increase CO_2 emissions, which ultimately are likely to bring about a less hospitable planet – severe water shortages for large parts of the world, dramatically rising tides of oceans and seas with periodic tsunamis, the gradual disappearance of fossil fuels, the scarcity of minerals, the lack of arable land, etc. (Klare 2002; Dyer 2011; Mann 2013). These major changes are likely not only to make the global ecosystem unsustainable but might also cause organisational collapse and potential disintegration of state structures in some regions of the world. Once these states prove unable to feed and protect their citizens, this is likely to spark large-scale migrations of people moving from uninhabitable to habitable parts of the globe. Such unprecedented population movement might trigger violent responses: 'Global warming will force mass migrations on a scale never seen in human history. Governments lack the organisational capacity and almost certainly the desire to accommodate those refugees; many however, will have the military means and popular support to repel needy migrants' (Lachmann 2013b: 3). Thus the future geopolitical and environmental transformations could bring about a very different world, with some states continuing to increase their organisational powers and channelling those powers in the direction of building large militaries and police forces, whereas others would struggle to survive in the remnants of failed states. In other words, one is likely to see a much more dystopian world in the future. On the one side, the expanded cumulative bureaucratisation of coercion is likely to be used to engage in new wars of conquest for scarce resources while simultaneously creating and keeping fortresslike borders to exclude potential refugees. On the other side, one might expect the appearance of quasi-Hobbesian organisational wastelands populated by stateless groups and organisations fighting for survival. Although this almost apocalyptic imagery might sound unrealistic and farfetched, its small-scale incarnation is already borne out in the social reality of several contemporary civil wars. From Somalia and the Democratic Republic of Congo to Syria, Iraq, Chad, Sudan and Yemen, one can encounter large areas of destroyed and environmentally desolate areas where people struggle to endure or escape the never-ending war-induced shortage of water and energy, periodic famine, untreated contagious disease, chronic homelessness and unemployment (Hendrix and Salenyan 2012; Hironaka 2005). In contrast to these zones of despondency, the ever-increasing organisational capacity of most powerful states creates conditions for the real and substantial transformation of warfare in the future: the gradual displacement of a human military and workforce with their robotic counterparts. The mass reliance on the use of unmanned drones in Afghanistan and Yemen navigated by 'civil servants' in Nevada is probably a reliable indicator of how some wars will be waged in the future. It is quite conceivable that human warfare might give way to armed conflicts between robotic soldiers (Kreps 2016; Coker 2013). In this context, where there is no direct human presence on the battlefields but where devastation and demolition continue to escalate, it will quickly become obvious how futile it is to rely solely on human casualty counts as the barometer of war's destructiveness.

The War–State–Society Nexus and Ideology

Wars cannot be waged without effective social organisations. However, the historical record demonstrates that organisational power on its own is rarely enough to succeed on the battlefield. What has also been highly important is the ability of those who wage wars to justify their violent actions and if possible also mobilise a substantial degree of support for their cause. Hence successful warfare often entails the presence of persuasive ideological doctrines. To be deemed justifiable, wars have to be fought in the name of something important – to defend one's nation, to uphold the royal dynasty, to fulfil a civilising mission, to preserve the existence of a particular collective, to impose social justice, to ensure racial purity, to expand specific religious doctrine, to defend national territory and so on.

However, for much of human history the rulers did not see it as necessary to justify their wars to the entire population under their control. Instead, the focal point of their attention were the fellow rulers of other polities and the domestic aristocrats. Hence in the European dynastic wars of succession, the central issue was the question of who has the birthright to claim the throne, and although this affected all subjects of the realm, legitimacy was secured only when the other European rulers and the domestic aristocrats, including the top clergy, had given their consent for the new monarch. For example, the Wars of Roses (1455–1487) were waged over the issues of dynastic entitlements to occupy the throne of England. The conflict arose between two rival branches of the same royal House of Plantagenet, the York and Lancaster, with each side making a claim to the throne. Although the causes of these wars were complex, including difficult economic conditions resulting from the Hundred Years' War, the nominal trigger was the mental illness of Henry VI of Lancaster, whose right to rule was challenged by Richard, Duke of York (Pollard, 2001). Although the conflict period was extremely long (thirty-two years), the actual warfare involved only a number of violent episodes and decisive battles such as the famous Battle of Bosworth Field (1485). What is worth emphasising is that these wars were fought exclusively by the landed aristocracy, including the feudal retainer armies and some international mercenaries, while the majority of the essentially peasant population were not involved. More significantly, the conflicts ceased when one of the throne claimants, Henry Tudor, defeated his principal opponent, Richard III of York, and this victory was recognised by other aristocrats. Consequentially, Henry Tudor assumed the throne as Henry VII, and to strengthen the legitimacy of his claim he married Elizabeth of York, the daughter of Edward IV, a move that allowed him to unite the two royal houses and reinforce his dynastic legitimacy. Hence, although coercive organisational might was crucial for winning the war, force alone would not have been enough to secure a lasting claim to royal power.

Premodern rulers had to justify the use of large-scale violence to their peers and to demonstrate occasionally that specific war undertakings were aligned with the dominant belief systems. Hence wars were often justified in reference to specific mythological narratives, religious teachings (i.e. the just war tradition in Christianity or jihad in Islam), imperial doctrines or proto-ideological principles. Nevertheless, it is only in the modern era that such justification encompasses wider sectors of population. Although there were sporadic instances of this before modernity, typically in city-states and other smaller polities, when the decisions to go to war required some form of popular legitimisation, this was more of an exception than a rule. In contrast, modern social orders are built around principles that demand a substantial degree of society-wide normative consensus about warfare. This doctrinal shift was already initiated by the Revolution of 1688 in England, which ultimately established the supremacy of parliament over the monarchy. Nevertheless, it was the turbulent experiences of the French and American revolutions that eventually brought about the transformation where the logic of the divine right of kingship was replaced by the idea of popular sovereignty. Obviously, this historical change was not instant, but it took another two centuries to incorporate most of the world, where different versions of divine right doctrine dominated or were still influential (from the Mandate of Heaven in China and East Asia to sultanism in Southeast Asia to the idea of caliph, rightful successor to the prophet Muhammad, in the Islamic world).

Since the notion of popular sovereignty transfers supreme authority over a particular polity from inherited dynasties towards populations who inhabit such polities, the issue of a ruler's legitimacy acquires a different logic. In the traditional world, decisions about war and peace were the royal, imperial or chief's prerogative, which usually did not demand large-scale public support. Although it was important that the rulers frame their military adventures in terms of particular religious or mythological principles, this procedure was largely confined to a very small audience: fellow aristocrats and top clergy. In contrast, the doctrine of popular sovereignty entails that all important decisions such as those about war and peace have to take into account the dominant views of population. However, this is not to say that such decisions are ever in the hands of the public. On the contrary, even in well-established democracies such judgements are made by a handful of individuals. For example, Mann (2012, 1993) demonstrates how geopolitical decision making largely remained the privilege of European rulers through the nineteenth and twentieth centuries, regardless of whether they presided over democratic or autocratic states. Obviously, in most democracies such judgements are made after consultations in parliaments, but governments ordinarily approach parliaments only to rubberstamp already made decisions. The recent experiences of the United States Congress and the U.K. and French parliaments in the context of wars in Iraq, Syria, Afghanistan, Libya and Mali are indicative examples of how such decisions are made.

Notwithstanding these similarities with the traditional polities, there is still substantial difference between the modern and premodern world. This difference stems from the role ideology plays in the modern orders. As I have argued previously (Malešević 2013a, 2010, 2006), there are organisational reasons why ideological power increases substantially in the modern world. For one thing, ideology expands as a byproduct of structural change, including the dramatic proliferation of complex social organisations in the last three hundred years of human history. As they expand and incorporate a large number of individuals, such organisations require effective means of communication. There is a need to gather and exchange large quantities of information, and the members of specific social organisations also need to be able to comprehend their role in such complex entities. Hence as the cumulative bureaucratisation of coercion increases, it necessitates the use of abstract, decontextualised communication. Simply put, individuals have to acquire certain basic skills, such as literacy, the ability to follow organisational rules, various everyday discursive competencies that allow individuals to achieve organisational tasks on time and in required space, a degree of self-discipline and so on. As Gellner (1983) points out, those generic skills are attained in specialised institutions which are established and often monopolised by the state, such as primary and secondary schools and colleges, all of which have become indispensable in the modern era. Moreover, the increased literacy rates and developed discursive capacities allow for mass production and mass reception of the printed word, including mass media, literary works and more recently digital modes of communication. Since these social changes are all happening in the context of dramatically transformed modes of political legitimation, where the principles of divine authority of kings are replaced by the ideas of popular sovereignty, this too fosters greater ideological awareness. In addition, all of these structural changes, together with greater urbanisation, stimulate the development of the public sphere. In other words, the collapse of the ancien regime also signalled the disintegration of the dominant legitimising narrative which inherently placed some human beings above others. In the new environment where all human beings are judged to be of equal moral worth, it becomes more difficult to establish unified societywide legitimising narrative that appeals to the majority of individuals. Consequently, instead of encountering a relatively small number of religious truths, one finds a proliferation of ideological doctrines offering often mutually exclusive interpretations of social reality.

Although previous historical transformations, such as the twelfth-century Renaissance in Western Europe or the "Italian" Renaissance of the fifteenth century, have managed to galvanise proto-ideological disputes, what was distinct about the postrevolutionary era is that in many important respects ideologisation becomes mass phenomenon. While during the Renaissance some ordinary individuals might have found the new liberalising cultural environment appealing, this in itself did not produce the utter delegitimisation of the existing order, as was the case after the French and American revolutions. In this new, Enlightenment-infused world where there is no unified doctrine, one is exposed to variety of competing ideological discourses. Although most of these modern ideologies appeal to the similar set of abstract principles, such as equality, justice, liberty, fraternity or common nationality, these ideas are articulated in very different ways. As Freeden (1996) convincingly argues, ideologies are modular in the sense that they compose similar abstract principles in different sets of hierarchies so as that, for example, for liberalism freedom comes above equality while for socialism it is the other way around. The emergence of these competing ideological programmes together with massive structural changes, where for the first time an ordinary individuals start thinking of themselves as being of equal moral worth to their former superiors, brings about significant ideological transformation. In this new environment, ideological discourses expand as they acquire a much wider popular base: instead of the relatively fixed social order where the divine right of monarchs is an unquestioned doctrine, modernity breeds ideological cacophony where ideologues and social organisations fight for the souls of every individual. Once the general principles of political legitimacy change and public opinion becomes relevant, rulers have to rely much more on ideological messages. Thus ideologies become important for both the mobilisation of a broader support base and also for the legitimisation of particular actions within the concrete ideological framework adopted by the social organisations. Even though nearly all modern ideologies are built around universalist principles such as liberty, equality, fraternity, authority, order, etc., their operative message is inevitably particularistic as they are framed around specific and geographically bound social organisations (Malešević 2013a). For example, the Enlightenment-shaped universalist discourses that underpinned both the French and Russian October revolutions had to give way to much more particularist messages once the revolutionaries took over the state. Hence instead of focussing on European *cityoens* and the world proletariat, the emphasis shifts towards French nationals and the Soviet working class. Therefore, as mass-scale ideologisation expands, the tendency is to embrace centrifugal tendencies: after the dominant ideological discourse is framed at the centre of particular social organisation, it permeates its organisational structure so that it can mobilise popular support and attain internal legitimacy while simultaneously trying to delegitimise competing social organisations. This is why I call this historical process a centrifugal ideologisation.

Why is this ideological transformation relevant for warfare? This change is highly significant because in the modern era wars acquire different modes of legitimation which allow for much greater popular acceptance of coercive power. Unlike premodern warfare, where war legitimacy hinged on the partial consent of aristocrats, in the modern age, war decisions tend to be grounded in particular ideological doctrines that often attain mass support. Moreover, as the justification is linked to abstract principles rather than the ruler's personal whim, it generates more determination to fulfil war aims than was the case in the premodern wars. As the experience of twentieth-century warfare demonstrates, in modernity one is able to reconcile mass murder with the Enlightenment-inspired ideals of autonomy, justice, liberty, authenticity and popular

Centrifugal ideologisation

sovereignty. At the heart of the modern project lies a paradox, a form of ontological dissonance, whereby the most devastating and most systematic extermination of human life is happening at the very time when that life is nearly universally considered sacred and precious (Malešević 2010: 141–144).

Nevertheless, as in previous historical periods, this paradox too is rooted in the war–state–society nexus. It is the prevalence of moral equality and ethical universality that creates the structural conditions for the proliferation and ultimate justification of mass murder. In the feudal Europe, the aristocrats were not interested in the annihilation of rebellious peasantry as they needed their labour and the peasantry as such was generally regarded (and often regarded themselves) as inferior to nobility in every respect.[7] As the two principal social strata were seen as occupying different places on the social ladder and inhabiting two different moral universes, there was no need to engage in the extensive delegitimisation of peasant rebellions. After all, all peasants were seen as no better than animals and torturing a small number of rebels and torching their villages proved to be a much better deterrent than killing hundreds of thousands of peasants. In contrast, as modernity brings about a new and profoundly different ethics where all human beings are now considered to be of equal moral worth, the only reliable way to delegitimise one's political opponent is to deny that opponent membership in the human race (Malešević 2010: 119–114). Hence it is precisely because of this moral universality that warfare becomes so rampant and indiscriminate in the modern era. In addition to controlling huge organisational powers, capable of historically unprecedented mass destruction, modern nation-states and various social movements are regularly guided by uncompromising ideological vistas determined to bring about a perfected social order. As these ideological blueprints are more often than not conceptualised as the ultimate truth delivering projects, buttressed either by scientific authority, moral humanist absolutism or both, then any attempt to stand in the way of such a noble endeavour can be interpreted as nothing less than deliberate evil. In this context, the Jacobin terror becomes 'cruel necessity' since the noble idea of an egalitarian and righteous Republic requires, as Saint-Just puts it, 'prompt, severe and inflexible justice', as the true ideal of the Republic 'can only be based on inflexibility' (Weber 2003: 85). The possession of ultimate truth and absolute justice calls for righteous zeal and no restraint. Similarly, to establish a classless world of proletarian justice

---

[7] This section draws in part on Malešević (2013b).

entails not only the 'expropriation of the expropriators' but also their ultimate destruction, as they are bourgeois stooges of the capitalist enemy nations. In the alternative modernist vista, the foundation of a new, better and racially pure world necessitates the implementation of genocidal policies against malicious 'Judeo-Bolshevik' conspirators.

Hence those who oppose the creation or existence of such a perfected social order can be nothing other than 'parasites', 'leeches', 'rats' and 'monsters', and as such they do not deserve treatment equal to that of humans; they have to be destroyed. Therefore, it is inclusivity, universalism and moral equality that paradoxically create the conditions for the greater dehumanisation of one's ideological enemy. When there is an acknowledged and visible hierarchy between social groups, there is no great need to dehumanise the (already inferior) Other. It is only when all human beings are universally considered to be of equal moral worth that one needs to deploy an elaborate ideological apparatus to deny a particular group full membership in the human community. It is only in modernity that dehumanisation becomes necessary for both the justification of organised, interpolity violence and for popular mobilisation to participate in such violence. How else could one reconcile the idea of building a more liberal, democratic world that respects human rights and the dignity of all human beings while simultaneously deploying atomic bombs to kill hundreds of thousands of civilians? It is no accident that the destruction of Hiroshima and Nagasaki was justified through dehumanisation.[8] When President Truman said that 'when you have to deal with a beast, you have to treat him as a beast' (Alperovitz 1995: 563), he was just reflecting the dominant perception of the Japanese shared by large sections of U.S. public. As various polls conducted at the end of the war show, most respondents enthusiastically supported bombings, with substantial numbers advocating dropping more atomic bombs and the extermination of all Japanese (Hixson 2003: 239). Furthermore, while in the premodern world both the infliction and legitimisation of violence remained essentially a vertical, status-based phenomena, in the modern era much violent action is inflicted and justified horizontally. That is, whereas in medieval Europe brutalising inferior Others within one's polity was regularly seen as legitimate and killing fellow aristocrats as a heinous crime, in the modern age it is the other way around: murdering

---

[8] A very similar attitude towards enemy civilians was present in the U.K. power echelons: 'Lord Cherwell – Prime Minister Winston Churchill's scientific advisor – argued that relentless bombing of cities would destroy German morale by rendering the population homeless. Of course, the British proposed to do much more than simply destroy German homes: the real targets were the occupants of these homes' (Downes, 2008: 30).

your fellow national provokes moral outrage and severe punishment while killing an enemy combatant is a heroic deed. Thus with the rise and expansion of modernity, both infliction and legitimisation of brutality become more organised and externalised.

Although in modernity violence has become less publicly invisible, it is, in fact, much more prevalent. The modern age differs from its premodern counterparts in hiding death, as both killing and dying are removed from the public eye. The animals we eat are killed in the closed and far away abattoirs, our old and sick die in hospices and hospitals, our morgues are removed from public view, we don't organise public hangings nor do we torture or burn people in town squares. Yet in times of war, the citizens of modern polities generally give tacit or explicit consent for the mass murder of those who inhabit other polities. Moreover, it is regularly those who are the least affected by the calamities of war who often support the most extreme forms of violent retaliation. For example, World War II surveys of the British public clearly show that there was substantially greater support for the reprisal bombings of German cities among individuals living in areas unaffected by the Luftwaffe's aerial bombardment than by those who lived in the cities that were excessively bombed (Garrett 1993). Similarly, in the wars of Yugoslav succession it is the civilians (academics, journalists, university students and teachers) rather than frontline soldiers who regularly expressed the most extreme attitudes towards the despised enemy (Popov 2000; Malešević and Uzelac 1997).

As both Collins (1974) and Bauman (1989) rightly emphasise, in the modern era visible and brutal infliction of pain is replaced by largely invisible and detached callousness. Modern social organisations require a depersonalised, disciplined and callous ethics that avoids moral responsibility through the bureaucratic delegation of tasks. In this context, the killing of a large number of 'enemy' soldiers and civilians becomes, ideologically grounded, a question of mere instrumental efficiency. This utilitarian, rationalist logic of mass murder reached its pinnacle in the Vietnam War, where military success was not measured by the territory that the soldiers occupied or the battle victories achieved but by the body count, that is, the number of enemy soldiers killed and 'the proportion between that number and the number of its own dead (the kill ratio)' (Caputo 1977: 160).[9] In the most recent wars, human casualties have

---

[9] This focus on kill ratios was already present during World War II, when the U.S. Joint Strategic Survey Committee was planning the invasion of Japan and calculating the potential number of casualties: 'Assuming that the Japanese would have roughly 3.5 million troops available, the planners applied what came to be known as the "Saipan

become even more depersonalised, as they are now simply reduced to 'collateral damage'. Hence greater ideological penetration, made possible by the increased organisational capacity of modern states, makes modern citizens more receptive to dehumanisation of the enemy. Since popular legitimacy is now shaped around abstract principles, dehumanisation is regularly interwoven into a broader ideological narrative where the destruction of the dehumanised enemy is often framed as the precondition for the full realisation of a particular ideological blueprint. Thus to achieve a Soviet socialist utopia, it was necessary to exterminate 'kulaks' and 'bourgeois spies'. Similarly, to realise a new thousand year Reich and attain the racial purity of Germans, it was vital that the inferior and 'infectious' races, such as Jews, Slavs, Gypsies and others, were obliterated. While state socialism and Nazism were particularly ruthless in the implementation of their ideological vistas, ideology has also played an important role in the justification of war aims in most modern states. Although the military organisations of the liberal democratic states operated under some constraints, they too were involved in numerous instances of mass killings that were legitimised in reference to specific ideological principals. For example, during World War II American soldiers would regularly kill captured Japanese soldiers rather than keep them as prisoners of war. This policy was driven by strong ideological conviction that unlike German soldiers Japanese were 'subhuman' and 'animals' undeserving of the humane treatment (Ferguson 2004; Weingartner 1992). As Ferguson (2004: 172) emphasises, 'Allied troops often saw the Japanese in the same way that Germans regarded Russians, as Untermenschen'. While racism was an important ideological constant on all sides during World War II and many other modern conflicts, the ideology that had much more impact was nationalism. Even though the mass killings of civilians in Dresden and Munich by the British and American air forces were often interpreted in the strategic terms (i.e. to destroy the systems of communications between the main German cities in order to paralyse the movement of troops and military supplies), it seems that nationalist motives played a more significant role. Most military historians believe that the destruction of the beautiful baroque city of Dresden had no military significance (McKee 1983). The killing of about thirty-five thousand people in Dresden was in part justified by British Air Commodore Grierson as an attempt to destroy 'what is left of German morale' (Taylor, 2005: 413). The fact that these two cities were seen to represent the centres of German high culture could have played

ratio" – "one American killed and several wounded to exterminate seven Japanese soldiers"' (Downes 2008: 122).

part in the decision, which probably had more to do with nationalist-driven revenge than any military strategy.

Many scholars make a direct link between the nationalism and war whereby for some nationalist ideology is a main deriver of organised violence (Wimmer 2013; van der Dennen 1995; Snyder 1968), while for others nationalism is a direct consequence of war experience (Mann 2012: Laitin 2007). However, as I have argued elsewhere (Malešević 2013a, 2011), the relationship between the two is more ambiguous and less direct. The view that strong national attachments inevitably cause violent conflicts is premised on two flawed and essentialist ideas: (a) that cultural differences are given and unchangeable in the sense that shared cultural markers inexorably generate organised social action; and (b) that cultural variation is in itself a source of violent discord. However, the fact that a number of individuals share the same national categorisation (i.e. Germans, Portuguese and Zimbabweans) does not in any way indicate that this category affiliation will instantly transform into a group-conscious social action. Nationalism entails successful and prolonged political mobilisation, and most attempts to mobilise a large-scale population end in failure. In a similar vein, the link between violence and cultural diversity is spurious: individuals do not injure or kill each other because they speak different languages or share incommensurable cultural practices but because they associate these differences with real economic, political or status disparities (Cohen 1969: 199: Brubaker and Laitin 1998). One should not take aggressive pronouncements of nationalist ideologues at face value and assume that the virulent rhetoric manifestly translates into real violence. There is nothing natural in nationalism: just like other ideological projects, it too requires a great deal of organisational work and skill. Even in the most recognisable cases of aggressive nationalism, such as Nazi Germany, Imperial Japan, late-1930s Austria and Romania, nationalism did not generate war by itself. As Mann (2012, 2004) demonstrates convincingly, it was only when nationalist ideas became mediated by geopolitical instability, the weakness of the old regime, class polarisation, corporatist statism and rampant paramilitarism that the link between war and nationalism comes to the fore. Rather than beings inherently linked, both nationalism and war are the product of the historical rise of organisational and ideological powers. War can trigger nationalist reactions if only a nationalist *weltanschauung* is there in the first place. The experience of war cannot create a sense of national solidarity if such a phenomenon did not exist before the outbreak of hostilities. The outbreak of wars can and often does intensify and crystallise nationalist sentiments, but it cannot create them ex nihilo.

The strong link between nationalism and twentieth-century warfare has less to do with the conflict itself and much more with long-term organisational and ideological processes that make such links possible and socially meaningful. As neither nationalism nor war comes naturally to human beings, the cumulative bureaucratisation of coercion and centrifugal ideologisation remain central in sustaining and reproducing both nationalism and war as well as in creating the conditions in which they reinforce each other.

Microsolidarity and the War Experience

While organisational capacity and ideological penetration are the key mechanisms that make nationalism and war gel, these two structural processes also require a micro-interactional dimension to succeed – microsolidarity. Although it is impossible to wage war without social organisation and some kind of ideological narrative, what also matters is how individuals respond to organisational demands and decide to fight. The conventional views on the personal motivation of soldiers to take part in wars clash over the question of whether actors are motivated by 'greed', that is, the individual's self-interest, or 'grievances', that is, noneconomic motives such as identity, religion or other cultural factors (Collier 2010; Collier et al. 2009). Hence Collier et al. (2009) analyse recent civil wars through the prism of an actor's material benefits, arguing that 'there is evidence ... that where a rebellion is financially and militarily feasible it will occur' (Collier et al. 2009: 1). In contrast, Cederman et al. (2013: 1) insist that the available data indicate that the primary individual motivation in most civil wars stems from social grievances: 'political and economic inequalities following group lines generate grievances that in turn can motivate civil war'. While both of these factors certainly play an important part in individual motivation, there is a need for a nuanced sociological understanding that takes into account the complexity of collective decision making, the changing historical dynamics of conflicts and geographical variation. For example, to account for the willingness of millions of British, French and German soldiers to fight and die in World War I, Michael Mann identifies five key reasons: the dominance of militaristic culture in the pre–World War I Europe; the youth's thirst for adventure as an attempt to escape the dull working- or middle-class life; the popularly shared belief, reinforced by mass media and government messages, that this was a war of self-defence and 'civilisation against barbarism'; and local community pressure, including the localised system of recruitment and the institution of regular pay and full employment generated by war (Mann 2012: 145–146). These factors were also present in World War II, although Mann argues that ideological commitment played a greater role in World War II when compared to World War I. However, even in this case, ideology mattered more for some than others, as he sharply distinguishes between the fascist regimes and the rest. More specifically, he accepts the view articulated by Bartov (1991, 1985) and others who see Wehrmacht soldiers as being more motivated by the Nazi ideology than the sense of a micro-, platoon-level comradeship associated with most other militaries (Mann 2012: 147; 2005: 273). In this view, the fascist states were characterised by a substantial degree of ideological unity between frontline soldiers and political elites. Mann illustrates this with available research that analyses diaries and letters of Wehrmacht soldiers who adored Hitler and remained loyal until the end of the war (Fritz 1995; Bartov 1991). This type of analysis is a major improvement on the very narrow greed versus grievance debates, as it emphasises the historical complexity of individual and group motivation in deciding to support or fight in wars. However, Mann's sharp distinction between the soldiers fighting in the fascist as opposed to nonfascist armies is too rigid. While there is no doubt that there were significant differences between the ideocratic militaries of fascist, Nazi and communist states, one could argue that the actual behaviour and motivation of ordinary soldiers on the battlefields exhibit more similarity than Mann and others envisage. To fully understand the microdynamics of battlefields and the complex motivations of frontline soldiers, it is necessary to briefly outline the microsocial sources of individual motivation.

As argued in Chapter 2, the success of large-scale historical processes such as cumulative bureaucratisation of coercion and centrifugal ideologisation is heavily dependent on their penetration and fusion with the patterns of microsolidarity. In other words, much social action is rooted in mechanisms of microgroup solidarities. Human beings thrive on small-scale, face-to-face interaction, and a great deal of individual motivation stems from one's sense of attachment, responsibility and emotional embedment in the micro-level groupings: families, friendships, neighbourhoods, peer groups, etc. Much of the recent microsociological research on intragroup behaviour shows that most human beings are substantially more motivated by chains of interpersonal interaction than by uncompromising doctrinal principles or narrow economic interests (Turner 2007; Collins 2004, 2008a, White 2000). From the early studies conducted during World War II to more recent analyses of the behaviour of soldiers on the frontline, it is clear that emotional bonds with one's platoon, regiment or even smaller military unit tend to outweigh other motives for individual and social action (Stouffer et al. 1949; Holmes 1985; Collins 2008a; King 2013).[10] To move away from overly rationalist and instrumentalist accounts, as articulated by the greed versus grievance debate, it is necessary to refocus one's attention to the emotional dynamics of microgroup solidarity. However, this is not to say that self-interest or inequality do not matter. On the contrary, such factors often feed into the emotional dynamics on the battlefields. Instead of focussing narrowly on whether soldiers' behaviour is motivated by the instrumental or normative concerns, the starting point of one's analysis should be the recognition that human beings are much more complex and malleable creatures.

In this context, it is the unusual character of the war experience that brings emotional attachments to the fore. As wars generate prolonged life-threatening situations of hardship and extreme conditions where questions of life and death are present on a daily if not hourly basis, emotional action is likely to temporarily overpower instrumental, value rational and habitual forms of social action. Both Max Weber and Georg Simmel recognised this quite well. For Weber (2004: 225), the war environment was decisive in creating intense feelings that generated communities of sacrifice: 'war ... is able to create in the modern political community pathos and feeling of community and thereby releases an unconditional community of sacrifice among the combatants ... [it] releases the work of compassion and love for the needy which breaks through all the barriers of naturally given groups'. In a similar vein, for Simmel (1917: 20) war constitutes 'an absolute situation' which contrasts with all previous human experiences and as such generates different emotional reactions. Hence writing in the midst of World War I, he describes this phenomenon: 'most of us are now living in what we might call an absolute situation. All the situations and circumstances in which we found ourselves in the past had something relative to them. ... None of this poses a problem now, since we are faced with an absolute decision. We no longer have the quantitative dilemma as to whether or when we must make a sacrifice or a compromise'. Hence the intensity of microgroup solidarity is largely based on emotional ties. In the whirlpool of armed violent conflicts, emotional energy constitutes the principal ingredient of individual and social action. As Collins (2008a, 2004) argues, emotions motivate much of social life, and emotional energy is the backbone of all successful patterned social encounters, which he calls interaction ritual chains, from commuters conversing on the train to

---

[10] This is elaborated more extensively in Chapter 9.

revolutionary uprisings. In this context, battlefield solidarity represents one of the most intensive forms of group attunement: a fully integrated and synchronised emotional bond. What is distinct about the frontline experience is that such strong emotional attachments tend to foster noninstrumental and nondoctrinal action. As a number of studies on the twentieth-century battlefield environment demonstrate, in extreme conditions there is a much greater willingness to die for others than to kill the adversary (Collins 2008a; Holmes 1985; Bourke 2000).

In this context, one could argue that despite the obvious political, ideological or cultural differences between the militaries involved in wars of the last two centuries, the bonds of microsolidarity are universal. While Wehrmacht or Japanese World War II soldiers might have been more prone to emphasise their ideological credentials, this in itself may not be the most reliable sign that their ideological commitment was stronger than their sense of microsolidarity. Bartov's studies have been criticised for taking the letters of frontline Wehrmacht soldiers at face value while ignoring the fact that sincere emotional expressions or criticisms of the Nazi regime could not pass the censors and could even lead to the courts martial. The fact that Nazis and Japanese military authorities shot 20,000 soldiers each for desertion or showing cowardice on the frontline while only 146 U.S. soldiers were given death penalty (Mann 2012) is in itself a powerful indicator that coercion was more significant than ideological devotion.

Much more recent research on both German and Japanese cases has questioned this image of uncompromising, highly ideological fascist soldiers. For example, Shimazu's (2009) and Hill's (2006) analyses of soldiers' diaries and interviews with the surviving kamikaze pilots demonstrate that their willingness to fight originated from a variety of sources, including vanity, a personal sense of pride or attempts to overcome humiliation. However, what stands out in this research is that ideological commitments played a less prominent role while a sense of loyalty and attachment towards one's family and friends dominates many personal narratives. In a similar vein, Neitzel and Welzer's (2012: 237, 319) recent analysis[11] of transcripts of secret recordings of German prisoners of war (POWs) indicate that the microsolidarity was a much more powerful source of individual motivation than any doctrinal principles. For example, key Nazi ideas such as *folksgemeinschaft*, 'global Jewish conspiracy' and 'Bolshevik promotion of Genetic inferiority' rarely if ever appear in the conversations of POWs. The authors

---

[11] Although Neitzel and Welzer (2012) provide excellent data, much of their own analysis is quite problematic and deeply rooted in the Hobbesian ontology.

demonstrate well that: 'As a rule German soldiers were not "ideological warriors". Most of them were fully apolitical' (Neitzel and Welzer 2012: 319). What really mattered is the sense of responsibility and duty towards one's comrades: 'Frontline soldiers felt an almost exclusive sense of duty to their comrades and their superiors who formed their social units'. Furthermore, decisions to continue resisting the enemy after the obvious military defeat were often made in relation to the anticipated reactions of family and friends. For example, when a tank commander explains his reluctance to aid Allied propaganda at the end of the war, he is not invoking ideological reasons but the emotional commitment to his family: 'I should consider it as an utterly dirty thing to do in every way. ... There are my wife and my children. I wouldn't dream of doing it. I should be ashamed to face my wife if I did' (Neitzel and Welzer 2012: 21). Even the views of SS soldiers were characterised by their diversity and heterogeneity, and in contrast to traditional interpretations, the willingness of SS soldiers to die for Hitler or Germany was not greater than that of ordinary soldiers (Neitzel and Welzer 2012: 301). In all of these cases, the microgroup dynamics were quite similar to what researchers observed in other militaries. While microsolidarity might operate differently in diverse social contexts, it remains a universal phenomenon present in all wars.

This leads us the final point: the relationship between ideological power and microsolidarity. Saying that the bonds of microsolidarity often trump officially proclaimed ideological creeds does not suggest that ideology does not matter. On the contrary, in addition to coercive-organisational might, ideological power is a cornerstone of much of social action. The point is that a great deal of ideological power does not stem from a set of uncompromising principles and beliefs. Instead, ideological processes work best when they are in perpetual motion and when they are able to amalgamate with other forms of social action. In other words, rather than assuming that ideology is an either/or singular phenomenon directly opposed to material interests or emotional, habitual or value rational action, it is much more fruitful to focus on ideologisation as a multifaceted process that blends with different forms of social action and taps into existing social relations. Most individuals do not absorb ideological doctrines *per saltum* (all at once), as a closed and coherent set of ideas, but take in ideological principles and acts in an unsystematic, fragmentary, contradictory and disjoined fashion (Billig et al. 1988). As I argue in Chapters 6 and 7, centrifugal ideologisation operates most efficiently when it is able to penetrate deeply into the microcosm of family life, kinship networks, peer groups or friendships. Hence ideological power is heavily dependent on the capacity to tie the diverse pockets of microsolidarity into a shared, wider, ideological narrative. In this context, nationalism has regularly proved to be the most potent social glue that brings together patches of microsolidarity into a societywide common narrative in which heterogeneous individuals and groups can instantly recognise their own personal experiences. Therefore, although the emotional bonds of microsolidarity help generate and maintain much social action, it is the long-term ideologisation, initiated and fostered by powerful social organisations, that synchronises and often successfully directs shared emotional energies so as to fulfil specific organisational demands. Obviously, this is not a simple and straightforward process, but something that encounters resistance and requires periodic spurts of mobilisation. Thus when trying to answer why soldiers fight in wars, it is necessary to explore these complex relationships between the competing coercive organisations that deploy mutually exclusive ideological practices to generate diverse forms of microsolidarity and utilise this solidarity for specific organisational purposes. This is not to say that the centrifugal ideologisation and the envelopment of microsolidarity operate in the same way all over the world. As these processes depend on infrastructural developments, substantial levels of literacy and organisational sophistication, as well as particular cultural traditions, some organisational contexts are likely to have greater ideological penetration of the microworld than others. Simply put, the extreme nationalist rhetoric present in the letters of Nazi soldiers or official declarations of Japanese Divine Wind pilots was not only an expression of quite particular forms of microsolidarity associated with each individual soldier but was also a broader reflection of the organisational and ideological capacity of the state and military organisations involved in waging World War II. In other words if ideology is not understood as a form of social pathology but as an integral process of organisational action, then it is not difficult to demonstrate that all militaries and soldiers are ideological to some extent.

Conclusion

War is not a biological phenomenon; it is a product of social relations. As such, wars emerge quite late in history, but once they appear on the historical stage they tend to expand and multiply. To understand this peculiar trajectory of warfare, it is crucial to recognise that its existence entails the continuous presence of the complex and durable social organisations, ideologies and a sense of group solidarity. While wars can and do experience periodic increases and decreases, the coercive organisational capacity that sustains warfare has continued to expand over the past twelve millennia. Hence the current decline in the number of war fatalities or interstate wars should not be automatically read as a radical break with the past. Instead, this looks more like a temporary phenomenon rooted in the same organisational logic that shaped our world over the last twelve thousand years. Rather than reflecting a permanent shift in historical development, this situation is a product of specific geopolitical and organisational constellations. Since these constellations are generated by the same long-term historical processes such as the cumulative bureaucratisation of coercion, centrifugal ideologisation and the envelopment of microsolidarity, as long as these processes are in motion it is unlikely that the institution of war will vanish. On the contrary, the ever-expanding coercive-organisational and ideological apparatuses provide a firm foundation for future violent conflicts.

6   Revolutions

Introduction

There is no doubt that most social and political revolutions throughout history have been defined by excessive violence. Stereotypical representations of a revolutionary event are usually associated with such images as French citizens storming of the Bastille or the mass assault against the Winter Palace in Saint Petersburg. Both of these events were later depicted by influential artists and as such gradually acquired mythological features. In the famous painting *The Storming of the Bastille*, Jean-Pierre Houël (1789) portrays a large number of armed citizens and soldiers confronting each other amidst the blaze of guns, fire, smoke and total destruction. In a similar vein, the 1920 reenactment of the Winter Palace attack directed by the Nikolai Evreinov involved over 2,500 participants (including numerous ballet dancers and circus people), replica weapons, tanks and armoured cars in order to signify the enormous scale and the excessively violent character of the event. In both of these cases, just as in many latter-day reenactments of revolutionary experience, the focus is on the voluntary action of ordinary individuals who take up the arms to resist the injustice, and in this heroic struggle they sacrifice their lives for revolutionary ideals. However, these mythological images bear very little resemblance to the realities of the actual revolutions, which are generally less grand and more chaotic, less planned and smaller-scale events involving initially less violence and a very little popular will to make sacrifices. This chapter aims to shed some light on the complex social dynamics of revolutions. In the first section, I critically engage with the leading sociological accounts of the revolutionary experience, while in the second section I offer an alternative interpretation that analyses revolutions as the distinctive forms of organised violence. As in the previous chapters, my argument centres on the role organisational capacity, ideological penetration and microsolidarity play in the rise and expansion of revolutions.

174

Defining Revolutions

The common sense understanding of revolution is inevitably tied with the image of France 1789–1799. In this vision, a revolution is perceived as a popular violent overthrow of an oppressive ancient regime, a profoundly changed and more inclusive structure of governance and deep social transformations bringing about a fairer and rational organisation of social order. Moreover, the outcome of such a revolutionary experience is often associated with the irreversible progress, greater enlightenment, social equality and individual autonomy. This model of revolutionary events has influenced generations of scholars and has been often used as an analytical yardstick to assess whether a particular rebellion, revolt or uprising constitutes a genuine revolution. From the classical analyses of Marx (1968 [1871]) and Trotsky (1931) to the later works of Brinton (1965) Gurr (1970) or Moore (1966) revolution was envisaged not only as a powerful vehicle of social change but also implicitly or explicitly as a stepping stone towards a better world. Karl Marx is generally identified with a proscriptive view of revolutionary change that foresaw the proletarian revolution repossessing and dismantling the capitalist state, as formulated in the *Communist Manifesto* (Marx and Engels 1998 [1848]). However, he also provided more analytical accounts of revolutionary situations as in 1848 European revolutions or 1871 Paris Commune (Marx 1968[1871]). Similarly, Trotsky too was both a communist agitator advocating a permanent revolution throughout the world and a more sober analyst attempting to explore the outcome of the 1917 October Revolution. Although later scholars such as Brinton, Gurr, Moore and others were firmly focussed on the analysis at the expense of activism, they too maintained a quite optimistic and to some extent teleological view of the revolutionary change.

Nevertheless, since the Mexican Revolution of 1910–1920, the Iranian Revolution of 1979, the postcommunist revolutions of 1989, the Colour revolutions of the early 2000s to the Arab Spring of 2010–2011 and many other cases in between, it has become apparent that the experience of late-eighteenth- century France is far from being typical. Instead, after more than two hundred years of revolutionary upheavals throughout the world, the French case looks ever more unusual. The long-standing heroic image of 1789 France as a beacon of progressive social change has clouded analytical judgement about the key features of revolutions in general but also about the French case in particular. With hindsight, it is clear now that actual revolutions do not much resemble those portrayed in teleological narratives that envisage a sudden, nearly automatic and irreversible leap towards a more humane order. On the contrary, most revolutions have ultimately resulted in social worlds that either do not substantially differ in terms of equality or individual autonomy from their prerevolutionary counterparts or have generated even more centralised, authoritarian, bureaucratic or ideologically purist social orders. Furthermore, it has become apparent that revolutionary outcomes can be, and often are, reversed: revolutionary rhetoric is regularly deployed to preserve the status quo or to reestablish the key features of an ancient regime under a new guise. De Tocqueville (1955[1856]) was already aware that even the French Revolution did not create the social equality it promised; instead, it just fostered a more speedy replacement of one dominant social strata (the nobility) by another (the bourgeoisie) while in the process making the state apparatus more centralised and powerful. Although the American Revolution of 1765–1783 was more socially inclusive in the beginning, with the cross-strata of settlers rebelling against a colonial power, its social outcome was similar, as the revolution 'produced little or no distribution of wealth or social status' (Goldstone 2014: 4). Even the most radical revolution of the early-twentieth century has not generated a socially equal society: despite the huge expectations triggered by the Russian October 1917 Revolution, its direct outcome was not the promised dictatorship of the proletariat but in fact the dictatorship of Communist Party officials. Max Weber (1995) was one of the few scholars who foresaw this outcome. In his essays on the 1905 and 1917 Russian revolutions, Weber argued that the Bolshevik ideological discourses promising the destruction of Tsarist bureaucracy and class liberation are quite feeble protection against the further bureaucratisation of a new social order. As he predicted, the revolution led towards the organisational monopoly of the Communist Party, thus creating an even more bureaucratic state.

In addition to this normatively optimistic misreading of revolutions, as modelled on the French example, another equally important problem is the lack of scholarly agreement on what exactly should count as a revolutionary process. As Rod Aya (2015: 627–628) rightly argues, there is widespread confusion on what constitutes a revolutionary experience and how revolutions differ from uprisings, rebellions, coup d'états, revolts, civil wars and other forms of violent usurpation of state power. For one thing, some analyses focus on the revolutionary movements in terms of their attempt to change the political regime or society as a whole regardless of whether they are successful in achieving these revolutionary ambitions (Palmer 2005; Zagorin 1982). Others are centred on revolutionary situations, 'a contest for state power by violence' (Aya 2015: 627). More specifically, they understand revolutions as a form of state breakdown or a profound political crisis involving multiple claims over sovereignty enacted by violent means (Goldstone 1991; Tilly 1978). In contrast to these two views, where the attention is not on the aftermath of revolutionary events but on social movements and processes, some scholars perceive revolutions exclusively in relation to the ultimate outcomes. In other words, there is no revolution unless there is a discernible transfer of power and a large-scale social change (Gouldner 1979; Skocpol 1979), or as Pipes (1991: xxi) puts it, the revolutionary outcome has to involve a 'complete redesign of state, society, economy, and culture'. Consequently, these three different views tend to emphasise different aspects of revolutionary events: revolutionary movements, revolutionary situations or revolutionary outcomes. In Aya's view, this difference in focus is crucial, as the dominant theories of revolution aim to explain one rather than all of these three phenomena: some are better at tracing the origins of revolutionary movements without accounting for revolutionary situations or outcomes, while others provide explanations of revolutionary outcomes or situations while paying less attention to the historical dynamics of particular movements.

Despite these pronounced differences, what the majority of the mainstream approaches share in common is the view that revolutions involve a substantial degree of violence (Aya 2015: 628). Nevertheless, if violence is defined in terms of severe physical injuries and death, and this is how most mainstream perspectives see it, then this further complicates the definitional issues. The obvious problem is the question of when violence transpires. If revolutionary movements advocate the use of physical violence but do not practice it, does this rule them out from one's analysis of revolutionary movements? If the violence appears only in the last stages of revolution and is not led by a specific revolutionary movement but by disorganised individuals or masses, would this count as a revolution? In other words, if revolutionary outcomes are produced by structural contingencies rather than by organised social movements, does this mean that the social movement advocating and initiating these societal changes is not revolutionary? In a similar way, if a revolutionary situation is fertile for violence but violent episodes do not include all the social actors involved (i.e. state authorities use violence against would-be revolutionaries while they might be too feeble or unprepared to respond), would this automatically constitute a nonrevolutionary situation?

Another problem is the extent of physical violence used. Is a single human casualty enough to deem a particular social uprising as revolutionary or not? If two societies experience a very similar dramatic social change that is accompanied with a relatively sudden transfer of political power, but in one case sporadic violence was present and in the other there was no violence, would only one of these two cases qualify as a revolution? For example, the 1989–1991 collapse of communism throughout Eastern Europe, with the exception of Romania and to a lesser extent Lithuania, was largely a bloodless regime change. This was followed by a radical social transformation in politics, economics, culture and other spheres of social life. The Eastern European experience immediately poses a question: do only Romania and Lithuania count as revolutionary uprisings, or can this label be equally applied to the other cases of 'velvet revolutions', such as those in Czechoslovakia, Hungary or Poland? Moreover, as the Romanian case involved more than one thousand casualties whereas the Lithuanian Singing Revolution amounted to fourteen killed protesters, does this imply that the former is a genuine revolution while the latter is not?

All these questions suggest that if violence is conceptualised in an extremely narrow sense, then it is difficult to properly capture the social dynamics of revolutionary experience. Just as the arbitrary cap of one thousand casualties per year is not particularly useful in accounting for the impact warfare has on society over time (see Chapter 5), so is the case with the revolutionary violence. Although most revolutions involve violence, not all revolutionary events are shaped by the physical destruction of human bodies. What is more important is that coercive action is deployed to successfully enact profound political or social change. In this context, physical violence might be a byproduct of coercive acts, but such acts do not necessarily generate physical injuries or destruction of human bodies. From the storming of Bastille in 1789 to the partial destruction of the Yugoslav parliament in 2000, much revolutionary energy was spent on capturing institutions that symbolically or actually represent the seats of political power: royal palaces, parliaments, presidential or prime-ministerial offices, police and military headquarters, notorious prisons, etc. More often than not, coercion was used by both the revolutionaries and the repressive apparatuses of the existing regime to secure the control of these institutions. In this process, human beings are often injured or killed, but even when there are no direct casualties, this does not mean that there is no coercive action involved. Burning or demolishing the seats of power can be achieved without killing human beings. Organising huge demonstrations, sit-ins, strikes, marches, boycotts, work stoppages, occupations of the public spaces, etc., can all be used to force revolutionary change. Nevertheless, all usurpations of power inevitably involve a coercive dimension, as the rulers are forced to comply with the will of revolutionaries. Hence, rather than defining revolutions exclusively in terms of the physical destruction of human bodies, it is important to shift the emphasis towards the wider forms of

coercive behaviour that bring about revolutionary outcomes. The significance of coercion over physical violence is not unique to recent 'velvet'
revolutions but was just as relevant in the past. For example, the French
Revolution has become an epitome of a profoundly violent historical
event, as its aftermath, the Reign of Terror, involved up to forty thousand
deaths. However, the actual event that started off the revolution, the
storming of Bastille, was not a particularly violent episode, amounting
to only one direct casualty and six more individuals who were killed after
the fortress prison was overtaken (Lusebrink and Reichardt 1997). As
the precise timeframe of revolution is never straightforward, one could
make an argument that the Reign of Terror was a new postrevolutionary
period which would make the 1879 French Revolution a much less
deadly, but still highly coercive, historical event. In a very similar way,
the October 1917 Russian Revolution initially did not involve any direct
casualties apart from a few injured red-guard soldiers. This event that
ultimately generated a profound historical change was so inconspicuous
at the time that it initially received very little media attention. Even the
American journalist who would later become one of the most significant
Western reporters of the revolution, publishing *Ten Days that Shook the
World* (Reed 1919), John Reed, allegedly slept through these events
(Moore 1966; Pipes 1991). In this case, too, mass-scale violence
emerged in the aftermath of the revolution with the civil war, the Red
Terror and the famine.

By replacing the narrow concept of violence used in mainstream
definitions, the issue of the extent of violence necessary to deem an event
a revolution can be resolved. Instead of setting up an arbitrary figure for
casualties that would differentiate revolutions from uprisings or rebellions, attention is to be given to the coercive processes that result in the
forced and major alteration of government structures. This is indirectly
acknowledged in Goldstone's (2014: 4) definition, where he describes a
revolution as 'the forcible overthrow of a government through mass
mobilisation (whether military or civilian or both) in the name of social
justice, to create new political institutions'. While Goldstone makes an
important step in the right direction, this definition still overlooks the
centrality of social organisations and a wider concept of ideological
motivation, both of which are indispensable for revolutionary events.
As I elaborate more extensively later, first and foremost revolutions
involve the usurpation of, and an attack on, existing social organisations.
Revolutions are also carried out by social organisations, including organised social movements. In order to mobilise wider support as well as to
justify their illegal overthrow of government, such organised groups
require potent ideologies. While the idea of social justice is a recurring

theme of many revolutions, it is not the only ideological narrative that has historically dominated the revolutionary movements. For example, in the 1979 Iranian Revolution, social justice was one of the themes incorporated in the dominant ideological narrative, but this theme was clearly subordinate to the idea of establishing a true Islamic social order, governed by the divine principles. Similarly, many nationalist revolutionary uprisings, from the Young Turks revolution of 1908, Indonesian National Revolution of 1945–1949, the Algerian Revolution of 1954 to the Singing Revolutions of the three Baltic states of 1989–1991 were driven less by the ideas of societal justice and much more by the principles of national sovereignty. Taking into account all these criticisms, a revolution can be defined as a scalar historical social process through which social organisations equipped with mobilising ideological discourses enact the forced toppling of a regime with an aim of establishing a new social and political order.

Theories of Revolution

Although most scholars agree that revolutions represent a significant and abrupt transformation of political and social structures, it is less clear why and when they happen. There are three distinct research traditions that provide different explanations of revolutions: the agency-centred, structuralist and culturalist approaches.

Agency-centred analyses had traditionally dominated both historical and social science explanations of revolutions. The early studies written in this vein usually focussed on the determination, individual abilities and motivation of specific revolutionaries, such as Robespierre or Lenin, to achieve a revolutionary outcome. From 1960s onwards, scholars have attempted to develop more generalisable models, emphasising the role of collective agents (i.e. middle classes, proletariat, peasants, professional revolutionaries, status groups, etc.). Hence Brinton (1965) and Edwards (1970) argued that the rising expectations of different groups lead towards pronounced tensions between social classes. Similarly, Smelser (1962) and Davies (1971) identified rising social discontent leading towards revolutionary situations as something caused by the individual frustrations, social strain and dysfunctional social roles. The most influential theory articulated in this tradition was Ted Gurr's (1970) approach developed in his book *Why Men Rebel?* In this book, Gurr argues that the revolutions stem from relative deprivation. More specifically, the argument hinges on the idea that when individuals are deprived of resources and amenities that they used to have or that are perceived to be one's legitimate entitlement, they are more likely to rebel against authority.

For Gurr (1970), changed social conditions are likely to generate turmoil, leading to greater individual frustrations as people experience discrepancy between their expectations and actual reality. In his own words: 'Men are quick to aspire beyond their social means and quick to anger when those means prove inadequate, but slow to accept their limitations' (Gurr 1970: 58). As frustrations rise, they are often channelled through aggression against those seen as responsible for one's deprivation. In this context, as conditions worsen, disgruntled individuals tend to organise themselves in social movements that aim at violent overthrow of the existing regime, which is deemed to be unjust. The focus here is clearly on the psychological responses of individuals as revolutions are understood through the prism of rising frustrations leading towards aggressive behaviour.

The agency-centred models have been criticised extensively for their inability to differentiate between the individual and structural processes involved. The frustration-aggression thesis, which underpins this model, cannot be simply imposed on the levels of social organisations and large-scale groups. Organisations and collectivities do not possess personality traits, singular wills or precise emotional responses in the way individual human beings do. Psychological approaches often tend to reify and essentialise complex social relations. Furthermore, the frustration-aggression thesis lacks much evidence even in the experimental trials conducted in psychological labs (Whitley and Kite 2010), whereas such evidence is largely nonexistent for the macrosocial world of revolutions (Aya 2015). The underlining supposition that revolutionary upheavals are brought about by the angry and frustrated individuals conflicts with the established empirical evidence indicating the significance of rational organisation, division of labour, planning, recruitment and many other processes that make revolutions possible. Moreover, by focussing on the role of revolutionary leaders and other social agents, one loses sight of the structural contexts that produce revolutionary conditions in the first place. While there were many historical situations where large sectors of the population were profoundly resentful of the existing regime and where relative deprivation was rampant, this did not lead to revolution. In fact, as revolutions are quite rare historical episodes, Gurr's thesis cannot explain why in most instances relative deprivation does not produce revolutions.

The structural theories offer more persuasive answers to many of these questions. From the early works of Moore (1966, 1978) and Skocpol (1979), to the later studies of Goldstone (2014, 1991), Goodwin (2001, 1997), Tilly (1995, 1992), Collins (1999) and Mann (2012) consensus has emerged that revolutions are rarely the product of the individual or collective will of agents. Instead, comparative historical studies indicate that revolutions often transpire as a byproduct of structural change. Both Barrington Moore (1978, 1966) and Theda Skocpol (1979) developed their structural arguments through the comparative analyses of several successful twentieth-century revolutions. Moore (1966) explored three different historical routes to modernity, arguing that the structural character of each individual revolution shaped directly its trajectory to modernity (i.e. the liberal, the fascist or the communist roads to modernity). Analysing the revolutionary outcomes of the French, Russian and Chinese revolutions, Skocpol (1979) found two key factors present in all three cases: (a) the chronic crises of the state generated by economic mismanagement, natural disasters, security issues, food shortages or similar processes; and (b) the fermenting social unrest from below. Although Skocpol recognises the role social agents play in revolutions,[1] the emphasis is clearly on structural constraints, such as the weakened state being unable to raise taxes and other crucial resources or the government's inability to pacify social order. In this context, Skocpol differentiates between social and political revolutions: whereas a political revolution involves the overthrow of political regime, a social revolution refers to more extensive social change. In her own words: 'Social revolutions are rapid, basic transformations of a society's state and class structures ... [they] are set apart from other sorts of conflicts and transformative processes above all by the combination of two coincidences: the coincidence of societal structural change with class upheaval, and the coincidence of political with social transformation' (Skocpol 1979: 4).

More recent structure-centred approaches identify a variety of organisational factors contributing to revolutionary outcomes. Thus Goldstone's (1991) influential theory singles out three interrelated structural processes that regularly precede revolutions: (a) the fiscally drained state being incapable of collecting revenue and other resources; (b) the existence of politically deeply divided ruling groups; and (c) the presence of societywide discontent. For Goldstone, revolutions often occur following major natural disasters or resounding defeat in war, both of which tend to further weaken the state, polarise political elites and deepen social discontent. More specifically, Goldstone (2014: 20–25) sees revolutions as events that emerge when number of structural causes coalesce: (a) a demographic change characterised by a substantial

---

[1] Even though Skocpol is highly sympathetic to Marxist-inspired historical analyses, she identifies peasants, not urban workers, as the dominant revolutionary force in all three revolutions she studied.

population increase that puts pressure on the state's resources; (b) significant geopolitical changes that can weaken the state authorities (with many revolutions arising in waves following large-scale wars and economic crises); (c) uneven economic development triggering popular resentment; (d) a rise in discrimination against specific groups in terms of religion, ethnicity, race, etc.; and (e) the entrenchment of personalist and highly corrupt regimes, which can foster popular resentment.

Many of these factors feature in other structural accounts of revolution. Thus both Tilly (1995, 1978) and Goodwin (2001, 1997) highlight geopolitical contexts, the state's capacity, economic weaknesses and elite disunity as important preconditions for revolutions. Nevertheless, Tilly also pays a great deal of attention to the relationship between established institutions and the social movements that challenge these institutions. His theory of contentious politics (Tilly 2008, 2004) focusses on the diverse strategies adopted by the social movements to challenge the state. Tilly (2008: 5) defines such contentious politics as 'interactions in which actors make claims bearing on someone else's interest, in which governments appear as targets, initiators of claims, or third parties'. In this context, revolutions are seen as one of several possible collective responses from the 'repertoire of contention' to changes to the state's policies. These repertoires are forms of collective action aimed at disrupting and disturbing the status quo and can range from the demonstrations, strikes, vigils, rallies, petitions and pamphlets to civil disobedience, terrorism, insurrection and revolution. Although contentious politics has been present throughout much of human history, its character and intensity have changed with the emergence of social movements in the eighteenth century. As social movements proliferate, they acquire organisational capacity to challenge the state, thus making contentious politics more frequent and occasionally more severe in the modern era. The increased intensity of social conflict creates conditions for a variety of noninstitutional disputes, some of which might evolve into a revolutionary situation. However, most revolutionary situations do not automatically lead to revolutionary outcomes. A revolutionary situation involves organised collective action against the government and can range from riots, civil disobedience and sit-ins to insurgencies and even civil wars, but it does not necessarily result in the transfer of political power. For Tilly (1995), this can only occur when social movements manage to mobilise coercive, material, organisational and other resources that are greater than those of the existing government. Nevertheless, as revolutionary situations regularly include politically divided state elites and polarised government structures, the segments of the state apparatus are often crucial for the transformation of a revolutionary situation into a revolutionary outcome, as they might indirectly provide a support for particular social movements. Hence whereas revolutionary situations are more frequent features of the modern world, revolutionary outcomes are quite rare.

This distinction between the actual and the potential in revolutionary movements also underpins Jeff Goodwin's (2001) model of revolution. In order to identify the key causal mechanisms present in revolutionary experiences, he undertook comparative empirical study of both successful and failed revolutions. For Goodwin, there are no revolutions without states, as revolutionary action is defined by a movement's ability to generate a state's breakdown or radical transformation of the state's structure. Moreover, popular support for revolutionary movements is often dependent on their promise to bring about a different form of state rule. In his view, the ultimate success of revolutionary movements is dependent on the character of the state involved. In contrast to agency-centred perspectives, which emphasise psychological and economic variables such as frustration, relative deprivation or economic exploitation, Goodwin argues that revolutionary movements often emerge as 'a response to political oppression and violence, typically brutal and indiscriminate'. In this interpretation, what matters the most is the character of the state as policies of some states generate revolutions while others do not. The states that are more likely to a produce revolutionary situation include those that engage in unpopular economic, social or cultural policies; those that repress and exclude mobilised segments of its population from state power or economic resources; those that discriminate or use violence against organised opposition; those that have weak infrastructural capacities and policing capabilities; and those that are defined by the presence of highly corrupt personalised regimes (Goodwin 2001: 49).

Most structural perspectives also emphasise the modernity of revolutions.[2] Even though violent rebellions, uprisings, revolts and sudden government overthrows have occurred throughout history and have happened on every continent, fully fledged revolutions emerged only in the late-sixteenth century. The key distinguishing trait here is the level of statehood. As structural approaches define revolutions largely in relation to the state power (i.e. revolution as the seizure or overthrow of state apparatus), there can be no revolutions without the developed state apparatuses. Although rudimentary statehood can be traced back to Mesopotamia twelve thousand years ago, there are substantial differences

---

[2] Goldstone (2014: 41) is an exception here, as he traces revolutions to ancient Egypt, Greece and Rome, arguing that 'revolutions are nearly as old as history itself'.

between pristine and modernising states. Following in part Mann (1986), Goodwin (1997) argues that 'until the modern era, there existed no institution with sufficient infrastructural power to remake extensive social arrangements in fundamental ways: the consolidated national state, however, made it possible to do – and to think of doing – just that'. Simply put, before early modernity, violent rebellions, uprisings or revolts did not possess infrastructural means nor ideology to achieve a genuinely transformative revolutionary outcome. While such rebellions could decapitate a particular monarch or a tyrant, they could not generate an unparalleled transformation of the entire social order. In this context, the rise and expansion of interstate systems have been conducive to a proliferation of revolutions over the last three hundred years.

The structural approaches have dominated the study of revolutions for the past forty years. Nevertheless, over the past two decades some central propositions of structural analysis have been questioned. From the 1979 Iranian and Nicaraguan revolutions, the 1989–1991 postcommunist and more recent Colour revolutions and the 2010–2011 Arab Spring, it has become apparent that revolutionary experience is not only political process. The critics have challenged structural approaches for their overemphasis on the role of the state and geopolitics, their neglect of the role that civil society plays in fermenting revolutionary situations and their separation of economic from political sources of revolution. However, most stringent criticisms have pointed out the structuralists' lack of attention to the centrality of culture and ideology in revolutionary upheavals. Consequently, the more recent studies of revolutions have embraced the cultural turn, arguing that revolutions are first and foremost defined and shaped by the cultural processes.

There is no doubt that the successful revolution predisposes the coalescing of different structural factors, such as substantial geopolitical shifts, demographic pressures, fiscal weakness of the state, military defeats or prolonged economic slumps. Nevertheless, as revolutions involve the social action of many nonstate agents, structural changes do not by themselves necessarily result in revolutionary events. As the historical record shows, revolutions are still very rare events, and even when several structural factors coalesce there is no certainty that this will automatically trigger a revolutionary outcome. In addition, from the 1979 Iranian Revolution onwards it has become apparent that revolutions can transpire even when many structural conditions are not in place. To understand these facets of revolutionary experience, a number of scholars have shifted their attention to cultural mechanisms – symbols, narratives, discourses and ideologies – and the role they play in generating revolutionary action as well as in legitimising the attempted takeovers of the state.

Hence Selbin (2010) argues that all revolutions require believable stories which can appeal to wide audiences. More to the point, for the mass mobilisation to happen in a particular society it is crucial that the society cherishes a culture of resistance, has a long tradition of rebellions and uprisings or celebrates resistance in folk idioms. In his own words: 'In societies where revolution is considered a viable response to oppression – due to a history of rebellious activities celebrated in folk culture, or to revolutionary leaders having employed such traditions in the local culture – revolutionary activities are more likely to be undertaken, receive broad popular support and conclude successfully' (Selbin 2010: 81). Although all revolutions entail the presence of coherent narratives which draw on the heroic and tragic past, Selbin distinguishes between four dominant revolutionary stories: (a) the foundation mythologies of modern liberal democracies that centre on the narratives of civilisation and democratisation (i.e. the English Glorious Revolution, the 1789 French and 1776 American revolutions, etc.); (b) the social revolution narrative with the focus on addressing social injustices, inequalities, poverty and hunger (i.e. the 1789 French Revolution, 1917 Russian October Revolution, 1958 Cuban Revolution, etc.); (c) national liberation stories emphasising the sacrifices made for independence, freedom and equality ranging from the narratives of slave revolts to anticolonial struggles (i.e. 1958 Cuba, Haiti, etc.); and (d) the tragic narratives of failed revolutions that still resonate among many discontent groups (i.e. the 1871 Paris Commune, etc.). While some revolutionary movements rely more on one of these narratives, most revolutions incorporate more than one revolutionary story. For example, the French Revolution is now associated with all four of these narratives. For Selbin (2010: 78), without a story, there is no revolution: 'stories are the reason why revolutions are made ... without them, there is no resistance, no rebellion, no revolution'.

In a similar vein, Foran (2005) and Foran, Lane and Živković (2008) insist that revolutions should be understood less as the unintended consequences of structural forces and more as intentional actions of groups endowed with social meanings. Pointing to the examples of the nonviolent revolutions that overthrew the communist governments in Eastern Europe and the former Soviet Union as well as the Colour revolutions of early 2000s, they emphasise the lack of structural preconditions for these revolutions. Both of these revolutionary waves emerged in the context of relatively stable state structures with governments in full control of their police, military and revenue collection and without any pronounced conflicts between the ruling elites. Moreover, unlike their classical predecessors these revolutionary upheavals were not driven by the distinct world-transforming utopian projects that were at the heart of major revolutions from 1789 France and 1917 Russia to 1979 Iran. In both of these revolutionary waves, social movements and civil society groups played an important role, while the role of state apparatuses seemed to be less pronounced. While acknowledging the importance of some structural and material factors for galvanising popular discontent (i.e. exclusionary rule, colonial domination, dependent development and economic decline), Foran (2005) argues that revolutions depend on political cultures of opposition, including coherent ideological doctrines, articulate cultural idioms, subjective historical experiences and messages that have strong emotional appeal. The researchers working in this tradition call attention to the role that shared myths, symbols, memories and historical figures play in mobilising civil society and the wider sectors of the population. The focus has shifted towards the study of subjective motivations of different agents involved in the revolutionary processes: elites, peasants, middle classes, workers, students, minorities, etc. (Foran, Lane and Živković 2008). Despite a relative failure of the Arab Spring revolutions, all of which with the exception of Tunisia have reverted back to the authoritarian rule, this particular revolutionary wave has been important in highlighting the complexity of revolutionary experience. The Arab Spring also defied the traditional patterns of revolutionary upheavals as it transpired in an environment of relative stability, with the governments in firm control of their military and police apparatuses. Furthermore, none of the states involved has recently experienced a military defeat, economic collapse or major natural disaster, and the governing elites were for the most part united. Although demographic changes played an important part, with the rapid population growth and the rise of unemployed educated urban youth spearheading the unrests (Goldstone 2014, 2011),[3] they were not the decisive factor, as this demographic change was equally present in those Middle Eastern states where there were no revolutions. What seems to have played a more important role in the Arab Spring were the new opportunities to voice and share one's discontent with similar others. Simply put, the availability of social media such as Facebook, Twitter, YouTube and other new technologies was crucial in communicating information about revolutionary events. It is no accident that the Arab Spring started in Tunisia, where there is a relatively large middle class and where 'the percentage of

---

[3] Goldstone (2014: 118) identifies another structural factor – 'the highest dependence on grain imports in the world' – which with the substantial rise in grain prices made the governments subsidies unsustainable. However, this too was a common policy affecting most of the Middle East.

Facebook users among young people was the highest in North Africa' (Goldstone 2014: 119). Social media was important in mobilising demonstrators against the governments in each country but also in keeping others informed about similar developments across the Middle East and North Africa. For culturalist approaches, such use of social media to channel the ideas, symbols and narratives of resistance indicates that revolutions are first and foremost a cultural phenomenon.

Cultural perspectives are useful in highlighting the fact that revolutions entail social meanings and that no revolutionary action is possible without symbols and believable narratives. However, just as traditional structuralist accounts were too rigid in their explanatory materialism, the same can be said about the rigidity of epistemological idealism that underpins most cultural approaches. Revolutions require stories and folk idioms, but ideas without organisation cannot enact profound social change. Culturalist perspectives neglect the obvious historical mismatch between the abundance of revolutionary narratives and symbolism on the one hand and successful revolutionary outcomes on the other. Ideas are important but by themselves insufficient for revolutionary undertaking. To understand the complex dynamics of revolutions, it is important to move beyond the three traditional interpretations of revolutions.

An Alternative Vision: The Longue Durée View

Since revolutions are historically highly contingent and rare events, it is difficult to identify their common patterns. Until the late-twentieth century, there was a degree of consensus that revolutions involve the sudden and violent overthrow of the government, mass mobilisation and institutional change. However, as discussed earlier, the use of violence has been questioned, as many of the late-twentieth and early-twenty-first century revolutions were not violent in the traditional sense. What seems to be more significant for revolutions is the collective attempt at the coercive usurpation of existing social organisations. In other words, all revolutions involve coercion in a sense that revolutionaries aim to take over control over the state apparatuses and other key social organisations. Sometimes when there is strong resistance from the government, this is achieved with a lot of bloodshed, but in other instances when the state leadership is deeply divided or profoundly delegitimized the revolutionary takeover can be accomplished without any human casualties. One of the key preconditions to succeed in this attempt is to galvanise a substantial degree of popular support. As revolution represents an illegal takeover of state power, it is paramount that revolutionaries create and deploy a believable ideological narrative capable of justifying such an act. Finally, to successfully link the organised revolutionary undertaking with the ideological message, it is crucial that revolutionary experience is integrated into the everyday microreality of ordinary individuals. Hence to better understand the complex workings of revolutions, it is vital to focus on the three processes that I have identified as decisive in shaping the social world over the past twelve thousand years: the cumulative bureaucratisation of coercion, centrifugal ideologisation and envelopment of microsolidarity. This is not to say that the dominant explanations of revolutions do not engage with some of these processes, as they clearly do with culturalists emphasising the role of ideas and beliefs, structuralists highlighting the institutional structures and agency-centred views focussing on individual leaders and group action. The point is that unlike the three dominant perspectives where organisations, ideologies and microgroup dynamics tend, in explanatory terms, to cancel each other out, in the longue durée perspective these three processes are analysed as being deeply interlinked. This strong linkage stems not from an abstract conceptual ambition to establish an eclectic grand theory that would provide a metasynthesis in the manner of several sociological attempts to reconcile structure and agency (i.e. Giddens 1985, Archer 2000, Elias 1978).[4] Instead, this connection emerges from the shared historical trajectory of the three processes involved. As argued throughout this book, these three long-term historical processes were contingent and interdependent products of social change over long stretches of time. Consequently, rather than establishing the causal mechanisms of revolutions by pinpointing agents, structures or culture, my goal is much more modest, which is to provide accentuated descriptions of specific historical trajectories that have characterised social development leading towards revolutionary upheavals. In this context, the longue durée perspective conceptualises organisations, ideologies and microgroup dynamics not as fixed and uniform structures or agents but as processual and relational categories prone to dramatic transformations. However, this is not to say that such forms of social relations are not stable. On the contrary, one of the key arguments made in this book is that organisational continuity matters a great deal and that more recent instances of organised violence are regularly rooted in organisational dynamics that has been shaped over very long periods of time. Hence, to come to terms with revolutionary change, it is important to reconceptualise and historicise structures, agents and cultures.

---

[4] I am highly sceptical that such grand synthetic attempts can be theoretically successful or empirically useful. For my criticism, see Malešević (2004: 168–181).

Revolutions and Social Organisations

The cumulative bureaucratisation of coercion is a process that involves state structures and changing geopolitical constellations, but as it predates state formation and encompasses other forms of social organisation (i.e. social movements, business corporations, religious institutions, etc.), it can account for the wider structural dynamics of revolutionary experience. Simply put, while in structuralist approaches states are the preeminent factor in the revolutionary upheavals, in the longue durée perspective a variety of social organisations can and often do play such a role. This is not to deny that revolutions are largely modern phenomena involving organised uprisings against the political authority of the infrastructurally developed polities. Goodwin (2001, 1997) is absolutely right that in order to overthrow a state apparatus, such an apparatus has to be in existence in the first place. The premodern social orders often lacked what we would now regard as the basic elements of statehood, including a legitimate monopoly on violence, taxation, legislation and education. However, neither revolutions nor social structures emerge out of historical thin air. Instead, they are both the byproducts of long-term organisational development. Although fully fledged revolutions proliferate only in the modern era, their organisational roots are deeper in the past. Just as the contemporary nation-state grew out of previous forms of political organization, so have present-day revolutions. The organisational knowhow of chiefdoms, city-states, city leagues, composite kingdoms and capstone imperial orders as well as modernising empires provided the organisational building blocks of contemporary nation-states (Malešević 2013a). In a similar vein, the premodern uprisings, rebellions, jacqueries, protests, revolts, risings and insurrections have paved the organisational way for revolutionary events over the last three centuries. Revolutions are for the most part modern phenomena, but their occurrence owes a great deal to the organisational buildup that has taken shape over thousands of years. As Lachmann (1997: 76) rightly argues revolutions are not to be identified exclusively with the states. Since premodern rulers usually controlled only segments of (quite small) state apparatuses and exercised elements of sovereignty over some territory (including mutually exclusive and competing claims over the same patches of land), a revolution is not necessarily an attack on the state. Instead, prior to 1789, 'revolutions were consequential to the extent to which they rearranged sovereign relations among elites and their organisational apparatuses rather than because (or whether) they decapitated and replaced the "head of state" '. For example, both the English Revolution of 1640–1649 and the Glorious Revolution of 1688–1689 were conflicts focussed on 'the local control of organisations of domination and extraction. The two revolutions ... did result in change of rulers, but had virtually no effect on the structure of national government which had been determined by the previous elite conflicts' (Lachmann 1997: 95).

Hence the nation-state is not the only organisational form conducive for the revolutionary overthrow, and organisational advancement is something that equally incorporates nonstate organisations. The first sociologically recognisable revolutions, such as the English Revolution of 1640–1649, the Glorious Revolution of 1688–1689, the American Revolution of 1775–1783 and the 1789–1795 French Revolution were events that unfolded not in the world of nation-states but empires. While in the English and French cases revolutionaries were set on changing the internal structure of their respective polities, in the American case the ambition was to secede from the existing imperial structure. Nevertheless, in all these three cases the transformation from the empire to nation-state was a protracted and asymmetrical process that initially generated polities that had features of both – the fledgling nation-state at home and the empire abroad. As Kumar (2010) and Burbank and Cooper (2010) show, the traditional differentiations between these two forms of polity have for the most part overemphasised revolutionary moments as bringing about completely new forms of the state structure, while in fact most nominal nation-states maintained many imperial features for many decades, if not centuries. Thus the transition towards a fully fledged nation-state took very long time and was often characterised by unprecedented organisational turbulence, wars and waves of revolutions throughout the eighteenth, nineteenth and twentieth century (Wimmer 2013). Revolutions have also occurred in modernising city-states, city-leagues, composite kingdoms and other forms of political organisation. For example, the 1848 failed revolutions in the Apennine peninsula involved short-lived revolutionary governments in the following city-states and city-leagues: Milan, the Republic of San Marco (in existence for seventeen months), the Roman Republic, the United Provinces of Central Italy or the Confederation of Central Italy. In a similar vein, the nineteenth and early-twentieth century witnessed many failed and successful revolutions in developing kingdoms, principalities and sultanates: the 1848 Duchy of Schleswig and the Principality of Wallachia revolutions; 1918–1919 revolution in the Sultanate of Egypt; or the 1964 revolution in the Zanzibar Sultanate. Simply put, although revolutions are principally attacks on the modernising structures, such structures involve much more than the nation-state model.

In addition, although revolutions often depend on internal conflicts at the top of state apparatuses, the success of a revolution entails the presence of competing nonstate social organisations. Despite popular perceptions of revolutions as spontaneous uprisings of discontented people, years of extensive research clearly indicate that revolutionary action necessitates meticulous organisation, planning, resources, mobilisation and external support. The fact that revolutions often come in waves indicates that the organisations involved in revolutionary activity interact with similar organisations outside of their respective polities. In some instances, this involves direct coordination and collaboration of ideologically compatible movements and associations, such as the liberal nationalist movements in 1848 revolutions or radical left-wing movements in the 1917–1923 revolutionary wave involving the October Bolshevik Revolution, the Bavarian Soviet Republic, the Hungarian Revolution, Biennio Rosso in Italy or the postcommunist 1989–1991 revolutions in Eastern Europe. In other instances, native revolutionary organisations borrow and copy from successful revolutionary movements, as was the case with some of the Colour revolutions of early 2000 and the Arab Spring of 2010–2011. For example, in both of these cases Serbia's Otpor! (Resistance!) youth movement, which was an influential actor in the overthrew of Milošević in 2000, provided extensive training to revolutionary organisations in Egypt, Georgia, Ukraine, Lebanon and Uzbekistan (Goldstone 2014: 122; Traynor 2005).

In this context, Goodwin's (2001) point about the infrastructural capacity of states applies equally to nonstate organisations, as they too can bring about a revolutionary outcome only when possessing such an organisational capability to mount an attack on the state structure. In other words, a revolutionary situation entails the existence of relatively complex organisational shells involving both polity and nonpolity structures. Moreover, as I argue throughout this book, such increased organisational capacity is deeply rooted in the coercive power that characterises all durable and effective social organisations. Hence the cumulative bureaucratisation of coercion is discernible in nonstate organisations just as in state apparatuses. The ever-increasing bureaucratic features of modernising polities are also reflected in social movements, political parties, trade unions, clandestine associations, churches and other social organisations involved in revolutionary action. As their organisational capacity continues to increases, so does the coercive power of all of these organisations. This is important, as it allows us to understand the dynamics of revolutionary action. While individual revolutions differ in the scale of violence produced, there has been a continuous increase in coercive actions that have accompanied revolutions over the past three hundred years or so. Revolutions emerge, are sustained by and succeed as a consequence of coercive organisational development.

In fact, revolution is first and foremost an organisational breakdown caused by the combination of internal organisational weaknesses and the coercive pressure of competing social organisations (from organised social movements to hostile neighbouring polities, private corporations and religious organisations to terrorist insurrectional groupings, etc.). A defeated and weakened polity unable to collect revenue, provide social protection to its citizens or secure law and order is likely to be a soft target for a revolutionary movement as well as for other competing social organisations. A state that loses its monopoly on the legitimate use of violence or taxation and cannot pay its civil servants, police, military and judiciary while also being unable to provide employment, health protection, transport, communications or educational opportunities to its citizens creates structural conditions for revolutions. Obviously, most such structural openings will not lead automatically towards the revolutionary situation, but some will. Although revolutions are still mostly rare phenomena, their occurrence has substantially increased in late modernity. One of the main reasons for this increase is the continuous cumulative rise of the coercive bureaucratic power that characterises most social organisations. Thus when social organisations such as the states lose their organisational (and ideological) grip, their coercive bureaucratic capacity does not disappear but is in fact mopped up by competing organisations. In other words, regardless of how radical the revolutionary rhetoric is, no revolutionary movement will, or even can, dispense with the coercive organisational capacity created by the previous regime. For example, despite Khomeini's virulent rhetorical attacks on the structure of Pahlavi's state and his prerevolutionary promises to mete out its foundations, much of the Shah's civil service and state apparatus was preserved in postrevolutionary Iran. Even the Islamic State (ISIS) has largely maintained Syrian civil servants on the condition that they pledge loyalty to new rulers. In rare instances, when the revolutionary radicals have attempted to make a clean sweep and destroy the existing organisational structures, such as in Cambodia under the Khmer Rouge or Afghanistan under the Taliban, this has quickly proved to be highly detrimental to the organisation's very existence. Since organisations are rooted in coercive power as they grow and expand, so does their coercive reach and capacity. In this sense, revolutions do not destroy states or other social organisations. Instead, they are nearly always organised attempts to attain more coercive organisational power. In line with the general argument of this book, it is my contention that as the organisational power expands through time so does the coercive potential of revolutionary events. Although the number of human casualties can and does vary from one revolution to another, the bureaucratisation of coercive power has largely maintained a cumulative character over the past three hundred years.

To illustrate this point, one can briefly compare and contrast the organisational contexts of the Russian October Bolshevik Revolution (1917) and the Romanian Revolution (1989). While the first is often seen together with the French Revolution as the beacon of worldwide social change that gave birth to the idea of the state socialist order, the second is usually interpreted as a relatively marginal and atypically violent episode in the otherwise peaceful postcommunist transition. Moreover, considering the size, geopolitical impact and economic strength of the two polities, the Russian Revolution is generally assumed to involve greater societal penetration and a more complex organisational grip than its less influential Romanian counterpart. The popular image of the Romanian Revolution is one associated with the chaotic and spontaneous uprising of discontented people, while the October Revolution is identified with the well-planned, disciplined and organised Bolshevik takeover of power.

However, when looking at the structural base of the two events as they unfolded over relatively short period of time,[5] it is clear that in coercive organisational terms the Romanian Revolution easily trumps its Russian counterpart. Whereas the Russian Revolution was essentially an elite opportunist undertaking hijacked by the Bolshevik leadership, who had no significant support among the overwhelmingly peasant population of Russia, the Romanian uprising involved wide, cross-class sectors of Romanian citizens, including dissatisfied leaders and members of the Romanian Communist Party. The October Revolution transpired in the context of unprecedented military losses during the World War I and severe food shortages, both of which triggered deep popular resentment against the ancient regime. As Moore (1978) shows, rather than planning and spearheading a revolutionary change of government, the small Bolshevik party was initially content to wait clandestinely for a more opportune historical moment to start a revolution while its leadership, including Lenin, were in exile in Switzerland. Hence the collapse of the regime was initiated by garrison desertions and food riots, and the Bolsheviks successfully utilised this organisational opportunity to assemble a small military force (the Petrograd Soviet's organisation of Red

---

[5] The two revolutions were both sudden events: the Russian Revolution took only two days (7–8 November), while the Romanian Revolution unfolded over eleven days (16–27 December). Obviously, the long-term impact of the two events was deeply asymmetrical, as the Russian Revolution profoundly changed not only Russian society but also much of the world, whereas its Romanian counterpart had some significant impact on Romanian society but almost no influence outside of its borders.

Guards controlled by the Military Revolutionary Committee) and take over the key symbols of state power, such as the Winter Palace. Nevertheless, the Bolsheviks did not have the organisational means to control the entire city of Petrograd, let alone the vast Russian countryside. The Bolshevik victory came about less through their organisational excellence and much more as a product of disorganisation and delegitimisation of the Tsarist state. It is only through the civil war of 1917–1922 that the Bolsheviks managed to create the potent military and bureaucratic apparatus to fully control the entire Soviet polity.

In contrast, the 1980s Romanian state was to use Mann's (1993) terms infrastructurally and despotically much more powerful than its 1917 Tsarist counterpart. Ceausescu's regime developed the most repressive police state in the communist world, with its secret police, the Securitate, monitoring nearly all aspects of everyday life. The Romanian secret police was even more effective than the German Democratic Republic's (GDR) Stasi, and it was estimated that in the 1980s one in thirty Romanian citizens was a Securiate informer (Deletant 1995). The Romanian communist state also possessed a huge civil and political bureaucracy, including a wide network of Communist Party cells, a large police force, USLA troops (antiterrorist special squads) and the military apparatus. In this context, where no alternative associations were allowed, revolutionary action was ultimately coordinated by the organised groups from within the omnipotent Communist Party of Romania. Although it is still not completely clear whether the National Salvation Front (NSF) was in operation six months before the revolution, as claimed by some of its leaders,[6] or was formally constituted during the revolution, its organisation was crucial during and after the revolution (Siani-Davies 2007). Despite the fact that the revolution was triggered by protests in Timisoara and other provincial towns, the key vehicles of revolutionary success were the coercive social organisations of the Romanian communist state – the party and the military. As ordinary protesting citizens were not armed or particularly well organised, it was decisive that key segments of the army and party leadership switched sides and in this way provided organisational and coercive means for the revolution. As in most other revolutionary events in Romania, too, the success of the revolution was premised on the deep divisions within the political and military leadership. The fact that both defence ministers appointed by Ceausescu decided to disobey his direct orders for the army to shoot at

---

[6] As Siani-Davies (2007: 167) reports, some leading members of the NSF have argued that its existence can be documented by the letters sent to Radio Free Europe six months before the revolution.

protesters was a significant moment that tilted the revolutionary events towards triumph.[7] Moreover, a very similar situation arose with the Communist Party of Romania where one faction took control of the revolution and rebranded itself as the National Salvation Front. It is this political organisation, with the help of military – hence both the coercive and bureaucratic apparatuses of the regime – that ultimately removed Ceausescu and his wife from power; organised their arrest, trail and execution; and took the reins of state power after the revolution. This organisational split was also reflected in the mass media, which proved to be an important mechanism for popular mobilisation of dissent once the main TV and radio stations were taken over by the supporters of the National Salvation Front. Therefore, when compared to the Romanian case and despite its lasting worldwide significance, the Russian Revolution was characterised by the lower level of coercive and bureaucratic capacity. This was also reflected in part in the number of human casualties in the two revolutions, with the October Bolshevik Revolution resulting in only several injured, whereas the Romanian Revolution involved 1,104 direct casualties and over 3,350 injured (Roper 2000). More importantly, as the Romanian coercive-bureaucratic apparatus had deeper reach and penetration within its society than its Russian counterpart, revolutionary change came about for the most part relying on the existing organisational structures, which was less of the case in the October Revolution.

Revolutions and Ideological Penetration

Until recently, most sociological theories have focussed on the material and structural causes of revolution. It is only in the last two decades that ideas, beliefs, discourses and cultural traditions have been identified as playing a decisive role in fermenting revolutionary action. In particular, Selbin (2010, 1997) and Foran (2005, 1997) have insisted that revolutionary ideas generate revolutionary outcomes. As Selbin (1997: 123) puts it in stark terms: 'ideas and actors, not structures and some broad sweep of history, are the primary forces in revolutionary processes'. Similarly, for Foran (1997: 214), revolutions cannot be explained without looking at their cultural underpinnings, as 'revolutionaries work within their pre-existing ideological horizons', and also create 'new, revisioned cultures of opposition to try to keep a revolutionary coalition together'. Although these ideas-centred accounts sound just as

---

[7] The first minister of defence committed suicide after rejecting Ceausescu's orders to use the military against the protesters.

determinist as some of the older structuralist interpretations of revolutions, there is no doubt that revolutionary action entails the presence of believable and motivating ideological narratives. It would be difficult to envisage the French Revolution without its key doctrinal principles centred on moral equality of all French citizens as formulated in the Declaration of the Rights of Man and of the Citizen, just as it would be impossible to understand the 1979 Iranian Revolution without examining the popular impact of Shia Islamic doctrine. However, ideas, symbols and cultural idioms cannot generate revolutionary action by themselves. The alternative discursive and symbolic frameworks are nearly always present in all societies, but it is only under specific social conditions and in quite rare situations that such alternative ideological understandings of social reality acquire popular resonance. In other words, ideology matters, but only when integrated into the effective organisational machinery.

Furthermore, as I have argued before, Malešević (2010, 2006, 2002), the focus on the contours of a specific doctrine might overshadow the significance of the process of ideologisation. Simply put, to have popular impact ideology cannot operate as a fixed and static set of principles but instead as a dynamic and multifacetted process that involves ideas as well as the practices. As Freeden (1996: 71–72) rightly argues, ideology is 'a form of thought-behaviour that penetrates all [social and] political practice'. Hence to get the grips of this process, it is critical to shift the attention from the general principles and ideas towards ideologisation as a long-term historical process that incorporates beliefs and actions. More specifically, I use the concept of centrifugal ideologisation to refer to an organisationally generated mass-scale process whereby specific ideological tenets and practices gradually start to permeate diverse social strata in a particular social order. While before the modern era much of this process remained at the level of political, religious and economic elites where the proto-ideological narratives are deployed to secure a degree of unity at the top, in modernity ideologisation casts a much wider net, aiming to forge ideological consensus among disparate individuals inhabiting the same social and political order. When successful, centrifugal ideologisation creates conditions which simultaneously provide means for legitimation of particular forms of social action as well as the motive for popular mobilisation for such an action. It certainly is true that the political, cultural, religious, economic or military elites usually play decisive roles in initiating revolutionary upheavals, but the success of any revolution hinges on the ability of these elite actors to achieve a degree of popular support. Although in the traditional social orders ideological penetration is not very deep, as it generally appeals to proto-ideological discourses (i.e. mythology, religious doctrines, civilising missions, etc.), it is still a crucial mechanism for preserving a level of doctrinal unity among the elite groupings involved in revolutionary activities. In modern contexts, as literacy rates and the public sphere dramatically increase and citizenry is better integrated into social and political systems, ideological principles usually resonate with much wider groups. As Gouldner (1976: 28–32) noted a long time ago, ideological power entails modern and literate citizens oriented towards betterment in their lifetime, not in the afterworld: such individuals 'must be more interested in the news from this world than in the tidings from another. The most obdurate enemy of ideology is illiteracy'.

One of the crucial features of modernity is the institutional and doctrinal recognition that all citizens of a particular polity are of equal moral worth. Although modern political and economic systems largely did not bring about economic and political equality, but have in many instances generated a wider social polarisation, they have ultimately institutionalised values that regard all human beings as morally equal. These principles were inaugurated by the Enlightenment movements and received their first organisational confirmation in the new French and American constitutions following the revolutionary upheavals in the two states. Nevertheless, even in these two cases the ideological shift was slow and incomplete, as the Declaration of the Rights of Man and of the Citizen did not apply to the native and slave populations of French colonies. In a similar way, the U.S. Bill of Rights was not envisaged as a document that would protect the rights of Native Americans or southern slaves. However, despite these slow, incomplete and gradual developments, both of these doctrinal documents have played significant part in mobilisation and legitimation of revolutionary actions throughout the world. For example, the Haitian Revolution (1791–1804) was directly inspired by the ideals advocated in the revolutionaries' French and American counterparts. The rebellion of the slave population led by Toussaint Louverture resulted in the independence of Haiti and the establishment of the first free society founded by former slaves in the new world. Louverture was profoundly influenced by the ideas of the Enlightenment and drafted Haiti's first constitution in this spirit. In some respects, most nineteenth and early-twentieth-century revolutionaries tended to refer either to the French or American revolutions as inspirations in terms of establishing a society governed by the principles of ethical equity, fraternity and liberty and deposing of the corrupt and authoritarian ancient regime. In this way, a variety of revolutionaries, from the conservative Catholics to communists, saw themselves as continuing in the footsteps of French or American revolutionaries. Hence the leaders of the Belgian

Revolution (1830–1831), who were mostly liberal and conservative Catholics, utilised the ideals of the French and American revolutions to win independence from the United Kingdom of the Netherlands and establish a parliamentary constitutional monarchy. While espousing very different ideological principles, many communist revolutionaries, from the 1917 October Revolution to the German 1918–1919 Revolution, to the short-lived Bavarian and Hungarian Soviet republics of 1919 to the Mongolian Revolution of 1921 to the Chinese Communist Revolution of 1919, perceived themselves as the direct heirs of the French Revolution bent on completing the job that their Jacobin predecessors have not finished.

What these diverse examples show is that the nominal content of each ideological doctrine was not as central to the revolutionary experience as the process of ideologisation itself. In other words, if we were to focus only on the individual doctrinal messages of the Soviet, Haitian or Belgian revolutionaries, it would be difficult to explain their different but equally persuasive popular appeal. Obviously, there are significant differences between their individual visions of the postrevolutionary order. The Soviet revolutionaries were striving to establish a communist proletarian society where each individual would contribute according to her ability and would receive according to her needs. In the Belgian case, the ambition was to establish a new order where the French-speaking Catholics would not be second-class citizens but would fully maintain their religious and linguistic exclusivity together with their Flemish counterparts. Finally, the Haitian revolutionaries engaged in the struggle to create an independent, slavery-free republic inhabited by the black citizens only. Nevertheless, despite these nominal doctrinal differences that advocate mutually incompatible principles – from communist universalism, to linguistic, religious and racial particularisms – these three revolutionary experiences are grounded in very similar ideological templates and practices. It is these templates and practices, initiated by the French and American revolutions, that were at the heart of nearly every nineteenth-, twentieth- and twenty-first-century revolution.

The key issue here is the ideological zeal and determination to create a completely new world that is usually associated with modern-day revolutionary movements. The post-Enlightenment world differs from its predecessors in a sense that it is generally premised on the idea that one can achieve social justice, dignity, prosperity and perfection in this world rather than only in the afterlife as formulated in teachings of the leading monotheistic religions. The modern revolutionaries strive to create such a better world here and now, not in the foreseeable future or in the afterlife. In this context, specific ideological doctrines serve as the topographic maps which indicate where to go and what the ultimate destination will look like. However, while these doctrinal destinations differ substantially, the means to achieve them usually do not. Since the French Revolution onwards, revolutionary projects were often envisaged not only as the morally superior but also as the most rational ways to organise social life. Grounded in Enlightenment philosophy (and later Romanticism as well), the revolutionaries took on themselves to mould the new world according to what they saw to be scientific blueprints providing the pathway to a better future. Since the key ambition of the modernist project was to create the most rational, equal, free, just and truthful social order, any organised resistance to this ideal world could only be interpreted as an attempt to stop the progress and reestablish the old tyrannical ancient regime. Hence the revolutionaries tended often to understand their role in deeply Manichean terms: they saw themselves as the possessors of the ultimate truth and justice fighting against the forces of darkness who intend to reverse the (progressive) wheel of history. In such an environment, ideological zeal was perceived as a precondition for the ultimate victory. Moreover, to successfully delegitimize the representatives of the ancient regime and others who challenge the new order, it becomes critical to deny them a membership in the human race. More to the point, as the new modernist ideologies conceptualise all human beings as morally equal, it is not enough anymore to emphasise the opponent's moral failings. Instead, to fully delegitimise the enemy's actions, it is now crucial to deny any humanity to the enemy. While in the deeply hierarchical premodern world such categorisations were not necessary, as peasants were universally perceived to be inferior to their lords, in the modern context where everybody is of equal moral worth, delegitimisation inevitably slides in the direction of dehumanisation. If all humans are equal, then our despicable enemy can only be something less than human (Malešević 2013b). The consequence of this ideological transformation was the justification of violence in new, universal terms. Hence the mass-scale massacres in regions that did not accept the legitimacy of the French revolutionary government, particularly in Vendee, were justified in strictly universalist terms. For example, one of the leaders responsible for the mass-scale violence of the revolutionary forces in Lyon stated that 'I am purging the land of liberty of these monsters according to the principle of humanity' (Townshend 2011: 39). Thus the representatives of the ancient regime and their supporters are not the respected opponents but monsters that need to be purged in the name of humanity.

This type of justification was also used by the revolutionary general Francois Joseph Westermann, who described his actions in a letter to the

Committee of the Public Safety announcing that 'There is no more Vendée ... According to the orders that you gave me, I crushed the children under the feet of the horses, massacred the women who, at least for these, will not give birth to any more brigands. I do not have a prisoner to reproach me. I have exterminated all .... Mercy is not a revolutionary sentiment' (Miller 2012: 334). In an almost identical way, the youngest leader of the French Revolution, Saint-Just, was a stringent proponent of the idea that revolution requires 'inflexible justice' and that 'whoever vilified or attacked the dignity of the revolutionary government should be condemned to death' (Spethens 1982: 470). The direct result of this uncompromising ideological crusade was as many as four hundred thousand casualties of this brutal civil war (Rapport 2013: 27).

This revolutionary radicalism was equally visible in the Haitian Revolution, where the enemy was also dehumanised. For example, one of the revolutionary leaders, Boisrond-Tonnerre, stated that 'For our declaration of independence, we should have the skin of a white man for parchment, his skull for the inkwell, his blood for ink, and a bayonet for a pen!' (Senauth 2011: viii).

Since revolutions are usually premised on the idea that the new post-revolutionary order will bring about a society able to transcend the existing social conflicts, their ideological mobilisation inevitably stimulates doctrinal radicalism. Since, as Mannheim (1966) recognised a long time ago, all ideological projects contain a kernel of utopianism, revolutionary violence is usually legitimised in terms of the possibility to realise such utopian visions. Furthermore, as revolutions generally transpire in an institutionally chaotic environment where leadership, commitment to revolutionary goals and loyalty to the revolutionary organisation are constantly questioned, revolutionary situations open the possibility for instant delegitimisation of individuals perceived to be deviating from the true path. Hence it is no accident that all major revolutions were accompanied by accusations of treason and physical removal of leaders judged to be disloyal, willing to compromise revolutionary ideals, or were simply too soft towards the enemies. Obviously, such accusations are always part of the game played by some leaders to attain more power by denouncing their direct competitors, but what is equally important is the popular pressure generated by revolutionary experience. Although the majority of those involved in revolutionary events rarely if ever possess great familiarity with the ideological doctrines underpinning the revolutionary demands, they are regularly responsive to the key symbols associated with the revolution. One such potent symbol is the notion of 'enemy of the people', a label that has regularly been attached to discredited revolutionaries who decided not to toe the official line. For example, the leaders of the French Revolution, Danton and Desmoulins, were accused by Robespierre of being the enemies of the people and were ultimately guillotined for engaging in counterrevolutionary activities, taking bribes and showing lenience towards the members of the ancient regime. In an almost identical way, Robespierre too ended on the guillotine as the enemy of the people. The revolutionaries involved in the Russian Bolshevik Revolution were often executed by the former comrades deploying the same syntagm. Hence Trotsky was assassinated on Stalin's order as the 'enemy of the Soviet people', as were Zinoviev and Bukharin before him. An almost identical pattern was repeated in numerous other revolutions, from North Korea and Vietnam to Iran and farther afield. In this sense, revolutions remain dependent on the ideological frames that establish and maintain their legitimacy as well as provide nodal points for the permanent mobilisation of large groups of people. Whereas in the premodern world, where ideological penetration was scant and ineffective, government overthrow did not require much popular mobilisation, in the modern world securing a substantial degree of public support is a crucial precondition for the success of revolutionary endeavour.

This point can be well illustrated with the brief comparison of the 1688 Glorious Revolution and the more recent Tunisian 2010–2011 Jasmine Spring. The former took place in what at that time was one of the most advanced and leading world powers, and the latter came about in a small North African state with a modest economy and negligible international influence. On the surface, the Glorious Revolution was all about (religious) ideology – replacing a disliked Catholic monarch with a new, legitimate Protestant ruler. In contrast, the Jasmine Spring is usually interpreted not in terms of ideology but as an economic and demographic phenomenon with the middle-class youth rebellion caused by rapid population growth and rampant unemployment (Goldstone 2014: 117–130). Yet I would argue that the ideological capacity of the Tunisian Revolution was much greater than that of its seventeenth-century English counterpart.

The Glorious Revolution was almost solely an elite undertaking involving a small cohort of Protestant aristocrats striking an alliance with another member of the Protestant nobility, William of Orange, and his English-born wife Mary to invade the country and depose a Catholic king, James. Despite its profound historical significance with the enactment of the Toleration Act and the Bill of Rights, which imposed severe limits on royal power, the actual revolutionary events were characterised by the relatively modest organisational infrastructure and a very low ideological penetration. The revolution was initiated not by a well-organised social movement but by the seven English aristocrats who issued a formal letter of invitation to William and Mary on behalf of the 'dissatisfied nobility and gentry'. Furthermore, despite the latter-day post-hoc interpretations which attribute too much coherence and strong ideological motivation to this highly contingent set of historical events, there was not much popular support for either of the two sides involved in this conflict. While the majority of the essentially peasant population were not involved in any meaningful way in these events, the gentry and the small merchant strata were eager to side with the ultimate winner regardless of religious affiliations (Jardine 2008: 15). Even the regents, provincial and town rulers of Dutch lands were not particularly keen on William's expedition and had to be persuaded. In other words, the ideological penetration was quite weak. Although the Dutch military force that landed on English soil was quite large, there was very little military engagement between the two opposing sides. The entire revolutionary episode included only two battles (at Wincanton and Reading), resulting in as many as fifty casualties. The financing of the military landing and the government overthrow was not secured through established state structures or revolutionary movements but instead relied on ad hoc loans from the individual bankers such as Francisco Suasso, who lent 2 million guilders to William and Mary for their planned invasion (Cruickshanks 2000). Even though William had put enormous resources in assembling an invading fleet, the underdeveloped transport and communication systems had made the entire operation slow, protracted and confusing. During the conflict, both King James and William were involved in prolonged negotiations with various aristocrats in order to secure their support, with religious commitments playing a secondary role to individual self-interests. Ultimately, the revolution was successful because James lost the support of his military and external powers such as the French monarch did not intervene. Although the entire event was a huge undertaking for its time, both organisational and ideological scaffolds were quite rudimentary.

In contrast, the Jasmine Spring was a revolution that involved large sectors of population ranging from teachers, civil servants and solicitors, workers, students, labour unions and the unemployed. For example, 95 per cent of Tunisia's eight hundred lawyers went on strike in January 2011, thus demonstrating their support for the revolution. The events that unfolded in 2011 were initially sparked by the self-immolation of a street vegetable seller, which galvanised popular movement against the authoritarian regime of Zine el Abidine Ben Ali. The well-organised campaign of civil resistance involved a series of street demonstrations which ultimately forced resignation of Bin Ali (who fled to Saudi Arabia) and his successors. Although the revolutionary movement shared a central goal of ousting the old regime, its support base was ideologically diverse, ranging from conservative and moderate Islamists to nationalist, liberal, socialist and reformist groupings. Since during his twenty-three years in power Ben Ali's establishment cracked down heavily on any form of dissent, much of Tunisian opposition was based either abroad or operated in a clandestine fashion. Despite their pronounced ideological differences, all of these groups demonstrated unity in supporting the key principles of revolution: the toppling of the authoritarian government, the drafting and passing of the new constitution, the organisation of free and fair elections, free speech and assembly and other principles associated with democratic political orders. Although liberal and secular middle-class youth were the vanguard of the revolutionary events, moderate Islamists were just as supportive of the revolutionary goals. Hence despite the external perceptions that ideological issues were not as dominant as economic ones, the available evidence indicates that the dissemination of ideas and images through social media, such as Facebook, Twitter and YouTube,[8] was an essential mechanism for mass mobilisation. In other words, the process of ideologisation, which was in place during the ancient regime, helped politicise large sectors of Tunisian population. While before the modern era most individuals had no organisational nor ideological capacity to get involved in revolutionary action, in the contemporary world, with substantially increased literacy rates, higher educational standards, improved communication networks and access to the international mass media (from Al Jezeera to the BBC) through the Internet, many individuals do have such capacity and can be mobilised for revolutionary action. Since Tunisian society has traditionally been more secular, moderate and economically more developed, it generated conditions for the most successful revolution of the Arab Spring. The strong ideological currents of the Jasmine Spring become quite visible after the revolution, with the two competing ideologies – moderate Islamist, represented by the Ennahda (Renaissance Party), and the secular nationalist, represented by Nidaa Tounes (Call of Tunisia) – dominating the ideological landscape of Tunisia. Hence increased organisational capacity often goes hand in hand with deeper ideological penetration, thus creating conditions where in modernity even small polities can trump much larger premodern entities. Although the Glorious Revolution remains an important symbolic watershed in world history, its ideological penetration and organisational capacity

---

[8] As Goldstone (2014: 119) emphasizes that Tunisia had a quite large middle class and a relatively high percentage of social media users.

were much weaker than those associated with contemporary revolutions such as the Jasmine Spring.

What Motivates Revolutionary Action?

Since all revolutions involve a radical change of organisational structure and/or ideological legitimacy of the regime, there cannot be a revolution without ideology or organisation. However, while organisational break- down and ideological delegitimisation are key preconditions of revolu- tionary experience, successful revolutions also require the ability to tap into the microcosm of everyday social action. In other words, just as with other forms of organised violence, revolutions entail a capacity to inte- grate grand ideological vistas and the large-scale organisational trans- formations with the social dynamics of the grassroots. Hence revolutions often succeed or fail depending on how well organisational and ideo- logical mechanisms are integrated with the microworld of daily inter- actions. This relates to the two different forms of social action: (a) the internal dynamics of small groups of revolutionary enthusiasts; and (b) the popular reception of revolutionary ambitions. Of course, the success- ful revolutionary project depends on the ability of revolutionary enthusi- asts to impart their massage to the wider sectors of the population.

Most revolutions generally simmer and explode at the top of organisa- tional pyramid rather than being caused by the external conspiracies of professional revolutionaries. Yet there are no successful revolutions without dedicated revolutionary movements. Although such movements usually do not cause or bring about revolutionary contexts, they tend to thrive in such unusual social environments. One of the principal features of such movements is their clandestine and conspirational character. Since revolutionaries plot government overthrows and deploy violence against state representatives, their actions are usually proscribed, thus forcing them to operate in a clandestine and secretive fashion. Neverthe- less, this environment of persistent threat, tension, fear of arrest and government intimidation fosters development of small but well- integrated revolutionary cells. Such secretive life in the underground helps enhance ties of solidarity among the members of revolutionary cells, thus making individual members emotionally attuned with their microgroup. What generally characterises such groups is the sense of loyalty, trust and emotional attachment, which all feed into a shared perception of the group's exceptionalism. For example, nineteenth- century revolutionary groups, such as the Italian Carbonari or the Greek Philiki Hetairia, both dedicated to the struggle against imperial rule, were secret fraternities of young men who developed highly intense feelings of attachment to their organisation's goals as well as to each other (della Porta 2013; Billington 1980). Such clandestine groups, which proliferated through Europe in the nineteenth century, have created elaborate initiation rituals and pledged to devote their lives to the organisation's causes. While both ideology and organisational cell-like structure contributed to their strong commitment to the revolutionary activity, it was these micro-level attachments that ultimately proved crucial in revolutionary events. While all such revolutionaries were inspired by a romantic and utopian vision of a world without imperial domination, their commitment was enhanced by the continuous joint action and by 'by the experience of camaraderie within their own small groups' (Billington 1980: 130).

Although revolutionary activity is often perceived through the prism of individual charismatic leaders such as Garibaldi, Che Guevara, Lenin, Mao or Khomeini, single individuals obviously could not mobilise the large-scale support necessary for revolutions. Hence revolutionary action is regularly shaped by smaller networks of dedicated and mutually interdependent groups – the Jacobins, the Bolsheviks, the Sandinistas, etc. Nevertheless, even such groupings are too large to develop genuine and intense ties of solidarity. So the overall cohesion of a particular revolutionary movement depends on the proliferation of very small and internally tight microgroups. Such groups are usually formed either through protracted joint social action or by already existing ties of friendships and kinships. Just as in the case of terrorist and insurgents (Chapter 8), revolutionary activists tend to join revolutionary organisations not as individuals but in groups of two, three or more. In this way, the clandestine nature of revolutionary activism helps bolster already strong emotional ties between revolutionaries engaged in daily face-to-face interaction. As della Porta (2013: 243) argues and documents well: 'Affective focusing is particularly intense in high-risk political activism. Throughout the networks of friends-comrades, friendship reinforces the relevance of political commitment, while political commitment strengthens some friendship ties, and the groups of political friends become closed units'. In other words, microsolidarity is the cornerstone of individual motivation and social action. It is these emotional ties that make revolutionary action possible and meaningful to those involved in such activities. This affective focussing generates a sense of individual responsibility towards one's comrades. In this way, revolutionary cells are internally conceptualised by its members as the nodal points of group morality. In such an environment, loyalty to the wider cause is interdependent with the feelings of attachment to one's friends who are regularly identified through the metaphors of close kinship – they are our brothers and sisters, our family, our children and so on. The intensity of these micro-level attachments is reinforced through hardships. A fallen comrade invokes a moral obligation to continue with the revolutionary activity regardless of the personal cost. The imprisonment of the fellow revolutionary only stimulates greater commitment to the revolutionary cause. In the words of a member of the Italian revolutionary far-left group Prima Linea: 'either we are all outside or we are all inside [prison], because if some of us are out and some of us are in, I don't give up my friends... This means that if my friends had drowned because of a belief that I shared with them, I would decide to drown; ... if they are there and I can't help them, I prefer to be with them' (della Porta 2013: 245).

The direct byproduct of this intensity of emotional attachments within microgroups is a heightened sense of morality. However, by amplifying moral commitments to each other, members of the microgroup decrease their sense of moral responsibility towards the outsiders. In this way, clandestine revolutionary cells acquire features similar to those of isolated religious cults, as both develop sense of moral superiority and elitism. Geographical and social isolation from mainstream society further fosters internal integration and the shared perception of the external world as being morally corrupt and polluted.

This deep internal cohesion of revolutionary cells is a precondition for successful revolutionary activity. Nevertheless, to be fully effective such cells have to be well integrated into the organisational and ideological structure of the revolutionary movement. As studies on revolutions demonstrate, successful movements tend to have a centralised but flexible organisational network structure that links individual cells together and can preserve its clandestine operations while also being capable of mobilising all cells for revolutionary action when the time is ripe (Thomassen 2012; Goodwin 2001). In a similar vein, the successful ideological penetration of revolutionary cells is dependent on the ability of revolutionary organisations to amalgamate the grand macro-ideological narratives with pouches of cell-level microsolidarity. Although this process is frequently ambiguous, contingent and contested, effective revolutionary organisations usually mange to reconcile the micro- and macroworlds and to project macro-level accounts into the emotional attachments of individual cells. In this context, centrifugal ideologisation is rooted in rhetoric that ties microgroup morality, a sense of exceptionalism and deep solidarity with doctrinal macronarratives that speak in the universalist discourses of fraternity or equality. A similar mechanism operates among the wider public too. For revolutions to succeed, it is crucial that macro-ideological narratives are effectively 'translated' into local microstories. The abstract concepts of popular sovereignty, anti-imperialism or liberalism have to be articulated in simple and recognisable terms that correspond to the everyday experience of millions of individuals. For example, the 1979 Iranian Revolution emerged in the context of the Shah's exclusion of clergy from the education, welfare and legal systems while simultaneously attacking traditional bazaar life. All of this galvanised popular resistance, which was articulated through the popular narrative frames of the Shia belief system. Thus the revolutionaries and wider masses were inspired by Shia mythology, which is firmly built on the idea that counterpoises the willing martyr Hussein against the unscrupulous usurper caliph Yazid. In this narrative, the Shah became the modern equivalent of Yazid, and the revolutionaries identified themselves with the martyrdom of Hussein (Skocpol 1982: 271–274). In other words, the local context of the bazaari life was well integrated with the wider ideological discourse that underpinned the Iranian Revolution. While in the Iranian case it is quite clear that both ideology and organisation were central for the revolution, this seems to be less the case with other revolutions.

For example, the 1959 Cuban Revolution is often interpreted as lacking in ideology since Castro's Twenty-Sixth of July Movement embraced Marxism-Leninism only after coming to power. Moreover, since the revolution was initiated by only twelve surviving exiled revolutionaries, the organisational capacity of such a small social movement is also questioned. Hence the materialist explanations of Cuban revolutions tend to stress the economic hardship of the Cuban population and the repressive character of Batista's regime. While it is certainly true that these two factors have contributed to the popular dissatisfaction and have ultimately fostered wider-ranging support for the revolution, they were not the determining causes of revolutionary events. Rather, for revolution to happen it was essential that popular dissatisfaction be channelled by an effective social organisation in possession of coherent ideological doctrine. The Twenty-Sixth of July Movement was well organised and disciplined, maintaining a highly centralised yet flexible hierarchical structure. Although the revolution was a byproduct of structural crises involving severe delegitimisation of Batista's regime, gradual withdrawal of U.S. support, economic collapse and political tensions between the military and the government, the presence of a well-organised revolutionary movement also played an important part. Castro's movement was in existence long before it started its first military operations: by 1952, it had over 1,200 members and large quantities of weaponry (Leonard 1999). Once exiled to Mexico, the Twenty-Sixth of July Movement's members underwent rigorous military and ideological training led by veterans of the Spanish Civil War. Although their initial attempt at invasion was not a success, the movement managed to regroup and reorganise in order to lead protracted guerrilla warfare, which ultimately brought down the Batista's rule. While Castro's movement remained quite small, usually no more than three hundred active fighters, its sophisticated organisation proved decisive in bringing about a successful revolution. In addition to its well-developed organisational capacity, the revolutionary movement was also capable of articulating a coherent, plausible and popularly appealing ideological message. This new doctrine fused the nineteenth-century revolutionary ideas of Jose Marti's anti-imperial nationalism and humanist ideals with twentieth-century notions of emancipation, popular sovereignty, social justice, gender equality, antiracism and social progress. The fact that the revolutionaries were in possession of the pirate radio station Radio Rebelde, the signal of which reached all of Cuba, further helped dissemination of these ideas to the wider audience. Since the Cuban public was highly responsive to these ideas, it was not difficult to depict Batista's regime in terms of being an exploitative puppet of imperial U.S. power. These organisational and ideological structures were shaped extensively by the Twenty-Sixth of July Movement, which proved highly successful in integrating its organisation and ideology with the local grassroots. The evidence for this comes directly from Che Guevara's manual *Guerrilla Warfare* (1961), where he documents his experiences of the Cuban Revolution and emphasises the centrality of revolutionary organisation and ideology. The central organisational and ideological principle was focalism – the idea that a small vanguard of well-organised, ideologically informed, fast-moving armed individuals should lead a revolutionary uprising from the rural areas. In this context, as Guevara (2006: 16) points out: 'the guerrilla band, as an armed nucleus, is the combative vanguard of the people'. To succeed, such a vanguard has to be highly disciplined: '. . . the guerrilla fighter, as the conscious element of the vanguard of the people, must display the moral conduct of a true priest of the desired reform. To the stoicism forced by the difficult conditions of warfare should be added an austerity born of rigid self-control that prevents a single excess, a single slip, whatever the circumstances. The guerrilla soldier should be an ascetic' (Guevara 2006: 49). Nevertheless, what also comes across in the Cuban experience is the link among organisation, ideology and microsolidarity. For example, Guevara (2006: 51) makes indirect yet regular observations about the significance of microgroup attachments: 'taking advantage of the heat of the war – those moments in which human fraternity reaches its greatest intensity – all kinds of cooperative work should be stimulated, as far as the mentality of the local people will allow'. Simply put, just as with other forms of organised violence, revolutions too emerge in the specific historical context that brings together ideology, organisation and microsolidarity.

Conclusion

To say that a revolution is a form of organised violence does not imply that all revolutions inevitably generate a large number of direct human casualties. In fact, most initial revolutionary episodes, from 1789 France and 1917 Russia to the 1989 Velvet revolutions or the 2000s Colour revolutions and many others in-between, were not particularly bloody events. However, this does not mean that such events are unrelated to violent action or that they could have taken place without the context of organised violence. As I argue in this chapter, a conventional, narrow, ahistorical and decontextualised understanding of violence cannot capture the changing long-term dynamics of the revolutionary experience. If one focusses only on the immediate causal relationships between violence and revolution, with violence being conceptualised in terms of intentionality and corporality, then such analyses cannot ascertain the changing and uneven trajectories of revolutionary experiences. Hence to analytically capture these developments, it is paramount to focus on the broader coercive powers of the organisations involved in revolutionary events, for it is the increased coercive capacities of revolutionary organisations as well as the existing states that generate violent outcomes. In this context, violence is a direct product of organisational power, and as the organisational (and ideological) powers grow, so does the potential for violence. This is illustrated well with the cases of the French and Russian revolutions, both of which started with relatively weak revolutionary and state organisations and rather minimal human casualties. Nevertheless, as the revolutionary context unfolded with the continuous substantial increase in coercive organisational and ideological powers, both revolutions ended in instances of mass murder. Hence to fully understand this dramatic social change, it is necessary to focus not only on the direct outcomes of violence but also on the long-term organisational and ideological potential for violence.

7   Genocides

Introduction

Genocide is the most extreme form of organised violence. While wars, revolutions and terrorism bring about images of destruction, carnage and death, the systematic mass murder of mostly unresisting civilians generates a truly horrific impression. As such, the act of genocide is generally regarded as a particularly senseless and heinous crime. However, genocide is not only a crime but also a particular, although extreme, form of social relationship. Hence to fully understand the origins and direction of each genocidal experience, it is necessary to reconstruct the structural contexts, social processes and practices that make genocides possible. While the legal and moral aspects of genocide research have received a great deal of scholarly and public attention, this has still not been the case with the sociological studies of genocide. Although sociologists have produced several comprehensive theories of genocide, their social impact has been limited and genocide is still largely understood as a legal rather than a sociological phenomenon. One of the aims of this chapter is to push the discussion firmly towards sociology. The first section of the chapter provides a sociological understanding of genocide including its social origins. The second section critically examines the leading sociological contributions to the study of this extreme form of organised violence. The final section of the chapter outlines a longue durée sociological approach that attempts to explain the historical dynamics of genocide through the analysis of the organisational, ideological and microsolidary processes.

What Is Genocide?

Unlike most other forms of organised violence, including warfare, terrorism and revolution, genocide is a relatively new concept. The term was coined by a Polish-Jewish lawyer, Raphael Lemkin, in 1943 as an attempt to find an adequate legal description of the unprecedented scale of mass murders of civilians committed during World War II. More specifically, Lemkin wanted to differentiate between the existing judicial categories of war crimes and the Nazis' unparalleled attempt to wipe out entire groups of people, something that Churchill described as 'a crime without a name'. In his *Axis Rule in Occupied Europe* (Lemkin 1944: 79–95), Lemkin defined genocide as 'the destruction of a nation or an ethnic group'. He emphasised that the intention was 'to denote an old practice in its modern development', and also qualified this general statement by specifying that 'genocide does not necessarily mean the immediate destruction of a nation, except when accomplished by mass killings of all members of a nation'. Instead, this concept was 'intended to signify a coordinated plan of different actions aiming at the destruction of essential foundation of the life of national groups, with the aim of annihilating the groups themselves'. As Shaw (2007: 18–36) rightly insists, Lemkin's original concept was quite broad, encompassing much more than a physical destruction of collectivities. For Lemkin (1944: 79), genocide referred to a variety of other processes, including the planned 'disintegration of the political and social institutions, of culture, language, national feelings, religion, and the economic existence of national groups, and the destruction of the personal security, liberty, health, dignity . . . .'

In addition to coining the term, Lemkin was also a highly effective campaigner who managed to persuade diplomats of the leading states to institutionalise this concept in the 1948 UN convention. Nevertheless, after prolonged wrangling between the representatives of major powers about the exact wording of this convention, the agreement was reached and Article 2 of the Convention on the Prevention and Punishment of the Crime of Genocide defines genocide as an act 'committed with intent to destroy, in whole or in part, a national, ethnical, racial or religious group'. The convention identifies five different forms of action that characterise genocide: (1) killing members of a specific group; (2) causing grave bodily or mental harm to members of that group; (3) intentionally forcing on that group conditions of life calculated to cause its physical destruction in whole or in part; (4) imposing measures aimed to prevent births within that group; and (5) transferring children of that group to another group by force.

Although the UN convention did include the substance of Lemkin's general proposal, it also significantly modified the meaning of this concept. For one thing, the definition adopted an extremely broad understanding of this phenomenon, as the term 'in part' is quite ambiguous, allowing for a great variation in the scale of destruction. While it is apparent that the Holocaust easily qualifies as an instance of genocide, such a wide definition has opened almost unlimited possibility for many other historical cases to make a similar claim. It is far from clear what exactly would count as 'destruction in part'. Does this refer to the clear intention to annihilate an entire group which was not achieved because of the group's resistance or external intervention? Or perhaps this implies that the aim always was a partial destruction in order to frighten the group or to force them to leave a particular territory? More importantly, this definition does not tell us how substantive 'the part' has to be. Is it enough to kill a few hundred individuals or is thousands or hundreds of thousands? For example, as throughout history ethnic categorisations have often been ambiguous, provisional and highly contingent it is far from obvious what exactly constitutes an ethnic group. If this label is applied to any kinship-related collectivity, would this suggest that the destruction of a small village of a 55 kin-related individuals could qualify as a genocide?

Paradoxically, while this definition widened the scope of genocidal action, the content of what constitutes genocide has simultaneously been narrowed. Shaw (2007: 22) has argued convincingly that the UN convention as well as much of the existing scholarship on genocide has focussed almost exclusively on the physical and biological destruction of groups while paying little or no attention to the broader contexts of social destruction. As he emphasises: 'The Nazis did not aim simply to kill subject peoples, even the Jews: they aimed to destroy their ways of life and social institutions'. Hence, instead of focussing on the means of destruction, as the UN Convention does, the point is to look at the aims that proceed these means: 'It was the other way round: when physical destruction came to be a distinct, eventually overriding end, this was an extreme development of pre-existing Nazi policies of social destruction' (Shaw 2007: 22).

In addition to this overwhelming focus on physical destruction, the UN definition also provides an unusually restricted understanding in terms of social targets of genocide. For example, Article 2 of the UN Convention makes no reference to killings or other forms of violent action in relation to ideological, political, class or gender reasons. These glaring definitional omissions were not accidental; they were the direct legacy of the post–World War II geopolitical arrangements. While the overemphasis on physical destruction allowed the Allies to avoid any responsibility for the mass expulsions of German civilians after World War II, the exclusion of references to class and political ideology prevented any legal consequences for Stalin's or Mao's internal purges. Since in 1945 close to 15 million German civilians had been forcibly removed, and some also killed in this process, from various European countries, maintaining a more inclusive definition of genocide would make the Allies culpable of criminal acts (Schabas 2009). Similarly, the restrictive definition also protected the rulers of communist states as the existing legal formulation left no room to account for Stalin's 1938–1939 Great Purge of 'kulaks', intellectuals and 'western spies', which amounted to about 1 million deaths; for Mao's responsibility for mass starvation of Chinese citizens during the Great Leap Forward, resulting in no fewer than 18 million casualties (and possibly 30 million); or for the latter-day ideological killing fields of the Khmer Rouge amounting to at least 1.5 million direct casualties (White 2012).

The long-term consequence of such restricted wording of Article 2 is the never-ending debate over which historical and contemporary cases count as genocide and which ones fall short of this category. There are thousands of books written to make a case that 'our tragedy' clearly constitutes genocide while the claims of 'our hostile neighbours' do not merit such designation. In some respects, the term 'genocide' has become as contested as the term 'terrorism', whereby the use of these terms provides justification for contemporary political action. While naming various forms of political dissent as 'terrorism' allows state authorities to clamp down on civil society groups and opposition, the claim to be a victim of genocide provides a powerful symbolic weapon to delegitimise any political action of those whose predecessors were tainted by such a horrible crime.

To move away from these highly politicised debates, it is crucial to differentiate between the legal and sociological concepts of genocide. It is apparent that this term originated in the judiciary context and was conceived as an attempt to legally define a particular form of crime. Nevertheless, as the concept aims to describe specific social processes involving the use of violence to create a different form of social order, it inevitably refers to a distinct sociological phenomenon. Hence genocide is simultaneously a legal and a sociological category. However, as legal and sociological categories differ substantially, there is a profound tension between the two understandings of this phenomenon. The legal meaning of genocide is centred on the culpability of perpetuators, the grievances of the genocide survivors and the families of the victims as well as the pursuit of justice in national and international courts. Thus the focus is on human agency, intentionality and the allocation of responsibility for violent acts. Such an approach aims to deliberately decontextualise the events that have led to genocidal outcomes and centres on identifying the legality and criminality of decisions and actions of specific individuals. For example, Ljubiša Beara was convicted of the 1995 Srebrenica genocide by the International Criminal Tribunal for the

Former Yugoslavia (ICTY) in 2010 on the basis that he 'was the most senior officer of the Security Branch and had the clearest overall picture of the mass scale and scope of the killing operation ... he became, in the opinion of the Trail Chamber, a driving force behind the murder enterprise' (ICTY 2010). In this legal judgement, the structural context is secondary; it is taken into account only as far as it impacts on the individual responsibility of the accused. Hence the central question here is: Who is responsible for genocide?

In contrast, the focus of sociological understandings is on the broader historical and social contexts that make genocides possible. Instead of individual culpability, the emphasis is on the variety of processes that have ultimately resulted in genocidal outcomes. While not denying the role of powerful individuals to initiate, coordinate and order genocidal acts, the main aim is to contextualise socially such events in order to understand their long-term dynamics. Thus instead of straightforward simple intentionality, premeditated murderous plans and preordained genocidal scenarios, sociological analyses explore the contingent, dynamic and complex trajectories of genocides. In this context, the role of agency is not replaced by structural conditions; rather, this becomes a question of empirical validation. Sociologists recognise that any social action, including a genocidal one, is a product of both agency and structure. What matters is which of these processes carries a greater explanatory strength. For example, it is now clear that the Rwandan genocide was spearheaded by the Akazu, a Hutu extremist grouping built around the relatives and close friends of the late Rwandan president Juvenal Habyarimana and his highly influential wife Agatha Habyarimana. Nevertheless, the genocide could not happen if it was not for the combination of the specific geopolitical, economic and ideological factors that coalesced in 1994. Hence, although the legal and moral responsibility for genocide lies squarely with the prominent members of the Akuzu, the sociological trajectory of the Rwandan genocide owes much more to specific structural contexts (Mann 2005; Mamdani 2001; Malešević 2006). In other words, for sociological analyses the key question is not who is culpable, but why genocides happen.

This chapter focusses on the sociological understandings of genocide. Nevertheless, even at this analytical level there is no consensus about what constitutes genocide and how genocides differ from alternative concepts such as ethnic cleansing, ethnocide, democide, gendercide, politicide, classicide, urbicide, and murderous cleansing, among others.

Since the 1990s wars in the former Yugoslavia, much of the debate has focussed on distinguishing genocide from ethnic cleansing. Hence some scholars sharply differentiate between the two concepts (Schabas 2009;

Blecher 2005; Hayden 1996), while others find this distinction problematic, arguing that the notion of ethnic cleansing is no more than a political euphemism coined to deflect media attention from ongoing, actual genocides (Bećirević 2014; Blum et al. 2007). However, most scholars accept that although the two phenomena exhibit some different features, it is often difficult to differentiate between the two as ethnic cleansings might be an early stage of genocide or lead directly towards genocidal action (Mann 2005; Naimark 2001). For example, Gellately and Kiernan (2003: 19–20) argue that genocide and ethnic cleansing are partially distinct in the sense that ethnic cleansing involves 'the "purification" of a territory, not necessarily population', and that deportation of population from a specific territory can but does not have to end in a fully fledged genocide.

Other scholars insist on a finer gradation between the different types of extreme collective violent action. Harff and Gurr (1988) make a distinction between genocides and politicides. In their view, genocide is conceptualised as state-organised murders based on victims ethnic, racial, national or religious identities, whereas politicides are state-sponsored killings centred on victims' political opposition to the regime or in terms of their social position within the society. Furthermore, Harff and Gurr distinguish between hegemonial and xenophobic genocides and among retributive, repressive, revolutionary and hegemonial politicides.

Michael Mann (2005: 10–18) offers an even more elaborate model. He differentiates between different types of violent group action (ranging from institutional coercion to premeditated mass killings) and types of group cleansing (from none to partial to total). The combination of these two scales produces a large number of categories ranging from mild discrimination, language restrictions and cultural suppression to more extreme actions such as forced conversions, politicide, classicide, ethnocide and genocide. Mann deploys the term 'murderous ethnic cleansing' to denote the variety of radical violent social actions. Among the most extreme are the intended mass killings, including classicide, defined as 'intended mass killing of entire classes'; politicide, understood as intended killings of an enemy's group leadership and potential leadership groups; and genocide, conceptualised as an intentional policy aiming to 'wipe out an entire group, not only physically but also culturally (destroying its churches, libraries, museums, street names)' (Mann 2005: 17).

There is no doubt that such fine-grained typologies are useful in the sense that they emphasise the complexity and nuances of extreme violent action. However, as Shaw (2007: 64) argues, having too many concepts can also obscure the significance of the phenomenon: 'the invention of new terms threatens ... to delineate as separate phenomena types of action that belong to genocide'. In his view, all these new concepts 'are, in fact, the many sides of genocide'. For Shaw (2007: 78), genocide is best conceptualised as 'the master-concept' which can be applied not just to ethnic groups and nations but 'to cover the destruction of any type of people or any group'. Thus he defines genocide as a 'violent conflict, in which the armed, organised side engages in intentional social destruction of the unarmed, group side – which the latter necessarily resists' (Shaw 2007: 92).

Even though the term 'genocide' was originally coined to make sense of extreme violence against civilians based on their ethnic or national designation, it makes sense to follow in part Shaw's recommendation and treat genocide as a generic metaconcept that incorporates a variety of more specific radical types of organised violent action against civilian populations. Shaw is also right that the more comprehensive sociological understanding of genocidal processes also has to include noncorporal actions. Just as with the other forms of organised violence, genocides involve a large gamut of acts that are not centred only on the destruction of physical bodies but on the devastation of social relations; cultural, economic and political institutions; historical memory; and many other products of shared collective action.

Another highly valuable feature of this definition, which Shaw shares with Leven (2005), is the shift away from the idea of groups. An overwhelming majority of genocide definitions, both legal and sociological, insist that genocides involve systematic destruction of ethnic, national, racial, religious and other groups. Nevertheless, since Weber (1968), sociologists have been aware that ethnicity, nation, race or religion are forms of social relationships, not ingrained static properties. Instead of reifying cultural markers, it is critical to recognise that the social world is dynamic and fuzzy. In other words, social categories such as 'Jew', 'Tutsi' or 'Croat' are not clearly bounded and fixed entities. Instead, as Weber demonstrates, even when category affiliation is based on a particular belief in a shared common descent, this cultural resource is activated only through socially meaningful collective action (Malešević 2004: 24–28; Brubaker 2004). The Nazis had tremendous difficulty in identifying who is and is not a Jew, as there were no objective parameters to differentiate 'Aryan' Germans from German-speaking secular Jews. In this sense, defining individuals as members of specific and mutually exclusive groups is one of the key ideological prerequisites for genocidal actions. It is the perpetrators of such actions who coercively transform social categories into fixed groups. While many citizens of early-twentieth-century Germany did not see themselves as Jews, the Nuremberg laws and other coercive acts have made them into a clearly bonded group of Jews. Hence, to understand the social dynamics of genocide it is crucial to move away from the notion of physical groupness: 'because groups are social constructions, they can be neither constituted nor destroyed simply through the bodies of their individual members' (Shaw 2007: 106).

However, what is missing in Shaw's definition are three other variables: (a) the recognition that genocide is generally a phenomenon premised on a specific, long-term, historical logic; (b) that although most genocidal processes involve a substantial degree of intentionality, there is more to genocide than intentional acts; and (c) genocide differs from other forms of organised violence in terms of its scale and its target.

Firstly, Shaw's definition of genocide as a violent conflict of armed and organised side against unarmed civilians implies that genocides occur in a historical vacuum. This definition does not say anything about the specific historical contexts and as such cannot adequately capture the phenomenon of genocide proliferation in the modern era. As will be argued later in this chapter, genocidal action presupposes a degree of organisational complexity and ideological penetration that simply did not exist in the premodern world. It is crucial to explain why genocides occur only under specific historical conditions.

Secondly, to define genocide solely in terms of intentional social destruction leaves out the possibility of indirect mass murder caused by the continuous reckless behaviour of various social organisations. For example, the unprecedented decimation of native populations in North and South America and Australia was only in part caused by intentional, planned and organised genocidal actions. For example, the German general von Trotha's spearheading of the Herero and Nama genocide in South East Africa between 1904 and 1907 resulted in as many as one hundred thousand direct casualties (Olusoga and Erichsen 2010). Most victims were chased to Namib Desert and were then prevented from leaving in order to die from thirst. Von Throtha's statements made clear that this was deliberate policy: 'I believe that the nation as such should be annihilated, or, if this was not possible by tactical measures, have to be expelled from the country. ... This will be possible if the water-holes from Grootfontein to Gobabis are occupied. The constant movement of our troops will enable us to find the small groups of nation who have moved backwards and destroy them gradually' (Mamdani 2001:: 11). However, most genocidal action in the imperial colonies was undertaken indirectly through the destruction of the native habitat; the spread of European diseases; and the introduction of new, often parasitic, animals and crops. In this way, the populations of the Americas and Australia and some parts of Africa and Asia were completely decimated. In regions of North America, where the majority of European settlers moved, 90 per cent of the native population died. In Australia, by 1920s only 20 per cent of the original Aboriginal population survived (Mann 2005: 76; Smith 1980: 69–70). As Mann (2005: 76) points out, the pre-Columbian native population of what is today the United States was somewhere between 4 to 9 million, while 'in the US Census of 1900 there were only 237,000 Indians, a loss of 95%'. The speed and scale of social destruction were most visible in California, where the 1849 gold rush intensified mass slaughter: 'By 1860, after 10 years of statehood, Californian Indians numbered only 31,000 – an 80 percent loss rate over only 12 years! The Third Reich also lasted 12 years and killed 70 percent of European Jews' (Mann 2005: 76). Hence, the more comprehensive definition of genocide has to incorporate this type of indirect violent action.

Thirdly, Shaw does not differentiate between small-scale ad hoc violent conflicts against civilians and large-scale social destruction driven by the particular ideological ambitions. In this sense, his definition displays a degree of vagueness that also characterises the UN Convention's Article 2. Obviously there is a big difference between the ad hoc total destruction of a small Vietnamese village organised by a revenge-seeking rogue U.S. military platoon and an ideologically and organisationally elaborate attempt to annihilate millions of individuals on the basis of their cultural or biological descent. While in legal terms both of these events might carry an identical designation of 'genocide', in the sociological sense it is important to differentiate between the two.

Taking all these caveats into an account, I would define genocide as a historically specific and an extreme form of organised violence involving armed and ideologically committed social organisations engaged in social destruction of unarmed populations, resulting in mass-scale human casualties and the devastation of social relations and the corresponding cultural infrastructure.

The Social Origins of Genocide

Genocide is universally acknowledged as the most extreme form of organised violence. It is also clear that while this concept is only seventy years old, the social processes it aims to define are substantially older than that. Nevertheless, scholars are sharply polarised on the issue of how old this phenomenon is. There is a general recognition that the mass murder, the coercive prevention of births, large-scale rapes, the abductions of children from their parents and the premeditated deprivation of entire collectivities have been in existence for the past ten thousand years.

However, there is no agreement on the question of whether such forms of violent action constitute genocide or not. For some analysts, there is no substantial difference between premodern and modern-day mass murders. For example, Kuper (1981: 9) insists that the historical record indicates that genocide has been around for very long time: 'the word is new, the concept is ancient'. Smith (1987: 21) is also adamant that 'genocide has existed in all periods of history'.

Many scholars point out that the earliest written records such as the epic *Gilgamesh*, Homer's *Iliad* and *Odyssey* or the Old Testament contain extensive descriptions of killings that might indicate presence of genocides in prehistory and very early history. For example, in *Iliad* (book IV), Agamemnon addresses Menelaus with the following words: 'My dear Menelaus, why are you so chary of taking men's lives? Did the Trojans treat you as handsomely as that when they stayed in your house? No: we are not going to leave a single one of them alive, down to the babies in their mothers' wombs – not even they must live. The whole people must be wiped out of existence, and none be left to think of them and shed a tear'. Similarly, the Hebrew Bible is full of extremely violent accounts where large groups of innocent civilians are slaughtered. Thus in 1 Samuel 15:2–3, the vengeful deity proclaims: 'I will punish the Amalekites for what they did in opposing the Israelites when they came up out of Egypt. Now go and attack Amalek, and utterly destroy all they have: do not spare them, but kill both man and woman, child and infant, ox and sheep, camel and donkey'. Nevertheless, as argued in Chapter 3, such literary texts cannot be taken at face value since rather than being accurate descriptions of reality, their purpose was often to provide hyperbolic images serving as powerful pedagogical devices. The aim was not to offer a truthful account of reality but to frighten, enlighten and amaze their audiences.

More evidence-based research has focussed on the verified cases of mass murders in early history. The large-scale Assyrian slaughter of Babylonians and Jews in the seventh century BCE and the Roman destruction of Carthage in the second century BCE stand out as the exemplary cases (Kiernan 2009; Jonasson and Bjornson 1998; Bell-Fialkoff 1996). While the Assyrian case is depicted in the literary texts such as the Hebrew Bible (the Books of Isaiah and Kings) these events were also recorded in the Assyrians' own bas-reliefs and inscriptions. Although this evidence is very fragmented and contested, it seems that the Assyrian armies were involved in at least two cases of mass slaughter after the prolonged sieges of Babylon (689 BCE) and Jerusalem (701 BCE). These violent attacks resulted in the mass murders of soldiers and civilians. In a similar fashion, the obliteration of Carthage in the

Third Punic War is a well-documented case of mass killings involving a large number of civilians. Here too the killings came about after a prolonged three-year siege of the town. Following the military victory, Roman soldiers destroyed all the buildings and city walls and burned the city for seventeen days.[1] Nevertheless, while these two cases represent examples of excessive violence against the civilians, they lack many organisational and ideological features of genocide. For one thing, unlike genocides, which focus on the annihilation of individuals on the basis of *who* they are, these mass killings were quite traditional in a sense of targeting people for *where* they were. In both instances, the centre of attention was territorial conquest, not ideological commitment to obliterating individuals on the basis of their ethnicity. This is quite apparent from the fact that rather than killing fifty thousand Carthaginians who survived the siege, the Roman soldiers sold these individuals into slavery, which was the standard practice with the war prisoners at that time (Scullard 2002: 316). Similarly, the Assyrian army was not driven by ambition to obliterate all Jews or Babylonians. The emphasis was on territory or material resources. As Oded (1979) and Mann (2005) show, the Assyrian military was specialised in deportations, being capable of deporting over a million individuals. These deportations 'eliminated troublesome states, not peoples. Elites and soldiers might be killed or enslaved, the images and statues of the rebels' gods were smashed to destroy the ideology of their state. But people were valuable resources, and deportations helped rebuild Assyria' (Mann 2005: 41). For another thing, both of these cases are quite typical of premodern large-scale slaughters as the killing of civilians was not accompanied by the committed ideological destruction of their culture. While towns were often burned and local deities were desecrated after major battles, there was no prolonged commitment to annihilate the entire cultural structure of such societies. Hence the Jewish, Babylonian and Punic cultural influences remained strong long after these slaughters, as both Assyrian and Roman administrators tolerated such cultural practices.

Other scholars who pursue a similar argument that genocides are ancient practice tend to focus on the religious pogroms and organised mass killings of people on the basis of their incongruent belief systems. Thus Goldhagen (2009), Kiernan (2009) and Freeman (1995), among others, insist that the slaughter and expulsion of Jews, Muslims (Moors) and recent converts to Christianity (*conversos*) in fifteenth-century Reconquista Spain, the murder of Protestant Huguenots in sixteenth-

---

[1] Although it seems that most civilians died from hunger during the siege rather than being killed by the Roman soldiers.

century France or Oliver Cromwell's religious cleansing of the Catholic population in seventeenth-century Ireland indicate that the practice of genocide was widespread before modernity. The religious wars involving the Crusades, the protracted struggle with the Moors over Jerusalem, and the prolonged violence between the Muslim Ottoman power and European Christian empires, as well as the intra-Christian religious violence among Catholics, Protestants and the Eastern Orthodox, have all been identified as causing numerous instances of civilian massacres. For example, the Thirty Years' War (1618–1648) resulted in a huge number of civilian casualties, with the population of the Holy Roman Empire declining by up to 4 million, or 20 per cent (Parker 1984). In all of these cases, one encounters large-scale killings of individuals on the basis of their religious affiliation.

While religious conflicts can intensify a sense of group attachments to the point of deliberate murderous targeting of individuals on the basis of their faith, it is only in the late-eighteenth century and early-nineteenth century that such acts could acquire the ideological and organisational underpinning to become mass practices. In the religious wars of early history, large-scale cleansings of individuals who belong to the 'wrong' faith are quite rare. Instead, the rulers of traditional empires preferred to convert and assimilate the elites of conquered lands while largely ignoring the rest of population (Levene 2005; Mann 2005). Typical examples were the Ottoman conquests of Bosnia and Albania, where the aristocracy converted to Islam en masse and largely retained their privileged positions. The main issue here is that in premodern contexts, religion is still conceptualised as a belief system rather than an ingrained badge of one's identity, meaning that as long as one converts, one's soul can be 'saved' and there is no organisational need for mass slaughter. It is only in the later periods that religious affiliation acquires ethnic and racial overtones. This is already visible in the later stages of religious massacres of Jews, Muslims and recent converts in Reconquista Spain. While initially the focus was on forced expulsions and conversions in the latter period, even a fully fledged conversion was no guarantee that one's life would be spared. This gradual shift from religion as belief to religion as an ascribed identitarian category was fuelled by elite conflicts within the Catholic establishment, and the aristocracy who used this issue as an opportunity to establish their power by denouncing their rival aristocrats as having *converso* roots (Perez 2006). This practice was also present to some extent in other cases of religious cleansing in Ireland, France and other European states. Nevertheless, in most instances religious conflict did not escalate in the direction of genocide. Instead, such violent episodes were largely orchestrated and contained by the aristocratic elites, and only rarely would they acquire prolonged popular support. Although salvation religions fostered a degree of proto-ideological unity, this was still the world dominated by sharp and rigid forms of social stratification where inborn social status easily overpowered any attempt at horizontally solidarity. As Mann (2005: 42) puts it nicely: 'States belonged not to the people, but to princes and aristocrats. Souls but not bodies were democratised ...'. Hence, while the late-sixteenth, seventeenth and early-eighteenth centuries witnessed a gradual shift towards a social environment conducive for the mass killing of civilians in some parts of Europe, there was still neither organisational capacity nor ideological penetration that would make proliferation of genocide possible.

In sharp contrast to these primordialist approaches, most sociological theories of genocide argue that genocide is a modern phenomenon (Mann 2005; Levene 2005; Bauman 1989). What distinguishes genocides from premodern massacres of civilians is their systematic, ideologically articulated, technologically effective, centralised and state-run character. While most large-scale murders of civilians in the traditional world were ad hoc, random, patchy, technologically feeble and with rather weak ideological grounding, modern-day genocidal acts entail sophisticated organisation, complex division of labour, meritocratic hierarchies, centralised authorities, elaborate doctrinal justification, advanced technology and many other elements of modernity.

In *Modernity and the Holocaust*, Bauman (1989) offered the first sustained modernist sociological account of genocide. Although his focus was almost exclusively on the Nazi extermination of European Jews, his intention was to articulate a more general argument about the modern foundations of genocidal projects. For Bauman, the inherent modernity of the Holocaust stems from its engineering ambitions and ideological blueprints aimed at bringing about a completely new world. Although the Nazi utopia of racial hierarchies and eugenic purity is often perceived as a fluke aberration and a regression from Europe's enlightened march forward, for Bauman the Nazi project too was a child of the Enlightenment. He argues that unlike the premodern pogroms and ad hoc massacres of Jews associated with the morbid rituals and individual instances of brutal rage, the 'Final Solution' was a systematic programme aimed at implementing a blueprint for a new world. Whereas the premodern pogroms were simple expressions of individual rage and hate, modern genocides are ideologically articulated and instrumentally executed exercises in social engineering. For Bauman, genocide is a modern project in two senses: (a) it entails rationally envisaged grand vistas; and (b) its implementation is dependent on the use of advanced technology and organisation. In his view, in genocides the principal ambition is not to capture one's territory or murder as many disliked enemies as possible; instead, the focus is on the implementation of the specific ideological design of the perfect social order. In this context, the genocidal apparatus is deployed in a similar way to how a gardener intentionally uses bleach or vinegar to destroy grubby garden weeds: as Jews, Roma Gypsies, Slavs, homosexuals and the disabled did not fit into this Nazi racial utopia, they had to be removed in the same way weeds are cleansed to create a perfect garden. Hence the Holocaust is a direct byproduct of an Enlightenment-induced ambition to create a perfect social order.

For Bauman, this modernist obsession is well reflected in the execution of the Final Solution, which was accomplished relying on conventional bureaucratic mechanisms and routines. The same principle of instrumental rationality that operates in private corporations, modern factories or state administration was utilised in the extermination camps of the Nazi regime: 'Rather than producing goods, the raw material was human beings and the end product was death, so many units per day marked carefully on the manager's production charts. The chimneys, the very symbol of the modern factory system, poured forth acrid smoke produced by burning human flesh. The brilliantly organised railroad grid of modern Europe carried a new kind of raw material to the factories' (Bauman 1989: 8).

Although Michael Mann shares Bauman's view that the institution of genocide is a product of modernity, his attention is less on the role of instrumental rationality and utopian vistas and much more on the macrosociological processes that produce genocidal outcomes. While both Bauman and Mann see the modern state as the principal vehicle of mass murder, their explanations of the role that states play in genocide are quite different. In contrast to Bauman, for whom territorial conquests and rival ideological vistas play a marginal role in the Holocaust, for Mann genocide often emerges in the context of geopolitical instability and competing ideological projects. Moreover, to understand the modernity of genocide, one has also to explore the significance of the society-wide modes of legitimation, most of which invoke the notion of popular rule. Therefore, for Mann (2005: 33) genocidal politics is often the outcome of situations 'where powerful groups within two ethnic groups aim at legitimate and achievable rival states "in the name of the people" over the same territory, and the weaker is aided from outside'. Mann advances a counterintuitive argument that genocides rarely, if ever, occur under authoritarian rule but instead are regularly the side-effect of incomplete democratisation. Mann's argument rests on the idea that premodern rulers did not engage in genocides because they did not derive their political legitimacy from the notion of popular sovereignty. In contrast, modern-day social orders entail such a form of legitimacy. Nevertheless, the idea of 'in the name of the people' is ambiguous in a sense that it can be interpreted in an ethnic or demotic sense (ethnos versus demos). In a geopolitically unstable environment with competing state-building projects, the people's rule often ends up as a call for ethnic homogenisation, creating a situation where violence against others is legitimised through nominally 'democratic' means. Hence for Mann genocides often emerge as 'the dark side of democracy'. Sometimes this is achieved indirectly, as when former imperial states such as Britain, France or Netherlands or their white dominions (the United States, Canada, Australia or South Africa) have accomplished national homogenisation through ethnic cleansing in their colonial possessions. In other instances, genocides have taken place more directly, as the nationalising states have killed and displaced ethnically diverse populations inhabiting their territories (i.e. Turkey, Germany, Rwanda, the former Yugoslavia, etc.). In all of these and other cases, genocide came as a corollary of the competing state ambitions of modernising and nationalising states. The 1915 genocide of the Armenian population did not happen under the authoritarian, Islamist but culturally diverse Ottoman Empire: instead, the genocide was undertaken by the modernist, secular and liberal Young Turks. Thus for Mann genocidal outcomes entail the presence of several factors, including the modernising, democratising and nationalising state; the deep divisions within the political and other elites; internal and external radicalisation caused by changed geopolitical pressures, often culminating in warfare.

A number of other scholars (Levene 2005; Weitz 2003; Kaye and Strath 2000) follow a similar line of argument by emphasising the modern character of genocidal experience. For example, for Levene (2005) genocides are modern events produced by several structural contingencies, including the intensive state building, ideological radicalisation and the presence of warfare. In his own words: 'genocide occurs when a state, perceiving the integrity of its agenda to be threatened by an aggregate population – defined by the state as an organic collectivity, or series of collectivities – seeks to remedy the situation by the systematic, en masse physical elimination of that aggregate, *in toto*, or until it is no longer perceived to represent a threat' (Levene 2005: 35).

The modernists also tend to differ from the primodialists in a sense that in their explanations the focus is more on structural contexts and less on the choices made by individual actors. Thus, in addition to the temporal axis of divide (i.e. are genocides ancient or modern), there is also a profound disagreement over the question of what generates geno-cidal action. While most primordialists (Dadrian 1995; Goldhagen 2009; Scheff 1994; Bećirević 2014) explain genocides through the prism of individual or collective intentions and premediated plans, modernists tend to emphasise contingent and gradual radicalisation leading ultim-ately to genocidal outcomes. For example, some insist that already in the 1920s Hitler had devised a plan to annihilate all European Jews; that Mehmed Talaat and Ismail Enver were committed to the genocide of Armenians long before they came to power in Turkey; and that Slobodan Milošević and Radovan Karadžić had a clear prewar plan to murderously cleanse Bosnian Muslims from Eastern Bosnia (Scheff 1994; Bećirević 2014; Dadrian 1995). In contrast, most historical sociologists are scep-tical of such claims, arguing that the path to genocides is much more complex and dependent on the changing social environment. For Mann (2005) and Shaw (2007, 2003), genocides transpire in dramatically changed geopolitical contexts. Analysing all the cases of twentieth-century genocides, Mann demonstrates that with the exception of Nazi Germany in all other instances genocides were perpetuated by social movements that originally set off as groups infused by democratic and even liberal ideals. Nevertheless, as the social conditions worsened, often followed by destructive warfare, these ideals were gradually perverted, leading to radicalisation and extremist policies. Moreover, it seems that in most cases the decisions to pursue genocide were a result of an organisational failure to 'solve' ethnic, racial, religious or ideological issues by other means. Since genocides generally happen in times of war, when the enemy side is often dehumanised and widely perceived as an imminent danger, such radicalisation is more likely to happen. In this sense, as Shaw (2007) argues, genocides could be conceptualised as a particular form of warfare where specific groups are redefined and violently targeted as the enemy of the state: 'when armed military force is being extensively used against organized armed enemies, then it is easier for leaders to take the extraordinary, generally illegitimate steps towards also using armed force against social groups as such' (Shaw 2003: 44). None of this is to say that individual decision making does not matter. Obviously political and military leaders are ultimately responsible for genocides. However, focussing exclusively on the role of individual agents cannot help us yield coherent and subtle sociological explanations. Such an approach can in fact be counterproductive in both legal and sociological senses, as it would ultimately fix blame on a very small number of individuals, thus proving unable to understand the large-scale societal transformations that make large numbers of individ-uals complicit in genocidal episodes.

There is no doubt that the modernist theories of genocide offer sociologically more plausible accounts than the primordial approaches. It is crucial to differentiate between premodern mass killings and modern-day ideological projects set on the extermination of entire collectivities. It is also important to study these phenomena not as fixed and static blueprints devised and implemented by pathological personalities but to see genocides as complex, contingent and contradictory dynamic processes shaped by structural changes and collective action. Nevertheless, while the modernist approaches represent a great advancement when compared to their primordialist counterparts, they are not immune to criticisms. One of the standard critiques is that modernists have difficulty explaining why and how exactly genocides emerge in modernity. As Huchinson (1994) claims, in the context of the rise of nationalism, strong modernist arguments are built on a problematic view of the premodern world as an explanatory tabula rasa. In other words, for many modernists, it is only modernity that matters, and everything that has happened before has little sociological relevance. However, it is important to recognise that although genocide is a quintessentially modern phenomenon, it is not something that just suddenly and unexpectedly appears on the historical stage in the late-nineteenth and early-twentieth centuries. Instead, to fully understand its social origins and trajectory, it is crucial to undertake a longue durée analysis to historically situate the development and expansion of genocide throughout the world.

Another criticism of modernist accounts is their apparent inability to explain the motives of social agents involved in genocidal processes. Simply put, such theories offer overly structuralist interpretations of historical reality. While it is certainly true that genocides are first and foremost products of structural contingencies, this in itself should not preclude finding out how social actors are mobilised to take part actively in such violent acts or to remain passive bystanders. While Mann, Shaw and Bauman tell us great deal about the role of ideological blueprints, state organisation, geopolitics and technology, there is very little information about social mechanisms that transform ordinary individuals into mass murderers. Even when the focus is on individual motivation, such as in Bauman's use of Milgram experiments or Mann's analysis of the 'core constituencies' of radicalism, providing a social profile of the perpetuators, their general arguments remain staunchly structuralist. What is missing in these studies is a more tangible link between the macro- and microprocesses.

Finally, the modernist approaches, and in particular that of Bauman, have been recently challenged by scholars of genocide who provide empirical evidence that most victims of Nazi killings did not die in the concentration and extermination camps but through the more traditional shootings and butchery throughout occupied Europe and particularly Eastern Europe. As Gerwarth (2014: 27) points out, many recent studies of the Holocaust question 'the long-held belief that the genocide was bureaucratic, impersonal, and sanitized – after all, a substantial number of those murdered in the Holocaust were killed by "ordinary men" in face to face shootings rather than in the SS-controlled death factories of Auschwitz'. In a similar vein, more recent genocides such as in Rwanda and Bosnia have often been depicted as lacking the modernist ethos, ideology, technology and organisation. For example, critics have pointed out repeatedly that most killings of Hutus and disloyal Tutsis were undertaken by direct physical confrontations with individual machetes rather than the gas chambers, for example, serving as the key weapon of mass murder. In order to provide a coherent answer to these challenging criticisms, it is important to rethink the conventional modernist inter- pretations of organisational and ideological power.

Beyond the Conventional Modernism: Genocide in the Longue Durée

Organisational Capacity

One of the most memorable and equally chilling images from Bauman's (1989) book is the depiction of the extermination camps as resembling modern-day factories. In his view, modern plastic or car factories and Auschwitz operated according to very similar principles: the complex division of labour, production lines, highly developed systems of com- munication and transport of goods, production charts, management planning, supply and processing of raw materials and so on. In this image, the chimney stands as a symbol of industrial power and a modern way of life. The fact that the chimney smoke might equally be generated by the burning of rubber or human flesh reflects for Bauman the key features of modernity: the prioritisation of instrumental rationality and technological efficiency ahead of any ethical principles. Although this is a powerful image, it does not capture fully the central characteristics of genocidal projects. For one thing, Bauman overestimates the functional- ity and efficiency of corporate systems. In his view, the Holocaust was possible because organisational discipline replaced a sense of moral responsibility, allowing ordinary individuals to substitute feelings of empathy with those of unquestioned loyalty towards their organisations. Hence by obeying the orders and by focussing only on their small professional tasks, individuals did not have to engage with the grand genocidal project. In this view, loyalty is linked to the instrumental efficiency of the system as a whole. Since the Nazi state was an effective, well-organised and prosperous one, it could, according to this view, successfully embark on such a gigantic project. Bauman also insists that such a project is legitimised through unprecedented efficiency in achieving its set tasks and targets.

Although modern factories do incorporate many features of the bureaucratic model of rule, there is much more to bureaucratic power than instrumental rationality, functionality and efficiency. In fact, if these categories were the primary components of bureaucratic order, such an order would not last for a very long time. As James S. Scot (1998) demonstrates convincingly, overly centralised bureaucratic systems of control that utilise instrumentally rational principles often end in complete failure: from collective farming in the Soviet Union; to Le Corbusier's influenced architectural designs, such as those in Brasilia or Chandigarh; to the Prussian model of scientific forestry; to state-induced villagisation in Tanzania. Powerful bureaucratic systems require much more than rules, regulations and targets. Scott (1998: 310–311) illustrates this well with the example of the work-to-rule strike: 'In a work-to-rule action . . . employees begin doing their jobs by meticulously observing every one of the rules and regulations and performing only the duties stated in their job descriptions. The result, fully intended in this case, is that the work grinds to a halt, or at least to a snail's pace. . . . [This action] illustrates pointedly how actual work processes depend more heavily on informal understandings and improvisations than upon formal work rules'.

Hence in many instances the bureaucratic systems 'speak' in the language of instrumental rationality and project the idea of efficiency and functionality while in fact their internal day-to-day actions might be more messy, chaotic and contradictory. These organisational features were equally prevalent in the Nazi administration. Despite the popular image of an extremely efficient militaristic state machine, the decision making in Nazi Germany was riddled with internal conflicts, contradictory policies and organisational confusion. Ian Kershaw's (1993) concept of 'working towards the Fuhrer' nicely captures these competing tendencies at the heart of the Nazi bureaucratic order. For Kershaw, Hitler was a 'lazy ruler' who apart from military strategy and foreign policy was not particularly interested in getting involved in the day-to-day running of the Nazi state. Consequently, the multitude of existing Nazi-created bureaucratic systems were constantly competing with each other to win the Fuhrer's attention and favour. Hence the state, party and military bureaucracies took various initiatives in order to anticipate Hitler's perceived plans and wishes. In this process, they would often pursue mutually opposed policies, thus rendering the entire system inefficient and at times even shambolic. For Kershaw (2008, 1993), it is these constant and fierce rivalries between different Nazi organisations that ultimately led towards a genocidal outcome. He argues that after 1938 the Nazi state was a polycentric conglomerate of fiercely rival agencies all competing against each other to win Hitler's support. Since Hitler tended to favour radical options, the competing Nazi organisations were attempting to win Hitler's favour by outbidding their competitors with proposals for increasingly radical solutions. This cumulative radicalisation ultimately gave birth to the genocidal policies of the Final Solution.

Hence Bauman's image of the cost-effective factory as a symbol of modern organisational power is inaccurate. While the discourse of efficiency is a highly significant justifying principle of bureaucratic rule, this is not the main source of its power. What really matters for social organisations is the acquisition of coercive might and the ability to legitimise this power through the existing social order. Focussing exclusively on modern images such as a factory gives a wrong impression that organisational power is a very recent development. Nevertheless, as argued persistently throughout this book, the cumulative bureaucratisation of coercion is a process that has been in existence for the past twelve thousand years. Although modern social organisations have unprecedented organisational capacity when compared to their traditional predecessors, the key features of the bureaucratic system have been in existence for much longer than Bauman would suggest.

In the previous chapters, the point was made about the gradual development of organisational capacity over the past twelve millennia. Although polity formations were the dominant vehicle of organisational expansion, this process was just as present and visible outside of the state domain – from religious organisations and private corporations to paramilitaries of various types. While many individual polities and non-state organisations have experienced decline or have been colonised or assimilated by rival entities, organisational power as such has been on the continuous increase for most of this long historical period. It is important to emphasise that this process was always uneven and riddled with conflicts and contradictions and that the cumulative bureaucratisation of coercion is not an evolutionary phenomenon. For example, if one compares the organisational capacity of the Roman Empire with the small polities of the pre-Carolingian world, it seems obvious that the Roman Empire was a much more powerful entity that its early organisational descendants. However, despite these periodic blind alleys, the organisational capacity of polities and other entities has continued to increase in general terms. This can be easily assessed by looking at a variety of indicators: the ability of social organisations to provide various services, the management of a large number of people and resources, the establishment and maintenance of complex infrastructure, the regulation of social behaviour, the ability to enforce rules and regulations as well as to police one's territory, the capacity to collect revenue, the capability to initiate and implement specific policies, etc. (Malešević 2013a; Mann 1993).

In this organisational sense, modernity does not represent as profound a break with the past as many social theorists, including Bauman, claim. There is no tabula rasa in historical development. Instead, one can identify the long-term organisational changes that have been in existence for centuries. Although modern-day organisations, from nation-states to private corporations, are distinctly novel institutional forms, they have not emerged out of thin air. Rather, there is an important element of continuity between premodern empires and contemporary nation-states as well as between traditional merchant guilds and present-day entrepreneurships (Malešević 2013a; Burbank and Cooper 2010). What makes modern organisations different are their organisational complexities, sizes, scopes, capacities and novel modes of legitimation. Hence instead of treating modernity as the beginning of organisational development, it is more fruitful to talk about the dramatic intensification of the processes that have been in existence for quite a long time. This is not to say that social changes that have taken place over the last three hundred years lack the revolutionary quality. On the contrary, the scientific, industrial, political and social revolutions that have taken place in the past three hundred years have changed this world beyond recognition. However, these revolutionary transformations were only possible because of the long-term organisational buildup that ultimately provided the organisational capacity for these revolutions to take place and that these dramatic changes were accepted as such at the popular level.

In this context, the phenomenon of genocide is not to be viewed as something that has no historical predecessors. Genocide is a modern phenomenon, but only because its organisational seeds were planted thousands of years ago. As Shaw, Mann, Levene and others recognise, there is no genocide without the state and without war. Although the overwhelming majority of states at war throughout history did not engage in genocidal acts, it is important to focus on the transformation of warfare and state formation in order to understand how their interactions have changed over time, leading in some instances towards genocides.[2] Since our foraging predecessors did not live in states nor have they engaged in warfare, it is apparent that genocidal action does not come naturally to human beings. However, as states develop and expand and as wars intensify, the number of human casualties dramatically increases. Until the end of World War II, the casualties of war tended to increase exponentially: from less than 60,000 in the tenth and eleventh centuries to 135 million in the twentieth century (Eckhardt 1992; Leitenberg 2006). Moreover, the number of civilians killed in these conflicts has escalated substantially – from close to 40 per cent in World War I to around 65 per cent in World War II to 77 per cent in Iraq (Sadowski 1998; Boot 2006; IBC 2016). The size of the war usually has a profound impact on the number of casualties, and protracted wars tend to be even more destructive. Nevertheless, although civilians were the target of warfare for centuries and in some historical contexts were considered to be the legitimate spoils of war, most premodern states did not have the organisational means (nor the ideology) to annihilate huge numbers of individuals. For rounding up and killing hundreds of thousands of people, it is necessary to possess a highly developed means of coercion, transport, communication, weaponry and storage, to name a few examples. In addition, this cannot be accomplished without the complex division of labour, centralised authority, a substantial degree of literacy and sizeable material resources. Most premodern states had only rudimentary forms of these organisational ingredients. Hence when civilians were massacred, this was usually achieved within already existing confinements – the burning down of walled towns or the destruction of villages on site. In many instances, these slaughters of civilians came about after they refused to surrender. For example, the storming of Drogheda by Oliver Cromwell's army in 1649 followed a conventional pattern: the summons were issued by the attackers for the town to surrender, and after this was rejected the Cromwell forces destroyed the town and killed the soldiers and many civilians. This particular case has been regarded as more brutal than most as it involved the deliberate murders of civilians and prisoners of war. However, despite its relatively unusual cruelty for its time, it still involved a very small number of civilian casualties, ranging from seven hundred to possibly two thousand (Barratt 2009).

---

[2] Although instead of referring to 'the state', it is more accurate to write about social organisations, as genocides are possible outside of the state context, as was the case with some colonial genocides which were initiated and undertaken by the private militaries and police forces of trading companies, pirates, mercenaries and other irregular social organisations.

Since the organisation of the large-scale killings was complex, costly and demanding, most traditional rulers preferred to focus on a small number of individuals used as the scapegoats. To demonstrate one's might and wrath and to deter others from straying, it was enough to excessively torture and then murder a handful of individuals. As Collins (1974) demonstrates, traditional hierarchical orders utilised torture as a mechanism of social communication and control. There was no need (nor organisational means) to kill a large number of peasants. To maintain existing social hierarchies and to prevent future dissent, it was enough to break a few bodies on the wheel, burn several witches or strategically display a pair or two of the severed human heads.

Although the premodern states were organisationally quite feeble when compared to their modern-day counterparts, some premodern states had greater organisational capacity than others, which created conditions for the mass killings of civilians. For example, the European imperial powers, such as Portugal and Spain among others, were able to colonise large areas of the world and to decimate their civilian populations by deploying their organisational and technological superiority against the native populations. In a similar fashion, the non-European empires, from Han Dynasty China, Safavid Iran, the Ottoman, the Aztec, the Inca to the Mongol empires, have all been involved in mass killings of populations they colonised. However, even in these cases their organisational might was limited, as the imperial and military administration was unable to penetrate deeply into the mainland or the countryside of the colonies under their rule. For example, the European imperial maritime powers tended to establish their presence in coastal areas, from where they had little control over the less habitable mainland. Similarly, the non-European empires, such as the Chinese or Safavid, preferred to rule indirectly through local notables, as they had no organisational means to make a permanent way into the countryside (Burbank and Cooper 2010).

Nevertheless, by encoring their presence in these nodal points, some of these empires were able to gradually expand their organisational capacity and to embark on the periodic incidences of mass killings of civilians. In some cases, this involved deliberate instances of large-scale killings, such as those committed during the Russian conquest of Siberia in the mid- and late-seventeenth century with the periodic slaughter of indigenous populations (i.e. Daurs, Yakuts, Itelmens), or the Chinese massacres of the Western Mongol ethnic groupings, including the Dzungar, between 1755 and 1757 (Stephen 1996). In a similar way, the soldiers of the British Empire and the American colonists were involved in mass shooting sprees of indigenous civilians, the former in Tasmania, Australia, and the latter in northwestern America, respectively. However, most cases of mass killings of civilians emerged in the later periods, while in the early stages of colonisation diseases, enslavement and repossession of arable land were the main causes of civilian deaths. Although initially the colonising powers were not aware that the diseases would have such a devastating effect on the indigenous populations, once this became apparent, smallpox, flu and cholera were deliberately utilised against the colonised populations. For example, in 1837 the U.S. government officials were involved in the distribution of blankets infected with small-pox while in 1830 the U.S. army intentionally routed the march of the Cherokee through the areas infested with a cholera epidemic resulting in at least eight thousand deaths, half of the entire Cherokee population (Valencia-Weber 2003; Stannard 1993). The Portuguese and Spanish colonisation of the Americas and Africa resulted in millions of deaths, mostly through infectious diseases. This was already noticeable in the sixteenth century when it was documented how the indigenous popula-tion of the Spanish colony of Hispaniola slumped from close to four hundred thousand to as little as two hundred individuals in just a few decades (Juang and Morissette 2008: 510). Other mechanisms generat-ing genocidal outcomes involved forced religious conversions and forced removal of the population to less inhabitable terrain. Thus the Spanish imperial administrators employed a so-called *encomienda* system devised to generate conversion to Christianity and cultural assimilation of the native population, leading to the legalised system of forced labour and the repossession of arable land. In a similar way, the implementation of the U.S. government's Indian Removal Act (1830) led to the forced removal of Cherokee, Creek, Seminole, Chickasaw and Choctaw ethnic groups from their lands to the Indian Territory in what is today Okla-homa. This long exodus resulted in four thousand deaths is often referred to as the 'Trail of Tears' (Prucha 1984).

While the overwhelming majority of colonial period deaths were not caused by deliberate, systematic and planned mass murder, they did pave the way for such a possibility. This is best illustrated with the genocidal trajectory of the German military from South West Africa to the Holocaust. As Olusoga and Erichsen (2010) show, there is substantial degree of organisational and ideological continuity between the two cases of genocide. The Nazi murderous project is often seen somehow as a unique aberration from the European norm. However, the path to Auschwitz and the killing fields of occupied Eastern Europe was for the most part cemented through the colonial experience. Colonial expansion gave birth to the institution of the concentration camp (the Anglo–Boer Wars), and the German occupation of what is today Namibia was central for the creation of death camps. The 1904 genocide in South West Africa had all the organisational hallmarks of other twentieth-century genocides: the creation of concentration and death camps, the use of slave labour for military and production purposes (i.e. building of the railway), the meticulous documenting of camp inmates, the systematic mistreatment according to the official policy of ethnic hierarchies, the deployment of overwhelming military force against unarmed civilians and the mass slaughter of dehumanised groups by military men in open fields. It is no accident that many colonial soldiers who were involved in the killings of Herero, Nama, the Basters and many other groups were later to form the core of paramilitary forces associated with Nazi ideology. Even the infamous brown shirts of the SA were in fact surplus uniforms of the German colonial troops, Schutztruppe (Olusoga and Erichsen 2010: 292).

While the mass murders in South West Africa were more extreme than other cases of colonial killings, this was far from being a unique experience. The acquisition of huge territories throughout the world and the nominal control over at least 600 million individuals provided a unique opportunity to develop new organisational capacities for violence. While the rise of civil society, mass media and parliamentary politics imposed severe constraint on the use of organised violence within one's own territory, colonial expansion opened enormous possibilities to test and perfect a variety of coercive policies and technologies on the bodies and minds of one's colonial subjects. While the notoriously violent actions of King Leopold II of Belgium in Congo Free State have often been singled out,[3] the periodic reliance on the extreme violence was the dominant mode of colonial rule for the most colonial organisations, including both public and private bodies. This organisational advancement in mass killings can be traced back to the early colonial rule of the Portuguese and Spanish empires when the colonial rulers and administrators were faced suddenly with the task of managing millions of culturally diverse individuals and almost inexhaustible resources. Hence in order to govern new territorial positions and efficiently extract and transport enormous resources, new coercive techniques had to be devised. Hence the organisational roots of genocide can be traced to the ever-increasing organisational capacity of the colonial powers, which ultimately developed improved infrastructure, modes of regulation and coercion. The relatively dramatic organisational advancement in post-seventeenth-century Europe was directly linked with the colonial experience.

---

[3] It is estimated that 60 per cent of Congo's population was lost during Leopold's rule (Hinton 2002).

Tilly's (1985) famous quote about the inherent link between war making and state making in premodern Europe applies even more to colonial expansion, as the organisational capacities of both imperial states and private colonial corporations have largely been built on top of the bodies of their colonial subjects. The direct consequence of this organisational development were millions of native deaths: it is estimated that by the beginning of the twentieth century the indigenous populations of the Americas has declined by more than 80 per cent (Thornton 1987). While in other parts of the world these figures may not be as stark, there is no doubt that the colonial experience had extremely violent outcomes. Although the institution of genocide emerged very late in human history, the organisational ingredients for its creation were largely forged throughout the centuries of violent colonialism.

Ideological Penetration

Since genocides typically involve killings of a large number of individuals, they entail presence of complex organisational power. Although many extremist groups have advocated coercive resettlements of entire populations or even their complete annihilation, this has generally proved to be very difficult to accomplish. Once in power, the new rulers have to operate within the already existing structures, and even the most genocidal regimes have to put enormous organisational effort and resources to achieve such a giant task. Despite the general perception of genocides as being well prepared and efficiently executed, the mass killings of huge numbers of people are always organisationally messy affairs. In this sense, all genocides from the Nazi Holocaust to the Khmer Rouge to the Hutu-orchestrated Rwandan genocide were heavily dependent on complex modern organisational tools. Although the Rwandan case is often misinterpreted as being a traditional interethnic conflict it, in fact, was quintessentially a modern project: the pregenocide Rwanda was a well-administered, centralised and orderly state, characterised by decent infrastructure and relatively high literacy rates with a developed mass media and stable economy (Malešević 2006: 213–214; Prunier 1997). In this context, 'the administrative machinery of the local state was key to organising the series of massacres that constituted genocide' (Mamdani 2001: 144). Genocide was accomplished relying on the institutions of the modern state – the central government and the hierarchical civil service, including *prefets, bourgmesters* and local councillors (Prunier 1997: 349). Here too, just as in the Nazi case, most killings came about not as a result of Bauman's factory-type mass murders but through mass shootings and the use of machetes (Stone 2004). Nevertheless, it is important to bear in

mind that both of these weapons were mass-produced modern armaments imported by the government for their low cost and operational
efficiency in a densely populated country (Malešević 2006: 213).

While a complex organisational machine is necessary for genocide,
this in itself is not sufficient to realise a genocidal project. The rulers of
the Roman Empire already had at their disposal organisational tools
adequate to undertake genocide. Although the Roman imperial state
had a tiny civilian bureaucracy consisting of less than four hundred civil
servants (Mann 1986: 266), it possessed an enormous military, admin-
istered by tens of thousands of soldiers-bureaucrats. Furthermore, this
military machine was sufficiently centralised yet flexible to utilise its
highly disciplined soldiers not only to fight but also to build roads,
bridges, canals, dams, walls and aqueducts, thus keeping hold on the
occupied territories. The empire did occasionally engage in the mass
murder of civilians, but this was never an official state policy, and its
actions were determined more by what is profitable in both economic
and military terms. Hence enslaving conquered enemies was always
preferred to killing them en masse. Simply put, the Roman Empire,
just as nearly all premodern polities, lacked the ideological tools for
genocide. Hence in addition to organisational capacity genocidal action
also entails the presence of a relatively coherent and societywide
entrenched ideology.

There is no doubt that all social orders throughout prehistory and
history relied on some kind of shared belief systems. In small face-to-
face communities, such beliefs would typically centre on the real or
metaphoric kinship, usually associated with totemistic or animistic religions. In large polities, such beliefs and corresponding ritualistic practices would operate differently, as the rulers had to balance highly diverse
local traditions with dominant and codified religions. Hence the rulers of
the Roman Empire were keen to incorporate the deities of conquered
peoples into their own pantheon of gods. While remaining firmly
attached to their Muslim faith, the Ottoman sultans and caliphs
attempted to accommodate their non-Muslim subjects by creating the
millet system of separate judicial and educational orders. The European
overseas empires also had to find a way to justify their territorial expansion in Africa, the Americas, Asia and Australia. While initially advocating conversion to Christianity, the latter-day imperial rule adopted the
notion of *mission civilisatrice* – spreading the values of civilisation to those
who, in their view, did not have it yet. Thus organisational power
generally goes hand in hand with ideological power. However, as premodern social orders are deeply hierarchical, not only in the economic,
political and military but also in the cultural sense, they often lack social

mechanisms for establishing a societywide ideological glue. In other words, large-scale complex social orders such as premodern empires, kingdoms or tribal confederacies were capstone polities where rulers had neither the interest nor means to forge ideological unity between different social strata (Malešević 2013a: 37–43; Hall 1985).

The principal feature of the capstone model of rule is the inability of political elites to penetrate deeply into the communal structures of their polities. Hence, instead of governing a single society, the traditional rulers had to rely on local notables to get things done. In this sense, most premodern polities were not societies of mutually interdependent individuals who shared the same cultural values but were the conglomerates of highly hierarchical and extremely diverse communities. This inherent diversity combined with the chronic lack of literacy, and the undeveloped communication and transport networks, meant that in the traditional polities, ideological penetration was quite limited. This was highly visible in the parallel existence of several social strata that had very little in common. As Gellner (1983) emphasised, in the traditional world culture was typically utilised to reinforce the status difference between the aristocratic elite and the rest. In sixteenth-, seventeenth- and early-eighteenth-century Europe, it was essential that the young aristocrats master various cultural practices, such as fencing, horse riding, elaborate ways of dressing, speech, make-up or dancing, to distinguish themselves from the socially inferior peasants and town dwellers. For this reason, it makes sense to speak about proto-ideology rather than fully fledged ideological doctrines and practices. Nevertheless, even in this rudimentary form, the doctrines and their corresponding practices had significant impact on the social order. For one thing, a degree of proto-ideological unity at the top of the social pyramid was a prerequisite for waging successful wars as well as for preserving internal order. Whereas in the early feudal and Ständestaat polities the decision to go to war was largely dependent on the sovereigns' ability to secure support from their fellow aristocrats, in the later historical periods the rulers had to provide a proto-ideologically sound justification for a variety of political, economic, religious and military decisions. Most of this justification was articulated in religious or mythological terms (i.e. Christianity and Crusades, Islam and the Ottoman conquest of southeastern Europe, etc.). For another thing, the proto-ideology mattered also at the other end of the social pyramid. Although the social life of premodern villages and towns was largely disconnected from each other, shared ideas and practices played an important role within the small communities (Hall 1985). Local interpretations of religious morality, kinship-centred social responsibilities and communal ethics have all been central to the social life of the traditional countryside and towns. The fact that that these two worlds of 'high' and 'low' cultures were disconnected prevented the emergence of societywide ideological penetration. However, within their own worlds, proto-ideologies had visible impact.

To understand the historical dynamics of genocide, one has to tackle the gradual shift from the different proto-ideological drives towards the modern-day ideological universes. The scholars of genocide often point out that such extreme violent social action entails a specific, modern mindset. While prejudice and disdain of difference might be universal to human beings, the ideological underpinning of genocide involves much more. The idea that the specific groups of human beings should be annihilated simply because they belong to a different ethnicity, religion or class is something that does not come naturally to human beings. Instead, such a worldview develops quite late in human history and, as I have argued elsewhere (Malešević 2013b), is premised on a paradox: the gradual societywide acceptance of principles of social inclusion ultimately generates greater groupcentric exclusion. It is no coincidence that the French and American revolutions simultaneously inaugurated ideas of moral equality of all citizens while also practising mass murder and genocide against those deemed not to belong to the free republic: the peasants of Vendee, Haitians and other colonised populations in the French case, or the Native Americans and African slaves in the American case. The proliferation of principles that advocate moral equality of all human beings have unwittingly paved the way for the mass slaughter of others (see Chapter 5).

This had two important consequences. Firstly, when all humans are deemed to be of equal moral worth, then the only way to denounce one's political opponents is to deny them membership in the human race. In the deeply hierarchical premodern world, such denials of membership were not necessary as peasants could not even contemplate crossing the hard social boundaries that separated them from the aristocracy. Hence as political conflicts intensify in modernity, elaborate ideological means are deployed to dehumanise one's enemy. In Goebbels's cinematography and radio broadcasts, ordinary individual German citizens of Jewish heritage are transformed into 'the swarms of disease ridden vermin and parasites'; in Stalin's Soviet Union, moderate landowning peasants (i.e. kulaks) were depicted as 'leeches' and 'rats' bent on destroying the socialist homeland; and in the 'Hutu power' controlled radio station Libre des Mille Collines and the influential magazine *Kangura,* Tutsis were described as cockroaches that needed to be exterminated. While delegitimisation of one's enemy is not a historically new phenomenon, what is distinct about modern contexts is the availability of sophisticated organisational and technological mechanisms to generate and distribute propagandistic messages and images. More importantly, only in modernity do such dehumanising images make popular sense as they become integrated into the wider ideological narrative.

And this leads us to the second consequence: unlike the proto-ideologies which are usually confined to relatively small groups of individuals and which mostly appeal to a single social strata, modern ideologies (nationalism, socialism, liberalism, conservatism, religious fundamentalism, etc.) draw their mass support base from a variety of social strata. For example, while nationalism was a doctrine that attracted a small number of intellectuals and members of the upper-middle classes in early-eighteenth century, by the end of the twentieth century this belief system has become a dominant ideology of its age (Malešević 2013a; Smith 2010). This widening of an ideological support base is crucial for the proliferation of genocidal projects, as genocides ultimately grow out of ideologies that have a substantial degree of popular support. This is not to say that modern individuals easily consent to mass murder. On the contrary, in Enlightenment-infused modernity, human life is deemed much more precious than in the previous historical epochs. However, precisely because life is so valued, it becomes critical to delegitimize and destroy all organisations and people associated with the imminent threats to, what ideologues perceive to be, a direct road to human happiness. Simply put, as modern ideological projects devise grand vistas of perfected social orders, the realisation of such ultimate societal goals fosters extreme intolerance towards opponents of such projects. Once a particular ideological outlook is taken to be the ultimate truth, any challenge to such a project is regularly interpreted as a malicious attempt to prevent the fulfilment of a noble goal. This way of thinking opens the door for the use of the most extreme measures to implement a particular goal: annihilating all ethnic minorities to build an ethnically uniform *folksgemeinschaft*; destroying all kulaks and Western spies to create a perfect communist utopia; sterilising genetically inferior populations to produce a eugenically perfected human race; etc. While Bauman (1989) makes a similar point about the centrality of ideology in genocide, what is missing in his staunchly modernist account is the long-term historical dynamics. It is true that the presence of elaborate ideological blueprints makes genocides possible in modern era. However, this shift from premodernity to modernity is never so stark, as nearly all modern ideologies have emerged out of proto-ideological ingredients.

A good example of this gradual development is the premodern and early modern Spain. While sporadic and disorganised massacres of Muslims and Jews were present throughout the Reconquista, it is only after Ferdinand II of Aragon and Isabella I of Castile became the joint Catholic monarchs that the systematic purge of Jews and Muslims gradually became a state policy. Being beset by continuous violent conflicts over territory on the Iberian peninsula on the one hand and having to accommodate the Catholic Church authorities on the other, the new rulers embarked on the coercive policies against Jews and Muslims with a view of strengthening their domestic legitimacy. Hence the Spanish state introduced variety of discriminatory policies against minorities: initially, the focus was on the voluntary conversions, then on the forced conversions and ultimately on expulsion and killings. As some converts from Judaism were relatively wealthy individuals, royal hierarchies and the top Catholic clergy tended to perceive them as an economic and political threat. Thus in order to mobilise elite support against *converses,* they were publicly accused of being crypto-Jews who secretly maintained their traditions and were involved in covert proselytism. In 1942, Alhambra Decree was issued ordering expulsion of all Jews from the Kingdoms of Aragon and Castile within a three-month period. The Jewish population were accused of subverting country's 'holy Catholic faith and trying to draw faithful Christians away from their beliefs' (Perez 1993: 114. The edict stipulated that any Jew who does not leave or converts to Christianity will be summarily executed. It is estimated that about two hundred thousand Jews were expelled while at least twenty thousand died en route or were killed.[4] Although periodic anti-Semitic purges were common throughout Europe at this time, the scale and character of the Spanish case is relatively unique. While material, geopolitical and other factors played a crucial role in this development, one cannot discount the role that religious proto-ideology played. The killings and ethnoreligious cleansing policies were justified directly in reference to the protection of the 'holy Catholic faith' and the assumed threat caused by the presence of an 'alien faith'.

There is no question that that this proto-ideology was largely confined to the elite level and that Reconquista Spain lacked the organisational means for the implementation of fully fledged genocidal projects. Moreover, even at the height of the anti-Semitic purge, individual Jews were still given opportunity to convert, and at least fifty thousand took up this option (Perez 2006). Although there was widespread public prejudice against Judaism, there were no means for the greater ideological

---

[4] Many Jews were killed and their stomachs cut open following the widespread rumours that they had swallowed their gold and diamonds, which they were not allowed to carry out of the country.

penetration of anti-Semitism as a relatively coherent doctrine. It is safe to say that at this time there was still no 'fusion of racism and fordism' (Olusoga & Erichsen 2010:9) that characterises genocidal vistas. Nevertheless, it is difficult to deny that these coercive state policies provided a stepping stone for the future genocides since religious anti-Semitism was established as a source of the latter-day, more secularised, anti-Semitic ideologies that were widespread in twentieth-century Spain and culminated in the Nazi-implemented Holocaust. The main point is that rather than emerging ex nihilo, genocidal ideologies have developed gradually over longer stretches of time.

Genocide and the Microsolidarity

It is difficult, if not impossible, to envisage genocide which does not involve a complex organisation and a potent ideological justification. The most memorable and best documented cases, such as the Holocaust and the Rwandan, Armenian or Cambodian genocides, were all defined by the organisational effectiveness and intense ideological penetration. The National Socialist movement, the Akazu, the Young Turks and the Khmer Rouge all developed operative and efficient social organisations (i.e. political parties, paramilitaries, pressure groups, etc.) and also captured the organisational vehicles of the state, both of which were crucial in the implementation of the respective genocides. In addition, in all four cases genocidal outcomes were rooted in specific ideological narratives that in one way or another had a great deal of popular support: the eugenic racism and anti-Semitism of the National Socialists, the Hutu power ideology that defined Tutsis as alien invaders, the Young Turks' doctrine of integral Turkish nationalism and the Khmer Rouge's agrarian socialism. Nevertheless, while ideology and organisation are essential building blocks of any mass-scale violent action, genocides also entail the presence of groups and individuals willing to undertake such acts of extreme violence as well as a general public that in some way tolerates genocidal outcomes.

There is a popular perception that *genocidaires* are inherently sadistic individuals who enjoy torturing and killing other human beings. However, without denying the fact that some killers suffer from various mental illnesses which might destroy their sense of empathy, there is abundance of empirical evidence indicating that the overwhelming majority of genocide perpetuators do not suffer from any mental disorders (Mann 2005; Levene 2005). Taking into account that genocides usually involve a large number of perpetuators and that serious mental illnesses affect only a small section of any general population, it seems highly unlikely that mental disorders play any significant role in such killings. For example, the Rwandan *gacaca* courts have tried at least 120,000 individuals accused of being directly involved in genocidal acts. No serious case could be made that such a large number of people were affected by mental disorders. Furthermore, as argued in Chapter 3, human beings as a species are not particularly good nor comfortable with violence. Even individuals who were ideologically highly committed and responsible for most mass-scale killings have shown an aversion towards face-to-face murders. For example, Heinrich Himmler, often named as the architect of the Final Solution, could not stomach the killing sprees that he witnessed in person. In one of his private letters to his wife Marga, he describes how during his visit to the eastern front in 1941 he saw SS firing squad killing Jews en masse and that made him vomit all over his uniform (Smith and Peterson 1974). So the question is, if *genocidaires* are normal or mostly ordinary individuals, and if ordinary humans are not at ease with killing, how do they became perpetuators of such extreme forms of violence? Part of the answer (in addition to already discussed coercive organisational pressure and ideological embedment) is a sense of emotional attachment and ethical responsibility towards one's microgroups.

As already argued, genocidal projects are rarely, if ever, developed well in advance. In most instances, they emerge through gradual radicalisation. If this were not the case, very few individuals would express any support for such extreme acts of violence. Step-by-step radicalisation regularly transpires in the context of large-scale warfare (Shaw 2003), when future genocide perpetuators are already organisationally and ideologically caged in the particular doctrinal project. The outbreak of war contributes to radicalisation in a variety of ways: the propagandistic discourses deployed to delegitimise the enemy foster dehumanisation; increased battlefield casualties relativise the universalist principles that hold all human life sacred, thus opening up the possibility that killing others does not breach moral norms; and deteriorating living conditions with an increased sense of fear foster a greater lack of empathy. In such an environment, radicalisation presents ordinary individuals with difficult choices: to embrace extremist doctrines, to reject such acts and risk punishment or to ignore the actual social reality and pretend that such violent events do not take place. As both Fulbrook (2012) and Browning (1992) demonstrate, most 'ordinary men' in 1940s Germany were not initially supportive of extreme violence against enemy civilians. However, once they joined the Nazi bureaucratic machinery (including the various armed forces), they gradually became more accepting of such extremist acts. Browning (1992) shows how some members of Reserve Police

Battalion 101 disliked killings of Jewish women and children and would initially shoot in the air, would vomit after the murderous actions and would apply for transfer to other units. Nevertheless, he also shows how killings of civilians gradually became normalised and how many 'ordinary men' embraced their role as killers. What is crucial in such a step-by-step radicalisation is the sense of attachment to one's microgroup. While human beings as individuals are not good at nor comfortable with killings of other human beings, once they are well integrated or aspire to be integrated into small groups, their actions change.

The classical psychological studies, from Adorno and Millgram to Zombardo and others, have focussed on the conformity and acceptance of authority as the principal motivations leading ordinary individuals to injure others. More recently, sociologists of emotions have identified other motives: feelings of shame, fear, anger, love, emotional reciprocity, etc. (Scheff 1994; Turner 2007). It seems plausible to conclude that the combination of different emotions, together with other more cognitive factors, plays a significant part in human motivation. Nevertheless, what matters more is the context in which such emotions develop and operate – the small-scale close-knit groups. Even though genocide perpetuators are usually engaged in profoundly different activities than, for example, soldiers on the frontlines, revolutionary conspirators or insurgents, their microgroup dynamics exhibit many similar traits (see Chapter 9). In each of these cases, individuals display a substantial degree of attachment and loyalty to one's group; they also feel a sense of moral responsibility to their fellow members; they are often willing to endure hardship to protect their microgroup, and they value their microgroup as a centre of their moral order. Hence in this instance, one could speak legitimately about 'the solidarity of killers', which is often maintained and reinforced after genocide has taken place. In this sense, behaviour of *genocidaires* resembles that of violent gang members, such as the Mungiki, who rule the slums of Nairobi; the Eighteenth Street Gang, which controls parts of Los Angeles; or the Salvadorian MS-13. All of these organisations combine intense coercive pressure and ideological justification with strong small-group bonding. Just as every member of the Mungiki gang has to prove his loyalty to the group through his active participation in regular killings, so do genocide perpetuators. This shared experience of bloodletting (as well as the periodic exposure to danger) reinforces group bonds as gangsters/genocide perpetuators articulate their own microgroup-centred moral universe. Thus many *genocidaires* become convinced that their actions were fully justified. This solidarity is often displayed through genocide denial and relativisation of crimes in which they were involved during the war.

The micro-level solidarity is also decisive in conducting specific genocidal acts as *genocidaires* utilise their intense group solidarity to overpower their victims. For example, Klusemann (2010) demonstrates how relatively small cohorts combine organisational supremacy with emotional dominance to subdue larger groups of 'enemy' individuals. Hence to bypass the nearly universal killing taboo, genocide perpetuators are engaged in forging a distinct situational emotional dynamic that allows them to build a strong internal bond and to perceive their violent acts as morally justified. This was quite visible with the behaviour of Serbian forces in Srebrenica, where 'we saw an emotional flow over time with a build-up phase and a situational trigger when the peace-keeping commander showed himself paralyzed in the face of an implicit threat to kill both U.N. troops and refugees, and the defeated Muslims themselves turned passive. It was at this moment that the local commander gave the order for the massacre. Locally given orders to kill, where they occur, are themselves the result of micro interactions and their emotional outcomes' (Klusemann 2010: 10).

In addition to this 'internal' dynamic of small-group solidarities, most genocide perpetuators are also responsive to their 'external' microgroups, including their families, friends and peers situated outside of the conflict zone. The initial decision to join the coercive apparatus of the state or the paramilitary forces is often determined by one's sense of responsibility towards others. This is not to deny that such decisions might rest on instrumental motivation or a sense of strong ideological commitment. Often one's decision to join involves combination of factors. For example, despite influential arguments that World War II German and Japanese soldiers were ideological killers, more recent studies indicate that for most ordinary recruits motives were complex and multiple. The newly available documentary evidence that combines secret recordings of prisoners of war (POWs), interviews with surviving suicide pilots and soldiers' private diaries demonstrate clearly that the individual decisions to join were motivated by a number of factors – from the personal sense of family pride to individual vanity, efforts to avoid humiliation, attempts to raise one's social status, etc. Nevertheless, in both the Japanese and German case, the most prevalent motivation was the feeling of responsibility, loyalty and attachment to one's family and friends (Neitzel and Welzer 2012; Shimazu 2009; Hill 2006). This is particularly evident in the secret recordings of German POWs, where the key ideological idioms such 'global Jewish conspiracy', the glorification of *folksgemeinschaft* or 'Bolshevik promotion of Genetic inferiority' rarely appear in conversations. Instead, most discussions are focussed on issues of one's responsibility towards his family and fellow soldiers (Neitzel and

Welzer 2012: 21). Even individual decisions to persist with the fight despite the obvious defeat of Nazi Germany were regularly described in the context of anticipated reactions of family and friends. Although these particular examples involve regular soldiers and not necessarily genocide perpetuators, there is a very similar logic of motivation and justification at work in both cases. This is primarily because *genocidaires* perceive themselves as the regular soldiers fighting for the same reasons other soldiers do. Interviews with the convicted war criminals show that the majority explain their actions either in terms of bureaucratic coercion or in the context of their responsibility towards their microgroups. It is well known that Nazis convicted at the Nurnberg trials made persistent reference to their hierarchical responsibility to follow orders. The trial of Adolf Eichmann in 1961 gave a full expression to this type of self-justification, with Eichmann's words: 'I cannot recognize the verdict of guilty . . . . It was my misfortune to become entangled in these atrocities. But these misdeeds did not happen according to my wishes. It was not my wish to slay people. . . . Once again I would stress that I am guilty of having been obedient, having subordinated myself to my official duties and the obligations of war service and my oath of allegiance and my oath of office, and in addition, once the war started, there was also martial law. . . . I did not persecute Jews with avidity and passion. That is what the government did. . . . At that time obedience was demanded, just as in the future it will also be demanded of the subordinate'. However, what is less known are his dying words, where he invokes his microgroup attachments: 'I greet my wife, my family and my friends. I am ready. We'll meet again soon, as is the fate of all men' (Cesarani 2005: 321). This appeal to the microgroup is just as present in many other cases. For example, as the Rwandan genocide perpetuator explains: 'What we did in 1994 caused a lot of harm to this country . . ., we thought that Tutsis were enemies — like the government used to tell us that they were our enemies. The (duty) we thought we had was eliminating our enemies . . . [but] . . . We lost people. We lost our friends. We lost neighbours. . . . And even after the genocide, many of us fled the country to Congo and other neighboring countries. We suffered there. We were separated from our wives. And children . . .' (Larson 2014: 1–2).

Once in custody, most genocide perpetuators tend to deny their responsibility for the mass killings. This is often interpreted as a profoundly dishonest but rational behaviour to evade lengthy prison terms or in some instances capital punishment. There is no doubt that most of those accused of genocide and other war crimes are motivated by such instrumental goals. However, this self-interest-driven behaviour is rarely the only motivation. Instead, most genocide perpetuators remain firm in their commitment that their actions were justified. Some of this justification stems from deep ideological commitments, but more often the ideological narrative is permeated with a sense of attachment to one's microgroups: friends, family and close others. Hence the murder of thousands of innocent civilians is understood through the prism of one's responsibility towards one's microgroup. It is no accident that most genocide perpetuators embrace the narrative of victimhood and portray their actions as an attempt to protect their kin or their close comrades. As Fiske and Rai (2015: xxii) emphasise, most violent action has a strong moral motivation: 'when people hurt or kill someone, they usually do so because they feel they ought to: they feel that it is morally right or even obligatory to be violent'. Since morality involves regulation of social relations, the use of violence is often a mechanism to regulate relationships. Thus the individual acts of genocide, much like other instances of violence, are rooted in a sense of ethical obligation. Most perpetuators of the Holocaust knew very well what they were doing and believed that it was morally justified to gas Jewish children. In their worldview, Jewishness (i.e. Judeo-Bolshevism) was perceived as an inherent threat to the German way of life. Although many Nazis found the personal experiences of mass murder difficult or even repugnant, they did not hesitate in its implementation because it was deemed to be the right thing to do. This attitude comes across in Himmler's 1943 Poznan speeches, where he repeatedly emphasises how the mass killings of Jewish women and children are extremely difficult but also necessary for Germany's existence:

I ask of you that that which I say to you in this circle be really only heard and not ever discussed. We were faced with the question: what about the women and children? – I decided to find a clear solution to this problem too. I did not consider myself justified to exterminate the men – in other words, to kill them or have them killed and allow the avengers of our sons and grandsons in the form of their children to grow up. The difficult decision had to be made to have this people disappear from the earth. For the organisation which had to execute this task, it was the most difficult which we had ever had. ... I felt obliged to you, as the most superior dignitary, as the most superior dignitary of the party, this political order, this political instrument of the Führer, to also speak about this question quite openly and to say how it has been. The Jewish question in the countries that we occupy will be solved by the end of this year. Only remainders of odd Jews that managed to find hiding places will be left over (Smith and Peterson 1974: 169).

There is no doubt that Nazi ideology looms large in this type of motivation. However, it is also important to recognise that such ideological narratives work only when they are couched in a sense of responsibility towards one's friends and family. While Himmler's speech is shocking in its explicit recognition of genocide, what is also important is his less explicit message to the troops. The demand is made to kill Jewish women and children in order to prevent the supposed future massacres of soldiers' own family members. Himmler makes reference to the future 'avengers of our sons and grandsons'. Hence although genocide is justified in the national/racial terms, its message is conveyed in much more personal terms by tapping into the sense of ethical obligation towards one's microgroup.

Conclusion

To most contemporary individuals, genocide is an irrational act of barbarity, something associated with uniquely wicked leaders and their followers. For example, U.S. President Bill Clinton described the 1994 Rwandan genocide, involving the systematic killings of around eight hundred thousand people, as an act of 'pure evil'. Clinton went on to acknowledge that this was something that could have happen elsewhere too, but only because 'we cannot abolish that capacity [for the pure evil], but we must never accept it' (Cushman 2009: 220). Nevertheless, genocides, just as with the other forms of organised violence, are not the irrational acts of the lunatic fringe nor are they inherent biological potentials of any individual. Instead, genocides are social phenomena that possess a distinct social logic of their own. As argued in this chapter, to understand how, why and when genocides happen, it is of paramount importance to shift our attention from individual pathologies and intrinsic immoralities towards the organisational, ideological and micro-interactional mechanisms that make genocides possible. While wickedness might or might not play a part in the genocide, there is no genocide without organisation, ideology and microsolidarity.

8 Terrorisms

Introduction

In contrast to genocides that involve an attempt to annihilate hundreds of thousands or even millions of individuals, terrorist attacks usually generate a very small number of casualties. Yet terrorism often attracts as much, if not more, public attention. For example, in 2003 several terrorist attacks in Israel and Russia gained much more worldwide publicity than the genocide that took place in the same year in Darfur. Although the Sudanese government forces and the Janjaweed militias were responsible for over four hundred thousand casualties and 2.5 million displaced people, this event was completely overshadowed by the actions of the two female Chechen terrorists who killed fourteen individuals in Russia or the Hamas suicide bomber, dressed as an ultra-Orthodox Jew, who detonated an explosive belt on a bus in Jerusalem, thus killing twenty-three Israelis. Although the chances of being killed by a terrorist attack are smaller than winning a lottery, many individuals seem to be more afraid of terrorist threats than of many other forms of organised violence. This chapter aims to address this puzzle by focussing on the sociological foundations of terrorism. More specifically, I critically explore the most influential theories of this phenomenon and then provide an alternative, longue durée, interpretation. I argue that the dominant nonsociological approaches to terrorism do not capture the complexity of social action involved in the terrorist acts, while most contemporary sociological approaches are too culturalist and too ahistorical to account for the role that organisational power plays in this process.

The Meaning of Terrorism

The term 'terrorism' has been heavily politicised and generally used by state authorities to delegitimise various types of dissent, even when such dissent was not expressed in a violent form. The label 'terrorist' is also deeply contextual, and its meaning has changed over time. For example, representatives of the same political movement are at one point dubbed 'terrorist' and at another 'freedom fighters' or 'politicians', as was the case with Nelson Mandela and African National Congress (ANC) before and after the apartheid eras; Yasser Arafat before, during and after the First and Second Intifada; or Gerry Adams in the 1980s and today (Boehmer 2005; Victoroff 2005). This rather vague concept is also often used to demonise one's political opponents regardless of whether they control state power or not. Thus competing political movements within a particular state might depict their competitors as 'employing terrorist models of action'. In a similar vein, state authorities might accuse other states of sponsoring or engaging in terrorism. Just like genocide, terrorism has become a catch-all pejorative word deployed regularly to vilify adversary social organisations: while genocide is used to claim one's own intrinsic victimhood, the idiom of terrorism is utilised to delegitimise the political actions of others. This misuse and overuse of the concept have led some scholars to abandon it all together and instead employ alternative terms such as 'clandestine political violence', 'radical violent movements' or 'violent insurgents', among others. However, as Jackson (2009) rightly argues, since there is no universally agreed-upon alternative and since this term has become so dominant in the public eye that discarding the concept of terrorism altogether would lead to even greater fragmentation of this research area. Moreover, as state security agencies all over the world are likely to continue to use this term, if academics agree to abandon it they might find it even more difficult to communicate their research to a wider audience.

Nevertheless, when using this problematic concept, it is important to specify its meaning and scope. For example, Vertigans (2011) defines terrorism as 'the targeted and intentional use of violence for political purposes through actions that can range in intended impact from intimidation to loss of life'. Although this definition is straightforward and specific, it does not account for the nonintended consequences of social action nor for the historically contingent character of this phenomenon. Since terrorism is a form of organised violence, it too exhibits typical features that I have attributed to all forms of organised violence: it is a scalar and historical social process shaped by specific structural conditions, and it encompasses a variety of violent social actions that intentionally or unintentionally produce coercively imposed behavioural change or physical, mental or emotional damage, injury or death. In addition to these features common to all types of organised violence, terrorism also has some distinctive traits. For one thing, it is for the most part premised on unpredictable spectacular events that intentionally or unintentionally cause fear and tension. For another, terrorism is rarely if ever conceived as an attempt to overpower one's political opponent but largely as a mechanism to communicate a particular political message through the violent means. That is why terrorist acts are selective and spectacular – assassinations, hijackings, bombings, suicide missions, rocket or mortar attacks, arsons, firebombings and so on. Such unprecedented and unpredictable violent episodes produce maximum effects in terms of widespread shock and fear among large sectors of the population.

Over the past two centuries, state authorities have regularly displayed substantial interest in terrorism and have also funded its study. Nevertheless, it is only in the aftermath of 9/11 that research on terrorism has gained prominence and public visibility. The spate of suicide missions and other bombings that have proliferated since 9/11 were followed by the dramatic increase in social science models devised to explain terrorist phenomena. Among these, three approaches have dominated: psychological and psychoanalytical approaches, doctrinal fanaticism models and economics-centred explanations. The psychological and psychoanalytical interpretations aim to identify personality types prone to terrorist activities. For some authors, such actions stem from paranoid delusions, narcissistic rage, shame, sexual repression or personality disorders (Bandura 2004; Scheff 1994; Kobrin 2002; Horgan 2009). For example, Merari (1990: 206) argues that 'terrorist suicide, like any other suicide, is basically an individual rather than a group phenomenon; it is done by people who wish to die for personal reasons'. In this perspective, terrorist actions are understood as personal traumatic responses by emotionally disturbed individuals. For some psychologists, terrorists suffer from mental illness that requires treatment while for others their behaviour is result of a low self-esteem originating in unstable and traumatic family circumstances (Israeli 1997; Davies 2003; Berko 2007). The explanations that focus on doctrinal fanaticism combine psychological and cultural arguments in order to make a case that terrorists differ from ordinary individuals in their unwavering irrational commitment to a particular doctrine. This is sometimes interpreted as a result of 'brainwashing', propaganda or the presence of a unique religious milieu. While religion is emphasised as being especially potent as an object of such fanaticism, some secular beliefs have also been identified as generating strong individual commitment to terrorist acts (Salib 2003; Juergensmeyer 2003; Lachkar 2002; Volkan 2002; Burleigh 2009).

Since terrorism is first and foremost a social phenomenon, such individualist explanations have largely proved inadequate. The available evidence indicates that the overwhelming majority of individuals involved in terrorism had no psychological disorders and did not suffer from paranoid delusions, sexual repression or excessive narcissism. On the contrary, in-depth empirical studies of Islamic terrorists demonstrate that the majority were raised in stable and loving families, were good or very good students, were married and had children and were regarded as the best and brightest in their communities (Atran 2010; Sageman 2004, 2011; Silke 2008). The available psychological evaluations show mentally healthy individuals who were perceived by their neighbours and acquaintances as moral and considerate citizens (Sageman 2004; McCauley 2007). Similarly, the approaches that emphasise deep doctrinal commitment have difficulty accounting for the fact that most deeply religious and ideologically rigid persons are not involved in violence, and despite intense indoctrination only a very small number of individuals become involved in terrorist acts (Vertigans 2011: 3). Moreover, the evidence indicates that the majority of terrorists have grown up in secular or moderately religious homes where they did not display any fanatical commitments (Hassan 2011; Atran 2010; Sageman 2004). While most terrorist acts are justified now in reference to a specific religious doctrine, it is important to historically contextualise this situation. The data show that before 2003 (the beginning of the Iraq War), only one-third of suicide bombings were undertaken by organisations that invoke religious principles, with the overwhelming majority of such missions being carried out in the name of secular ideas involving such nationalist organisations as the Tamil Tigers, the Kurdistan Workers Party (PKK) or Chechen independence movements (Gambetta 2005: 261–262).

Although these individualist centred explanations remain highly popular outside of academia, most social scientists tend to emphasise the social contexts of terrorism. The majority of such explanations invoke economic reasons as being highly influential. For some scholars, instrumental rationality is the principal motivational factor behind most forms of terrorism, as this is relatively cheap and one of the few available effective methods to fight a much more powerful enemy (Laitin 2007; Wintrobe 2006; Gambetta and Hertog 2009). More specifically, rational choice explanations see terrorism as a conscious and calculated strategy to achieve specific instrumental goals. They point to cases such as the Irgun's violence against the British occupation resulting in the independent Israeli state; Hezbollah's use of terrorism to force withdrawal of Israeli, American and French forces from Lebanon; and the ANC's violent activism contributing to the collapse of apartheid system (Victoroff 2005). Other analysts explore the structural variables involved arguing that terrorism is a product of long-term relative deprivation and social inequalities that foster intense grievances, some of which are channelled in violent ways (Gurr 1970; Thompson 1989; Li and Schaub 2004; Burgoon 2006). Hence Li and Schaub's (2004) study of a sample of 112 countries indicates that economic development is inversely proportional to the number of terrorist attacks. In a similar vein, Burgoon (2006) argues that the increase in social welfare is positively correlated with the decrease in terrorist acts.

Without intending to dispute the often observed finding that sharp class or status polarisation and inequalities contribute to popular discontent, it is not self-evident why these factors matter more in some cases and have very little impact in others. As argued in Chapter 6, economics-centred explanations of revolution, which also focus on economic disparities and deprivation, cannot provide plausible answers to the question of why popular discontent rarely translates into rebellion or revolutionary upheaval. In the same way, such theories cannot account for the nonexistence of terrorism in some of the poorest and most unequal societies in the world. Why is there so much terrorism in Iraq, Pakistan and Afghanistan and almost none in Namibia, Lesotho or Botswana, which top the list of the most unequal countries in the world (CIA 2016)? Although social injustice and economic inequality can under particular circumstances contribute substantially to the proliferation of violence, there is no reliable evidence that poverty, inequality and deep economic disparities by themselves cause a terrorist response. On the contrary, several important recent studies show the opposite trend, with an increase in living standards being positively correlated with involvement in and support for terrorist activities (Hassan 2011: 39: Malečkova 2005; Kruger and Malečkova 2003). There is also robust evidence demonstrating convincingly that rather than being uneducated and impoverished individuals, most terrorists come from the relatively affluent backgrounds. For example, Al Qaeda membership was disproportionally staffed by voluntary recruits from the upper and middle classes who were well educated, possessing science, medicine or engineering degrees from respectable universities (Sageman 2004). A similar pattern was established for other Islamic radical groupings involved in terrorism who in some important respects resemble their late-nineteenth- and early-twentieth-century anarchist counterparts. Gambetta and Hertog (2009) have analysed the demographic and biographical details of over four hundred jihadists involved in violence and have found that a large majority had engineering degrees. Since terrorist activities entail a substantial degree of technological, organisational and communicational skills, it seems reasonable to assume that the educated middle classes are better equipped to take part in such activities. Nevertheless, this does not explain their motivations.

While the economics-centred explanations are a major improvement on psychological and psychoanalytic interpretations of terrorism, they are still too narrow in their approach and as such cannot account for the broader social context that shapes terrorism. To do so. one requires engagement with sociological analyses. Over the past ten to fifteen years, sociologists have produced influential theoretical models aimed at identifying and dissecting the social and cultural conditions that give rise to such violent activities.

The Sociology of Terrorism: Culture and Violence

Contemporary sociological approaches to terrorism focus extensively on the cultural context of this phenomenon. Although most sociological interpretations of terrorism insist on the socially constructed and culturally mediated character of this phenomenon, they differ substantially in how they conceptualise this relationship. While for some culture is understood in terms of stable normative patterns of collective behavior, for others the cultural processes are more fluid, inherently contested, discursively dynamic and shaped according to the specific situational logic. There are many culture-centred sociological interpretations of organised violence in general and terrorism in particular, but three distinct perspectives stand out: the Neo-Durkhemian, interactionist and antifoundationalist approaches.

The Neo-Durkhemian Analyses

Author of many of the classics of sociology, Emile Durkheim (1997 [1893]) was the pioneer in the study of group solidarity. Strongly influenced by the spirit of the Enlightenment but also equally opposed to the individualist interpretations of social change, he argued that social cohesion is at the heart of all, traditional and modern, social orders. In his now famous formulation, he distinguished between the mechanical solidarity of premodern societies based on the simple in-group resemblance and organic solidarity of modern complex societies shaped by networks of mutual interdependence. In this context, violence, including the anarchist bombings which were the dominant form of terrorist activity in his day, were perceived as a form of anomie, a transient anomaly indicating that a particular society is in transition to modernity and experiencing a temporary moral malaise.

Contemporary neo-Durkhemians are deeply influenced by such ideas in the sense that they too develop norm-centred explanations of violent conflicts, including terrorism. However, they go beyond the classical

Durkhemian view, as their models are more reflexive, less functionalist and less deterministic. Instead, the focus here is on identifying particular symbols associated with violence, which gradually acquire intense collective meanings. Hence in this view a terrorist act is less of a material event and more of a cultural artefact. This means that the events do not generate collective action by themselves but instead require a particular cultural coding which will transform them into socially meaningful acts. For example, Alexander (2011) and Smith (2008) interpret the aftermath of large-scale terrorist events in terms of the popularly resonant cultural frameworks. In this context, Alexander (2004a: 10) argues that there is no automatic collective trauma resulting from particular catastrophes such as 9/11 or the Bali bombings of 2002. Instead, such traumas have to be socially mediated in order to be understood as collective experiences: 'It is the meanings that provide the sense of shock and fear, not the events in themselves'. For Alexander (2004b: 88), terrorism is a form of postpolitical action, as 'it reflects the end of political possibilities'. Thus the focus should shift to the analysis of its symbolic performance: 'We need to theorise terrorism differently, thinking of its violence less in physical and instrumental terms than as a particularly gruesome kind of symbolic action in a complex performative field'. More specifically, the argument is that terrorist acts represent a model of political performance which relies on the specific cultural scripts, dramatic executions, symbolic productions of martyrdom, wide audiences and clearly defined positive and negative actors. For neo-Durkhemians, terrorism is dependent on mutually exclusive cultural categories which frame particular agents in terms of friend versus foe and their actions through the prism of sacred versus profane. Hence the 9/11 attacks entailed a socially mediated articulation built around contrasting dramaturgical scripts. Al Qaeda depicted the United States as a symbol of polluted power that constantly breaks universal moral norms and spreads injustice throughout the world, while the U.S. authorities portrayed the hijackers as fanatical, bitter, cowardly, irrational monsters hell-bent on senseless destruction. Alexander (2004b: 100) argues that the conflict between these two performative counternarratives resulted in the greater social cohesion of the American public, as terrorist acts generated 'purification after pollution'. In this way, rather than shattering the fabric of the social order, terrorism has helped reinforce imagined ideals of American values: 'After 9/11, the national community experienced and interpreted itself as united by feeling, marked by the loving kindness displayed among persons who once had only been friends, and by the civility and solicitude among those who once merely had been strangers'. In a similar vein, Smelser's (2007: 87–88) social strain theory of terrorism emphasises the role that values play in generating terrorist acts. Although his approach is wider in the sense that he also focusses on material resources, ideational logic still retains the upper hand. For Smelser (2007: 87–88), terrorism inevitably entails the presence of an extremist belief system that would justify the use of violence. Such ideological doctrines offer diagnoses of contemporary social reality, identify the main culprits of present injustices and provide visions of 'a more perfect world' to be achieved in the near future. Moreover, terrorism necessitates 'polarisation into systems of good and evil, deification and demonization. It is this package of beliefs that commands the moral engagement of terrorists in the cause'. In this way, extremist ideologies manage to translate popular discontent into collective action.

Interactionism

Unlike the neo-Durkhemians, who understand cultures as distinct moral macro-universes, interactionists focus on the diverse micro-level interpretations of social reality. In other words, for interactionists social reality is not necessarily underpinned by collective normative patterns of understanding. Instead, the social world is perceived as being constituted by a multitude of contextual situations where shared understanding is dependent on collective action. As one of the early proponents of the interactionist paradigm argues: 'it is the social process in group life that creates and upholds the rules, not the rules that create and uphold group life' (Blumer 1969: 19). Nevertheless, this approach too privileges ideas and values over material factors. For example, in their interpretation of terrorism and counterterrorism, Constanza and Kilburn (2005) identify cultural resources such as 'symbolic security' and 'moral panic' as the crucial mechanisms in the construction of the collective definition of the situation. The key argument is that security policies are often guided not by actual threats but by collective perceptions of, often imagined, threats. In this environment, where the public sphere is dominated by fear, political leaders are driven towards responding to such collective definitions of reality rather than the actual dangers.

The most sophisticated contemporary interactionist theory of terrorism is developed by Randall Collins (2011, 2008a, 2008b, 2004). For Collins, violence does not come naturally to human beings. Instead, in face-to-face interactions, most individuals will find it difficult to engage in violent acts, as violence is a 'set of pathways around confrontational tension and fear' (Collins 2008a: 8). This means that humans are not particularly competent at violence, as such acts generate intense emotional discomfort. The focus here is not on individuals or groups as carriers of violent acts but on the social situations that produce violent outcomes. Since violent situations are wrought with fear and tension, successful violent action is dependent on one's ability to transform this emotional tension into emotional energy: 'Successful violence battens on confrontational tension/fear as one side appropriates the emotional rhythm as dominator and the other gets caught in it as victim' (Collins 2008a: 19). In this view, the emotional energy, which is forged in the interaction rituals, is the backbone of social interaction. More to the point, for Collins successful interaction ritual chains generate potent symbols of group membership and in this way help foster emotional energy. Violence is difficult because it goes 'against the grain of normal interaction rituals', and those who are proficient at violent interactions are individuals 'who have found a way to circumvent confrontational tension/fear, by turning the emotional situation to their own advantage' (Collins 2008a: 20).[1]

Although Collins recognises that terrorism depends on the existence of effective organisations, he argues that such behaviour entails a particular interactional dynamic. Even though all terrorist activities include clandestine preparation, there is a substantive difference between those engaged in long-standing confrontations such as hostage-taking, kidnapping or hijacking and those such as suicide bombings, targeted assassinations or remote-detonated explosives, where violent acts happen in a very short period of time. While all these activities require proper navigation of the tension/fear continuum, this is achieved differently for the two forms of terrorism. As hijacking or hostage taking is often a prolonged activity, it regularly includes a small group rather than a solitary individual. As Collins argues, this is necessary not so much for organisational reasons but primarily to utilise the group's emotional solidarity to overcome this confrontational tension. In contrast, assassinations and suicide bombings are often carried out by lone individuals who navigate this emotional discomfort in a different way. By refocusing their attention on routine preparations, a would-be suicide bomber detaches himself from the object of his action and from the entire violent context. In this way, he psychologically shields himself from an emotionally disturbing confrontational experience while also making sure that the terrorist act is conducted in the most efficient way. For Collins, this relatively unique

---

[1] To overcome this universal aversion towards killing, the U.S. military is conducting research into developing a 'anti-remorse pill' that would help eradicate the guilt arising from killing other humans: 'As Leon Kass, chairman of the President's Council on Bioethics, explained, it's the morning-after pill for just about anything that produces regret, remorse, pain or guilt' (Bourke, 2015: 154).

feature of suicide bombings makes such activity more suited for ordinary individuals wary of direct face-to-face confrontation. Drawing on empirical findings that the large number of such killings were undertaken by university graduates and other professionals, Collins (2008b: 2) argues that there is a sociological reason why terrorist suicide bombings are predominantly a middle-class phenomenon: 'Clandestine, confrontation avoiding violence such as suicide bombing is … a pathway around confrontational tension. It succeeds only because the attacker is good at pretending that he or she is not threatening at all'.

Antifoundationalist Perspectives

Although the neo-Durkhemian and interactionist approaches provide different interpretations of terrorism, they share the standard social science ambition of attempting to explain this phenomenon. In contrast, the antifoundationalist perspectives are suspicious of what they call totalising ambitions. Instead of explaining, they focus on deconstruction of the dominant narratives. Following Foucault and Derrida, such perspectives see all truth claims as provisional, relatively arbitrary and contingent. Hence, to deconstruct means to identify the hegemonic and arbitrary practices that underpin various discursive projects. The emphasis here is on the particularity and plurality of knowledge and truth: to highlight the inherent discrepancies, randomness and contradictory nature of metanarratives. For antifoundationalists, what really matters are the competing modes of signification which allow hegemonic domination of one narrative over the other. In this context, terrorism is conceptualised as a particular form of discursive practice deployed by both the state and the clandestine organisations. For example, for cultural analysts influenced by this perspective, terrorism is always a culturally constructed, context-dependent and unstable concept which changes its meanings over time and space (Sluka 2009a; Jackson 2009, 2007). In this view, the truth claims about terrorism can never be neutral or objective as they are always grounded in particular discursive experiences (Toros and Gunning 2009). Hence they argue for a much broader understanding of this phenomena that includes both state and nonstate forms of terrorist activity.

Among the antifoundational approaches, representatives of the Copenhagen School have articulated the most influential theory of this phenomenon. At the centre of this perspective is the notion of securitisation. For Buzan (2006; Buzan and Wæver 2009) and Wæver (2011), terrorism requires contextualisation whereby individual or collective subjects are transformed into objects of security. Securitisation means that certain individuals, groups, organisations or social relations become framed as threats to state security even though they might not actually pose such a threat. In other words, securitisation is about prioritising and giving great deal of attention to particular subjects regardless of whether or not such subjects generate actual or potential damage. For example, as Zwitter and de Wilde (2014: 8) argue: 'In 2005 41,600 people died in traffic accidents in the EU, while in the same year 56 people died in Western Europe from the terrorist attack. While a major political discourse is going on regarding terrorism, road safety is hardly securitized'. For theorists of securitisation, the key issue is how a particular phenomenon is framed and widely perceived as an existential problem. Although attempts to securitise various issues are present in all societies, the capacity to establish a particular issue as the central security concern is linked with status of those making such discursive claims as well as the audiences' willingness to accept these claims. For Buzan and Wæver, the success of securatisation, often achieved through elaborate speech acts, allows legitimate use of extraordinary means to deal with security treats. Hence the Patriot Act in the United States and similar legislation establishing the state of emergency or martial law in other parts of the world are regularly justified in reference to the perceived danger of the terrorist threat. Other anti-foundationalist analyses focus on the genealogy of discourses on terrorism where the emphasis is not on why such discourses emerge but how they operate. For example, Ditrych (2014) historicises discourse on terrorism by exploring the changing interpretations of this phenomenon throughout twentieth and twenty-first centuries (with a spotlight on 1930s, 1970s and 2000s). Drawing on Foucault, he argues that terrorism has no essential origin, nor does it develop in evolutionary fashion. Instead, his study aims to trace continuities as well as discontinuities in the dominant discourses of the three periods. While in all three cases terrorism 'was rendered as an exceptional threat that warranted extraordinary responses', the outcomes produced were highly contingent. Ditrych identifies the three basic discourses shaped around logic of identity versus difference associated with each period. In the 1930s, the state's discourses on terrorism utilised the following dichotomies: civilisation versus barbarism, order versus chaos and political enemy versus *hostis humani generis*. For the 1970s onwards, the last category has given way to the two new categories of innocence versus harm and regime versus people. After 9/11, Ditrych (2014: 4) sees the dominant discourses embracing similar rhetoric espoused in the 1930s: 'as in the 1930s, a counter-construction of the civilized and ordered mankind is juxtaposed with this global threat, disciplining both the "inside" of particular political orders and the "outside" of the international order'.

Is Terrorism a Cultural Phenomenon?

There is no doubt that terrorist activity, whether it involves clandestine organisations or internationally recognised political entities, does not happen in a cultural vacuum. Terrorism depends heavily on cultural representations and tends to invoke intense symbolic reaction. Since acts of terror regularly include spectacular and unpredictable events that aim to spread fear among the wider population, it is essential that such acts are coded and delivered as initially planned. In other words, since terrorist organisations rely on terror to send a particular political message, it is critical that this message reaches its targeted audience and that the message is also framed as the organisation has envisaged it. When this does not happen, the terrorist act will have no desired impact or can also significantly damage the organisation involved, as was the case with several bombings by ETA or PIRA, to name a few. Hence to achieve such goals, terrorist cells require the presence of mass media, access to the Internet or vociferous reaction by state authorities. In all of this a particular cultural context plays a significant part: violent acts have to be justified or delegitimised, the spectacular events have to be framed in the broader narratives or presented as the irrational and senseless acts of deranged individuals and the targeted audience has to strongly identify with or against the terrorist act.

Nevertheless, while culturalist perspectives help us understand these complex social relations and the necessary cultural frames that underpin them, they are more limited in terms of providing an explanation of the origins and the long-term social dynamics of terrorism. Whereas antifoundationalist approaches are generally and explicitly ill disposed towards any attempts to explain terrorist phenomena, other cultural perspectives tend to downplay the noncultural processes involved. In particular, culturalist models suffer from the following three weaknesses: epistemological idealism, the lack of robust empirical validation and the inability to elucidate the macro/micro dynamics of terrorism.

Even though some antifoundationalist approaches highlight the significance of the materiality of events and processes, an overwhelming majority of cultural perspectives on terrorism are epistemologically idealist.[2] Simply put, they see ideas, beliefs, norms or discourses as being principal

---

[2] This idealism is most explicit among the neo-Durkhemians. For example, when attempting to explain the American response to 9/11 bombings, Alexander (2004b: 100) emphasises dominance of ideas over the material experience: 'The ideal inner core of America was still intact. ... the social centre was being reconstructed as an ideal and not as a material thing. Because the centre of society existed in the imagination, in the nation's soul, it certainly would be rematerialized in the days ahead'.

generators of social action. For the neo-Durkhemians, human beings are first and foremost moral creatures influenced by the normative universes they inhabit; for interactionists, collective action is the product of meaning-centred social construction of reality and for the antifounda-tionalists social behaviour is discursively framed and enacted. Although ideas and values play an indispensable role in making particular violent acts symbolically resonant, politically legitimate and socially meaningful, there is no terrorism without the material reality. Terrorist acts are intended to disseminate a particular message, but it is very unlikely that such communication would have any impact if it did not involve physical violence. In other words, terrorism can never be reduced to a narrative, discourse, cultural code, mode of interaction or ethical claim, as all such cultural frames firmly rest on the presence of a distinct material event. The hijacking of Israeli athletes at the 1972 Munich Olympics or the 1983 barrack bombings in Beirut instantly attained worldwide attention not because of the cultural codes associated with these events, but primarily because they involved unprecedented killings of a large number of individuals. Being centred on the shared values, group interactions and collective metanarratives, cultural approaches cannot adequately explain when and why acts of terror happen. Cultural codes by them-selves do not create terrorism; their role is important but for the most part auxiliary. To fully understand the origins and changing dynamics of terrorist action, it is crucial to explore the variety of noncultural factors: the geopolitical and historical contexts, the political and economic inter-ests, the structural disparities and so on.

Another weakness of the culturalist paradigm is its quite thin empirical validation. Although some anthropological studies of terrorism are built around in-depth ethnographies of specific case studies (i.e. Sluka 2009b on Northern Ireland or Atran 2010 on Islamist groups), most cultural analyses of terrorism rely on common sense or anecdotal evidence. As the cultural approaches emphasise the centrality of values, beliefs and shared ideas underpinning both the terrorist activity and the popular response to such events, it is crucial that the link between the two is properly estab-lished. However, this is rarely the case, as most such studies simply assume that the audience is highly responsive to particular narratives, frames and cultural codes. For example, Alexander (2004b: 100) argues that 'After 9/11, the national community experienced and interpreted itself as united by feeling, marked by the loving kindness . . . and by civility and solicitude among those who once merely had been strangers'. This rather strong generalisation about the U.S. population is verified by a single quotation from a *New York Times* article (a book review on United Flight 98) and the reassuring statement that 'thousands of examples of such generalisation and abstraction can be culled from the communicative media in the days, weeks, and months that followed 9/11'. The problem here is not the issue of whether one can find examples from the mass media indicating increased national solidarity after a terrorist attack, as these usually follow every such event. The problem is the fact that many culturalists take such public media pronouncements at the face value instead of analysing in a greater detail how, when and why such statements are made and what they actually mean. To do so one requires much more in-depth empirical analyses. Furthermore, even when researchers from this paradigm engage in extensive empirical corroboration, this is regularly done through the analysis of various cultural products: newspapers, website networks, TV programmes, books, pamphlets, advertising messages, etc. While it certainly is useful to acquire such information, it is also important to distinguish between the cultural artefacts and the actual human beings. For example, Smith (2005: 36, 212) argues that 'social life can be treated like a text', and that organised violence 'is not just about culture, but it is all about culture'. However, human beings are not one-dimensional texts. Culture matters, but so do politics, economics, biology, etc. Deconstructing texts and dominant discourses is not the same as analysing complex social relations, and for this we need much more empirical verification.

Finally, although cultural perspectives centre on group solidarities, they do not persuasively explain how exactly solidarity is linked with terrorism. If terrorism is a result of mismatched solidarities, then why and how do similar social contexts foster different outcomes? Why individuals socialised in the same cultural milieu embrace different ideological paths, with some joining terrorist cells while most do not? Why some political symbols attract public attention while others are ignored? Why are both terrorist and counterterrorist activities on some occasions perceived as legitimate and in other contexts as profoundly unjustified? Why do particular dominant discourses and metanarratives have impact on some terrorist organisations but none on others? Culturalists attempt to answer some of these questions by focussing either on the macro (neo-Durkhemians and antifoundationalists) or micro level (interactionists) of group solidarity. Thus interactionists such as Collins (2004) and Klusemann (2010) explain these differences invoking the unique situational contexts and the degree of emotional energy of specific individuals that foster development of strong interaction ritual chains. Nevertheless, it is far from clear how these small-scale interactional ritual chains are linked to the wider organisational macrostructures. Why and how does the rhetoric of group solidarity such as 'nation' or 'umma' appeal to huge numbers of people? Can Al-Baghdadi's emotional energy spread wide enough to include all members of Nigerian Boko Haram, Libyan Ansar al-Sharia or Islamic Movement of Uzbekistan? This does not seem very persuasive.

In contrast, the neo-Durkhemians and antifoundationalists see social order as being governed by widely shared universal norms or by discursively established metanarratives, respectively. In this context, terrorism is viewed as a societal aberration (neo-Durkhemians) or as an attempt to challenge hegemonic narratives (antifoundationalism). Interestingly enough, both of these approaches focus on pinpointing mutually exclusive dichotomies that shape the cultural repertoire of terrorism and counterterrorism: sacred versus profane, civilised versus barbarian, etc. These ideological categorisations are obviously important, but unless they are linked with the microsociological processes involved, they remain static categories with little explanatory power. Why and when such discourses acquire popular resonance, and when this does not happen? When the neo-Durkhemians attempt to engage with the micro level, this is far from convincing. For example, Smelser (2007: 95) argues that 'disturbed individuals with chaotic personal pasts are susceptible to the meaning, comfort, and rewards the extremist groups have to offer'. However, as already indicated, there is now overwhelming evidence that most terrorists are not only mentally healthy individuals but also that the majority had happy and fulfilled childhoods (Vertigans 2011; Sageman 2004; McCauley 2007). Thus to understand the relationship that exists between terrorism and group solidarity, it is necessary to integrate these macro and micro levels of analysis.

Beyond Culturalist Explanations: Terrorism in the Long Run

Terrorism is something that threatens the state's monopoly on the use of violence and also, when successful, can make state authorities look weak and incapable of protecting their citizens. For this reason, much of the terrorism research tends to focus on the instrumental character of this phenomenon: Who are the terrorists? What motivates their actions? How and why do they join terrorist organisations? Who benefits from terrorism? How can we stop it? While it is very important to establish the motivations of the individual terrorists, or the utilitarian reasoning behind the groups engaged in such acts, one cannot explain terrorism without understanding the broader social and historical contexts involved. As human beings are not only *homo economici* but are also cultural beings, all terrorist actions have a significant cultural component. However, just as the rigidly instrumentalist explanations cannot fully capture the complexity of social action, culturalism too remains overly reductionist in its interpretations of terrorism. In other words, to adequately explain the impact values and ideas play in violent processes, one cannot focus on ideas alone. Instead, values, ideas and cultural representations are segments of the larger social processes that shape violent action. As terrorism is a particular form of organised violence, it is crucial to situate its development within the wider historical frame.

As I have argued throughout this book, the dynamics of organised violence require a longue durée analysis. More specifically, to get to grips with the phenomenon of terrorism, one should avoid an overly present-centred focus and instead look at the long-term organisational, ideological and microsocial dynamics. All organised violence, including terrorism, entails presence of the three long-term historical processes: (a) the cumulative bureaucratisation of coercion; (b) centrifugal ideologisation; and (c) the envelopment of microsolidarity. These three processes are interdependent and as such impact on the direction of terrorist activity. Nevertheless, as terrorism is usually a response to the activities or deliberate inactivity of other organisations (i.e. the state, a private corporation, a religious association, etc.), the analysis of terrorist action inevitably involves exploration of these three processes as they operate in such 'adversary' organisations.

Bureaucracy and Terror

As emphasised earlier, the cumulative bureaucratisation of coercion stands for an open-ended historical process that encompasses the constant increase of bureaucratic and coercive power that characterises all large-scale, durable social organisations. Their coercive organisational capacity is also revealed through their power to internally pacify the social environment under their control. For nation-states, this means a monopoly on the legitimate use of violence over their territory, while for the other organisations this is reflected in their organisational ability to successfully dominate their membership and to inflict symbolic or real damage on competing social organisations. Although this is not an evolutionary process but something defined by the periodic rises and falls – as some organisations have expanded and others have disappeared – organisational power as such has been cumulative for the past twelve thousand years. Moreover, this cumulative character has dramatically increased in the last 250 years, with modernity fostering an intense proliferation of bureaucratic systems of organisation throughout the world (Malešević 2013a, 2010).

In this context, terrorism represents a particular from of organisational response to the ever-increasing bureaucratic expansion of states and nonstate structures. Simply put, terrorism cannot exist without effective social organisation, and in the world of ever-expanding organisational power, this means greater reliance on knowledge, technology, science and efficient bureaucracy. Whereas the early-nineteenth-century anarchists still relied on makeshift weapons (i.e. crudely assembled dynamite, knifes and handguns) and highly improvised action plans, today's terrorism entails elaborate division of labour, sophisticated organisation and technology and well-planned deployment of the most effective armaments available. In this way, the terrorist organisations resemble other bureaucratic units. They are hierarchical, meritocratic, professionalised, rule-obeying entities that employ advanced division of labour and provide expert training and protection for their members. As Mayntz (2004: 12) demonstrates, there is a great deal of similarity between various terrorist entities in this respect:

They have a clearly defined leadership – e.g. the cupola (SL), army executive (IRA), majlis shura (Islamic Jihad), council or again majlis shura (Al Qaida). They are differentiated both vertically and functionally. All terrorist organisations ... have specialised units directly below the top leadership level. In some cases the main distinction is between a military and a support branch, in other cases various units distinguished by functions such as finance, procurement, propaganda etc. are related to the operative units in a matrix-like fashion. All terrorist organisations have furthermore a clearly circumscribed third level of operative units, the famous cells.

Furthermore, such organisations perceive their competitors, be they state authorities, private corporations or other terrorist entities, in a manner similar to how other complex social organisations do. This means that they observe the organisational and ideological weaknesses of their adversaries and look for ways to diminish their impact. Just like other social organisations, they have political ambitions, ideological goals, economic interests and coercive capacities. Internally, terrorist organisations work towards establishing an effective, legitimate and flexible bureaucratic structure capable of implementing specific violent tasks. Externally such entities are engaged in surveillance, intelligence gathering, propaganda, recruitment, popular mobilisation, technological advancement, business ventures, collection of funds and so on.

Although terrorist organisations are in many ways similar to other bureaucracies, they also exhibit some differences. Since terrorist activities usually reflect a sharp asymmetry in the military capacities between the organisations involved in conflict, terrorism is not aimed at destroying the organisations' adversaries. Instead, the focus is on transmitting a particular political message in a way that will maximise the attention of opponents as well as one's own political constituency. To achieve this goal, terrorist organisations deploy a spectacular use of violence aimed at generating profound traumatic experience and fear. In addition, as terrorist organisations directly challenge the authority of the state and other large-scale organisations and as they utilise violent means to advance their goals, terrorist organisations are by definition deemed illegitimate. In this environment, their activities are as a rule clandestine and secretive. To successfully operate under such conditions, terrorist cells have to exhibit greater organisational flexibility than ordinary bureaucracies. Thus they generally assume a more compartmentalised structure. Della Porta (2013: 158) shows how increased state repression pushed the Red Brigades in Italy and the Red Army Faction (RAF) in Germany towards greater decentralisation. Similarly, the Provisional Irish Republican Army (PIRA) was established in 1970 as a mass membership organisation but was soon forced to assume a smaller, covert and lissom cell structure in order to avoid the British forces (O'Dochartaigh 2015). This is also the case with the violent jihadist organisations, most of whom operate as the clandestine flexible networks of smaller cells.

Such organisational plasticity of terrorist networks has led many analysts to argue that in the contemporary globalised world, terrorism does not require much organisational structure, but that most forms of terrorism are accomplished by grassroots improvisations of individuals and ad hoc groupings. For Sageman (2011), this is a 'leaderless jihad' waged by fully independent local groups utilising the Al Qaeda – and one could add more recently, ISIS – brand. Atran (2010: 50) too dismisses the importance of organisational structures, arguing that hierarchical organisations 'tend to lose wars', whereas 'the egalitarian jihad prospers because, like Google, its leadership is distributed over a social network in ways that are fairly fluid and flat'. Nevertheless, such sweeping generalisations do not reflect the reality on the ground. Although there are many instances of small, relatively isolated terrorist units all over the world, most successful terrorist networks depend heavily on a coherent and resilient organisational structure. In this respect, Islamist radical groups are not profoundly different from their secular counterparts, as they all had to devise decentralised, flexible cell-focussed modes of operation. However, this did not imply weakening of the hierarchical structure. On the contrary, in the cases of the PIRA, Red Brigades, ETA and many other violent movements, clandestine compartmentalisation fostered militarisation and tighter hierarchy, as the organisation's very existence was dependent on the leadership's control of its actions (Della Porta 2013: 159). This is even more pronounced with the leading jihadi movements, as they have gradually become more violent, more hierarchical and better organised to sustain intensified conflict with the repressive apparatuses of the states in which they are based. The outcome of this enhanced hierarchisation, more developed division of labour and increased organisational capacity, is well illustrated by the transformation of ISIS from a relatively small terrorist outfit into a parastate organisation capable of defeating the armed forces of both Iraq and Syria and establishing a fully functioning administrative and military structure over vast territory. The military successes of the reinvigorated Taliban in Afghanistan and Pakistan and the expansion of Boko Haram in Nigeria are other notably visible examples of terrorist networks whose military advancement is a direct result of increased organisational structure. Although highly decentralised grassroots-led cells might attract a great deal of public and media attention, their coercive and political efficiency still remains quite minimal when compared to well-organised bureaucratic terrorist machines such as ISIS or the Taliban. Even though ISIS has recently transformed from a terrorist outfit into a parastate structure, this development was possible precisely because from its establishment this social organisation had a typical bureaucratic structure. Rather than having 'fluid and flat' network formation, ISIS is a profoundly hierarchical entity built around a pyramid structure. At the top of this organisation is Caliph Ibrahim (al-Baghdadi), who is the ultimate decision maker. The principal organisational units of ISIS include the military council; the Shura (Consultative) Council; the Judicial Authority; the Defence, Security and Intelligence Council; and the Islamic State Institution for Public Information. The power structure is fully centralised and the caliph's decisions are implemented through the war office and six governors appointed to rule over six provinces under ISIS control. The organisation relies on the complex division of labour, aims to utilise meritocratic principles when rewarding its soldiers and administrators and follows a relatively consistent system of abstract (Islamic) rules in everyday life (Singh 2014). Obviously, as ISIS operates in the environment of incessant warfare and is governed by ideological principles that are hostile to legal-rational order, this is certainly not a Weberian-style modern bureaucracy, but it is bureaucracy nonetheless.

Since ISIS is in some respects an unusual entity involved now more in state terrorism than in traditional forms of antistate violence, it might be pertinent to take a brief look at the organisational structure of other, more typical, terrorist movements. As della Porta (2013: 152) rightly points out, terrorist social organisations develop a variety of organisational forms: 'some look more like an army, and some more like a party, some are more compartmentalised, and others less; some ask their members to go underground, and others do not'. Nevertheless, to be politically and militarily effective in the long term, all such organisations require a hierarchical structure defined by a developed division of labour, specialisation of tasks and responsibilities, professionalism and coercive enforcement of rules. For example, PIRA started off as a relatively democratic association with an almost flat structure, with its commanders being directly involved in armed action. Over time, and under external pressures, the organisation became much more hierarchical and formalised. As PIRA gradually adopted a formalised bureaucratic form, with a pronounced division of labour and pyramidal military structure, the organisation became more effective in achieving its military and political ambitions. It established a structure of brigades and battalions modelled on the British Army, with companies based in a specific local neighbourhoods, and it introduced variety of new organisational roles, from surveillance, intelligence, counterintelligence, planning of operations, propaganda operations to storage and release of weapons, etc. By the 1990s, most members of PIRA were involved in bureaucratic roles where they had no contact with violence (Malešević and O'Dochartaigh 2017). This gradual shift to a more formalised, meritocratic and strategically rational mode of organisation resulted in a highly successful campaign that ultimately brought about substantial political change in the Northern Ireland peace process.

In contrast, Al Qaeda is a terrorist organisation that experienced almost the exact opposite developmental trajectory. Contemporary perceptions of this organisation as 'fluid and flat' are largely based on the post-9/11 realities, when Al Qaeda was for the most part destroyed as a functioning terror network. However, as all available evidence shows, its early success was to a great extent rooted in its organisational might. Al Qaeda was initially set up at the end of the 1980s as a strictly hierarchical and centralised entity. As Chhabra (2011: 2) emphasises, the organisation had a clearly established pyramidal power structure, 'a well-defined, top-down system of communication; well-defined and rigid positions and responsibilities; a rigid command chain; and clear time horizons for operations'. With bin Laden's move to Sudan in 1992, Al Qaeda increased its organisational capacity, economic resources and military strength (Sageman 2004). As the organisation expanded geographically, it transformed into a network of relatively autonomous cells that still largely were controlled and directed by the central authority. Nearly all its prominent terrorist acts, from the 1992 hotel attacks in Yemen, the 1993 World Trade Center bombing, the 1998 U.S. embassy attacks in

East Africa, the 2000 suicide mission that killed seventeen U.S. service-men on the *USS Cole* to 9/11, were planned, organised, financed and approved for execution by the central command. Like other effective and durable terrorist entities, Al Qaeda was a complex but well-structured organisation consisting of the chief commander (emir) Osama bin Laden, his deputy Ayman al-Zawahiri, the military committee, the finan-cial committee, the law committee, the Islamic study committee and the media committee (which at one point published its own newspaper, *Newscast*). It is only after the U.S. occupation of Afghanistan and the worldwide military hunt of its leadership that Al Qaeda was forced to decentralise its power structure and for the most part to abandon its bureaucratic mode of organisation (Eilstrup-Sangiovanni and Jones 2008). In other words, and contrary to widespread perception, the suc-cess of Al Qaeda as a terrorist outfit is not rooted in its flat and loose organisational structure. On the contrary, this was a post-9/11 transform-ation that came about as a response to unprecedented external pressure. Over the past decade or so, the successful, cohesive, well-structured, centralised and hierarchical Al Qaeda has given way to the weak, decen-tralised, ad hoc groupings that attempt to utilise the Al Qaeda brand.

Hence despite some organisational specificities, terrorist organisations demonstrate a pattern of development very similar to that of other bureaucracies. Even though some such entities have disappeared over time (Red Brigades, RAF, etc.), the organisational structure of an ideal typical terrorist network has increased its bureaucratic and coercive capacity. Here too, just as with other social organisations, one can witness cumulative effects of this change.

Ideology and Terrorism

Apart from requiring organisational power, terrorism also entails the presence of a relatively distinct set of normative principles. Precisely because terrorist activities are generally regarded as being illegitimate or senseless, terrorist organisations devote a great deal of attention to ideology. Although such ideological principles regularly draw on the familiar cultural archetypes, it is important to differentiate culture from ideology. Unlike culturalists, for whom culture shapes, or even deter-mines, social behavior, it is better to conceptualise social action through the prism of the selective use of cultural resources. In other words, cultural processes and shared ideas are highly significant, but only when they are integrated into broader organisational structures and specific micro-interactional contexts. Thus unlike culture, which encompasses entire ways of living and being, ideology is a more specific set of values, principles and practices that are organised as distinct cognitive and normative maps that guide social action.[3] To understand how terrorist organisations rely on such maps, it is necessary to look at what I refer to as centrifugal ideologisation (Malešević 2013a, 2010). As already explained, this concept stands for an organisationally channelled long-term process that involves not only the formulation of distinct ideological narratives that justify the use of violence but also a structural change whereby such ideas and practices take root among wider sectors of population. The upshot of this transformation is a greater degree of ideological consensus among members of diverse social organisations, leading towards better ideological mobilisation and greater popular receptiveness of the doctrinal legitimacy of the organisation's activities. Simply put, ideology matters a great deal to all social organisations, but this has sociological relevance only as far as ideological penetration spreads to the wider groups of individuals and is fully integrated into organisational mechanisms.

This means that, in contrast to culturalist arguments, texts and narratives do not speak for themselves, nor do they generate violent action. Having an expert knowledge of the Koran, Bible or Torah does not make one more susceptible to religiously inspired violence. On the contrary, as evidence indicates, most individuals involved in direct violent actions are not deep thinkers well versed in theological debates but are politically motivated doers bent on the concrete action (Atran 2010; Hassan 2011). Such cultural resources and discourses are relevant only in the context of already existing and politically defined violent social organisations. Although terrorist outfits deploy intense ideological rhetoric and justify their violent acts through direct references to central principles of their respective ideological doctrines, one should not take such pronouncements at face value. Since all social organisations have to reconcile their doctrinal principles with the bureaucratic models of management, ideological messages are almost never popularly absorbed as they are presented. As Billig et al. (1988) demonstrated a long time ago, the reception of doctrinal ideas is never a smooth process but something characterised by contradictions, resistance, misunderstanding, reinterpretations, dilemmas and 'contradictions of common sense'. Hence ideologisation is a regularly contingent, uneven and contested process that remains dependent on the coercive prop of the organisational shell. There is no doubt that ISIS puts enormous emphasis, and financial resources, on its Takfirist/Salafist ideology. However, if it was not for

---

[3] A more comprehensive definition of ideology is provided in Malešević (2013a: 170–172; 2010: 8–12).

its organisational might, displayed on the battlefields as well as in its spectacular and macabre beheadings of Westerners, such ideas would attract very little attention. Ideology is also important in recruiting new members and in maintaining a degree of internal cohesion. Nevertheless, as ideologisation is a complex and contingent process, not a set of fixed principles, its social impact is dependent on broader historical and geopolitical contexts. For example, the emergence of radical militant Islamist organisations is deeply linked to secularised political space in the Middle East and further afield. The doctrinal fixation on religious Puritanism that characterises Salafist-influenced terrorist organisations is often a response to intense modernisation and secularisation. As Hassan (2011) and Sageman (2004) show, a majority of Islamist suicide bombers were raised in secular environments, and their radicalism was often result of ideological conversion. Centrifugal ideologisation is premised on this ongoing internal and external dialogue which is also reinforced by the presence of a coercive organisational scaffold.

The success of ideologisation is dependent on the popular receptiveness to key doctrinal principles but also on the ability of social organisations to establish themselves as the dominant or only legitimate conveyor of these ideas. For example, Irish Republican ideology appeals to a wide sector of population in Northern Ireland (and to some extent in the Republic of Ireland and among Irish diaspora in the United States and United Kingdom). Over the past forty years, many clandestine organisations have advocated implementation of these Republican ideological ambitions: Official IRA, Real IRA, Provisional IRA, Continuity IRA, the Irish National Liberation Army (INLA), Oglaigh na hEireann, etc. However, while some of these organisations remained marginal and have eventually disappeared from the public scene, others have managed to establish themselves as the principal representatives of the Republican movement (initially Official IRA and later Provisional IRA). Obviously, the degree of ideological commitment of these organisations is not the only reason why some have attracted more support than others, but ideological purity or flexibility play an important part in how a specific organisation is perceived by its constituency. One of the reasons for the 1969 split between the Official and Provisional IRA was the doctrinal principle of abstentionism whereby the PIRA members opposed the motion to end the long-term principle of not taking part in the parliamentary life of the United Kingdom, Northern Ireland or the Republic of Ireland. This commitment to ideological purity attracted more support among the grassroots in the early 1970s, and PIRA emerged as the dominant Republican force in Ireland. Interestingly enough, as the geopolitical situation changed in the late 1980s and early 1990s, PIRA embraced a more flexible attitude by gradually disengaging from violence and by ending its support for abstentionism in Ireland (North and South). Consequently, its political wing, Sinn Fein, took seats in both parliaments while maintaining abstentionist policies vis-a-vis the Westminster representation. Despite this huge ideological shift, PIRA and Sinn Fein maintained the popular support, which was well reflected in Sinn Fein's successive electoral gains in North as well as the South. Similar ideological and organisational splits were just as present among many other clandestine political movements, from ETA to the Tamil Tigers to jihadist groups.

To demonstrate one's ideological purity, or when the situation changes to demand flexibility, terrorist organisations require access to the mass media and other outlets for dissemination of their messages. When such organisations control a piece of territory, as is the case with Hezbollah in Lebanon, Hamas in Gaza or until 2009 the Tamil Tigers in the north of Sri Lanka, they can monopolise access to the mass media and can also control the educational system and the public sphere, both of which are the central organisational pillars that sustain the process of ideologisation. In most situations where this is not the case, terrorist organisations print their own newspapers and magazines, set up their radio and TV stations and most of all rely on the Internet to spread their messages. Whereas all coercive social organisations utilise these media outlets, terrorism is much more dependent on publicity than others. Precisely because most terrorist organisations are clandestine, the visibility and impact of their actions entail the involvement of mass media. For example, although there were numerous instances of serial killing throughout the world, if it were not for extensive media reports, not much attention would have been given to the violent anarcho-primitivism espoused by Ted Kaczynski (the Unabomber), who was responsible for mailing home-made bombs that killed three people and wounded another twenty-three. Terrorism thrives on media attention, and all terrorist organisations are well aware of this. That is why Ted Kaczynski demanded that his thirty-five thousand–word manifesto 'Industrial Society and Its Future' be published by the leading U.S. newspapers *The New York Times* and *The Washington Post*. Jihadist organisations put even more effort and resources in information and devise violent actions in a way that will maximise mass media attention. As Saudi general Alhumaidan puts it: 'The front is in our neighbourhoods but the battle is the silver screen. If it doesn't make it to the six o'clock news, then Al Qaeda is not interested' (Atran 2010: 290). The mass media serves two main purposes. On the one hand, journalists, government officials and some analysts unwittingly contribute to spreading fear, panic and insecurity as they generally tend to provide overblown portrayals of terrorists. After every terrorist attack, the culprits are usually depicted as if they are equally subhuman (in terms of their morality and lack of humanity) and superhuman (in terms of their military prowess). In this way, the violent terrorist act is not the end product of a terrorist enterprise but in fact often represents the beginning of a protracted violent cycle. As Atran (2011: 278) rightly observes: 'by amplifying and connecting relatively sporadic terrorist acts into a generalised "war", the somewhat marginal phenomenon of terrorism has become a primary preoccupation of our government and people'. Although terrorism as a rule causes a very small number of casualties, the aftermath regularly results in dramatic social changes: increased funding for security services, expensive and often not particularly useful enhancing of surveillance and border controls, decline of trust among people, curtailing of some individual liberties, loosened public control of government officials, the narrowing of public debate, increased public hostility towards critical and dissenting voices, etc. In this sense, terrorism is much more successful than usually recognised.

On the other hand, terrorist organisations aim to convey a similar fear-inducing message to the 'enemy' public while simultaneously attempting to address grievances expressed by their own constituents. Spectacular violent episodes, such as 9/11, the Bali bombings of 2002, the 1984 Brighton Hotel bombing by PIRA or the Liberation Tigers of Tamil Eelam's (LTTE) 1990 massacre of Sri Lankan police officers, sent a message to both sides that each of these clandestine organisations is strong enough to organise a large-scale attack on the 'enemy state'. By attracting an enormous amount of attention from government officials and the mass media, the terrorist organisations position themselves as the principal representatives of their particular ideological position. In other words, through their acts, what nineteenth-century anarchists called propaganda of the deed, clandestine organisations manage to establish themselves as radical or extreme but nevertheless sincere defenders of a specific ideological doctrine. For example, although PIRA, ETA or Al Qaeda had a relatively small direct following, they did appeal to genuine grievances of many Irish Catholics, Basques and Sunni Muslims, respectively. Despite general condemnation of their violent methods, such organisations were perceived by their constituents as expressing legitimate concerns and existing structural injustices. In this context, centrifugal ideologisation fosters a degree of consensus between terrorist organisations and their constituencies. While such organisations have little interest in legitimising their actions to their 'enemies', they are very concerned about how their acts will be viewed by their potential sympathisers. The key issue here is that, just like any other coercive social organisation, terrorist outfits require and search for popular legitimacy. Even the most violent terrorist organisations seek an approval for their actions. From the Jacobins' Reign of Terror in 1793–1794 to Carbonari's 1858 theatre killings to the Bentalha massacre by the Armed Islamic Group in Algeria, the use of violence is usually justified in reference to the immorality or injustice of 'the enemy'. Even ISIS, famous for the most horrific and ruthless killings and torture, devotes a great deal of attention to justification of such brutal acts. For example, in its magazine *Dabiq*, which is published in six languages, ISIS provides an extensive explanation for the particularly gruesome character of its hostage executions. Rather than being ad hoc and impulsive forms of murder, each execution is well planned and utilised ideologically.

Hence the burning alive of the captured Jordanian pilot Yusuf al Kasasibah was legitimised in the following way: 'In burning the crusader pilot alive and burying him under a pile of debris, the Islamic State carried out a just form of retaliation for his involvement in the crusader bombing campaign which continues to result in the killing of countless Muslims who, as a result of these airstrikes, are burned alive and buried under mountains of debris. This is not to even mention those Muslims – men, women, and children – who survive the airstrikes and are left injured and disabled, and in many cases suffering from severe burns that cause them pain and anguish every minute of every day' (*Dabiq* 2014: 5). In addition to this application of the principle of 'an eye for an eye', the organisation also deploys Islamic ideological justification, aiming simultaneously to validate its use of violence in reference to various religious texts and to discredit alternative interpretations provided by some Islamic scholars. Thus the magazine lists numerous historical examples from the Islamic tradition where fire was used against the enemy. It provides extensive quotes from religious texts and concludes:

This āyāh sufficiently demonstrates the shar'ī validity of burning someone alive in a case of qisās (retribution). The confusion perpetuated by the hizbiyyīn, the palace "scholars," and the ignorant defeatists, is with regards to the authentic statement of Allah's Messenger (sallallāhu 'alayhi wa sallam), "None should punish with fire except Allah" [Sahīh al-Bukhārī]. As a result of their dishonesty in conveying the truth, the deviants concealed the fact that there is a famous exception to this ruling made in the case of qisās and maslahah (overwhelming benefit), and that in addition to the aforementioned āyah from Sūrat An-Nahl, the fuqahā' used as evidence for these exceptions the following āyah from Sūrat Al-Baqarah. {So whoever has assaulted you, then assault him in the same way that he has assaulted you} [Al-Baqarah: 194]'. .... Thus, the Islamic State not only followed the footsteps of Allah's Messenger (sallallāhu'alayhi wa sallam) in his harshness towards the disbelievers, but also emulated the example of his righteous Sahābah (radiyallāhu 'anhum) by punishing with fire in retaliation, and for the purpose of terrorizing the murtaddīn and making examples out of them (Dabiq 2014: 6–7).

Microsolidarity and Terrorism

As ideological doctrines tend to be shaped around abstract and highly general principles, they cannot so easily penetrate everyday mundane social life. Although human beings are ideological creatures who require clearly defined ethical principles and collective meanings, they are also creatures of habit who spend most of their lives in trivial activities. At the heart of these banal, everyday interactions are personalised networks of individuals who care about each other. Randall Collins (2008a) is right that emotional attachments play an indispensable part in human actions. Individuals are much more motivated when their concerns are personal and involve people who they know and care about. Since both bureaucracy and ideology are abstract impersonal forces built around ideas that foster anonymity and structural functionality, they are not sufficient as such to generate or justify organised violent action. For this to happen, it is crucial to tap into the microcosm of daily interactions. Unlike the macroworld of social organisations, which is by necessity formal, bureaucratic and detached, the micro-universe of family, friends, neighbours, lovers or kinship is informal, familiar and intimate. Since most human beings achieve emotional fulfilment and a sense of security and attachment in such small-scale, face-to-face groupings, it is difficult if not impossible for social organisations to attain such a degree of emotional connection with its members.

Hence to keep organisations internally cohesive and externally powerful, it becomes important to find the way either to imitate such bonds or to penetrate the microworld. This is usually accomplished through the combination of both with social organisations deploying centrifugal ideologisation to portray the organisations in the language of close friendships, kinship and other intimate groups. It is no accident that the representatives of violent nationalist and religious institutions and associations rely extensively on the kinship metaphors and address their members and supports as 'brothers', 'sisters', 'sons' and 'daughters'. Moreover, the most successful social organisations find a way to blend small-scale networks of microsolidarity with the macrostructural mechanisms of their organisations. The existing empirical studies on terrorism indicate that microsolidarity is by far the most significant motivational factor in both joining the terrorist organisations and in being involved in violent activities. While ideological messages are important in attracting new recruits, it is peer groups and family networks that have been the most common routes towards terrorism. In other words, people do not volunteer to join terrorist organisations as individuals but as members of such small collectivities (Sageman 2004; Hassan 2011; Hopgood 2005). Radicalisation is a long-term process which is heavily dependent on the emotional, cognitive and moral support of other individuals (Hassan 2011; Ricolfi 2005). For example, data gathered from interviews with surviving jihadists involved in terrorism in Saudi Arabia between 2004 and 2006 show that close to two-thirds joined such groups through friends and one-quarter joined with family members (Atran 2010: 114). In a similar vein, foreign volunteers who came to fight in Iraq and later in Syria as well often arrived in small groups of friends or family members. In some instances, a majority of volunteers came from the same towns or even the same neighbourhoods (Felter and Fishman 2007). Five out of seven suicide members who organised the 2004 Madrid train attacks grew up in the same neighbourhood, Jamaa Mezuak, in Moroccan city of Tetouan, where they used to regularly play soccer together (Elliott 2007).

Regardless of whether terrorist organisations are inspired by religious, nationalist, communist, anarchist or some other ideology, the patterns of recruitment and the motivation to take part in violence are very similar in most cases: a sense of attachment and responsibility towards friends, peers, family members, admired teachers, disciples or guardians. The fact that terrorists operate in a secretive, clandestine environment which is usually removed from the mainstream world fosters an even greater sense of a small-group solidarity: 'The relative isolation of the individuals from the surrounding society beforehand appears to play an important role in creating group cohesion, solidarity and a sense of common purpose' (Hassan 2011: 40). As most terrorist cells consist of several individuals who spend a great deal of time together dedicated to what they consider to be a noble mission, the dynamics of their everyday life stimulate development of intense friendship bonds. In this context, microsolidarity matters more than the ideological principles. Although both ideologisation and bureaucratisation are crucial for bringing volunteers together and for maintaining their organisational function, it is interpersonal emotional and ethical ties that motivate individuals to engage in violence and self-sacrifice. Hence individuals join terrorist organisations as members of small groups and also engage in violence via their group membership. Just as was the case with the soldiers on the battlefield, revolutionary cells' and even *genocidaires'* willingness to kill and die is rooted in one's sense of emotional attachment and moral responsibility towards his or her microgroup. Even though in most of these cases individuals seem to be strongly wrapped in the language of specific ideology and their dying words might suggest a deep doctrinal commitment to religion, nation, race, class or some other abstract entity, their personal obligation usually is much more concrete – one's family, friends or peers. This rather paradoxical discrepancy between rhetoric and reality is for the most part generated by social organisations. Successful organisations, whether they are nation-states, business enterprises, churches or terrorist networks, operate in a similar way: they utilise organisational scaffolds and ideological know-how to penetrate the micro-universe of interpersonal relationships. In this process, ideologisation and bureaucratisation create conditions that allow for the effective organisational mimicking of human emotional and moral ties. Thus all terrorist organisations deploy the language of kinship, friendship, discipleship, neighbourly relations or peer bonds. They also invoke the images and memories associated with one's family, friends and significant others. Although in some instances this might be a deliberate attempt to manipulate one's feelings, in most cases this is a product of organisational logic whereby ideology inevitably infuses its organisational cells.

Some clandestine organisations rely more on this fusion of ideology and microsolidarity than others. There is also pronounced difference in the metaphors and images deployed in different ideological narratives. Nevertheless, to be militarily and politically effective all terrorist organisations have to organisationally and ideologically penetrate the micro-world of personal attachments. In order to galvanise support for organisational causes, it is essential that one's interpersonal commitments overlap with those of the violent organisation as a whole. For example, LTTE's elite terrorist unit the Black Tigers was universally regarded as militarily the most efficient suicide bombers in the 1990s and early 2000s. They carried out to two hundred missions and were feared by the Sri Lankan army and politicians. The unit's members were all volunteers who were strictly vetted and trained by LTTE's leadership and whose identities were concealed until they were killed in mission. In selecting among volunteers, the emphasis was on the personal discipline and moral fibre of individuals. As a rule, the Black Tigers were not lone suicide bombers but operated in small, cohesive groups, and as Hopgood (2005: 67) describes, 'the camaraderie of Black Tigers training' was highly significant 'in encouraging a sense of duty and obligation on missions, especially to one's comrades rather than to the more abstract goal of Tamil Eelam'. Before each mission, most volunteers would pursue ascetic lifestyles and would have a last meal and a picture taken with the leader of LTTE, Pirabakaran. As they operated and lived in small units, their emotional commitment and moral responsibility towards their comrades was well infused with the broader ideological and organisational goals of LTTE. In one of the rare clandestine interviews with a Black Tiger by a BBC journalist, one can encounter justification for the suicide killings that incorporates the organisational and ideological aims with more personal motivations. The interviewee mentioned his killed relatives and 'wanted to show his strength to safeguard not only his family but his community. . . . the suicide bomber said he was not scared to die for the cause and although his parents did not know he was a member of the Black Tigers they would be proud of his achievements when his time came' (Harrison 2002: 1). As Hopgood (2005: 76) shows, the Black Tigers were driven by 'a heightened sense of personal responsibility', and the selection for suicide missions brought about a collective feeling of being chosen, 'of being one of the elect with others, and therefore of having a special obligation to one's own comrades to uphold the honour of the unit'.

Although suicide bombings and other forms of terrorist attacks have gained great deal of attention, the importance of microsolidarity is just as visible in instances of 'dying without killing' – self-immolations. This practice has a long history involving in particular Buddhist- and to some extent Hindu-inspired resistance movements. Self-immolation is regularly perceived as a profoundly individualised form of violent protest, with notable historical examples of the Vietnamese Buddhist monk Quang Duc, who burned himself in a busy Saigon street to protest persecution of Buddhists by the South Vietnamese government in 1963; Jan Palach setting himself alight to oppose the Soviet invasion of Czechoslovakia in 1968; or more recently the self-immolation of Mohamed Bouazizi that ignited 2010 Tunisian Revolution. Hence some authors insist that while suicide attacks are generally organised, 'self-immolation is inherently individualistic' (Biggs 2005: 207). Nevertheless, since Durkheim's (1952 [1897]) early studies on suicide, sociologists have become aware that an overwhelming majority of such acts have a strong social component. Although suicide is by definition an individual act, based on a personal decision to cease one's existence by violent means, such decisions are frequently a direct response to the broader social environment. Hence Durkheim emphasised the significance of what he termed the 'altruistic suicide' – killing one's self for the benefit or preservation of others. For Durkheim, this form of suicide was prevalent in the premodern world of mechanical solidarity where the 'individual personality' tended to overlap with the 'collective personality'. Thus if there was a societal expectation for a member of a group (tribe, clan, lineage, etc.) to kill himself or herself for the sake of the group's well-being, he or she would go along with this. The typical examples are the practice of *sati*, which used to be widespread in some parts of Asia, in which a recently widowed woman kills herself by jumping into her husband's pyre, or Japanese tradition of *seppuku* (*hara-kiri*), a ritual disembowelling to preserve the honour of one's family. With hindsight, it is clear that Durkheim was wrong about the premodern character of this practice, as altruistic suicide has been just as present in the modern era as it was in the past. Moreover, over the last three decades such acts have gained in political significance, and since the Iran–Iraq War of the 1980s, martyrdom was institutionalised as a potent weapon of war and terrorism.

Although much public focus has been on suicide bombings, self-immolations have also proved to be a potent instrument of social and political action. From Quang Duc's demonstrative death in 1960s Vietnam to the 2010–2011 Arab Spring's self-immolations in Tunisia, Saudi Arabia, Syria and Mauritania, this form of altruistic suicide has proliferated as a social mechanism of protest. Biggs (2005: 174) estimates that up to 3,000 individual acts of self-immolation have occurred throughout the world since Quang Duc's suicide in 1963. He compiled a database of 533 individual cases of self-immolation (from 1963–2002), which shows that the pattern of clustering of such acts in space and time with self-immolation occurring in waves and through the copy-cat imitation of others. In his view, most such activities have a strong instrumental dimension as they tend to advance the collective cause by demonstrating the intensity of popular grievances and by inciting sympathisers to feel guilty about their inaction. What is also crucial, and this is omitted by Biggs, is that most such self-immolations rely on the emotional support of one's close friends, family and peers. Even in Quang Duc's case, the immolation was well planned and agreed upon with his friends and colleagues. As Browne (1993: 9) describes, his fellow Buddhist monks discussed his proposal and after long deliberation agreed to go ahead with the plan. They also tested different fuels, informed journalists beforehand and organised nuns and other monks to stop firefighters from reaching the burning Quang Dac. The precisely organised spectacle also involved a monk with a loudspeaker proclaiming the five key requests, while other monks distributed the English translation of Quang Duc's declaration. A similar pattern of action was just as visible with PIRA and INLA hunger strikers in Long Kesh prison, who too were well organised and were able to publicise widely their political messages. The deaths of Long Kesh hunger strikers such as Bobby Sands and Francis Hughes galvanised the Irish nationalist movement and had worldwide appeal. Thus while on hunger strike Sands was elected as a Westminster member of parliament (MP), and two other Republican candidates were elected in the Republic of Ireland. Moreover, commemorations of hunger strikers became a powerful and important recruiting tool for the Republican cause. However, this organisational and ideological scaffold was built extensively on the microsolidarity of hunger strikers, whose personalised emotional bond was crucial for initiating and persisting in the hunger strike until the very end (O'Hearn 2009, 2006).

Conclusion

Terrorism is a complex phenomenon that requires the use of the socio-logical tools of analysis. There is no doubt that the leading cultural-centred, sociological accounts make an important contribution to this analysis. It would be difficult to imagine a terrorist activity which does not rely on the specific cultural codes, does not make an appeal to the particular moral norms or does not offer distinct narrative scripts to justify the use of violence. In many important respects, there is no terrorism without culture as all organised collective violence entails elaborate cultural appeals to social meanings. Since human beings are meaning oriented creatures their actions require meaningful goals and ends. The main strength of culture-centred perspectives is this analytical attempt to capture the impact of values on violent action and vice versa. However, being overly focussed on such values may also lead to the neglect of the more materialist, structural, historical and geopolitical sources of terrorism. Hence culturalism displays some explanatory weaknesses, such as pronounced epistemological idealism, the lack of robust empirical validation and the inability to elucidate the macro/micro dynamics of terrorism. In order to circumvent such pitfalls, it is necessary to articulate an alternative, longue durée interpretation which focusses on the role of social organisations, ideological power and microsolidarity. In this chapter, I have attempted to develop this approach in order to show how terrorism, just like other forms of organised violence, operates according to similar sociohistorical dynamics. Despite its inherent particularities, terrorism too is a social and historical phenomenon moulded by the cumulative bureaucratisation of coercion, centrifugal ideologisation and the envelopment of microsolidarity.

9   Why Do Humans Fight?

Introduction

This chapter focusses on the social dynamics of group cohesion in the context of organised violence. While recent debates on social cohesion have highlighted the relevance of solidarity, the existing parameters of this debate have been historically too narrow and sociologically too thin. Hence to fully understand the character and significance of group ties, it is critical to bring in historical sociology. I argue that when one looks through the lens of the longue durée sociological analysis, it is possible to make a case that violence-induced social cohesion is a universal phenomenon and also one of the main sources of an individual's will to fight. Nevertheless, this is not to say that the human beings are naturally gregarious creatures. On the contrary, this chapter attempts to show how micro-level solidarities are shaped by macro-level organisational and ideological processes. The aim is to explore the historical origins of social cohesion and its relationship with the organised violence. In this context, I briefly compare and contrast different social orders throughout time and space to assess how diverse social structures mould group cohesion. I argue that the microsolidarities are deeply linked with specific forms of social development and that their military significance increases with organisational and ideological expansion.

Social Cohesion and the Military Organisation

There is an interesting paradox underpinning much military thinking and writing. On the one hand, most high-ranking officers and traditional military scholars espouse a strong version of the Hobbesian ontology where violence is understood to be a natural and inevitable part of social life. For Hobbesians, the natural state of a human being is one of war – *homo homini lupus est*. On the other hand, military thinkers and officers are also aware that most human beings are unlikely to fight other humans unless they are strongly induced to do so. In some respects, this paradox is understandable, as any attempt to recognise that violence is not a necessity of social relations might unwillingly stimulate defeatist attitudes among future recruits and soldiers. In other respects, the unspoken recognition that most individuals require strong inducements to fight means that much of military scholarship had to focus on the issue of soldiers' motivation to engage in violence. From Sun-Tzu to Thucydides to Machiavelli and Clausewitz and beyond, a great deal of attention was devoted to questions such as: Why do soldiers fight? How can the fighting capacity of individuals be increased? Under which conditions soldiers are likely to fight better and longer?

Throughout history, most military leaders were interested in answers to these questions. However, the issue of soldiers' motivation gained in importance once governments started relying on mass mobilisations. The emergence of all-citizen armies in the late-eighteenth and early-nineteenth century signified a substantial change in the military affairs. Whereas in the previous historical epochs the possession of an aristocratic lineage automatically implied a degree of military responsibility, now all male (and in some instances, also female) citizens were the subject of potential recruitment. Hence to secure a successful mobilisation and the continuous performance of their military tasks, it was essential to identify what motivates recruits' behaviour on the battlefield. Since the early studies of French colonel Charles Ardant du Picq (2006 [1880]), analysts became aware that success on the battlefield was often determined by the intensity of social cohesion of soldiers. Du Picq emphasized the mental state of soldiers and 'moral force' as the decisive factors governing success and failure on the frontline. In contrast to the traditional views that simply assumed that once on the battlefield soldiers would automatically fight and support each other, Du Picq understood the social complexity of group motivation. Thus he states that 'Man does not enter battle to fight, but for victory. He does everything that he can to avoid the first and obtain the second' (p. 55). Therefore, one of the chief responsibilities of military commanders is to make clear how this victory can be achieved and what the goals of each battle, and the entire war, are. Moreover, Du Picq was adamant that group cohesion does not develop instinctively but is something that requires intense social action: 'The soldier is unknown often to his closest companions. He loses them in the disorienting smoke and confusion of a battle which he is fighting, so to speak, on his own. Cohesion is no longer ensured by mutual observation' (p. 110).

De Picq's reflections generated a more systematic study of soldiers' motivation on the frontline. The development of military psychology and sociology throughout the twentieth century has resulted in numerous empirical analyses of individual and collective behaviour in the theatres of war. The pioneering studies conducted during World War II by Marshall (1947) and Shils and Janowitz (1948) dominated this field of research for decades. These two influential contributions have set the foundation of the so-called primary group model of social cohesion. The key issue advanced by both studies emphasised the centrality of small-group interactions as a primary driving force of soldiers' willingness to fight. Shils and Janowitz attempted to show how the determination of the Wehrmacht units to fight until the very end of the war was not the result of their ideological fanaticism but had much more to do with their sense of attachment and responsibility towards their military comrades. In a similar vein, Marshall focussed on the motivations of American soldiers who were deployed to fight far away from their homeland. Marshall shocked his readers and the military establishment with the now-famous claim that less than 25 per cent of the frontline U.S. combatants were willing to shoot at their enemy. However, their general unwillingness to fight was counterbalanced by their feeling of attachment and responsibility towards their fellow platoon members. So in this case, too, the findings pointed away from strong ideological commitments and towards primary group solidarity. Hence these two studies established the model whereby the principal motivational factor in warfare for most soldiers was a sense of loyalty and belonging to one's military unit: a squad, a platoon or company. Most latter-day studies attempted to confirm or challenge this finding.

With the outbreak of the Vietnam War, a new wave of scholarship emerged, some of which was highly critical of the pioneering studies. For example, Madej (1978) argued that the early studies were wrong in their claim that greater social cohesion produces more efficient soldiers. Instead, he attempted to demonstrate the reverse effect: it is the already existing military skills, discipline and efficiency that generated more cohesive military units. Others criticised the original model as being overly static since the social cohesion tends to oscillate in time and space, with some groups also exhibiting greater bonds than other similar units (Tuckman 1965; Siebold and Lindsay 1999). Some research, mostly historical, such as Bartov (1991), revisited the archival material in order to show that many Wehrmacht units had very high death ratios, which would suggest that they could not develop strong bonds in such a short time and that Nazi ideology was much more influential in their motivation than what pioneering studies claimed. Other studies explored more specific links (i.e. the relationship between leadership and social cohesion, the connections between the unit goals and their performance, the difference between social cohesion and task cohesion, etc.), but they generally tended to confirm the basic tenets of Marshall's and Shils and Janowitz's studies. Simply put, there is an accumulated wealth of evidence indicating that much of soldiers' motivation remains centred on small-group affection (Moskos 1975; Tziner and Vardi 1982; Henderson 1985; Griffith 1989; Stewart 1991; Winslow 1997; Wong et al. 2003). These studies focus on the different military conflicts (from Vietnam to the Falklands War, Iraq, Afghanistan, etc.) and different social and political contexts, yet they have produced quite similar findings – soldiers are more committed and better fighters when they are well integrated and can rely on small-group bonds. As Stewart (1991: 17) concludes: 'Disparate men from varied socioeconomic backgrounds, of different ethnic origins and levels of education, are expected to become not just a collective of individuals but a unit in which an individual will sacrifice his life and die in order to preserve the group. Because of well-developed friendship or camaraderie, men will fight individually as a part of a unit to defend the group as a unit'.

Nevertheless, more recent scholarship has questioned the link between motivation and social cohesion (King 2013; Segal and Kestnbaum 2002; Janis 1985). Anthony King (2013: 32) argues that group cohesion cannot be reduced to interpersonal motivation, as these two phenomena are independent: 'since interpersonal motivation can at best be only one factor in explaining combat performance, it cannot be the sole focus of attention in this analysis'. For example, highly cohesive groups might prioritise solidarity over performance and thus disrupt the goals of a particular military organisation (Winslow 1997; Janis 1985). As Fuller (1990) shows, it was the intense solidarity of its infantry units that contributed to the collapse of the French army in World War I, as soldiers' loyalty to their microgroup was much stronger than their sense of responsibility towards the military organisation as a whole. Moreover, empirical studies indicate that the opposite relationship is also not unusual: the high levels of military performance combined with low intensity of social cohesion. This is particularly the case in contemporary wars, where professional soldiers do not interact much with each other and rely extensively on sophisticated technology to achieve high-performance targets (i.e. pilots, drone and missile navigators, etc.). In order to circumvent this problem King (2013: 36–37) suggests that cohesion should be redefined so that the focus on motivation is replaced with that of performance itself. In other words, 'cohesion is no longer taken to refer to motivation or to interpersonal bonds but exclusively and specifically to the successful coordination of actions on the battlefield'. Simply put, for King, who draws on Durkheim and Parsons, cohesion is a form of social action: 'cohesion refers most accurately to collective action itself, and specifically, to successful collective performance, not to sentiments which encourage that performance'.

While King's contribution to this debate is valuable and his criticisms are pointed, one could argue that the debate itself is still framed too narrowly. One of the main problems here is that the dynamics of group solidarity in most of these studies are largely reduced to its military utility. In other words, instead of analysing how and why small-group solidarity develops, transforms, oscillates or collapses, the main focus is on how specific group ties aid the military effort. In this endeavour, there is not much difference between the two leading representatives of the recent social cohesion debate – King and Siebold. While Siebold insists that the personal bonds between soldiers motivate high military performance, for King the quality of combat performance itself is the most reliable indicator of social cohesion. Nevertheless, to understand how microgroup dynamics operate in violent contexts, such as battlefields, but also terrorist actions, direct genocidal experience or active participation in violent revolutionary upheavals, it is necessary to move away from the obsession with the military performance. For one thing, 'performance' is really a technical euphemism for a soldier's willingness to take part in shooting, injuring and killing other human beings ('the enemy'). For another, 'performance' implies readiness to accept hierarchical commands and to comply with the orders. Once these two types of activity are integrated with one's sense of responsibility towards the other members of the military unit, then 'performance' is usually deemed to be of a very high standard.

While military organisations are primarily interested in the question of a soldier's utility (to fight), this is not where sociology's focus lies. Hence the key sociological questions are: Why and when human beings are willing to injure and kill other humans? Is this related to their sense of attachment to small groups? Under which circumstances are humans willing to sacrifice themselves for others? Is the micro-level group the primary source of an individual's motivation to kill and die for others? How are micro-level dynamics related to the macrostructural contexts? Is micro-level solidarity a universal phenomenon or something specific to the particular historical and geographic contexts? What role do social organisations and ideologies play in the formation and maintenance of microsolidarity? Let us try to provide answers to some of these questions.

Violence and Microsolidarity

From the early works on social cohesion until more recent debates, the idea of a 'primary group' has acted as a springboard for most analyses.

Shils and Janowitz's argument was largely built on the Chicago school sociologist Charles Cooley's (1909) concept of the primary group. Cooley conceptualised the primary group as a small unit defined by intimacy and direct face-to-face interaction: 'by primary groups I mean those characterized by intimate face-to-face association and cooperation. They are primary in several senses, but chiefly in that they are funda-mental in forming the social nature and ideals of the individual. The result of intimate association, psychologically, is a certain fusion of individualities in a common whole, so that one's very self, for many purposes at least, is the common life and purpose of the group' (Cooley 1909: 25). In his view, the typical examples of a primary group are 'the family, the play-group of children, and the neighbourhood or community group of elders'. Although Cooley's original concept was largely associ-ated with the intimate groups central to one's early socialization, such as family and peers, military sociologists and psychologists tended to apply the same concept to the close-knit social relations that emerge among individuals on the battlefield (Siebold 2011). While there is no doubt that the intense emotional ties that develop among soldiers exposed to mortal danger often resemble those among caring family members, the two types of group solidarity do not necessarily operate according to the same principles. While close family attachments and deep childhood friend-ships rarely if ever involve imminent threats to one's life, this is one of the key components of microgroup solidarity on the frontline. Furthermore, whereas civilian friendships and family ties entail long-term daily inter-actions, the small groups associated with violent experiences tend to forge intense emotional ties over much shorter periods of time. Hence to better understand how microsolidarity works in units exposed to violence, it is important to keep them distinct from other forms of intimate social groupings.

Another equally important problem with the primary group model is its largely essentialist and inflexible understanding of social ties. King (2007: 641) has already criticised the psychological essentialism that often underpins the primary group model of social cohesion: 'it seems likely that social psychologists, like Siebold, who define social cohesion as an emotional essence, which pre-exists practice, simply fail to observe or acknowledge the social practices in which cohesion is actually created and sustained'. In both instances of the primary group model, the civilian and military, deep emotional attachments entail shared social practice. There is no solidarity without practice. However, King's cri-tique does not go far enough. In addition to the rampant essentialism, the primary group model is also too groupcentric to account for the subtlety of social interaction on and off the violent contexts. As

Brubaker (2015, 2004) convincingly shows, no group has fixed and inherently stable properties. Although his focus is on large-scale entities, such as nations and ethnicities, where a simple category designation such as 'Serb' or 'Hutu' is regularly misread as a group attribute, the same principle applies to much smaller units. The notion of a 'primary group' as something defined by primordial emotional bonds, or as Cooley put it, by 'the relatively simple and general condition of the social mind' (p. 31), is deeply flawed. The contemporary reincarnation of this idea is also present in the decline of violence paradigm, as both Pinker (2011) and Gat (2006) understand group formation in biologically static and essentialist terms. However, rather than being overly stable and given property of a particular collective unit, group-ness is a variable category. A group, regardless of how small it may be, is never a fixed and bounded entity shaped by intuitive bonds. Instead of reifying 'primary groups' as corporal entities, it is important to explore the dynamics of social action that generates temporarily strong forms of group-ness. In this sense, any distinction between the primary and secondary groups can only be provisional and thus not particularly valuable. Instead, the focus is to shift towards the social mechanics of group formation, and in this case particularly how the shared experience of violence, or the imminent threat to one's existence, impacts on the dynamics of microsolidarity.

While the intense emotional ties of the small, violence-experiencing, groups are important for the existence of military units, terrorist outfits, revolutionary organisations or genocidal troops, this process also works the other way around. It is the social organisations (and ideologies) that help sustain pockets of concentrated microsolidarity. If one discounts the rigid sociobiological and other primordialist concepts of sociability à la Pinker and Gat, it becomes apparent that human beings do not have a genetic propensity towards group formation. In contrast to the conventional, and rather crude, primordialist interpretations which base much of their judgement on simple analogies between humans and other animals, the more sophisticated biological studies of social relations emphasise sharp differences between hominids and other simians (see Chapter 3). Turner and Maryanski (2005) summarise these findings, which show that unlike monkeys, which are more gregarious, the life of early hominids was much less social. Since most monkeys live on trees rich with fruit, they were often in position to grow and sustain large packs. In contrast, the walking apes, who originated in African savannahs where there were no trees and an abundance of predators, had to move in very small and highly flexible groupings in order to survive. The legacy of this divide is still visible among the surviving species of apes, such as orangutans, chimpanzees and gorillas, where social ties between adults are quite weak. The direct consequence of life spent in a hostile environment was the emergence of fluid and porous social bonds. Hence the early humans did not live in the 'primary groups'; instead, they populated small foraging bands, which, apart from the mother–child dyad, were highly flexible and whose internal composition was in constant flux. Since humans were poorly equipped for survival in African savannahs, their lack of sharp teeth, speed, horns or claws was ultimately compensated for by the gradual development of their unique emotional and cognitive abilities. The ability to generate but also read emotions of constantly changing others combined with ever-more complex cognitive capacities has been a decisive mechanism for the survival of humans as a species (Collins 2004; Damasio 2003; Turner 2007). The defining feature of emotional interactions is proximity. In order to utilise cognitive and emotional abilities, it was necessary for early humans to intensify face-to-face interactions in order to read the visual cues which indicate different emotional reactions. This emotional and cognitive fine-tuning took hundreds of thousands years to perfect, but once fully developed it gave birth to a new form of social interaction – microsolidarity. However, while microsolidarity is dependent on the intense emotional relations and cognitive exchange, its existence entails prolonged joined social action. In other words, the mere presence of emotions and cognitions does not by itself generate microgroup solidarities. Instead, such ties require coordinated and shared action. For most human beings, bonds of microsolidarity are built around the individuals they grow up with – their parents, siblings, close relatives, childhood friends, neighbours, early peers, etc. Nevertheless, even these very close bonds are far from being automatic or genetic: they all entail protracted emotional and cognitive work. Although parents and children usually form strong emotional (and cognitive) ties, the loving relationships they share are built on years of shared emotional (and cognitive) action. This is not to say that these relationships are inevitably symmetrical nor that such shared feelings do not oscillate and change. On the contrary, all emotional ties are dynamic and variable. Moreover, specific microgroup bonds can change content over time so that what initially was a desire and love might gradually transform into a sense of responsibility, attachment through interdependence or habitual satisfaction, to name a few. All emotional and cognitive bonds involve social action even when one of the sides does not regularly reciprocate. The intensity of many microgroup attachments often hides the fact that all social relations are fragile. While two lovers might constantly express their unconditional love for each other, their affective bond is as strong as the social action they put into this relationship. Simply put, a more shared emotional and cognitive action is likely to forge stronger and more durable bonds of microsolidarity.

While in many respects microsolidarity is a universal phenomenon that transcends time and space, there are significant differences between the social microbonds developed through habitual and prolonged experience of shared life and those generated in violent environments. Much of microsocial interaction is built around emotional and cognitive needs that involve sense of security, overcoming of fear, emotional comfort and trust, among others. In this sense, violent environments such as war, terrorism or revolution generate threatening situations that foster more intense emotional reactions. Consequently, individuals who find themselves in such hostile environments are prone towards developing intense microsocial ties over much shorter periods of time. What in everyday 'civilian' life usually takes years of interactive work and personal dedication in times of violent crises such intense bonds develop in a matter of months or even weeks. As pointed out in Chapter 5, the classics of sociology such as Simmel and Weber were already aware that wars bring about 'absolute situations' which heighten one's experience and serve as a 'unifying, simplifying and concentrating force' (Simmel 1917: 20). For Weber (2004: 225), warfare creates 'feeling of community' and 'releases an unconditional community of sacrifice among the combatants'. The emotional and cognitive experience of those involved in the terrorist campaigns, revolutionary overthrows, direct genocidal practices or street gang fights has often been described in the similar terms (Stephenson 2015; Mann 2005; della Porta 2013). Obviously there are sound psychological and physiological reasons why human beings behave differently when they find themselves in life-threatening situations. Moreover, such frightening social environments stimulate one's emotions and cognitions. For example, the meticulous studies of Grossman (1996) and Grossman and Christensen (2000) demonstrate how in direct violent contexts human physiognomy and psychology change in enable affected individuals to survive. Thus Grossman identifies regularly occurring phenomena on the battlefield, such as the experience of the slow motion time, tunnel vision, heightened visual clarity, memory loss, auditory exclusion (i.e. the shots are not heard), increased cortisol levels (to help blood clot quickly) and the loss of bladder and bowel control, among others. In such a threatening environment, when emotions and cognitions are regularly heightened, microsocial bonds tend to develop and grow within much shorter periods of time. Hence people who have a shared life-threatening experience often tend to develop and maintain friendships built almost solely around that experience. This seems to be the case not only for soldiers, terrorists or revolutionaries but also for airplane crash survivors or former concentration camp inmates. While external hostility does by itself foster the rise of microsolidarity, the bonding mechanisms present in military, terrorist or revolutionary units entail more complexity. Instead of appearing as an automatic response to a dangerous external threat, the networks of microsolidarity developed in squads, platoons or regiments are often an organisationally and ideologically generated phenomenon. This is not to say that emotions that individual soldiers, revolutionaries or terrorists experience in relation to their buddies are fake or artificial, but only that such feelings (and cognitions) have more of macrostructural rather than only microinteractional origins. Hence to understand how microsolidarity works, it is crucial to focus one's attention on the social organisations that create, sustain and utilise the organisational and ideological means that make such microgroup bonds possible.

The scholars of social cohesion in the military tend to disagree over the question of what is the appropriate level of analysis for cohesion. So Siebold (2011: 455) differentiates between the 'primary group cohesion model', which relates to squads and platoons, and 'the secondary group cohesion model', involving organisational bonding generated at the higher level of organisational unit, such as the company or battalion. He argues that much of the existing research on the U.S. military indicates that although cohesion is present at all unit levels, the surveys indicate 'that military cohesion was best assessed at the small group level such as the squad (about ten members) or platoon (a little over thirty members)'. While Siebold (2007: 288–289) makes some interesting points about the different levels of integration, he tends to assume that a particular military unit and a group are the same thing. Nevertheless, unlike a military unit (i.e. squad, platoon or battalion), which is a fixed and formal bureaucratic entity created and sustained by the wider organisational structure, groupness is much more flexible, dynamic and informal unit of sociality. In other words, whereas a platoon is an organisational shell produced by the military bureaucracy that pays little or no attention to respective individuals who populate that unit of organisation, the group-ness is dependent on the very characteristics of individuals who compose that entity. A military unit is a formal bureaucratic vessel that is replaceable and can be populated with any set of individuals who meet the standard criteria of military recruitment. In this sense, its composition is relatively arbitrary, as it is largely built around the principles of military utility and quantity of armed and trained physical bodies. Thus, from the organisational point of view, all platoons have a similar value – the focus is on having more and better trained military units so that they can overpower the adversary military organisations and their respective units. In this sense, a platoon is almost the exact opposite of a close-knit group: while the intensity of group-ness is defined by one's sense of emotional and cognitive attachments, the bureaucratic units are valued by their organisational functionality. Simply put, while group ties entail warmth, deep friendships, love, care and sense of personal loyalty, a bureaucratic units stand for detachment, professional coldness, instrumental rationality and the strict following of rules (Malešević 2013a, 2011).

To overcome this deep paradox at the heart of the military and other coercive systems, it is critical to make these arbitrary organisational vessels into social cohesive groups. However, as human beings are complex and dynamic creatures whose senses of group attachment change and oscillate, it is difficult to make such personal bonds overlap with the instrumental goals of the military bureaucracies. As Kirke (2009: 748, 751) rightly argues, social cohesion is never absolute nor constant: 'it varies among groups and within a single group at different times ... it is not a matter of fixed blocks of cohesion but of a variable and flexible set of loyalties that are manifested in cooperation and opposition according to context'. Furthermore, even though members of a particular squad or platoon can develop a strong sense of attachment, this does not mean that they are equally attached to all their squad/platoon members. On the contrary, individuals are always likely to have people who they feel closer to than others within the same tightly integrated unit. In addition, these individual preferences can also change so that the soldiers break off old friendships and make new close ones.

Nevertheless, as success in war and other organised violent activities frequently depends on social cohesion and the morale of small-scale fighting units, military organisations have devoted a great deal of energy and resources in making such small-scale units resemble close-knit groups. In some respects, this is obvious as many contemporary military organisations invest heavily into developing systems that allow for such forms of social cohesion to develop. For example, the U.S. army allocates substantial resources for the Cohesion, Operational Readiness and Training (COHORT) manning system that studies how networks of microgroup solidarity relate to military performance. Moreover, over the last twenty years, different branches of U.S., U.K., French and other militaries have implemented significant changes in their armed forces so as to utilise micro-level cohesion for military tasks. Hence the recruiting military agencies focus now on drafting recruits not as individuals but where possible as a group of established friends from the same towns and villages. Complex weapons such as the anti-aircraft missiles, which can be manned by a single individual, are regularly allocated to two or more soldiers to forge and utilise their small-scale group attachments (Collins 2008a).

All these examples indicate that rather than being an innate propensity of human life, microsolidarity is often a structurally generated phenomenon. Moreover, one could argue that much of history has not been shaped by the inherently cohesive natural primary groups, as claimed by many military psychologists and sociologists, but by social organisations capable of generating, using and justifying the use of such micro-ties for the specific organisational ends. Since our prehistoric predecessors did not live in the 'primary groups', but generally tended to inhabit very fluid, flexible and unstable networks of survival, it is no historical accident that the strong bonds of microsolidarity emerge together with the development and expansion of the first durable social organisations. One could argue that the more intense forms of micro-level solidarity materialise with, but also against, the emerging macrostructural organisational forces. From the complex settled hunter-gatherers, some of which developed into chiefdoms, over the first imperial capstone empires, to a variety of kingdoms, sultanates, city-states or city-leagues, human beings were exposed to the process that Mann (1986) calls social caging. By this, he means the organisational entrapment that human beings gradually experience as they move away from nomadic to state-controlled sedentary lifestyles. With the rise of state power, often reinforced through the expansion of warfare, organisational capacities increase, thus generating particular territorial and social relations that ultimately force individuals to 'trade' their original freedoms for security and safety. Although Mann's focus is on the development and expansion of state structures throughout the world, this idea applies equally to all forms of durable and complex social organisations – from business enterprises and religious institutions to terrorist networks (Malešević 2013a, see also Chapter 3).

None of this is to say that social organisations intentionally forge pockets of microsolidarity. Even today, the most sophisticated and well-organised military establishments, such as the U.S. army or Israeli Defence Forces, have great difficulty in creating cohesive military units by design. Despite the enormous resources, the availability of modern scientific apparatuses at their disposal or the sophisticated training practices and facilities, there are no simple recipes for the production of social cohesion in the military forces. The further one steps into history, this intentionality becomes even more chimerical.

Violence and Social Cohesion in the Premodern World

Thus for much of human history the rulers and other individuals in charge of their respective social organisations lacked the means or even interest to forge or utilise small-group cohesion. As Hall (1985) rightly emphasizes, one of the key features of premodern empires is their inability and lack of ambition to build a societywide and shared normative and organisational structure. Hence unlike contemporary nation-states, which have highly developed infrastructural powers and the capacity to penetrate their civil societies, including the pockets of microsolidarity within their territorial domain, the ancient empires were, in this sense, feeble leviathans. While the Chinese or Sumerian emperors had enormous despotic powers, including the right to behead the individuals they deemed to be a threat to their rule, such emperors had great difficulty enforcing their will across the large territories under their nominal control. Since they were organisationally (and ideologically) weak, they had to rely on the local notables to collect taxes, mobilise recruits for wars or implement specific religious edicts. Hence when effective small-scale cohesive groups emerged, they ordinarily developed at the top of social pyramid – either in opposition to the imperial structures or as an unintended byproduct of imperial order. For example, the two very cohesive social and political groups that emerged in imperial China, the court eunuchs and the bureaucrat scholars, mandarins, were direct byproducts of the organisational structure of the Chinese imperial court. Although these two professional orders consisted of many diverse individuals who displayed varying degrees of loyalty within their order, their different structural positions fostered antagonistic relationships between the two collectivities (Darwin 2008; Jones 1987). While these elite groupings were not directly involved in organised violence, they emerged through similar organisational processes that gave birth to the more specialised, violence-wielding social units. The typical examples here would be the elite warrior strata such as the Japanese samurai and the Egyptian mamluks.[1] Both of these warrior organisations consisted of highly cohesive and loyal individuals who were also very accomplished and effective soldiers capable of defeating much larger enemy forces. The samurai were the nobility who were organised in hierarchical structures with the feudal lords (*daimyo*) dominating individual clans. The clan memberships were strong, and the loyalty towards one's own clan was beyond dispute. The sense of duty towards one's lord and the entire clan was installed into samurai from early childhood. In addition, the early martial

---

[1] It is important to note that both Mamluks and samurai were not confined to a single polity. While samurai originated in China and were present in Korea, they achieved much of their influence in Japan. In a similar way, Mamluks were present throughout the Islamic world from Persia and the Ottoman Empire to India and the Caucasus.

training encouraged loyalty to lords and other clan member samurai and celebrated self-discipline and a disdain for pain, fear and material possessions (Clements, 2010).

Unlike the samurai, who were often members of the warrior elite by birth, the Mamluks were slave soldiers who only became military (and occasionally political) elite by merit. The Mamluk soldiers were often forcibly removed as boys from their families and brought to the imperial centres for military training. Over the centuries (the ninth through the nineteenth), this practice generated a distinct warrior caste capable of fighting prolonged wars and even capturing political power, as was the case with the Mamluk Sultanate (1250–1517) in what is today Egypt and Syria. Similarly to the samurai, these elite military units were run by the lords (i.e. patrons), who were responsible for ensuring that the soldiers underwent rigorous and austere military training and education. The military advancement of an individual Mamluk was dependent on the patron's support but the reputation and influence of patrons themselves were also dependent on the military prowess of the Mamluks under their control. Since mamluks grew up together in the military schools, separated from their families, they developed strong sense of attachment to their mamluk comrades. As Behrens-Abouseif (2008: 76) emphasises, each mamluk was 'bound by a strong spirit de corps to his peers in the same household'. As a rule, the mamluk armies lived separated from society in their garrisons, where they spent most of their time with each other, thus reinforcing already intense friendships. Thus in both the cases of the samurai and the mamluks, one can encounter highly cohesive military units which exhibited a strong sense of loyalty to each other and to their order.

Nevertheless, what is less apparent here is that in both of these cases social cohesion emerged not through the bottom-up 'primary group' bonding but was largely created by existing social organisations. The institution of samurai grew out of the Japanese military reform during the Asuka and Nara periods. The Taika reform under Emperor Tenji led to issuing of Taiho Code (702 CE), which introduced a requirement that one in four adult males had to be drafted into the state military. Imitating the existing Chinese system, the rulers introduced the imperial bureaucratic system with twelve ranks, where the last six ranks were termed 'samurai' (Turnbull 2013). Over time, these civilian public servants gradually became an elite military order. In a similar way, the Mamluk system was a product of the top-down coercive organisational change aimed at increasing the military efficiency of the empire. It seems that the system originated in ninth-century Abbasid caliphate, in which the caliph al-Mu'tasim (833–842 CE) used his best slaves (*ghilman*) to supplement its existing military units. While initially the ghilman system was an ad hoc arrangement which included mixed units of slaves and freemen who had little or no systematic military training, once slave soldiers proved valuable warriors the caliph al-Muwaffaq established a new system in the 870s CE where young slaves were systematically trained in military arts. In addition to being highly respected for their martial capabilities, the slave army was highly sought after because the soldiers had no family attachments and as such were more reliable, trustworthy and loyal to the emperor.

Hence in both of these cases, the internal cohesion of military units was the product of the specific historical and structural developments. Those involved coercive-organisational mechanisms, such as the creation of a slave army from forced abductions in one case and the imperial decree for mobilisation of civil/military servants in other case. Moreover, in addition to the organisational force, in both cases proto-ideology played a crucial role in mobilising social action and in maintaining the respective social orders. The samurai's famous Bushido code underpinned much of their daily activity. This proto-ideology centred on the eight key virtues: righteousness, courage, benevolence, respect, sincerity, honour, loyalty and self-control (Benesch 2014; Clements 2010). This 'way of the warrior' drew on the ethical prescriptions articulated by neo-Confucianism, Shinto and Zen Buddhism, and as such provided moral legitimacy to the institution of the samurai. Since Bushido was a set of value prescriptions that emanated from the wider Japanese social and political order, it also served as a mechanism of politywide organisational justification. That is, in addition to the coercive-organisational structures that made the institution of samurai possible, this proto-ideology also facilitated development of social cohesion at the micro level. In other words, the strong networks of microsolidarity that characterised samurai clans were generated and maintained by structural forces: the presence of coercive social organisations which were legitimised through effective proto-ideological doctrines and practices.

The Mamluk social order was created and maintained through similar structural contexts. On top of the coercive organisational structure that gave birth to and facilitated its existence, the Mamluk units legitimised their actions in relation to a specific proto-ideological doctrine – a particular version of Islam. As Broadbridge (2008: 12) explains, since Mamluks were slaves, they could not invoke lineage as a source of status legitimation. This was particularly visible in cases where Mamluks rose to the top of social pyramid and embraced key ruling positions. Hence during the early years of the Mamluk Sultanate, its leaders, former slaves or descendents of slaves, had to devise alternative models of political legitimation in order to secure both external and internal recognition. For example, when Mamluk sultan Baybars approached King Hetum I of Armenia, he was rejected not because of his Muslim faith but only because of his lowly origin: Hetum called Baybars 'a dog and a slave' and as such 'refused to have any dealings with him' (Broadbridge 2008: 13). To eliminate the stigma of servitude and the lack of distinguished lineage, the Mamluks had no other choice but to rely on Islam. In this context, the dominant mode of political legitimacy, the idea of the divine origins of rulers, had to be modified so as that lineage was downplayed at the expense of excessive loyalty to one's true faith. Hence the proto-ideology of the early Mamluk sultans emphasised 'antiquated Islamic concepts' and the 'vision of the Mameluk sultan as a martial guardian of Islam and Islamic society'. This shift in focus from lineage to faith was also pronounced among the ordinary Mamluks, who tended to accentuate their loyalty to their clan, order, religion and the polity. Since many Mamluks were forced converts whose lineage was either forgotten or deemed to be lowly, their sense of solidarity was enhanced through the shared attachment to their clan, order, faith and polity. Hence, in both of these cases, micro-level social cohesion was a direct product of structural developments.

While the large size of empires was an obstacle for development of the militarywide bonding mechanisms, before modernity this was less the case with smaller polities such as city-states or small chiefdoms. Nevertheless, even in these cases social cohesion did not emerge through the 'natural' ties of 'primary groups' but principally through the combination of the coercive and the proto-ideological mechanisms of the specific social organisations. For example, much military mythology glorifies the social cohesion of Spartan warriors, who at the height of their power were described by the legislator Lycurgus as so internally cohesive that Sparta maintained 'a wall of men, instead of bricks'. It is certainly true that Spartan soldiers were deeply attached to their military units and were often willing to sacrifice themselves for their fellow soldiers or fight to the last man. However, this relatively unique development was a direct product of the organisational work that underpinned the Spartan polity. The fact that all soldiers underwent identical training and shared a lifestyle from their infancy was the most significant element for forging lifelong bonds. The *agoge* system of military training, which involved rigorous and ascetic daily activities from the age of seven until thirty, helped create a fierce military machine but was also crucial in establishing deep microsocial ties between individuals who would spend years of harsh training and an austere lifestyle together. The young boys lived in small units (*agélai*, meaning herds) where they were expected to develop a sense of attachment to their fellow students with whom they shared the communal mess hall (*syssitia* or *pheiditia*). This daily shared meal ritual was compulsory, so as that even the kings could not be absent without a very good excuse. The small organisational units of young boys (*agelai*) were led by mature men who were also responsible for the ideological training of their pupils, helping them to conceptualise key values and principles of the Spartan city-state (Lazenby 2012). The Laconian proto-ideology stood for militarism, austerity, self-restraint and the moral virtues of masculinity and loyalty to one's group and the Spartan state. The agoge system of military education was effective in stimulating long-term microgroup ties, but what is apparent is that such ties were the direct product of coercive and proto-ideological structural contexts. Simply put, the small-group cohesion was largely generated by two external, structural forces: the coercive organisation of the Spartan polity and the proto-ideological value system that emphasised the moral quality of an ascetic and collectivist ethos. As Birgalias (2002) shows, the Spartan model of social cohesion was byproduct of the polity's devastating defeat at Leuctra and was initially devised to prevent internal conflicts within the polity. The main point here is that rather than simply utilising humans' alleged natural propensity to group formation, the Spartan city-state not only created organisational space for the development of microsolidarity but in fact generated that microsolidarity itself.

Violence and Social Cohesion in the Modern Era

All large-scale social organisations face difficulty in generating and maintaining social cohesion within their realms. This is particularly the case with organisational entities that utilise violence on a regular basis. Since most human beings are not particularly good at or comfortable with the use of violence (Collins 2008a), any mobilisation of violent social action entails the use of coercive pressure and/or ideological justification. In the premodern world, coercion often outweighed justification, and when justification was provided the tendency was to limit it to the elite. When the rulers were perceived to be god's representatives on Earth or gods themselves, as was the case in ancient Egypt, imperial China and Japan, Nepal, the Incas or the post–Julius Caesar Roman Empire,[2] there was less need to legitimise one's political and military actions.

---

[2] Caesar was deified in 42 BCE as 'Divine Julius'. This practice was followed by a number of other Roman emperors, including Caesar Augustus, deified as *Divi filius* (Son of the Divine One), Tiberius (14–37), Caligula (37–41), Claudius (41–54), Hadrian (117–138), Commodus (161–192), Constantine I (306–312) and Julian the Apostate (361–363).

The advent of modernity brought about substantial change. On the one hand the rulers were deprived of the traditional modes of justification as their actions had to be legitimised in relation to the new principles such as – the popular sovereignty, political equality, liberty, social justice or nationality to name a few. On the other hand, as the new social orders were built on the heritage of the Enlightenment, which glorifies reason, logic and peace, any large-scale use of violence entails deploying much more elaborate mechanisms of justification. Hence, unlike their traditional counterparts, who prioritised coercion, modern social organisations had to focus their attention on developing effective systems of control able to camouflage coercion behind complex ideological scaffolds. This is not to say that coercion is less present in modernity. On the contrary, precisely because the use of coercive action requires more popular legitimacy, its deployment is possible only when coercive acts become integrated into specific ideological practices. In other words, while in the traditional world (proto-)ideological justification is a useful but often not essential requirement for the use of violence, in modernity ideology is a sine qua non of any large-scale violent action.

As argued throughout this book, coercive-organisational power often merges with ideological power in the modern era. This merger takes a variety of forms and can range from the more explicit mobilisation of entire societies in times of large-scale interstate wars to less discernible processes such as when ideology and coercion come together in the everyday life of contemporary legal systems. Since those who control modern social organisations possess greater infrastructural capacities, including sophisticated technology, communications, transport, division of labour or complex hierarchies, they can generate and maintain huge coercive apparatuses, including those that specialise in the use of violence (i.e. police, military, terrorists, revolutionaries, etc.). Since such large bureaucratic systems are costly, they can be sustained only through the regular taxation (i.e. the states), through established consumerist practices (i.e. private corporations) or through voluntary or coerced financial contributions (i.e. religious organisations, terrorist groups, nationalist insurgencies, etc.). Furthermore, such organisations also require labour, commitment and support of many individuals. In some instances, this is achieved through material or symbolic incentives, but in most cases organisational success is dependent on shared ideological beliefs and practices. Thus, in times of war, a major natural disaster or a terrorist attack, the citizens of modern states tend to show that they share some key principles and they regularly express a sense of responsibility towards their fellow citizens. In this, modern societies differ substantially from their premodern counterparts. In the traditional world, one's sense of attachment was largely confined to small-scale, face-to-face collectivities such as close kinship networks, village communes, guilds, smalltown associates or the networks of nobility and clergy. In contrast, modernity is defined by large-scale associations where individuals become members of abstract and anonymous entities, such as nation-states, private corporations, military organisations, trade unions or political parties.

Such wide-ranging organisations, which can consist of thousands or even millions of individuals, do not lend themselves to protracted social action easily. Instead, all social organisations require a great deal of coercive and ideological work. While the exceptional durability of such organisations such as the Catholic Church, the University of Bologna or the Japanese imperial system might imply that they are inherently stable entities resistant to major changes, the historical sociology of these social organisations shows that their sturdiness was rooted in their ability to adapt to changing structural contexts (Delanty and Isin 2003). In this sense, all social organisations are intrinsically fragile, and even those that have been in existence for hundreds or thousands of years, from the Roman Empire to Lehman Brothers, can (and in the latter case, did) collapse over a relatively short period of time. This built-in fragility is often hidden by the apparent coercive might and ideological resilience. When one observes a particular nation-state (i.e. France or Germany) or megacorporation (i.e. IBM or Toyota), they generally seem stable, powerful, durable and ideologically coherent. Hence nation-states possess large militaries, police forces, legal and fiscal systems and other institutions that show coercive prowess. Moreover, the prevalence of a specific form of nationalist ideology provides a substantial degree of societywide ideological legitimacy. In a similar vein, big private corporations maintain huge bureaucratic machineries that involve coercively established and enforced hierarchical systems of order which are regularly policed by line mangers, auditors, CEOs and many other coercive agents. Such organisations are also successful in justifying their existence in terms of the wider capitalist ethos focussed on profit maximisation and wealth generation as well as on the more specific ideological practices tied into the organisational culture of specific corporations. However, this coercive capacity and ideological strength rest on the willingness of individuals to obey orders and on their belief that such orders are legitimate. As the experience of many revolutions and successful general strikes demonstrate, once citizens and employees stop following orders, such coercive and ideological scaffolding can easily fall to pieces. The Foucauldian (Foucault 1998: 63) view that 'power is everywhere' and it 'comes from everywhere' might be overly relativistic, as it does not distinguish between different forms of coercive power. Nevertheless, such understanding is close to the truth in the sense that all coercive human power[3] entails consent to follow the orders. Once this consent is withdrawn, the weapons can be turned against the rulers and bosses. The same applies to ideology. Although nationalism or capitalist culture might be deeply entrenched in organisations such as the nation-states or private corporations, respectively, once the leaders are perceived as not fulfilling such ideological goals, their actions can be quickly delegitimized.

This point leads us closer to the main issue: How do modern organisations generate social cohesion? There is no question that both coercive and ideological power play crucial roles in sustaining large-scale social organisations. However, such huge organisations are by definition impersonal, formal, instrumentally rational and detached while most human beings are the opposite, as they thrive on deep emotional connections, informality and spontaneity and value rationality. Hence to circumvent this organisational obstacle, it becomes critical that the coercive and ideological powers tap into the microcosm of small-group attachments and emotional bonds. This is a crucial feature of all successful organisations. Once they are able to link the pockets of microsolidarity into a relatively coherent ideological narrative and set of practices, social organisations can mobilise long-term social action. Thus in times of interstate wars, the leaders of nation-states can utilise the familiar tropes of nationalist narratives that blend the micro- and macroworld and project an abstract and anonymous entity, such as a nation-state, as a close community of friends and family. This is well reflected in the common use of kinship metaphors in such contexts: the fight to protect our motherland, our brothers dying to preserve the lives and honour of our mothers and daughters, etc. Another common practice involves camouflaging organisational demands as a moral responsibility so that new recruits have to join the military in order not to shame and dishonour their family and friends. At the same time, their families and friends have to support the war effort so as not to betray those same recruits (their family and friends) who are sacrificing their lives for them (Malešević 2013a, 2013b, 2011, 2010). The similar blending of the organisational requirements and microsocial attachments is just as present in other organisations specialised in the use of violence: from terrorist cells to genocidal units, revolutionary cliques, insurgency outfits, etc. In all of these cases, the cumulative bureaucratisation of coercion and centrifugal ideologisation foster strong linkages with the pockets of genuine microsolidarity.

---

[3] Obviously this only applies to human relations, as individuals can still utilise technology to achieve their aims – i.e. robots, drones, etc.

When successful, social organisations manage to integrate thousands, and even hundreds of thousands, of small-scale group interactions into the relatively uniform organisational machine (Malešević 2013a).

Nevertheless, in modern social environments, more can be achieved. While many organisations attempt to channel existing microsolidarities in the directions of their own macrocauses, some organisations are able to create new forms of microsolidarity. In some instances, this is a product of deliberate policy, but in most cases such forms of group cohesion are side-effects of organisational development. Since the U.S. military invests the most in the research on social cohesion as a factor of a unit's military capacity, it has developed a variety of specific policies aimed at creating small-group solidarity and then utilised these bonds for organisational (military) purposes. For example, all branches of the U.S. military have introduced the 'buddy system' of recruitment, which allows 'friends who joined at the same time to complete their basic and job training together' (Levinson 2014: 17). Hence the U.S. navy recruitment strategy emphasises this policy:

The Navy Buddy Enlistment Program provides for the enlistment of small groups of not more than four male individuals or four female individuals who wish to remain together for as long as possible during their enlistment. The program should be conducive to stimulating enlistments among high school graduates and others from a local area, and assists enlistees during the transition period of adjustment from civilian status to military status (usmilitary.about.com/cs/navyjoin/a/navybuddy.htm).

The focus here is not only on exploiting already existing friendships but also on using such very small networks of solidarity to build a bit larger but highly cohesive military units. In other words, this type of recruitment policy works as a deliberate mechanism for the creation of military unit micro-level solidarity. While in this instance the social organisation still builds on the elements of microgroup bonds that were forged outside that organisation, this is not the case in the U.S. military's policy to deploy a number of individuals to man antiaircraft weapon systems, machine guns, bazookas, rocket launchers, mortars and other group-operated weapons (Collins 2013: 40–41; 2008a: 55–56). Although many such weapons can be manned by a single individual, the aim is to generate micro-level solidarity in order to increase fighting efficiency. As Collins (2008a: 56) emphasises: 'group-operated weapons are important, then, not so much because of the specific technology but because they facilitate a mood of solidarity; there is some evidence that just getting going at firing is a catalyst, and that soldiers in these weapons teams switched from one weapon to another as the fighting went on'. Obviously this policy was aimed at increasing the firing and fighting capacity of soldiers, and in this regard it has proved highly successful (Grossman 1998). Since most soldiers, as individuals, are reluctant killers, it is critical that small-group cohesion be generated to foster the degree of conformity conducive for one's willingness to shoot. However, what is equally important, and less recognised, is that this intense form of microsocial cohesion does not develop automatically but is built by specific organisational processes. While the 'buddy system' still utilises already formed bonds, the group-operated weapon systems largely forge the ties of microsolidarity by design. This is not to say that all such units exhibit the same degree of attachment nor that such ties will inevitably persist as soldiers move from their respective military roles. Clearly, some such units are likely not to gel at all, others will fizzle out as individuals move on and some individuals will remain more attached to their civilian buddies. Nevertheless, what often makes a difference is the shared traumatic experience. Hence, regardless of how such units were created, once they engage in a protracted social action involving life-threatening situations, their emotional commitment to each other tends to increase (Grossman 1996; Holmes 1985; Weber 1968). While this shared traumatic experience is a decisive element likely to help forge lasting bonds, it is the macro-organisational contexts that make such microsolidarity possible in the first place. The shared tragedies and triumphs of war trenches, the distribution of last rations over the campfires or the carrying of a severely wounded comrade under direct fire from the enemy are all microsituations produced by macrostructural contexts: wars between the nation-states, civil wars, insurgencies, terrorist actions, revolutionary uprisings, etc. Hence much of microsolidarity in the modern era is mediated by workings of organisational and ideological structures. As our world becomes ever more satiated with complex and coercive social organisations, there is less and less room for the formation of microsolidarities that are completely disconnected from formal bureaucratic institutions.

This sturdy link between microgroup cohesion and large-scale social organisations is to some extent quite apparent in contemporary militaries. From the United States, the United Kingdom, France and Israel to Russia and China, military establishments invest resources, time and research to utilise the military benefits of these links. Nevertheless, the structural underpinning of the microgroup cohesion can also be traced to less obvious examples such nineteenth-century African polities as the Zulu and Dahomey kingdoms or the Ethiopian Empire. The late British historian John Keegan (1993: 28–32) identified Zulus as representing a distinct form of military culture that emerged sui generis and as such had little to do with the wider geopolitics. In his view, war is not the Clause-witzian extension of politics by other means but 'an expression of culture'. Thus for him, Zulu warfare 'defied altogether the rationality of politics as it is understood by Westerners' (Keegan 1993: 24). However the military experience of these three African military structures shows otherwise. Rather than being an authentic expression of distinct traditional culture, the military might of the three states was a direct product of the geopolitical and organisational change that took place in the nineteenth century. Whereas the Dahomey under the rule of Gezo (1818–1858) developed on the back of the intensified transatlantic slave trade, the rise of the Zulu Kingdom was a consequence of the political bifurcations caused by European colonial expansion. Similarly, the staggering expansion of the Ethiopian polity under Emperor Tewodros is also linked with the geopolitical changes brought about by European colonialism. What is common to all three states is the gradual development of organisational capacity, which resulted in the increased military might. Hence under Gezo, Dahomey became the leading exporter of slaves, and war was a primary means of slave supply. After the British blockade of Dahomey ports in 1851, this was augmented with palm oil production, leading to further conflicts over the commercial highways. Gezo built an effective military, capable of defeating its powerful neighbour, the Oyo Empire. Almost uniquely in the world, Gezo's armed forces included female units that proved to be a highly disciplined, deeply cohesive and fierce fighting force. As Edgerton (2000) shows, Dahomey 'Amazons' consisted of exceptionally loyal units where new recruits took 'the blood oath' that symbolised one's willingness to die for her comrades. These women soldiers had to be celibate, and their devotion to their military units was expressed in the favourite martial song stating that 'thunder and lightning kill us if we break our oaths' (Edgerton, 2000: 25).

Even more impressive was the rise of the Zulu state under Shaka kaSenzangakhona (1816–1828). Although Shaka's military exploits have become mythologised, he was responsible for the creation of a highly organised, centralised and effective military force capable of the speedy conquest of its neighbours. At the heart of this military system were the age cohort regiments (*ibutho*), where all Zulu men had to serve until the age of forty. The Zulu military was defined by strict organisational discipline, including regular drills, forced marches and extensive military training with a novel weapon – the long swordlike spearhead (*iklwa*). Moreover each army unit had distinctive name and corresponding insignia that helped foster social cohesion. As Reid (2012: 120) emphasises, Shaka's military was particularly effective in conscripting and integrating 'young men into a regimental system' that 'inculcated a new sense of loyalty and identity' in this 'highly militarised society'. In addition, the military was largely built on meritocratic principles, as defeated clans were integrated into the empire on equal terms, allowing for promotion on the basis of one's military skill. Organisational might was supplemented with ideological power as Shaka took on the spiritual leaders and witchdoctors, making sure that they were subservient to the idea of the expanding Zulu polity. In this context, the traditional beliefs of ancestor worship were integrated into the new political project of empire building.

This increased organisational and ideological capacity combined with the strongly cohesive military units was also present in the Ethiopian military under Tewodros II. Just as Shaka came from a small clan of Zulus who managed to impose themselves on much larger populations, so did Tewodros. Born Kassa Hailu, an outlaw from a minor aristocratic Oromo family, he fought with the Oromo cavalry against the Ethiopian armies in the 1840s and 1850s. Relying on the effective fields of fire, cavalry in flanking manoeuvres and reliable military intelligence, his armies defeated regional powers, and he was crowned Emperor of Ethiopia in 1855. As an emperor, he had notable military successes, including the conquests of the Kingdom of Shewa and the Province of Gojjam. He also brought under his direct control the rebellious regions of Begemder and Simien and defeated the warlords of Wollo and Tigre. Although the Oromo remained at the core of the Ethiopian imperial military, Tewodros was successful in centralising military power while also maintaining internal cohesion in individual units. In the early years of his reign, the state was militarily efficient: 'Tewodros professionalised the army, creating more regular units, and was successful insofar as he demonstrated the feasibility of a larger, centralised polity based on the more effective use of force' (Reid 2012: 124). He focussed on importing modern weaponry from Europe and had an ambition to bring the European craftsmen to build cannons. In addition to the organisational changes, the new emperor attempted to legitimise his rule through genealogical myths and Solomonic lineage linking him to Tewodros I (who ruled from 1413 to 1414) and even more directly to King David and Solomon as in the later years he added to his title 'the Son of David and Solomon'. Just as in the other two cases, the expanding organisational and ideological powers were used to forge social cohesion of individual military units. Hence Ethiopian armies were composed of highly motivated, loyal and cohesive troops. For example, in conflicts with the technologically much more advanced British colonial army, these soldiers would continue to fight despite the enormous losses.

In the famous Battle of Magdala (1868), Tewodros's army attacked the British (mostly with spears), losing more than seven hundred soldiers in less than two hours of fighting.

What is interesting about these three non-European cases is not their cultural uniqueness, as emphasised by Keegan, but the exact opposite – the ever- increasing modern organisational standardisation. The fact that these African militaries were technologically still far behind their European or American counterparts should not cloud one's judgement about the staggering organisational change taking place here. Rather than reflecting the indigenous cultural traditions, the new Ethiopian, Dahomey and Zulu armies were largely the product of worldwide geopolitical and organisational transformations. Rulers such as Shaka, Tewodros or Gezo might have been military geniuses who introduced some new modes of fighting, new weapons or new techniques of recruitment and training. They might have also been personally responsible for the novel tactical, strategic, operational or logistical developments. Nevertheless, in all of this they were largely reflecting the broader structural changes taking place around them: the intensified colonial expansion, the struggle for new resources, the unprecedented migrations of populations, the introduction of new technologies and so on. Simply put, the onset and proliferation of modernist principles and modes of organisation had a profound impact on warfare in Africa, just as much it did in other parts of the world. While Shaka was not keen to imitate 'the Western way of war', this was less of the case with Tewodros and Gezo, both of whom were influenced by and aspired to adopt some of the Western technology and modes of fighting. However, regardless of their individual preferences, they all had to address distinctly modern problems such as the continuous coordination of huge numbers of individuals, complex division of labour, the maintenance of social order involving different ethnicities, the execution of specific and long-term political agendas, etc. Most of all, they had to focus their entire societies towards implementing specific military goals. In this context, Shaka was no different from other leaders of modern military organisations. He had to devise the most rational and most effective ways to achieve these military targets. As Morris (1965) argues, in this process Shaka 'changed the nature of warfare in Southern Africa' from 'a ritualised exchange of taunts with minimal loss of life into a true method of subjugation by wholesale slaughter'. Hence the intense micro-level solidarity that characterised the Ethiopian, Dahomey and Zulu armies was largely a top-down, modern-day creation. The three rulers utilised the traditional ways of social organisation in order to forge novel institutions capable of maintaining centralised yet flexible and effective military capacity. Thus Shaka transformed the existing age cohorts, which were common in the Bantu culture of the day, into distinctively named, unified and loyal military regiments that maintained their separate identities and were stationed in special military *kraals* (Morris 1965: 50–53). In a similar way, Gezo supported the formation of all-female units in order to offset the exceptional number of male casualties through increased warfare and slave trade. Here too existing traditions were supplemented with the modern technologies of organisation and ideology. In each of these cases and many others throughout Africa and the world, the cumulative bureaucratisation of coercion and ideologisation were deployed to generate micro-level social cohesion (Malešević 2015, 2013a, 2010).

Conclusion

Much of the contemporary debate on social cohesion has focussed on the question of whether group solidarity stems from interpersonal motivation, as argued by Siebold (2007), or from the successful collective performance, as insisted by King (2013). Although these two perspectives differ sharply over the question of soldiers' impetus to fight, they both subscribe to an overly groupist and utilitarian understanding of social action and neglect the macrohistorical contexts that make social cohesion possible in the first place. In this chapter, my intention was to move this debate further: one the one hand, I problematise the dynamics of group formation, and on the other hand, I explore the macro-organisational and ideological forces that underpin small-scale solidarities. Hence in contrast to the two dominant perspectives, I argue that there is nothing innate and self-evident about group attachments. When compared to many other advanced species, human beings are not particularly social creatures as such. Instead, our sociability entails intense and protracted social action as well as lasting organisational and ideological props. This is quite apparent in the processes that shape the patterns of social cohesion among individuals who are regularly exposed to violence. Hence soldiers, terrorists, revolutionaries, insurgents and *génocidaires* all tend to develop intense microgroup bonds. In this sense, one could find a great deal of evidence that micro-level social cohesion in such violent contexts is universal. Nevertheless, despite the widely shared assumptions that such bonds stem from the human's natural propensity to seek group attachments, I argue that in most instances such forms of microsolidarity have structural roots. In other words, since groupness is a highly variable and amorphous state of being, its prolonged existence regularly requires organisational and ideological scaffoldings. Hence when social cohesion is analysed over long historical periods, it becomes

palpable that violence-related social bonds remain dependent on organisational and ideological structures. It is these structures that often initiate, maintain and make social action possible. It is true that human
beings are emotional and cognitive creatures who often thrive in face-
to-face interactions. However, it is the organisational shells and ideological legitimation that make these elements of human sociability into
long-lasting forces of social cohesion. This process has been in existence
since the formation of the first durable and complex social organisations
twelve thousand years ago. However, with the onset of modernity and the
rise of organisational and ideological capacities of states and nonstate
actors, this link with microsolidarity has only increased. In the premodern world, it took generations to forge and then utilise military benefits
of the micro-level cohesion, as the cases of the Mamluks, samurai or
Spartiates show. This process was slow, uneven and inherently fragile,
and most attempts to benefit organisationally from micro-level solidarities ended in failure. In contrast, the era of modernity has witnessed
proliferation of this phenomenon, as modern militaries and violent nonstate actors can rely on expanded infrastructural capacities and ideological know-how to generate and then use the benefits of small-unit
cohesion for their military ambitions.

Conclusion: The Future of Organised Violence

Violence is a variable, situational and contextual phenomenon. There is a general consensus that killing a human being is a violent act. However, there is less agreement about what other types of action constitute violence. This is particularly pronounced the further one moves from the more visible acts towards the less discernible types of violent behaviour. Most societies regard torture and deliberate physical injuries against humans as a type of violence, but in some social contexts such acts might not be regarded as violent at all: sadomasochistic relationships, voluntary acceptance of extremely painful rituals of initiation (i.e. the North American hanging by flesh at sun dance festivals, Hindu Thaipusam ritual painful body piercings, Muslim and Jewish circumcision practices, Filipino voluntary crucifixions and many others). With nonphysical forms of social action, this variability is even more prominent. On the one hand, the emotional and mental anguish that one experiences as a result of the nonphysical coercion is difficult to empirically capture and measure, and as such it can also be faked. On the other hand, individuals and groups exposed to the same noncorporal coercive pressure may react very differently, with some feeling genuine pain, leading to various physical disorders and even death, and others not experiencing much, or any, discomfort. For this reason, the scholars of violence tend to focus on more extreme instances of violent action, such as homicides or the battlefield fatalities. There is no doubt that such statistics on death rates are very valuable and when collected properly highly useful for social and historical research. However, since violent deaths represent a quite small segment of violent social action, such data can also mislead. This is particularly the case with late modernity, where the development of science, medicine and pharmacology has dramatically improved one's chances of survival and where technological advancements have made the use of extreme violence strategic and selective. Hence the fact that the fewer soldiers have died in recent wars does not automatically mean that violent conflicts have also declined. As Fazal (2014: 100) argues that in the context of civil wars, the decline in the number of casualties does not

308

mean that violent attempts at territorial control have also decreased. On the contrary, successful attempts at territorial redistribution today are likely to generate fewer casualties than prolonged, unsuccessful conflicts. Hence she documents how the number of such territorial wars 'has actually increased over course of the twentieth century' and beyond (see also Hansel et al. 2009).

One can push this argument further and envisage how future advancements in science, technology and medicine might impact the transformation of organised violence. The gradual and continuous expansion of nonhuman devices in wars and other forms of organised violence might ultimately lead to wars without any human casualties. As Coker (2013: xxiii) predicts, 'robots will be fighting robots in 2035'. Developments in robotics, cybernetics, nanotechnology and pharmacology are likely to substantially reduce the presence of human beings in the theatres of war, in terrorist actions and insurgencies or possibly even in future revolutions. As Singer (2009) argues, the proliferation of unmanned robotic systems such as drones, unmanned submarines, patrol robots, robotic mine sweepers and autonomous sniper systems, among others, is likely to redefine the nature of future violent conflicts[1]. With robots replacing humans, one might expect a dramatic reduction in the number of fatalities and even greater human emotional and physical distance from the epicentres of organised violence. While in principle such developments might save countless human lives, extensive reliance on robots might also lead towards more frequent conflicts. If only robots are destroyed and there are no human fatalities, there would be less need to justify the use of violence, as robotic casualties could be easily, and possibly cheaply, replaced. This gradual but continuous shift away from direct human presence in wars, revolutions, terrorisms and other forms of organised violence is likely to further decouple coercive power from bloodshed. However, the possible disappearance of human casualties on the battlefields would not automatically imply the end of violence. On the contrary, such a social transformation would only make apparent how the current focus on the corporality and intentionality of violence is insufficient to account for the diversity of violent action. Hence the social experience of violence cannot be reduced solely to the destruction of human bodies. One of the key reasons why collective violence has been

[1] As Kreps (2016: 1) points out, it is estimated that 'the number of drones in US airspace could reach 30,000 by 2020'. U.S. military investments are now primarily focussed on the air systems: 'in 2014, air system funding amounted to $3.8 billion compared to just $13 million for ground and $330 million for maritime, with air making up the lion's share of the $4.12 billion total' (Kreps 2016: 6).

so prevalent and so powerful throughout history is its organisational flexibility and capacity to adapt to different social and historical conditions. Looking from the safe historical distance, one can judge the medieval Europeans or the pre-Columbian Mesoamericans as 'barbaric', 'cruel', 'impetuous', 'uninhibited' and 'childlike'(Pinker 2011; Elias 2000), but such deeply normative characterisations cannot help us understand how organised violence changes over time. There are specific organisational and ideological reasons why different social orders deploy different regimes of violence. The polities with the weak infrastructural capacities, low levels of societywide ideological penetration and deep social hierarchies often utilise excessive torture and other macabre practices (Brown 2011; Malešević 2013b; Mann 1986; Collins 1974). This use of expressive violence is intended to communicate a particular message to populations that cannot be easily controlled through the other means. By burning a heretic or a disobedient peasant at the stake, rulers aim to frighten those who they cannot organisationally or ideologically reach. This form of violence might look ghoulish to us, as it also did to our predecessors, but its use was not particularly effective or efficient. The popular personification of such a ghastly violence, the Spanish Inquisition, was responsible for a very small number of deaths: 'the death penalty was passed in 3.5 per cent of cases, but only 1.8 per cent of those contemned were actually executed'. Thus, between 1540 and 1700, only 810 individuals were killed by the Inquisition (Perez 2006: 173). In many respects, medieval excessiveness demonstrated its organisational and ideological weakness, not its strength.

In contrast, modern polities have at their disposal enormous coercive organisational capacity, intertwined with deep ideological penetration, that tap into grassroots microsolidarities, all of which allow for the unprecedented use of violence. Whereas the medieval European butcheries generally resulted in the hundreds of casualties or less, twentieth-century organised violence generated millions of fatalities. With the continuous and cumulative rise of organisational and ideological powers, the late-twentieth and early-twenty-first centuries have witnessed a gradual shift towards more selective and clinical use of extreme forms of violence. When one is in possession of highly advanced military technology, worldwide organisational reach and a great deal of popular justification at home, there is no need for mass armies and mass military casualties. Such modern coercive organisational machines might kill less but displace, injure, deprive, torment, agonise and ultimately control more people. As science and technology expand, one can expect further development of nonlethal weapons, which would be much more effective precisely because they can control individuals without killing them.

U.S. Department of Defense's Non-Lethal Weapons Program has already developed lasers that produce temporary blindness, disabling heat rays that cause temporary pain, large-scale nonlethal riot control devices, nonlethal grenades and active denial systems (ADS), among many others (jnlwp.defense.gov/). These and other future technological advancements are likely to change the nature of organised violence. In this sense, future conflicts might become focussed more on degrading the cognitive and emotional capacities of enemy populations rather than on having been entrapped into indiscriminate and inefficient killing sprees. However, this change would not mean the end of violence: on the contrary, it would pave the way for a much more efficient system of coercive control. If one can coercively manipulate millions of individuals, there is no need to completely destroy their bodies. The rise of pharmacology, biological engineering, artificial intelligence and personalised medicine may all contribute to even more selective and targeted forms of violence that can cause genetically targeted sterility of the enemy, trigger new types of incurable but externally controlled diseases, produce drug-induced mass-level hallucinations and so on. Moreover, the shift towards incessant robotic wars might also cause permanent civilian migrations and destruction of the environment and human habitats. In this context, the long-term consequences of organized violence might be even less visible but ultimately more devastating.

To fully comprehend these structural changes, it is necessary to move away from overly static concepts of violent action. Hence when violence is understood in historically dynamic terms, then it is possible to realise that the lower death tolls do not automatically signify the extinguishing of violence. Instead, as violence becomes more organisationally and ideologically embedded in our everyday lives, it also becomes less visible. This transformation is particularly apparent today when corporal forms of violent action have experienced a societywide delegitimisation. In this context, physical expressions of violence, such as killings, dying and bodily injuries, tend to be more and more removed from the public eye: the billions of animals we consume yearly are killed in closed and segregated industrialised slaughterhouses; our old and sick die in specialised, isolated hospices and hospitals; our morgues and crematoria are located far away from the housing estates; the graphic images of dead civilians killed by long-distance drone warfare do not appear on our TV screens; nor do we ever see victims of torture on our streets. Since violence is firmly tied to physical injuries, contemporary citizens find such expressions of violence particularly disturbing. However, this organisational and ideological invisibility of corporal violence does not mean that violence as such disappears. On the contrary, by removing physical forms of violence to the margins and by not recognising non-corporal forms of violent action, one creates room for the proliferation of coercive power. Hence to avoid any contact with physical violence, citizens of modern polities demand and then legitimise the ever-increasing coercive organisational diffusion in our everyday lives: from the policing of sexuality and parenthood to the daily surveillance of individuals at work, in the school, in the street; to more rigorous punishments against 'antisocial behaviour'; to ever more rigid border controls and prevention of migration; to the multiplying of prison populations; to the increasing suicide rates; and so on.

When these changes are explored historically, then it becomes clearer that organised violence has not declined through the course of history. On the contrary, as I argue in this book, organised violence continues to grow and expand. Since durable violent collective action is dependent on the presence of specific organisational shells and adequate ideological cohesion, as long as these two are in place, violence is unlikely to disappear. Despite geographical oscillations and historical variability, the last twelve thousand years of human history have witnessed a continuous and cumulative increase in the organisational and ideological powers that make violence possible. Although the character of violence changes through time and space, its persistence and expansion remain firmly dependent on these organisational and ideological powers. Since these powers have not experienced any decline but have continued to increase, it is difficult to envisage how organised violence can disappear. Violence is a form of social action, and as such it can change its character, direction and intensity but cannot be obliterated. Human beings are born and die in violent contexts. We come to this world through the physical and mental pain of childbirth. The baby is born through the violence it inflicts on its mother, and the very experience of coming to this world is an arduous and traumatic event. We also leave this world through the violence of the death experience that is inflicted on our bodies and our minds. Throughout our lives, we also encounter violence in a variety of forms. Hence, whether we like it or not, violence is also a part of what it means to be a human.

References

Alexander, J. 2004a. Toward a theory of cultural trauma. In J. C. Alexander, R. Eyerman, B. Giesen, N. J. Smelser and P. Sztompka (eds.), *Cultural Trauma and Collective Identity*. Berkeley: University of California Press, pp. 1–30.

2004b. From the depths of despair: performance, counterperformance, and 'September 11'. *Sociological Theory*, 22(1): 88–105.

2011. *Performance and Power*. Cambridge, UK: Polity Press.

Allworth, E. 1967. *Central Asia: A Century of Russian Rule*. New York: Columbia University Press.

Alperovitz, G. 1995. *The Decision to Use the Atomic Bomb*. New York: Knopf.

Anderson, F. and A. Cayton. 2005. *The Dominion of War: Empire and Liberty in North America, 1500–2000*. New York: Viking.

Andreski, S. 1968. *Military Organization and Society*. London: Routledge & Paul.

Archer, M. 2000. *Being Human: The Problem of Agency*. Cambridge, UK: Cambridge University Press.

Ardrey, R. 1976. *The Hunting Hypothesis: A Personal Conclusion Concerning the Evolutionary Nature of Man*. New York: Atheneum.

Arendt, H. 1970. *On Violence*. New York: Harvest.

Armstrong, J. 1982. *Nations before Nationalism*. Chapel Hill: University of North Carolina Press.

Arrighi, G. 1994. *The Long Twentieth Century: Money, Power, and the Origins of Our Times*. London: Verso.

Atran, S. 2010. *Talking to the Enemy: Violent Extremism, Sacred Values, and What It Means to Be Human*. London: Penguin.

Aya, R. 2015. Theories of Revolutions. In J. White (ed.), *Encyclopedia of Social and Behavioural Sciences*, 2nd edition. Philadelphia, PA: Elsevier.

Axelrod, A. and J. Kingston. 2007. *Encyclopedia of World War II*. London: H W Fowler.

Baker, S., J. Burt, D. Donald, E. Fudge, G. Marvin, R. McKay, C. Palmer and C. Wilbert. 2006. *Killing Animals*. Urbana-Champaign: University of Illinois Press.

Bandura, A. 2004. The origins and consequences of moral disengagement: a social learning perspective. In F. M. Moghaddam and A. J. Marsella (eds.), *Understanding Terrorism: Psychosocial Roots, Consequences, and Interventions*. Washington, DC: American Psychological Association.

Baraz, D. 2003. *Medieval Cruelty: Changing Perceptions, Late Antiquity to the Early Modern Period*. Ithaca, NY: Cornell University Press.

Barratt, J. 2009. *Sieges of the English Civil Wars*. London: Pen and Sword.

Bartov, O. 1991. *Hitler's Army: Soldiers, Nazis, and War in the Third Reich*, Oxford, UK: Oxford University Press.

Bauman, Z. 1989. *Modernity and the Holocaust*. Cambridge, UK: Polity Press.

Bećirević, E. 2014. *Genocide on Drina River*. New Haven, CT: Yale University Press.

Behrens-Abouseif, D. 2008. *Cairo of the Mamluks: A History of Architecture and Its Culture*. New York: Macmillan.

Bell, D. 2007. *The First Total War: Napoleon's Europe and the Birth of Warfare as We Know It*. Boston: Houghton Mifflin.

Bell-Fialkoff, A. 1996. *Ethnic Cleansing*. New York: St. Martin's Press.

Benesch, O. 2014. *Inventing the Way of the Samurai: Nationalism, Internationalism and Bushido in Modern Japan*. Oxford, UK: Oxford University Press.

Berko, A. 2007. *The Path to Paradise. The Inner World of Suicide Bombers and Their Dispatchers*. Westport, CT: Greenwood Press.

Berndt, R. 1962. *Excess and Restraint: Social Control among a New Guinea Mountain People*. Chicago: University of Chicago Press.

Bible Online. www.biblegateway.com/

Biggs, M. 2005. Dying without killing: self-immolations, 1963–2002. In D. Gambetta (ed.), *Making Sense of Suicide Missions*. Oxford, UK: Oxford University Press.

Billig, M. et al. 1988. *Ideological Dilemmas: A Social Psychology of Everyday Thinking*. London: Sage.

Billington, J. 1980. *Fire in the Minds of Men: Origins of Revolutionary Faith*. New York: Basic Books.

Birgalias, N. 2002. Helotage and Spartan social organization. In A. Powell and S. Hodkinson (eds.), *Sparta: Beyond the Mirage*. London: IB Taurus.

Blecher R. 2005. Citizens without sovereignty: transfer and ethnic cleansing in Israel. *Comparative Studies in Society and History*, 47(4): 735–750.

Blickle, P. 1981. *The Revolution of 1525: The German Peasants War from a New Perspective*. New York: Johns Hopkins University Press.

Bloch M. 1961. *Feudal Society*. London: Routledge and Kegan Paul.

Blum, R., G. Stanton, S. Sagi and E. Richter. 2007. Ethnic cleansing bleaches the atrocities of genocide. *European Journal of Public Health*, 18(2): 204–209.

Blumer, H. 1969. *Symbolic Interactionism*. New Jersey: Prentice Hall.

Boehmer, I. 2005. Postcolonial terrorist: the example of Nelson Mandela. *Parallax*, 11(4): 46–55.

Bonta, B. D. 1996. Conflict resolution among peaceful societies: the culture of peacefulness. *Journal of Peace Research*, 33(4): 403–420.

Boot, M. 2006. *War Made New: Technology, Warfare, and the Course of History, 1500 to Today*. New York: Gotham.

Bourdieu, P. 1990. *Language and Symbolic Power*. Cambridge, MA: Harvard University Press.

Bourdieu, P. and L. Wacquant. 1992. *An Invitation to Reflexive Sociology*. Chicago: Chicago University Press.

Bourke, J. 2000. *An Intimate History of Killing*. London: Granta.

2011. *What It Means to Be Human: Reflections from 1791 to the Present*. London: Virago.

2015. *Deep Violence: Military Violence, War Play and the Social Life of Weapons*. Berkley: Counterpoint.

Bowden, B. 2013. *Civilization and War*. Camberley Surrey, UK: Edward Elgar.

Bowles, S. 2009. Did warfare among ancestral hunter-gatherers affect the evolution of human social behaviors? *Science*, 324(5932): 1293–1298.

Braudel, F. 1973. *The Mediterranean in the Time of Philip II*. Berkeley: University of California Press.

1979. *Civilisation and Capitalism*. Berkeley: University of California Press.

Breuilly, J. 1993. *Nationalism and the State*. Manchester: Manchester University Press.

Brinton, C. 1965. *The Anatomy of Revolution*. New York: Prentice Hall.

Broadbridge, A. 2008 *Kingship and Ideology in the Islamic and Mongol Worlds*. Cambridge, UK: Cambridge University Press.

Brown, W. 2011. *Violence in Medieval Europe*. Harlow, UK: Longman.

Browne, M. 1993. *Muddy Boots and Red Socks*, Random House: New York.

Browning, C. R. 1992. *Ordinary Men: Reserve Police Battalion 101 and the Final Solution in Poland*. New York: Harper Collins.

Brubaker, R. 2004. *Ethnicity without Groups*. Cambridge, MA: Harvard University Press.

2015. *Grounds for Difference*. Cambridge, MA: Harvard University Press.

Brubaker, R. and D. Laitin. 1998. Ethnic and nationalist violence. *Annual Review of Sociology*, 24: 423–52.

Brzezinski, Z. 1993. *Out of Control*. New York: Simon and Schuster.

Burbank, J. and F. Cooper. 2010. *Empires in World History*. Princeton, NJ: Princeton University Press.

Burleigh, M. 2000. *The Third Reich: A New History*. London: Macmillan.

2009. *Blood and Rage: History of Terrorism*. New York: Harper.

Burgoon, B. 2006. On welfare and terror. *Journal of Conflict Resolution*, 50(2): 176–203.

Buzan, B. 2006. Will the 'global war on terrorism' be the new Cold War? *International Affairs*, 82(6): 1101–1118.

Buzan, B. and O. Wæver. 2009. Macrosecuritization and security constellations: reconsidering scale in securitization theory. *Review of International Studies*, 35(2): 253–276

Caputo P. 1977. *A Rumour of War*. New York: Ballantine.

Carman, J. 1997. Introduction: approaches to violence. In J. Carman (ed.), *Material Harm: Archeological Studies of War and Violence*. Glasgow: Cruithne Press.

Carneiro, R. L. 1970. A theory of the origin of the state. *Science*, 169(3947): 733–738.

2012. The circumscription theory: a clarification, amplification, and reformulation. *Social Evolution & History*, 11 (2): 5–30.

Carrel, H. 2009. The ideology of punishment in Late Medieval English towns. *Social History*, XXXI: 301–320.

Cederman, L., H. Buhaug and N. Gleditsch, 2013. *Inequality, Grievances, and Civil War*. Cambridge, UK: Cambridge University Press.

Centeno, M. A. 2002. *Blood and Debt: War and the Nation-State in Latin America*. University Park: Penn State University Press.

Centeno, M. and E. Enriquez. 2016. *War and Society*. Cambridge, UK: Polity Press.

Cesarini, D. 2005. *Eichmann: His Life and Crimes*. London: Vintage.

Chagnon, N. 1967. Yanomamö social organization and warfare. *Natural History*, LXXVI: 44–48.

  1992. *Yanomamo: The Last Days of Eden*. New York: Harcourt Brace Jovanovich.

  2013. *Noble Savages: My Life among Two Dangerous Tribes – the Yanomamö and the Anthropologists*. New York: Simon and Schuster.

Chapman, B. 1970. *Police State*. London: Pall Mall Press.

Chase-Dunn, C. 1989. *Global Formation: Structures of the World-Economy*. New York: Basil Blackwell.

Chatterjee, P. 1993. *The Nation and Its Fragments: Colonial and Postcolonial Histories*. Princeton, NJ: Princeton University Press.

Chhabra, S. 2011. Adept-Qaeda: analysing the relationship between organisational transformation and the exploitation of information technology. *Cornell International Affairs Review*, 4(2): 1–16.

CIA (Central Intelligence Agency). 2016. Country report: Namibia, Lesotho, Botswana. www.cia.gov/library/publications/the-world-factbook/geos/hr.html

Cioffi-Revilla, C. and D. Lai. 1995. War and politics in Ancient China, 2700 bc to 722 bc: measurement and comparative analysis. *Journal of Conflict Resolution*, 39(3): 467–494.

Cirillo, P. and N. N. Taleb. 2016. On the statistical properties and tail risk of violent conflicts. Physica A: statistical mechanics and its applications. www.fooledbyrandomness.com/violence.pdf

Claessen, H. J. M. 2000 *Structural Change, Evolution and Evolutionism in Cultural Anthropology*. Leyden, Netherlands: CNWS.

Clark, C. 2012. *The Sleepwalkers: How Europe Went to War in 1914*. London: Penguin.

Clausewitz, C. von. 1997. *On War*. Ware, UK: Wordsworth.

Clements, J. 2010. *The Samurai: A New History of the Warrior Elite*. Philadelphia: Running Press.

Clodfelter, M. 1992. *Warfare and Armed Conflicts: A Statistical Reference. Vol I*. Jefferson, NC: McFarland and Company.

Cobbing, J. 1988. The Mfecane as alibi: thoughts on Dithakong and Mbolompo. *Journal of African History*, 29(3): 487–519.

Cohen, A. 1969. *Customs and Politics in Urban Africa*. Berkeley: University of California Press.

Cohen, L. 2010. Administrative development in 'low intensity' democracies: governance, rule of law and corruption in the western Balkans. *Simons Papers in Security and Development*, 5(1): 1–48.

Cohen, M. and G. Armelagos. 1984. *Paleopathology and the Origins of Agriculture*. Orlando, FL: Academic Press.

Coker, C. 2013. *Warrior Geeks*. London: Hurst.

Collier, P. 2010. *Wars, Guns and Votes: Democracy in Dangerous Places*, New York: Vintage.

Collier, P., A. Hoeffler and R. Rohner, 2009. Beyond greed and grievance: feasibility and civil war. *Oxford Economics Paper*, 61(1): 1–27.

Collins, R. 1974. Three faces of cruelty: towards comparative sociology of violence. *Theory and Society*, 1: 415–40.

  1986. *Weberian Sociological Theory*. Cambridge, UK: Cambridge University Press.

  1999. *Macro History: Essays in Sociology of the Long Run*. Stanford, CA: Stanford University Press.

  2004. *Interaction Ritual Chains*. Princeton, NJ: Princeton University Press.

  2008a. *Violence: A Micro-Sociological Theory*. Princeton, NJ: Princeton University Press.

  2008b. Suicide bombers: warriors of the middle class. *Foreign Policy*. January, www.foreignpolicy.com/story/cms.php?story_id=4131

  2011. Forward panic and violent atrocities. In H. Strang, S. Karstedt and I. Loader (eds.), *Emotions, Crime and Justice*. Oxford, UK: Hart.

  2013. Does nationalist sentiment increase fighting efficiency? A sceptical view from the sociology of violence. In J. Hall and S. Malešević (eds.), *Nationalism and War*. Cambridge, UK: Polity Press.

Conquest, R. 1992. *The Great Terror: A Reassessment*. Oxford, UK: Oxford University Press.

Conrad, S. 2006. *Globalisation and Nation in Imperial Germany*. Cambridge, UK: Cambridge University Press.

Constanza, S. and J. Kilburn. 2005. Symbolic security, moral panic and public sentiment: toward a sociology of counterterrorism. *Journal of Social and Ecological Boundaries*, 1(2): 106–124.

Cooley, C. 1909. *Social Organization: A Study of the Larger Mind*. New York: Charles Scribner's Sons.

Corry, S. 2013. Why Steven Pinker, like Jared Diamond, is wrong. www.truthout.org/opinion/item/16880-the-case-of-the-brutal-savage-poirot-orclouseau-or-why-steven-pinker-like-jared-diamond-is-wrong

Courville, C. B. 1967. Cranial injuries in prehistoric man. In D. Brothwell and A. T. Sandison (eds.), *Diseases in Antiquity*. Springfield, IL: Charles C. Thomas.

Cruickshanks, E. 2000. *The Glorious Revolution*. New York: Palgrave Macmillan.

Cudworth, E. 2015. Killing animals: sociology, species relations and institutionalised violence. *Sociological Review*, 63: 1–18.

Cushman, T. 2009. Genocidal rupture and performative repair in global civil society: reconsidering the discourse of apology in the face of mass atrocity. In T. Brudholm and T. Cushman (eds.), *The Religious in the Responses to Mass Atrocities: Interdisciplinary Perspectives*. Cambridge, UK: Cambridge University Press.

Dabiq. 2014. Issue 8. www.clarionproject.org/news/islamic-state-isis-isil-propaganda-magazine-dabiq#

Dadrian, V. 1995. *The History of Armenian Genocide*. Providence, RI: Berghahn.

Damasio, A. 2003. *The Feeling of What Happens.* New York: Vintage.

Dandeker, C. 1990. *Surveillance, Power and Modernity: Bureaucracy and Discipline from 1700 to the Present Day.* New York: St. Martin's Press.

Darwin, J. 2008. *After Tamerlane: The Rise and Fall of Global Empires, 1400–2000.* London: Bloomsbury.

Davies, J. C. (ed.). 1971. *When Men Revolt and Why.* New York: Free Press.

Davis, J. 2003. *Martyrs: Innocence, Vengeance, and Despair in the Middle East.* New York: Palgrave Macmillan.

Davis, M. 2001. *Late Victorian Holocausts: El Niño Famines and the Making of the Third World.* London: Verso.

Davis, N. 1996. *Europe: A History.* Oxford, UK: Oxford University Press.

de Crespigny, R. 1991. The three kingdoms and western Jin: a history of China in the third century AD ~ I. *East Asian History* 1(2): 1–36.

Delanty, G. and E. Isin (eds.). 2003. *Handbook of Historical Sociology.* London: Sage.

Deletant, D. 1995. *Coercion and Dissent in Romania, 1965–1989.* London: Routledge.

Della Porta, D. 2013. *Clandestine Political Violence.* Cambridge, UK: Cambridge University Press.

Dentan, R. K. 1968. *The Semai: A Nonviolent People of Malaya.* New York: Holt, Rinehart and Winston.

de Tocqueville, A. 1955 [1856]. *The Old Regime and the French Revolution.* New York: Anchor.

De Waal, F. 2005. *Our Inner Ape.* New York: Riverhead.

2013. *The Bonobo and the Atheist.* New York: Norton.

Diamond, J. 2012. *The World until Yesterday: What Can We Learn from Traditional Societies?* New York: Viking.

Ditrych, O. 2014. *Tracing the Discourses of Terrorism.* New York: Palgrave.

Downes, A. B. 2008. *Targeting Civilians in War.* Ithaca, NY: Cornell University Press.

Doyle, W. 2001. *The French Revolution.* Oxford, UK: Oxford University Press.

Dunbar, R. 1992. Neocortex size as a constraint on group size in primates. *Journal of Human Evolution,* 22(6): 469–493.

1998 *Grooming, Gossip, and the Evolution of Language.* Cambridge, MA: Harvard University Press.

Du Picq, A. 2006 [1880]. *Battle Studies.* New York: Bibliobazar.

Durkheim, E. 1952 [1897]. *Suicide.* London: Routledge and Kegan Paul.

1997 [1893]. *The Division of Labor in Society.* New York: Free Press.

Dyer, G. 2011. *Climate Wars.* New York: One World.

Eckhardt, W. 1992. *Civilizations, Empires and Wars: A Quantitative History of War.* Jefferson, NC: McFarland.

Edgerton, R. B. 2000. *Warrior Women: The Amazons of Dahomey and the Nature of War.* Boulder, CO: Westview Press.

Edwards, L. P. 1970. *The Natural History of Revolution.* Chicago: University of Chicago Press.

Eilstrup-Sangiovanni, M. and C. Jones. 2008. Assessing the dangers of illicit networks: why Al-Qaeda may be less threatening than many think. *International Security,* 33(2): 7–44.

Eisner, M. 2003. Long-term historical trends in violent crime. *Crime and Justice*, 30: 83–142.

2009. The uses of violence: an examination of some cross-cutting issues. *International Journal of Conflict and Violence*, 3(1): 40–59.

2014. From swords to words: does macro-level change in self-control predict long-term variation in levels of homicide? *Crime and Justice*, 43(1): 65–134.

Elias, N. 1978. *What Is Sociology?* London: Hutchinson.

1987. The retreat of sociologists into the present. *Theory, Culture and Society*, 4. (2): 223–247.

1991. *The Society of Individuals*. Oxford, UK: Blackwell.

1996. *The Germans: Power Struggles and the Development of Habitus in the Nineteenth and Twentieth Centuries*. Cambridge, UK: Polity Press.

1998. The civilising of parents. In J. Goudsblom and S. Mennell (eds.), *The Norbert Elias Reader*. Oxford, UK: Blackwell.

2000 [1939]. *The Civilising Process: Sociogenetic and Psychogenetic Investigations*. Oxford, UK: Blackwell.

2005 [1969]. *The Court Society*. Dublin: University College Dublin Press.

Elliott, A. 2007. Where boys grow up to be Jihadis. *New York Times*. www.nytimes.com/2007/11/25/magazine/25tetouan-t.html?_r=0

Ellman, M. 2007. Stalin and the Soviet famine of 1932–33 revisited. *Europe-Asia Studies*, 59(4): 663–693.

Elvin, M. 1972. The high-level equilibrium trap: the causes of the decline of invention in the traditional Chinese textile industries. In W. E. Willmott (ed.), *Economic Organization in Chinese Society*, Stanford, CA: Stanford University Press.

Epstein, R. 2011. Book Review of *The Better Angels of Our Nature*. *Scientific American*. www.scientificamerican.com/article/bookreview-steven-pinker-the-better-angels-of-our-nature-why-violence-has-declined/

Esdaile, C. 2008. *Napoleon's Wars: An International History, 1803–1815*. London: Penguin.

Fairbank, J. K. 1992. *China: A New History*. Cambridge, MA: Belknap Press of Harvard University Press.

Farb, P. 1991 [1968]. *Man's Rise to Civilization: The Cultural Ascent of the Indians of North America*. London: Penguin.

Farrell, G., A. Tseloni, J. Mailley and N. Tilley. 2011. The crime drop and the security hypothesis. *Journal of Research in Crime and Delinquency*, 48(2): 147–175.

Fazal, T. 2014. Dead wrong? Battle death, military medicine, and exaggerated reports on war's demise. *International Security*, 3991: 95–125.

Felson, R. 2009. Violence, crime, and violent crime. *International Journal of Conflict and Violence*, 3(1): 23–39.

Felter, J. and B. Fishman. 2007. *Al Qa'ida's Foreign Fighter in Iraq: A First Look at the Sinjar Records*, West Point, NY: Harmony Project, Combating Terrorism Center, Department of Social Sciences, US Military Academy.

Ferguson, B. 1995. *Yanomami Warfare: A Political History*. Santa Fe, NM: School for American Research Press.

2013. Pinker's list: exaggerating prehistoric war mortality. In D. Fry (ed.), *War, Peace, and Human Nature: The Convergence of Evolutionary and Cultural Views*. Oxford, UK: Oxford University Press.

Ferguson, N. 2004. Prisoner taking and prisoner killing in the age of total war: towards a political economy of military defeat. *War in History*, 11(2): 148–192.

Fiske, A. and T. Rai. 2015. *Virtuous Violence*. Cambridge, UK: Cambridge University Press.

Fitzgerald, C. 1985. *China: A Short Cultural History*. New York: Praeger.

Fligstein, N. 2001. *The Architecture of Markets: An Economic Sociology of Capitalist Societies*. Princeton, NJ: Princeton University Press.

Foran, J. 1997. Discourses and social forces: the role of culture and cultural studies in understanding revolutions. In J. Foran (ed.), *Theorising Revolutions*. London: Routledge.

2005. *Taking Power: On the Origins of Third World Revolutions*. Cambridge, UK: Cambridge University Press.

Foran, J., D. Lane and A. Živković (eds.). 2008. *Revolution in the Making of the Modern World: Social Identities, Globalization, and Modernity*. London: Routledge.

Foucault, M. 1975. *Discipline and Punish: The Birth of the Prison*. New York: Random House.

1980. Truth is in the future. In S. Lotringer (ed.), *Foucault Live (Interviews, 1961–1984)*. Cambridge, MA: MIT Press.

1982. The subject and power. *Critical Inquiry*, 8(4): 777–795.

1998. *The History of Sexuality: The Will to Knowledge*. London: Penguin.

France, J. 2010. Casualty rates. In C. Rogers (ed.), *The Oxford Encyclopedia of Medieval Warfare and Military Technology*. Oxford, UK: Oxford University Press.

Freeden, M. 1996. *Ideologies and Political Theory: A Conceptual Approach*. Oxford, UK: Clarendon Press.

Freeman, M. 1995. Genocide, civilization and modernity. *British Journal of Sociology*, 46(2): 207–225.

Fritz, S. 1995. *Frontsoldaten: The German Soldier in World War II*. Lexington: University Press of Kentucky.

Fry, D. P. and P. Söderberg. 2013. Lethal aggression in mobile forager bands and implications for the origins of war. *Science*, 341: 270–273.

Fry, D. S. 2007. *Beyond War: The Human Potential for Peace*. Oxford, UK: Oxford University Press.

2013a. Dangerous tribes. *European Journal of Sociology* LIV(3): 531–536.

2013b. War, peace, and human nature: the challenge of achieving scientific objectivity. In D. Fry (ed.), *War, Peace, and Human Nature: The Convergence of Evolutionary and Cultural Views*. Oxford, UK: Oxford University Press.

Fuchs, C. 2012. Google capitalism. *Triple C*, 10(1): 42–48.

Fukuyama, F. 2011. *The Origins of Political Order*. New York: Farrar, Straus and Giroux.

Fulbrook, M. 2012. *A Small Town near Auschwitz: Ordinary Nazis and the Holocaust*. Oxford, UK: Oxford University Press.

Fuller, J. 1990. *Troop Morale and Popular Culture in the British and Dominion Armies 1914–18*. Oxford, UK: Claredon Press.

Gabriel, R. 1990. *The Culture of War: Invention and Early. Development*. Westport, CT: Greenwood Press.

2002. *The Great Armies of Antiquity*. Westport, CT: Praeger.

Gambetta, D. 2005. Can we make sense of suicide missions? In D. Gambetta (ed.), *Making Sense of Suicide Missions*. Oxford, UK: Oxford University Press.

Gambetta, D. and S. Hertog. 2009. Why are there so many engineers among Islamic radicals? *European Journal of Sociology*. 50(2): 201–230.

Galtung, J. 1969. Violence, peace, and peace research. *Journal of Peace Research*, 6(3): 167–191.

1990. Cultural violence. *Journal of Peace Research*, 27(3): 291–305.

Galtung, J. and T. Høivik. 1971. Structural and direct violence: a note on operationalization. *Journal of Peace Research*, 8(1): 72–76.

Gardner, P. M. 2000. Respect and nonviolence among recently sedentary Paliyan foragers. *Journal of the Royal Anthropological Institute*, 6(2): 215–236.

Garland, D. 2001. *The Culture of Control: Crime and Social Order in Contemporary Society*. Oxford, UK: Oxford University Press.

Garrett S. 1993. *Ethics and Air Power in World War II*. London: Macmillan.

Gat, A. 2006. *War in Human Civilization*. Oxford, UK: Oxford University Press.

2013. Is war declining and why? *Journal of Peace Research*, 50(2): 149–157.

Gates, D. 2011. *The Napoleonic Wars 1803–1815*. New York: Random House.

Geary, P. 1988. *Before France and Germany*. Oxford, UK: Oxford University Press.

2002. *The Myth of Nations*. Princeton, NJ: Princeton University Press.

Gellately, R. and B. Kiernan (eds.) 2003. *The Spectre of Genocide: Mass Murder in Historical Perspective*. Cambridge, UK: Cambridge University Press.

Gellner, E. 1983. *Nations and Nationalism*. Oxford, UK: Blackwell.

1988. *Plough, Sword and the Book: The Structure of Human History*. London: Collins Harvill.

Gerlach, M. 1992. *Alliance Capitalism: The Social Organization of Japanese Business*. Berkeley: University of California Press.

Gerwarth, R. 2014. Cold empathy: perpetrator studies and the challenges in writing a life of Reinhard Heydrich. In D. Baratieri, M. Edele and G. Finaldi (eds.), *Totalitarian Dictatorship*. London: Routledge.

Gibbon, E. 2003 [1776]. *History of the Decline and Fall of Roman Empire*. New York: Random House.

Giddens, A. 1985. *The Nation-State and Violence*. Cambridge, UK: Polity Press.

Ginsberg, B. 2013. *The Value of Violence*. New York: Prometheus.

Giustozzi, A. 2011. *The Art of Coercion*. New York: Columbia University Press.

Gleditsch, N. P., P. Wallensteen, M. Eriksson, M. Sollenberg and H. Strand. 2002. Armed conflict 1946–2001: a new data set. *Journal of Peace Research*, 39(5): 615–637.

Goldhagen, D. 2009: *Worse Than War: Genocide, Eliminationism, and the Ongoing Assault on Humanity*. New York: PublicAffairs.

Goldstein, J. S. 2001. *War and Gender: How Gender Shapes the War System and Vice Versa*. Cambridge, UK: Cambridge University Press.

2011. *Winning the War on War*. London: Penguin.

Goldstone, J. 1991. *Revolution and Rebellion in the Early Modern World*. Berkley: University of California Press.

2011. Understanding the revolutions of 2011: weakness and resilience in Middle Eastern autocracies. *Foreign Affairs*, 90(May/June): 8–16.

2014. *Revolutions: A Very Short Introduction*. Oxford, UK: Oxford University Press.

Goldsworthy, A. 2007. *The Fall of Carthage: The Punic Wars 265–146 BC*. London: Cassel.

Goodal, J. 1986. *The Chimpanzee of Gomb: Patterns of Behaviour*. Cambridge, MA: Harvard University Press.

Goodwin, J. 1997. State-centered approaches to social revolutions: strengths and limitations of a theoretical tradition. In J. Foran (ed.), *Theorizing Revolutions*. London: Routledge.

2001. *No Other Way Out: States and Revolutionary Movements, 1945–1991*. Cambridge, UK: Cambridge University Press.

Gouldner, A. 1976. *The Dialectic of Ideology and Technology: The Origins, Grammar and Future of Ideology*. London: Macmillan.

Gouldner, A. W. 1979. *The Future of Intellectuals and the Rise of the New Class*. New York: Continuum.

Goncalves, B. et al. 2011. Modeling users' activity on Twitter networks: validation of Dunbar's number. *Ploseone*, 6(8): e22656.

Grafstein, R. 1981. The failure of Weber's conception of legitimacy: its causes and implications. *Journal of Politics*, 43: 456–472.

Graulich, M. 2000. Aztec human sacrifice as expiation. *History of Religions*, 39(4): 352–371.

Gray. C. 2002. *Strategy for Chaos*. London: Frank Cass.

Green, D. 2010. *The Hundred Years War: A People's History*. New Haven, CT: Yale University Press.

Griffith, J. 1989. The army's new unit personnel replacement and its relationship to unit cohesion and social support. *Military Psychology*, 1(1): 17–34.

Grossman, D. 1996. *On Killing: The Psychological Cost of Learning to Kill in War and Society*. Boston: Little, Brown.

Grossman, D. and L. W. Christensen. 2000. *On Combat: The Psychology and Physiology of Deadly Conflict in War and in Peace*. Millstadt, IL: Warrior Science.

Guevara, C. 2006[1961]. *Guerrilla Warfare*. New York: Ocean Press.

Gurr, T. 1970. *Why Men Rebel*. Princeton, NJ: Princeton University Press.

Guthrie, R. D. 2005. *The Nature of Paleolithic Art*. Chicago: Chicago University Press.

Hacker, D. 2011. A census-based count of the Civil War dead. *Civil War History*. 57(4): 307–384.

Hajjar, L. 2013. *Torture: A Sociology of Violence and Human Rights*. London: Routledge.

Hall, J. A. 1985. *Powers and Liberties: The Causes and Consequences of the Rise of the West*. London: Basil Blackwell.

1988. States and societies: the miracle in comparative perspective. In J. Baechler, J. A. Hall and M. Mann (eds.), *Europe and the Rise of Capitalism*. Oxford, UK: Basil Blackwell.

2000. Globalisation and nationalism. *Thesis Eleven*, 63: 63–79

2013. *The Importance of Being Civil*. Princeton, NJ: Princeton University Press.

Hall, R. 2000. *The Balkan Wars 1912–1913: Prelude to the First World War*. London: Routledge.

Hansel, P. R., M. E. Allison and A. Khanani. 2009. Territorial integrity treaties and armed conflict over territory: conflict management and peace. *Science*, 26(2): 120–143.

Hanson, V. 2001. *Carnage and Culture: Landmark Battles in the Rise to Western Power*. New York: Knopf.

Harff, B. and T. Gurr. 1988. Towards empirical theory of genocides and politicides: identification and measurment of cases since 1945. *International Studies Quarterly*, 32(3): 359–371.

Harris, M. 1984. A cultural materialist theory of band and village warfare: the Yanomamo test. In B. Ferguson (ed.), *Warfare, Culture, and Environment*. Orlando, FL: Academic Press.

Harrison, F. 2002. 'Black Tigers' appear in public. BBC. news.bbc.co.uk/2/hi/south_asia/2516263.stm

Hassan, R. 2011. *Suicide Bombings*. London: Routledge.

Hayden, R. 1996. Imagined communities and real victims: self-determination and ethnic cleansing in Yugoslavia. *American Ethnologist*, 23(4): 783–801.

Hebrew, Bible. www.scripture4all.org/OnlineInterlinear/Hebrew_Index.htm

Henderson, D. 1985. *Cohesion: The Human Element*. Washington, DC: National Defence University Press.

Hendrix, C. and I. Salehyan. 2012. Climate change, rainfall, and social conflict in Africa. *Journal of Peace Research*, 49(1): 35–50.

Hensel, P. et al. 2009. Territorial integrity treaties and armed conflict over territory. *Conflict Management and Peace Science*, 26(2): 120–143.

Herbst, J. 2000. *States and Power in Africa: Comparative Lessons in Authority and Control*. Princeton, NJ: Princeton University Press.

Herman, E. and D. Peterson. 2014. Reality denial: apologetics for the Western-imperial violence. www.globalresearch.ca/reality-denial-apologetics-for-western-imperial-violence/32066

Herwig, H., C., Archer, T. Travers and J. Ferris. 2003. *Cassell's World History of Warfare*. London: Cassell.

Hill, P. 2006. Kamikaze, 1943–45. In D. Gambetta (ed.), *Making Sense of Suicide Missions*. Oxford, UK: Oxford University Press.

Hinton, A. L. 2002. The dark side of modernity: toward an anthropology of genocide. In A. L. Hinton and K. Roth (eds.), *Annihilating Difference: The Anthropology of Genocide*. Berkeley: University of California Press.

Hironaka, A. 2005. *Neverending Wars*. Cambridge, MA: Harvard University Press.

Hirst, P. 2001. *War and Power in the 21st Century*. Cambridge, UK: Polity Press.

et al. 2009. *Globalisation in Question*. Cambridge, UK: Polity Press.

Hixson, W. 2003. *The American Experience in World War II: The Atomic Bomb in History and Memory*. London: Routledge.

HL (History List). historylist.wordpress.com/2008/05/29/human-deaths-in-the-us-caused-by-animals/

Hobsbawm, E. 1994. *The Age of Extremes*. New York: Vintage.

2002. *Interesting Times: A Twentieth-Century Life*. London: Allen Lane.

Hochschild, A. 1999. *King Leopold's Ghost: A Story of Greed, Terror, and Heroism in Colonial Africa*. New York: Houghton Mifflin.

Holmberg, A. R. 1968. *Nomads of the Longbow*. Washington, DC: Smithsonian Institution Press.

Holmes, R. 1985. *Acts of War*. New York: Free Press.

Hopgood, S. 2005. Tamil Tigers 1987–2002. In D. Gambetta (ed.), *Making Sense of Suicide Missions*. Oxford, UK: Oxford University Press.

Horgan, J. 2009. *Walking Away from Terrorism: Accounts of Disengagement from Radical and Extremist Movements*. London and New York: Taylor and Francis.

2012. *The End of War*. New York: McSweeney.

Howard, M. 1976. *War in European History*. Oxford, UK: Oxford University Press.

Huntington, S. 1996. *The Clash of Civilizations and the Remaking of the World Order*. Chicago: University of Chicago Press.

Hutchinson, J. 1994. *Modern Nationalism*. London: Fontana Press.

2005. *Nations as Zones of Conflict*. London: Sage.

Iadicola, P. and A. Shupe. 2012. *Violence, Inequality and Human Freedom*. New York: Rowman & Littlefield.

IBC (Iraq Body Count) 2016. www.iraqbodycount.org/database/

ICTY (International Criminal Tribunal for the Former Yugoslavia) 2010. www.haguejusticeportal.net/Docs/Court%20Documents/ICTY/Press%20release%20Seven%20Senior%20Bosnian%20Serb%20Officials%20Convicted%20of%20Srebrenica%20Crimes.pdf

Israeli, R. 1997. Islamikaze and their significance. *Terrorism and Political Violence*, 9(3): 96–121.

Jackson, R. 2007. The core commitments of critical terrorism studies. *European Political Science*, 6(3): 244–251.

2009. The study of terrorism after 11 September 2001: problems, challenges and future developments. *Political Studies Review*, 7(2): 171–184.

Janis, I. 1982. *Group Think*. Boston: Houghton Miffin.

Jarausch, K. 1990. *The Unfree Professions: German Lawyers, Teachers and Engineers, 1900–1950*. Oxford, UK: Oxford University Press.

Jardine, L. 2008. *Going Dutch: How England Plundered Holland's Glory*. London: Harper.

Jarvis, J. 2009. *What Would Google Do?* New York: Harper Collins.

Jenkins, R. 2014. *Social Identity*. London: Routledge.

Jonassohn, K. and K. Bjornson. 1998. *Genocide and Gross Human Rights Violations in Comparative Perspective*. New Brunswick, NJ: Transaction.

Jones, E. 1987. *The European Miracle*. Cambridge, UK: Cambridge University Press.

Juang, R. and N. Morrissette (eds.) 2008. *Africa and the Americas: Culture, Politics, and History*. Santa Barbara, CA: ABC-CLIO.

Juergensmeyer, M. 2003. *Terror in the Mind of God: The Global Rise of Religious Violence*. Berkeley: University of California Press.

Jurmain, R. 2001. Paleoepidemiological patterns of trauma in a prehistoric population from central California. *American Journal of Physical Anthropology*, 115: 13–23.

Kalyvas, S. 2001. 'New' and 'old' civil wars: a valid distinction? *World Politics*, 54: 99–118.

2006. *The Logic of Violence in Civil War*. Cambridge, UK: Cambridge University Press.

Kaye, J. and B. Strath (eds.) 2000. *Enlightenment and Genocide, Contradictions of Modernity*. Brussels: Peter Lang.

Keegan, J. 1993. *A History of Warfare*. London: Vintage.

Keeley, L. H. 1996. *War before Civilization: The Myth of the Peaceful Savage*. Oxford, UK: Oxford University Press.

Kelly, R. C. 2000. *Warless Societies and the Origin of War*. Ann Arbor: University of Michigan Press.

Kertzer, D. and D. Arel. 2002. *Census and Identity: The Politics of Race, Ethnicity, and Language in .National Censuses*. Cambridge, UK: Cambridge University Press.

Kershaw, I. 1993. Working towards the Führer: reflections on the nature of the Hitler dictatorship. *Contemporary European History*, 2(2): 103–118.

2008. *Hitler, the Germans, and the Final Solution*. New Haven, CT: Yale University Press.

Kiernan, B. 2009. *Blood and Soil: A World History of Genocide and Extermination from Sparta to Darfur*. New Haven, CT: Yale University Press.

King, A. 2007. The existence of group cohesion in the armed forces. *Armed Forces and Society*, 33(4): 638–645.

2013. *The Combat Soldier*. Oxford, UK: Oxford University Press.

Kirke, C. 2009. Group cohesion, culture and practice. *Armed Forces and Society* 35(4): 745–753.

Kissane, B. 2016. *Nations Torn Asunder: The Challenge of Civil War*. Oxford, UK: Oxford University Press.

Klare, M. 2002. *Resource Wars*. New York: Owl.

Kleinschmidt, H. 2008. *Understanding the Middle Ages*. Woodbridge, UK: Boydell Press.

Klemettilä, H. 2009. *Cruelty in the Middle Ages*. Jyväskylä, Finland: Atena.

Klusemann, S. 2010. Micro-situational antecedents of violent atrocity. *Sociological Forum*, 25(2): 272–295.

Kobach, K. 1993. *The Referendum: Direct Democracy in Switzerland*. Aldershot, UK: Dartmouth.

Kobrin, N. 2002. A psychoanalytic approach to bin Laden, political violence, and Islamic suicidal terrorism. *Clio's Psyche*, 8(4): 181–183

Kohler, G. and N. Alcock. 1976. An empirical table of structural violence. *Journal of Peace Research*, 13(4): 343–356.

Kradin, N. N. 2004. Nomadic empires in evolutionary perspective. In L. Grinin (ed.), *Alternatives of Social Evolution. The Early State: Its Alternatives and Analogues*. Volgograd: Uchitel.

Kreps, S. E. 2016. *Drones: What Everyone Needs to Know*. Oxford, UK: Oxford University Press.

Krieger, H. 2001. *The Kosovo Conflict and International Law: An Analytical Documentation 1974–1999.* Cambridge: Cambridge University Press.

Krueger, A. and J. Malečková. 2003. Education, poverty, and terrorism: is there a causal connection? *Journal of Economic Perspectives,* 17(4): 119–144.

Kumar, K. 2010. Nation-states as empires, empires as nation-states: two principles, one practice? *Theory and Society,* 39(2): 119–43.

Kuper, L. 1981. *Genocide: Its Political Use in the Twentieth Century.* Harmondsworth, UK: Penguin.

Lachkar, J. 2002. The psychological make-up of a suicide bomber. *Journal of Psychohistory,* 29, 349–367.

Lachmann, R. 1997. Agents of revolution: urban and rural elites and masses. In J. Foran (ed.), *Theoriing Revolutions: Disciplines, Approaches.* London: Routledge.

Lachmann, R. 2010. *States and Power.* Cambridge, UK: Polity Press.

2013a. *Mercenary, citizen, victim: the rise and fall of conscription in the West.* In J. Hall and S. Malešević (eds.), *Nationalism and War.* Cambridge, UK: Polity Press.

2013b. *What Is Historical Sociology?* Cambridge, UK: Polity Press.

Lacina, B., N. P. Gleditsch and B. Russett. 2006. The declining risk of death in battle. *International Studies Quarterly,* 50(3): 673–680.

Laitin, D. 2007. *Nations, States, and Violence.* Oxford, UK: Oxford University Press.

Larson, M. 2014. Rwanda genocide perpetrator: 'I asked for forgiveness'. www.worldvision.org/news-stories-videos/rwanda-genocide-perpetrator-interview.

Lazenby, J. 2012. *The Spartan Army.* Mechanicsburg, PA: Stackpole.

Leaky, R. 1981. *The Making of Mankind.* New York: Elsevier-Dutton.

LeBlanc, S. A. 2007. Why warfare? Lessons from the past. *Daedalus*(Winter): 13–21.

Lee, S. 1991. *The Thirty Years War.* London: Routledge.

Leitenberg, M. 2006. Deaths in wars and conflicts in the 20th century. Cornell University Working paper.

Lemkin, R. 1944. *Axis Rule in Occupied Europe: Laws of Occupation – Analysis of Government – Proposals for Redress.* Washington, DC: Carnegie Endowment for International Peace.

Leonard, T. 1999. *Castro and the Cuban Revolution.* New York: Greenwood Press.

Levene, M. 2005. *Genocide in the Age of the Nation State,* vol. 2: *The Rise of the West and the Coming of Genocide.* London: IB Taurus.

Levy, J. and W. Thompson. 2012. *The Arc of War.* Chicago: Chicago University Press.

Levinson, N. 2014. *War Is Not a Game: The New Antiwar Soldiers and the Movement They Built.* New Brunswick, NJ: Rutgers University Press.

Lewis, M. E. 1999. *Writing and Authority in Early China.* New York: State University of New York Press.

Li, Q. and D. Schaub. 2004. Economic globalization and transnational terrorism: a pooled time-series analysis. *Journal of Conflict Resolution.* 48(2): 230–258.

Lillie, M. C. 2004. Fighting for your life? Violence at the Late-Glacial to Holocene transition in Ukraine. In M. Roksandic (ed.), *Violent Interactions in the Mesolithic: Evidence and Meaning*. British Archaeological Reports International Series 1237.

Lizot, J. 1985. *Tales of the Yanomami: Daily Life in the Venezuelan Forest*. Cambridge, UK: Cambridge University Press.

Lusebrink, H. and R. Reichardt. 1997. *The Bastille: A History of a Symbol of Despotism and Freedom*. Durham, NC: Duke University Press.

Lyon, D. 2001. *Surveillance Society: Monitoring Everyday Life*. London: Oxford University Press.

MacFarlane, A. 2003. *The Savage Wars of Peace: England, Japan and the Malthusian Trap*. New York: Palgrave.

Maddern, P. 1992. *Violence and Social Order: East Anglia 1422–1442*. Oxford, UK: Clarendon Press.

Malečková, J. 2005. Impoverished terrorists: stereotype or reality? In T. Bjorgo (ed.), *Root Causes of Terrorism: Myths, Reality, and Ways Forward*. London: Routledge.

Malešević, S. 2002. *Ideology, Legitimacy and the New State: Yugoslavia, Serbia and Croatia*. London: Routledge.

2004. *The Sociology of Ethnicity*. London: Sage.

2006. *Identity as Ideology: Understanding Ethnicity and Nationalism*. New York: Palgrave.

2008. Solidary killers and egoistic pacifists: violence, war and social action. *Journal of Power*, 1(2): 207–216.

2010. *The Sociology of War and Violence*. Cambridge, UK: Cambridge University Press.

2011. Nationalism, war and social cohesion. *Ethnic and Racial Studies*, 34(1): 142–161.

2012. Did wars make nation-states in the Balkans? Nationalisms, wars and states in the 19th and early 20th century South East Europe. *Journal of Historical Sociology*, 25(3): 299–330.

2013a. *Nation-States and Nationalisms: Organisation, Ideology and Solidarity*. Cambridge, UK: Polity Press.

2013b. Forms of brutality: towards a historical sociology of violence. *European Journal of Social Theory*, 16(3): 273–291.

2013c. Obliterating heterogeneity through peace: nationalisms, states and wars in the Balkans. In J. Hall and S. Malešević (eds.), *Nationalism and War*. Cambridge: Cambridge University Press.

2014. Is war becoming obsolete? A sociological analysis. *Sociological Review*, 62(S2): 65–86.

2015. Where does group solidarity come from? Ernest Gellner and Ibn Khaldun revisited. *Thesis Eleven*, 128(1): 85–99.

2016. Nationalism and military power in the 20th century and beyond. In R. Schroeder (ed.), *The Global Powers: Michael Mann's Anatomy of the 20th Century and Beyond*. Cambridge, UK: Cambridge University Press.

Malešević, S. and N. O'Dochartaigh. 2017. *Why Soldiers Fight: The Irish Republican Army and the Army of the Serbian Republic in Bosnia Compared* (in preparation).

Malešević, S. and K. Ryan. 2013. The disfigured ontology of figurational sociology: Norbert Elias and the question of violence. *Critical Sociology* 39(2): 165–181.

Malešević, S. and G. Uzelac. 1997. Ethnic distance, power and war. *Nations and Nationalism*, 3(2): 291–298.

Malkin, M. and J. Miano. 2016. *Sold Out*. New York: Mercuri Ink.

Mamdani, M. 2001. *When Victims Become Killers: Colonialism, Nativism and Genocide in Rwanda*. Princeton, NJ: Princeton University Press.

Mandel, E. 1968. *Marxist Economic History*. London: Merlin Press.

Mann, M. 1986. *The Sources of Social Power I: A History of Power from the Beginning to* A.D. 1760. Cambridge, UK: Cambridge University Press.

Mann, M. 1993. *The Sources of Social Power II: The Rise of Classes and Nation-States, 1760–1914*. Cambridge, UK: Cambridge University Press.

2003. *Incoherent Empire*. London: Verso.

2004. *Fascists*. Cambridge, UK: Cambridge University Press.

2005. *The Dark Side of Democracy: Explaining Ethnic Cleansing*. Cambridge, UK: Cambridge University Press.

2006. The social sources of life, the universe and everything: a conversation with Michael Mann (interviewed by G. Lawson) *Millennium*, 34(2): 487–508.

2012. *The Sources of Social Power III. Global Empires and Revolution, 1890–1945*. Cambridge, UK: Cambridge University Press.

2013. *The Sources of Social Power IV. Globalizations, 1945–2011*. Cambridge, UK: Cambridge University Press.

2014. Have societies evolved? Paper presented at the Conference 'History as Sociology, Sociology as History', University College, Dublin, 27 August.

2016. *Have Wars and Violence Declined?* Unpublished manuscript.

Mannheim, K. 1966. *Ideology and Utopia*. London: Routledge.

Marshall, S. 1947. *Men against Fire: The Problem of Battle Command*. New York: Morrow.

Marx, K. 1968 [1871]. *The Civil War in France: The Paris Commune*, New York: International Publishers.

Marx, K. and F. Engels. 1998 [1848]. *The Communist Manifesto*. London: Verso.

Mayntz, R. 2004. *Organisational Forms of Terrorism*. Cologne: Max Planck Institute for the Study of Societies.

Mayo, E. 1949. *Hawthorne and the Western Electric Company: The Social Problems of an Industrial Civilisation*. London: Routledge.

McCarty, C. et al. 2000. Comparing two methods for estimating network size. *Human Organisation*, 60(1): 28–39.

McCauley, C. 2007. Psychological issues in understanding terrorism and the response to terrorism. In C. Strout (ed.), *Psychology of Terrorism*. New York: Oxford University Press.

McKee, A. 1983. *Dresden 1945: The Devil's Tinderbox*. London: Granada.

McNeill, W. 1982. *The Pursuit of Power*. Chicago: University of Chicago Press.

Madej, V. 1978. Effectiveness and cohesion of the German ground forces in World War II. *Journal of Political and Military Sociology*, 6: 233–248.

Mennell, S. 2007. *The American Civilising Process*. Cambridge, UK: Polity Press.

Merari, A. 1990. The readiness to kill and die: suicidal terrorism in the Middle East. In W. Reich (ed.), *Origins of Terrorism: Psychologies, Ideologies,*

Theologies, States of Mind. Washington, DC: Woodrow Wilson Center Press.

Meredith, M. 2005. *The State of Africa: A History of the Continent since Independence.* New York: Free Press.

Meyer, J. et al. 1997. World Society and the Nation-State. *American Journal of Sociology,* 103(1):144–81.

Michels, R. 1939. *Political Parties: A Sociological Study of the Oligarchical Tendencies of Modern Democracy.* London: Dover.

Mill, J. S. 1836. Civilization. www.laits.utexas.edu/poltheory/jsmill/diss-disc/civilization/civilization.html

Miller, B. 2012. *The Tea Party Papers: The American Spiritual Evolution versus the French Political Revolution.* Bloomington, IN: Exlibris.

Mohr, N. 2012. Average and total numbers of land animals who died to feed Americans in 2011. www.upc-online.org/slaughter/2011americans.pdf

Moore, B. 1966. *Social Origins of Democracy and Dictatorship.* Boston: Beacon.
1978. *Injustice: The Social Bases of Obedience and Revolt.* London: Macmillan.

Morris, D. 1965. *The Washing of the Spears: The Rise and Fall of the Zulu Nation.* New York: Simon and Schuster.

Morris, I. 2014. *War! What Is It Good For? Conflict and the Progress of Civilization from Primates to Robots.* New York: Farrar, Straus and Giroux.

Moskos, C. 1975. The American combat soldier in Vietnam. *Journal of Social Issues,* 31(4): 25–37.

Mueller, J. 2009. War has almost ceased to exist: an assessment. *Political Science Quarterly,* 124(2): 297–321.

Müller-Hill, B. 1998. *Murderous Science: Elimination by Scientific Selection of Jews, Gypsies, and Others in Germany, 1933– 1945.* New York: Cold Spring Harbor Laboratory Press.

Munkler, H. 2007. *Empire.* Cambridge, UK: Polity Press.

Naimark, N. 2001. *Fires of Hatred: Ethnic Cleansing In 20th Century Europe.* Cambridge, MA: Harvard University Press.

Nairn, T. 1977. *The Break-up of Britain.* London. Verso.

Neill, H. U. and J. Wardenaer. 2015. Global conflict fatalities increase by more than 35% in 2014. International Institute for Strategic Studies www.iiss.org/en/iiss%20voices/blogsections/iiss-voices-2015-dda3/february-04dc/acd-2014-fatalities-3023

Neitzel, S. and H. Welzer. 2012. *Soldaten: On Fighting, Killing and Dying.* New York: Knopf.

Obeyesekere, G. 2002. *Imagining Karma: Ethical Transformation in Amerindian, Buddhist, and Greek Rebirth.* Berkeley: University of California Press.

Oded, B. 1979. *Mass Deportations and Deportees in the Neo-Assyrian Empire.* Wiesbaden, Germany: Dr Ludwig Reichert Verlag.

Ó Dochartaigh, N. 2015. Radical milieu and mass mobilisation in the Northern Ireland conflict. In L. Bosi, N. Ó Dochartaigh and D. Pisoiu (eds.), *Political Violence in Context: Time, Space and Milieu.* Colchester, UK: ECPR Press.
2016. Northern Ireland since 1920. In R. Bourke and I. McBride (eds.), *The Princeton History of Modern Ireland.* Princeton, NJ: University of Princeton Press.

O'Hearn, D. 2006. *Nothing but an Unfinished Song: Bobby Sands, the Irish Hunger Striker Who Ignited a Generation.* New York: Nation Books,

2009. Repression and solidary cultures of resistance: Irish political prisoners on protest. *American Journal of Sociology*, 15(2): 491–526.

Oksala, J. 2012. *Foucault, Politics, and Violence*. Evanston, IL: Northwestern University Press.

Olusoga, D. and K. Erichsen. 2010. *Kaiser's Holocaust: Germany's Forgotten Holocaust and the Colonial Roots of Nazism*. New York: Faber and Faber.

Osborne, R. 2006. *Civilization: A New History of the Western World*. New York: Pegasus.

Overy, R. 1997. *Russia's War*. London: Penguin.

2004. *The Dictators: Hitler's Germany and Stalin's Russia*. New York: Allen Lane.

2005. Total War II: The Second World War. In C. Townshend (ed.), *The Oxford History of Modern Warfare*. Oxford, UK: Oxford University Press.

Palmer, R. R. 2005. *Twelve Who Ruled: The Year of the Terror in the French Revolution*. Princeton, NJ: Princeton University Press

Parker, G. 1984. *The Thirty Years War*. London: Routledge.

Perez, J. 1993. *History of a Tragedy: The Expulsion of the Jews from Spain*. Chicago: University of Illinois Press.

2006. *The Spanish Inquisition: A History*. London: Profile.

Pinker, S. 2011. *The Better Angels of Our Nature: The Decline of Violence in History and Its Causes*. New York: Allan Lane.

Pipes, R. 1991. *The Russian Revolution*. New York: Vintage.

2001. *Communism: A History*. New York: Random House.

Phillips, C. and A. Axelrod. 2005. *Encyclopedia of Wars*. New York: Zenda.

Poggi, G. 2001. *Forms of Power*. Cambridge, UK: Polity Press.

Pollard, A. J. 2001. *The Wars of the Roses*. London: Macmillan.

Pollard, E. et al. 2015. *Worlds Together Worlds Apart*. New York: Norton.

Popov, N. 2000. *The Road to War in Serbia*. Budapest: CEU Press.

Posen, B. 1993. Nationalism, the mass army, and military power. *International Security*, 18(2): 80–124.

Prucha, F. 1984. *The Great Father: The United States Government and the American Indians*. Lincoln: University of Nebraska Press.

Prunier, G. 1997. *The Rwandan Crisis 1959–1994: History of a Genocide*. London: Hurst.

Purdue, P. 2005. *China Marches West: The Qing Conquest of Central Eurasia*. Cambridge, MA: Harvard University Press.

Rapport, M. 2013. *The Napoleonic Wars: A Very Brief Introduction*. Oxford, UK: Oxford University Press.

Ray, L. 2011. *Violence and Society*. London: Sage.

Ricolfi, L. 2005. Palestinians, 1981–2003. In D. Gambetta (ed.), *Making Sense of Suicide Missions*. Oxford, UK: Oxford University Press.

Reed, J. 1919. *Ten Days that Shook the World*. London: Penguin.

Reid, R. 2012. *Warfare in African History*. Cambridge, UK: Cambridge University Press.

Robarchek, C. A. and C. J. Robarchek. 1998. Reciprocities and realities: world views, peacefulness, and violence among Semai and Waorani. *Aggressive Behavior*, 24(2): 123–133.

Rogers, C. 2010. *The Oxford Encyclopedia of Medieval Warfare and Military Technology*. Oxford, UK: Oxford University Press.

Roper, S. 2000. *Romania: The Unfinished Revolution*. London: Routledge.

Rosenburg, T. 1995. *The Haunted Land: Facing Europe's Ghosts after Communism*. New York: Vintage.

Rosenstein, N. 2004. *Rome at War: Farms, Families, and Death in the Middle Republic*. Chapel Hill: University of North Carolina Press.

Rummel, R. 2005. *Ending War, Democide, & Famine through Democratic Freedom*. Fort Lauderdale, FL: Llumina Press.

Sadowski, Y. 1998. *The Myth of Global Chaos*, Washington, DC: Brookings Institution Press.

Sageman, M. 2004. *Leaderless Jihad: Terror Networks in the Twenty-first Century*, Philadelphia: University of Pennsylvania Press.

2011. *Understanding Terror Networks*. Philadelphia: University of Pennsylvania Press.

Sahlins, M. 1972. *Stone Age Economics*. Chicago: Aidine Atherton.

Salib, E. 2003. Suicide terrorism: a case of folie à plusieurs? *British Journal of Psychiatry*, 182: 475–476.

Sand, S. 2008. *The Invention of the Jewish People*. London: Verso.

Schabas, W. 2009. *Genocide in International Law*. Cambridge, UK: Cambridge University Press.

Scheff, T. 1994. *Bloody Revenge: Emotion, Nationalism and War*. Boulder, CO: Westview Press.

Scheper-Hughes, N. 2004. Dangerous and endangered youth: social structures and determinants of violence. *Annals of the New York Academy of Science*, 1036: 13–46.

Scheper-Hughes, N. and P. Bourgois. 2004. *Violence in War and Peace: An Anthology*. London: Basil Blackwell.

Schild, W. 2000. Die eiserne Jungfrau. Dichtung und Wahrheit (Schriftenreihe des Mittelalterlichen Kriminalmuseums Rothenburg o. d. Tauber Nr. 3). Rothenburg ob der Tauber.

Schinkel, W. 2010. *Aspects of Violence: A Critical Theory*. New York: Palgrave.

Scott, J. S. 1998. *Seeing Like a State: How Certain Schemes to Improve the Human Condition Have Failed*. New Haven, CT: Yale University Press.

2012. *Decoding Subaltern Politics: Ideology, Disguise, and Resistance in Agrarian Politics*. London: Routledge.

Scullard, H. 2002. *A History of the Roman World, 753 to 146* BC. London: Routledge.

Segal, M. and M. Kestnbaum. 2002. Professional closure in the military markets: a critique of pure cohesion. In D. Snider (ed.), *The Future of Army Profession*. New York: Primis.

Selbin, E. 1997. Revolution in the real world: bringing agency back in. In J. Foran (ed.), *Theorizing Revolutions*. London: Routledge.

2010. *Revolution, Rebellion, and Resistance: The Power of Story*. London: Zed.

Senauth, F. 2011. *The Making and Destruction of Haiti*. Bloomington, IN: Author House.

Service, E. R.1978. *Profiles in Ethnology*. New York: Harper and Row.

Sewell, R. 1987. *India before the English*. Berkeley: University of California Press.

Shaw, M. 2003. *War and Genocide: Organized Killing in Modern Society*. Cambridge, UK: Polity Press.

2005. *The New Western Way of War: Risk-Transfer War and Its Crisis in Iraq Cambridge*. Cambridge, UK: Polity Press.

2007. *What Is Genocide?* Cambridge, UK: Polity Press.

Shaw, R. P. and Y. Wang. 1989. *Genetic Seeds of Warfare: Evolution, Nationalism, and Patriotism*. Boston: Unwin Hyman.

Shils, E. and M. Janowitz. 1948. Cohesion and disintegration in the Wehrmacht in World War II. *Public Opinion Quarterly*. 12: 280–315.

Shimazu, N. 2009. *Japanese Society at War*. Cambridge, UK: Cambridge University Press.

Siani-Davies. P. 2007. *The Romanian Revolution of December 1989*. Ithaca, NY: Cornell University Press.

Siebold, G. 2007. The essence of military cohesion. *Armed Forces and Society*, 33(2): 286–295.

2011. Key questions and challenges to the standard model of military group cohesion. *Armed Forces & Society*, 37(3): 448–468.

Siebold, G. and T. Lindsay. 1999. The relation between demographic descriptors and soldier perceived cohesion and motivation. *Military Psychology*, 11(1): 109–128.

Silke, A. 2008. Holy warriors exploring the psychological processes of jihadi radicalization. *European Journal of Criminology*, 5(1): 99–123.

Simmel, G. 1917. *Der Krieg und die geistigen Entscheidungen*. Munich: Duncker and Humblot.

Sinclair, R. K. 1988. *Democracy and Participation in Athens*. Cambridge, UK: Cambridge University Press.

Singer, P. 2009. *Wired for War: The Robotics Revolution and Conflict in the 21st Century*. London: Penguin.

Singer, J. and M. Small. 1972. *The Wages of War 1816–1965*. New York: Wiley.

Singh, M. 2014. The Islamic state's triple threat. *Foreign Policy:* shadow.foreignpolicy.com/posts/2014/09/05/the_islamic_states_triple_threat

Sinno, A. 2008. *Organisations at War in Afghanistan and Beyond*. Ithaca, NY: Cornell University Press.

SIPRI (Stockholm International Peace Research Institute) 2016. *Military Expenditure Database*. www.pgpf.org/Chart-Archive/0053_defense-comparison#sthash.cgDq2KLF.dpuf

Skocpol, T. 1979. *States and Social Revolutions: A Comparative Analysis of France, Russia, and China*. Cambridge, UK: Cambridge University Press.

1982. Rentier state and Shi'a Islam in the Iranian Revolution. *Theory and Society*, 11(3): 265–283.

Sluka, J. A. 2009a. The contribution of anthropology to critical terrorism studies. In R. Jackson, B. Smyth and J. Gunning (eds.), *Critical Terrorism Studies*. New York: Routledge.

2009b. In the shadow of the gun: 'not-war-not-peace' and the future of conflict in Northern Ireland. *Critique of Anthropology*, 29(3): 279–299.

Smelser, N. 2007. *The Faces of Terrorism: Social and Psychological Dimensions*. Princeton, NJ: Princeton University Press.

Smelser, N. J. 1962. *Theory of Collective Behavior*. New York: Free Press.

Smith, A. D. 2010. *Nationalism*. Cambridge, UK: Polity Press.

Smith, A. D. 1986. *The Ethnic Origins of Nations*. Oxford, UK: Blackwell.

2009. *Ethnosymbolism and Nationalism: A Cultural Approach*. London: Routledge.

Smith, B. and A. Peterson (eds.). 1974. *Heinrich Himmler: Geheimreden 1933– 1945*. Frankfurt am Main: Propyläen Verlag.

Smith, J. 2009. Facebook's 'in-house sociologist' shares stats on users' social behaviour. inside Facebook.com. www.adweek.com/socialtimes/facebooks-in-house-sociologist-shares-stats-on-users-social-behavior/217813?red=if

Smith, L. 1980. *The Aboriginal Population of Australia*. Canberra: Australian National University Press.

Smith, P. 2005. *Why War? The Cultural Logic of Iraq, the Gulf War, and Suez*. Chicago: Chicago University Press.

2008. *Punishment and Culture*. Chicago: University of Chicago Press.

Smith, R. 1987. Human destructiveness and politics: the twentieth century as an age of genocide. In M. Dobkowski and I. Walliman (eds.), *Genocide in the Modern Age*. New York: Greenwood Press.

Snyder, L. 1968. *New Nationalism*. New Brunswick, NJ: Transactions.

Sofsky, W. 1997. *The Order of Terror: The Concentration Camp*. Princeton, NJ: Princeton University Press.

Sorokin, P. 1957. *Social and Cultural Dynamics*. Boston: Porter Sargent.

Speierenburg, P. 2008. *A History of Murder: Personal Violence in Europe from the Middle Ages to the Present*. Cambridge, UK: Polity Press.

Spencer, H. 1882. *Principles of Sociology*, vol. 5: *Political Institutions*. archive.org/details/principlesofsoci02spen

Spengler, O. 1991 [1918]. *The Decline of the West*. New York: Oxford University Press.

Spierenburg, P. 2004. Punishment, power, and history: Foucault and Elias. *Social Science History*, 28(4): 607–636.

Sponsel, L. 1998. Yanomami: an arena of conflict and aggression in the Amazon. *Aggressive Behavior*, 24(2): 97–122.

2015. Peace and nonviolence, anthropological aspects. In J. Wright (ed.), *International Encyclopedia of the Social and Behavioral Sciences*. Amsterdam: Elsevier Press.

Stannard, D. 1993. *American Holocaust*. Oxford, UK: Oxford University Press.

Stephan, J. 1996. *The Russian Far East: A History*. Stanford, CA: Stanford University Press.

Stephens, H. M. 1982. *A History of the French Revolution*. Westport, CT: Greenwood Press.

Stephenson, S. 2015. *Gangs of Russia*. Ithaca, NY: Cornell University Press.

Stewart, N. K. 1991. *Mates and Muchachos: Unit Cohesion in the Falklands/Malvinas War*. New York: Brasseys.

Stone, D. 2004. Genocide as transgression. *European Journal of Social Theory* 7(1): 45–65.

Stone, L. 1971. Prosopography. *Daedalus* 100(1): 46–71.

Stouffer, S. et al. 1949. *The American Soldier: Combat and Its Aftermath*. Princeton, NJ: Princeton University Press.

Strathern, A. J. 1971. *The Rope of Moka: Big Men and Ceremonial Exchange in Mount Hagen, Papua New Guinea*. Cambridge, UK: Cambridge University Press.

Sutherland, D. 2003. *The French Revolution and Empire: The Quest for a Civic Order*. London: Blackwell.

Taagepera, R. 1997. Expansion and contraction patterns of large polities: context for Russia. *International Studies Quarterly*, 41(3): 475–504.

Taylor, A. 2002. *American Colonies*, vol. 1: *The Penguin History of the United States, History of the United States Series*. London: Penguin.

Taylor, F. 2005. *Dresden: Tuesday 13 February 1945*. London: Bloomsbury.

Thomassen, B. 2012. Notes towards an anthropology of political revolutions. *Comparative Studies in Society and History*, 54(3): 679–706.

Thompson, D. 2010. The politics of the census: lessons from abroad. *Canadian Public Policy*, 36(3): 377–382.

Thompson, J. 1989. Deprivation and political violence in Northern Ireland, 1922–1985: a time series analysis. *Journal of Conflict Resolution*, 33(4): 676–699.

Thornton, R. 1987. *American Indian Holocaust and Survival: A Population History since 1492*. Norman: University of Oklahoma Press.

Tilly, C. 1978. *From Mobilization to Revolution*. Reading, PA: Addison-Wesley.

1985. War making and state making as organized crime. In P. Evans, D. Rueschemeyer and T. Skocpol (eds.), *Bringing the State Back In*. Cambridge, UK: Cambridge University Press.

1992. *Coercion, Capital and European States*. Oxford, UK: Blackwell.

1995. *European Revolutions, 1492–1992*. Oxford, UK: Blackwell.

2003. *The Politics of Collective Violence*. Cambridge, UK: Cambridge University Press.

2004. *Contention & Democracy in Europe, 1650–2000*. Cambridge, UK: Cambridge University Press.

2008. *Contentious Performances*. Cambridge, UK: Cambridge University Press.

Tin-bor Hui, V. 2005. *War and State Formation in Ancient China and Early Modern Europe*. Cambridge, UK: Cambridge University Press.

Toros, H. and J. Gunning. 2009. Exploring a critical theory approach to terrorism studies. In R. Jackson, B. Smyth and J. Gunning (eds.), *Critical Terrorism Studies*. New York: Routledge.

Townshend, C. 2005. People's war. In C. Townshend (ed.), *The Oxford History of Modern Warfare*. Oxford, UK: Oxford University Press.

2011. *Terrorism: A Very Short Introduction*. Oxford, UK: Oxford University Press.

Toynbee, A. J. 1950. *War and Civilization, Selections from a Study of History*. New York: Oxford University Press.

Traynor, I. 2005. Young democracy guerrillas join forces. *The Guardian*. www.mjaft.org/pdf/the_guardians_activism_festival.pdf

Trotsky, L. 1931. *The Revolution in Spain*. New York: Pioneer.

Tucker, S. 2010. *Battles That Changed History: An Encyclopedia of World Conflict*. Santa Barbara, CA: ABC-CLIO.

Tuckman, B. 1965. Developmental sequence in small groups. *Psychological. Bulletin*, 63(6): 384–399.

Turnbull, S. 2013. *The Samurai: A Military History*. London: Routledge.

Turner, J. 2007. *Human Emotions: A Sociological Theory*. London: Routledge.

Turner, J. and A. Maryanski. 2005. *Incest: The Origins of Taboo*. Boulder, CO: Paradigm.

Tziner, A. and Y. Vardi. 1982. Effects of command style and group cohesiveness on the performance effectiveness of self-selected tank crews. *Journal of Applied Psychology*, 67(6): 769–775.

Valencia-Weber, G. 2003. The Supreme Court's Indian law decisions: deviations from constitutional principles and the crafting of judicial smallpox blankets. *University of Pennsylvania Journal of Constitutional Law*, 5(2): 1–78.

Van der Dennen, J. 1995. *The Origin of War*. Groningen, Netherlands: Origin Press.

Van Hooff, J. 1990. Intergroup competition and conflict in animals and man. In J. van der Dennen and V. Falger (eds.), *Sociobiology and Conflict: Evolutionary Perspectives on Competition, Cooperation, Violence and Warfare*. New York: Chapman and Hall.

Vansina, J. 1966. *Kingdoms of the Savanna*. Madison: University of Wisconsin Press.

Van Vugt, M. and J. Park. 2008. The tribal instinct hypothesis: evolution and the social psychology of intergroup relations. In S. Sturmer and M. Snyder (eds.), *New Directions in Helping and Intergroup Behavior*. London: Blackwell.

Vertigans, S. 2011. *The Sociology of Terrorism*. London: Routledge.

Victoroff, J. 2005. The mind of the terrorist: a review and critique of psychological approaches. *Journal of Conflict Resolution*, 49(1): 3–42.

Vogel, S. 1996. *Freer Markets, More Rules: Regulatory Reform in Advanced Industrial Countries*. Ithaca, NY: Cornell University Press.

Volkan, V. 2002. September 11 and societal regression. *Group Analysis*, 35: 456–483.

Wæver, O. 2011. Politics, security, theory. *Security Dialogue*, 42(4–5): 465–480.

Waiko, J. D. 1993. *A Short History of Papua New Guinea*. Melbourne, Australia: Oxford University Press.

Walker, C. J. 1980. *Armenia: The Survival of a Nation*. New York: St. Martin's Press.

Wallerstein, I. 1989. *The Modern World-System*, vol. III: *The Second Great Expansion of the Capitalist World-Economy, 1730–1840's*. San Diego, CA: Academic Press.

Walmsley, R. 2013. *World Prison Population List*. London: Institute for the Criminal Policy Research.

Walter, E. V. 1969. *Terror and Resistance: A Study of Political Violence*. New York: Oxford University Press.

Wakely, J. 1997. Identification and analysis of violent and non-violent head injuries in osteo-archeological material. In J. Carman (ed.), *Material Harm: Archeological Studies of War and Violence*. Glasgow: Cruithne Press.

Weatherford, J. 2004. *Genghis Khan and the Making of the Modern World*. New York: Crown.

Weber, C. 2003. *The Terror and Its Discontents*. Minneapolis: University of Minnesota Press.

Weber, M. 1930. *Protestant Ethic and the Spirit of Capitalism*. New York: Citadel Press.

1946. *From Max Weber: Essays in Sociology*. Translated and edited by H. H. Gerth and C. W. Mills. New York: Galaxy.

1968. *Economy and Society*. New York: Bedminster Press.

1994. *Weber: Political Writings*. Cambridge, UK: Cambridge University Press.

1995. *Russian Revolutions*. Cambridge, UK: Polity Press.

2004. *The Essential Weber: A Reader*. London: Routledge.

Weingartner, J. 1992. Trophies of war: U.S. troops and the mutilation of Japanese war dead, 1941–1945. *Pacific Historical Review*, 61(1): 53–67.

Weiss, K. M. and A. V. Buchanan. 2009. *The Mermaid's Tale: Four Billion Years of Cooperation in the Making of Living Things*. Cambridge, MA: Harvard University Press.

Weitz, E. 2003. *A Century of Genocide: Utopias of Race and Nation*. Princeton, NJ: Princeton University Press.

Wendorf, F. 1968. Site 117: a Nubian Final Paleolithic graveyard near Jebel Sahaba, Sudan. In F. Wendorf (ed.), *The Prehistory of Nubia*. Dallas, TX: Southern Methodist University.

Wertham, F. 1966. *A Sign for Cain: An Exploration of Human Violence*. London: Macmillan.

White, M. 2012. *Atrocitology: Humanity's 100 Deadliest Achievements*. New York: Norton.

White, R. W. 2000. Issues in the study of political violence: understanding the motives of participants in small group political violence. *Terrorism and Political Violence*, 12(1): 95–108.

Whitley, B. and M. Kite. 2010. *The Psychology of Prejudice and Discrimination*. Belmont, CA: Wadsworth.

Wimmer, A. 2013. *The Waves of War: Nationalism, State Formation and Ethnic Exclusion in the Modern World*. Cambridge, UK: Cambridge University Press.

Winegard, B. and R. O. Deaner. 2010. The evolutionary significance of Red Sox Nation: sport fandom as a by-product of coalitionary psychology. *Evolutionary Psychology*, 8: 432–446.

Winslow, D. 1997. *The Canadian Airborne Regiment in Somalia: A Socio-Cultural Inquiry*. Ottawa: Canadian Government Publishing.

Wintrobe, R. 2006. *Rational Extremism*. Cambridge, UK: Cambridge University Press.

Wolpert, S. A. 2004. *New History of India*. Oxford, UK: Oxford University Press.

Wong, L. et al. 2003. *Why They Fight? Combat Motivation in the Iraq War*. Castle Barracks, PA: Strategic Studies Institute, US Army War College.

Zagorin, P. 1982. *Rebels and Rulers, 1500–1700*, 2 vols. Cambridge, UK: Cambridge University Press.

Žižek, S. 2008. *Violence: Six Sideways Reflections*. London: Picador.

Zwitter, A. and J. De Wilde. 2014. *Working Paper, Securitization and the Local Level: A Prismatic Approach to Psycho-Social Mechanisms of Securitization*. Groningen, Netherlands: University of Groningen.

Index

absolutism, 29, 34, 162
Afghanistan, 148, 150, 152, 157, 159, 193, 253, 267, 269, 284
Africa, 1, 74, 78, 82, 93, 109, 114–116, 124–125, 188, 218, 225, 234–235, 237, 269, 305, 316, 323–324, 329
aggressiveness, 27, 69
Al Qaida, 20, 64, 153, 265
Albania, 222
Alexander, Jeffrey, 106, 255, 261, 313
Al-Qaida, 255, 266, 268
American Civil War, 123
American Revolution, 191
An Lushan revolt, 102–103, 107
ancient China, 1, 59, 84, 106
Annales school, 42
Arendt, Hannah, 8, 313
Armenian genocide, 129
Ashoka's Hell, 1–2
Asia, 103, 114–116, 158, 219, 237, 279, 313, 319
Atran, Scott, 252, 261, 266, 270, 272, 276, 313

Balkans, 112, 128, 316, 327
Bartov, Omer, 168, 170, 283, 314
Bastille, 174, 178, 327
Bauman, Zygmunt, 31, 164, 223–224, 227–231, 236, 240, 314
Boko Haram, 263, 267
Bolsheviks, 129, 194, 206
Bosnia and Herzegovina, viii, 222, 226, 228, 327
Bourdieu, Pierre, 11, 13, 314
Braudel, Fernand, 42, 315
Brazil, 103, 124, 154
Brittany, 121
Brubaker, Rogers, 44, 88, 166, 217, 287, 315
bureaucratic power, 26, 49, 153, 193, 229

bureaucratisation, 5–6, 26, 43, 49, 54, 58, 62, 65–66, 97, 110, 115, 142, 147, 149–150, 152, 155, 159, 167–168, 173, 176, 189–190, 192, 230, 264, 276, 280, 300, 306

carceral power, 35, 38–39
Carthage, 108, 220, 322
Ceausescu, Nicolai, 195
Centeno, Miguel, viii, 86, 144, 151, 316
centrifugal ideologisation, 6, 43, 54, 58, 64, 66, 110, 140, 161, 167, 171–173, 189, 197, 207, 264, 270, 273, 275, 280, 300
chiefdoms, 47, 81, 91–94, 97, 105–106, 109, 144–145, 155, 190, 292, 296
China, 30, 44, 47, 103, 107, 110, 115–116, 118, 122, 124, 127, 131–132, 138–139, 153–154, 158, 233, 293, 297, 302, 318, 326, 330, 332, 334
citizenship, 43, 89, 128, 145–147
civil wars, 96, 104, 129, 136, 144, 151, 156, 167, 176, 183, 302, 308, 314
civilising mission, 53, 157
Civilising Process, 27, 30–32, 133, 319, 328
civilization, 27, 33, 35, 186, 329
Clausewitz, 84, 282
Clausewitz, Carl von, 31
Coker, Chris, viii, 157, 309, 317
collective violence, 8, 19, 30, 66, 84, 141, 280, 309
Collins, Randall, viii, 15–16, 21–22, 42, 60–61, 72, 112, 143, 154, 164, 168–169, 181, 233, 256–258, 262, 275, 288, 291, 297, 301, 310, 315, 317, 321
concepts of violence, 5, 11, 14
Congo Free State, 124, 127, 235
Correlates of War, 102
Cromwell, Oliver, 23, 222, 232
Cuban revolution, 208

cumulative bureaucratisation of coercion, 6–7, 43, 49, 62, 66, 97, 110, 115, 147, 152, 155, 159, 167, 173, 189, 192, 230, 264, 280, 300, 306

de Saint-Pierre, Charles, 99
De Tocqueville, Alexis, 176
death tolls, 97, 101, 103, 106, 109, 126, 128, 311
decline of violence, 4, 33, 120, 132, 135, 141, 287
della Porta, Donatella, 19, 61, 206–207, 266–267, 289, 318
democide, 127, 215
disciplinary power, 34–35, 38
discipline, 22, 24, 35, 46, 48, 82, 97, 126, 160, 228, 277, 283, 294, 303
discourse, 39, 44, 55, 121, 161, 208, 230, 259, 261
du Picq, Charles Ardant, 61, 282
Dunbar, Robin, 61, 318, 322
Durkheim, Emile, 58, 61–63, 135, 254, 278–279, 284, 318

Eisner, Manuel, viii, 11, 29, 100, 133–134, 138, 319
Elias, Norbert, 3, 6, 27–33, 35–36, 38, 40, 50, 113, 133–134, 147, 189, 310, 319, 328
England, 5, 111–112, 114, 157–158, 324, 327
Enlightenment, 2, 8, 24, 54, 56, 99, 120, 151, 160–161, 198–199, 223, 240, 254, 298, 325
envelopment of micro solidarity, 6, 43
Estonia, 112
ETA, 20, 64, 260, 266, 272–273
ethnic cleansing, 31, 38, 215–216, 225, 314, 323
Europe, 1, 3–4, 23, 27, 29–30, 43, 55, 74–75, 100, 111–118, 120–122, 127, 133, 148, 151, 153–154, 160, 162, 167, 178, 186, 192, 195, 206, 212, 223–224, 228, 234–235, 238, 241, 259, 304, 314–316, 318–319, 322, 326–327, 329, 333–334

Falklands war, 17, 333
FARC, 155
Flanders, 112
Foran, John F., 186–187, 196, 320, 322, 326, 331
Foucault, Michel, 6, 33–39, 137, 258–259, 320, 330

France, 102, 111–112, 150, 154, 175, 187, 210, 222, 225, 299, 302, 320–321, 328, 332
French revolution, 176, 179, 186, 197, 200–202

gacaca courts, 243
Galtung, Johan, 11–12, 14, 100, 321
Gambetta, Diego, 252–253, 314, 321, 323–324, 330
Gaza, 272
Gellner, Ernest, 53, 58, 147, 160, 238, 321, 327
Genghis Khan, 48, 105, 115, 145
genocide, 7–8, 19, 31–32, 38–39, 41, 50, 77, 99, 124–125, 127, 129, 132, 141, 211–228, 231, 232, 235–236, 239–240, 242–246, 248–250, 314, 317, 320–321, 324–326, 328, 330–331, 333, 336
Germans, 21, 32, 45, 112, 124, 163–165, 167, 170, 199, 213, 217–218, 234–235, 239, 245, 247, 314, 320, 324, 328
Giddens, Anthony, 139, 146, 149, 189, 321
globalisation, 38, 149
Goldstone, Jack, 176–177, 179, 181–182, 184, 187–188, 192, 202, 204, 322
Goodwin, Jeff, 181, 183–185, 190, 192, 207, 322
Great Recession, 2008, 59
Guevara, Che, 206, 209, 322
Gurr, Ted, 175, 180–181, 216, 253, 322–323

Hall, John A., viii, 21, 23, 42, 49, 116, 128, 149, 238, 293, 314–315, 317, 322–323, 326–327, 335
Hamas, 155, 249, 272
Hassan, Riaz, 252–253, 256, 270–271, 276, 323
Herero and Nama genocide, 218
Hezbollah, 155, 252, 272
Hobbes, Thomas, 87
Holocaust, 31–32, 39, 130, 212, 223–224, 228, 234, 236, 242, 247, 314, 320, 330, 333

ideologisation, 5, 54–55, 59, 64–65, 140, 142, 160, 171, 197, 199, 204, 270–272, 276, 306
ideology, 26, 33, 39, 58, 66, 121–122, 128–129, 131, 159, 165–166, 168, 171, 185, 197, 202, 205–206, 208,

213, 221, 228, 232, 235, 237–238,
240–242, 247–248, 269–271,
275–277, 283, 295–299, 306
Iliad, 76–77, 220
India, 1, 30, 53, 82, 103, 106, 114, 118,
124, 154, 293, 331, 336
Ireland, viii, 137, 222, 261, 268, 271, 280,
329, 334
iron cage, 24, 26, 51, 63
Iron Maiden, 1–2, 113
ISIS, 64, 153, 155, 193, 266–267, 270,
274
Islamic world, 108, 159, 293

Jacobins, 206
Japan, 134, 154, 164, 166, 293, 297, 314, 327
Jenkins, Richard, viii, 45, 324

Kaczynski, Ted, 272
Kalyvas, Stathis, viii, 151–152, 325
Kant, 99
Khmer Rouge, 193, 214, 236, 242
King, Anthony, 152, 169, 284–286, 306,
324–325
Kublai Khan, 115
Kumar, Krishan, viii, 191, 326

Lachmann, Richard, 37, 190, 326
Leibniz, Gottfried W., 99
Lemkin, Raphael, 211–212, 326
longue durée analysis, 6–8, 41–43, 49,
189–190, 211, 227, 249, 264,
280–281
LTTE, Tamil Tigers, 273, 277
lynching, 10, 100

Machiavelli, Niccolo, 282
Mamluk Sultanate, 294–295
Mamluks, 114, 314
Mann, Michael, viii, 31–33, 37–38,
42–43, 47, 49, 51, 60–61, 92, 94,
101–104, 106, 110, 115–116, 120,
128–129, 132–133, 139–140,
142–143, 145–147, 149–150, 154,
156, 159, 166, 167, 168, 170, 181,
185, 195, 215–216, 219, 221–227,
231, 237, 242, 289, 292, 310, 322,
327, 328
Mannheim, Karl, 201, 328
martyrdom, 2, 208, 255, 279
Marx, Karl, 58, 175, 328
Mayo, Elton, 63, 328
medieval Europe, 1, 112–114, 163
micro-solidarity, 7, 58, 61–62, 64–66, 121,
142, 167–168, 170–171, 173–174,

189, 206–207, 209, 248, 264,
275–278, 280, 285–287, 289,
292–293, 295, 297, 300–302, 306
Middle East, 44, 77, 84, 114–115, 178,
188, 271, 318, 328
Mill, John Stuart, 2–3, 99, 329
Moore, Barrington, 175, 179, 181, 194,
329
Mughal empire, 119

National Socialism, 170, 213, 217,
246–247, 314, 320
nationalism, 17, 53–54, 64, 122, 165–167,
172, 209, 227, 240, 242, 300, 332
North America, 92, 122–123, 148, 151,
153, 219, 313, 319
Nuremberg laws, 218

organisational power, 7, 18, 20, 47, 49,
51, 89–90, 92, 94–97, 106, 139–140,
147, 149, 153–155, 157, 193, 210,
230, 236–237, 249, 264–265, 269,
298
organised violence, 4–8, 15–16, 18–21,
23–24, 27–31, 33, 36, 39–41, 43, 48,
57, 59, 66, 78–79, 94, 99, 101–102,
104, 106, 108–109, 114–115,
117–118, 120, 122, 124, 132, 134,
141, 144, 166, 174, 189, 205,
210–211, 217–219, 235, 248–250,
254, 262, 264, 280–281, 309–310,
312
Ottoman Empire, 116, 225, 292

Pakistan, 253, 267
Palaeolithic, 60, 76, 78
Panopticon, 34, 36
Pax Americana, 134, 154–155
Pax Romana, 110, 134, 154
Pax Sinica, 111
Pinker, Steven, 3, 11, 29, 50, 69, 76,
80, 87, 99–103, 107, 113, 115, 120,
129–130, 132–134, 136, 145,
151–152, 154, 287, 310, 317, 320, 330
PIRA, 260, 266, 268, 271, 273, 279
Plague, 111
Poggi, Gianfranco, 36, 330
Poznan speeches, 247
prison population, 34, 45, 48, 53, 88, 138,
179, 207, 246, 279, 312
Punic wars, 108

Ray, Larry, viii, 11, 330
Red Brigades, 266, 269
refugees, 85, 156, 245

revolution, 7, 31, 38–39, 41, 45, 50, 54, 56,
    99, 102, 104, 120, 126, 158, 160–161,
    174, 176–194, 196–199, 201–202,
    205–208, 210–211, 231, 239, 299, 309
Roman Empire, 23, 49, 105, 108–111, 117,
    155, 222, 237, 297
Romania, 166, 178, 195, 318, 331
Romanticism, 54, 56, 200
Russia, 104, 137–138, 150, 154, 182, 187,
    194, 210, 249, 302, 330, 332–333
Rwandan genocide, 19, 215, 236, 246

Sageman, Marc, 252–253, 263, 266, 268,
    271, 276, 331
Sandinistas, 206
Scot, James S., 229
Selbin, Eric, 186, 196, 331
Shaw, Martin, 87, 152, 212–213, 216–219,
    226–227, 231, 243, 331
Siebold, Guy L., 283, 285–286, 290, 306, 332
Skocpol, Theda, 177, 181, 208, 332, 334
slavery, 123–124, 221
Smelser, Neil, 180, 256, 263, 313, 332
Sofsky, Wolfgang, 45, 129, 333
Soviet Union, 131, 148, 154, 186, 229, 239
Spain, 20, 77, 114, 221–222, 233, 240–241,
    334
Sparta, 145, 296, 314, 325
Spencer, Herbert, 3, 99, 333
Srebrenica, 214, 245
structural violence, 12, 14, 100
suicide, 16, 31, 63, 82, 104, 135, 196,
    245, 249, 251–252, 257, 269, 271,
    276–279, 312, 326
Sun-Tzu, 282
symbolic violence, 13, 100
systemic violence, 13–14

Taiping rebellion, 125
Taliban, 155, 193, 267
Tamil Tigers, 252, 272, 324
Tanzania, 229
terrorism, 7–8, 13, 15, 19, 31, 38, 50, 99–
    100, 141, 183, 211, 214, 249–254,

256–258, 260–263, 265–267, 269,
    272, 275, 279–280, 289, 309, 315,
    328, 331
Thucydides, 282
Tilly, Charles, 11, 19, 31, 42–43, 116, 120,
    128, 146–147, 150, 177, 181, 183,
    236, 334
Timur, 115
Tonnerre, Boisrond, 201
Torquemada, Tomas de, 113
torture, 1–2, 30, 32, 35, 55–56, 76, 100,
    104, 111–112, 164, 233, 274, 308,
    310–311
Trotsky, Leon, 22, 175, 202, 334
Tunisia, 187, 202–203, 279
Turner, Jonathan H., 46, 60, 72, 168, 244,
    287–288, 334

Uppsala Conflict Data Programme, 102
Utøya massacre, 20

Vendée, 121, 201

warfare, war, 2, 7, 18, 24, 30–32, 43, 48,
    59, 77, 79, 81, 83, 86, 94, 107,
    111–112, 118–121, 123, 126, 128,
    130, 133–134, 141–148, 150,
    152–155, 157–158, 161–162, 167,
    172, 178, 209, 211, 225–226,
    231–232, 243, 267, 283, 289, 292,
    303, 305, 311, 323, 326, 332
Weber, Max, 6, 21–28, 33, 35–36, 40, 44,
    47–48, 51–52, 57, 89–90, 136, 144,
    147, 162, 169, 176, 217, 234, 289,
    302, 322, 335
Wehrmacht, 168, 170, 283, 332
Wimmer, Andreas, viii, 166, 191, 336
Winter Palace, 174, 195
world system theory, 42

Yemen, 100, 156, 268

Žižek, Slavoj, 11, 13–14, 336
Zulu kingdom, 125, 302–303, 305, 329